CROSSWORD DICTIONARY

GILLIAN CLARK

ERIC DOBBY REFERENCE BOOKS

First published in Great Britain 1993
Reprinted 1994
by Eric Dobby Publishing Limited
12 Warnford Road
Orpington, Kent, BR6 6LW

ISBN 1-85882-019-7

Text typeset in Courier by Kevin O'Connor
Printed and bound in Great Britain by
BPC Paperbacks Ltd

Acknowledgements

I would like to acknowledge the help of the following people in the preparation of this book. For their contributions to the research that made possible the inclusion of so many specialist terms in the compilation, I would like to thank Betty Bawden, Muriel Hoadley and, in particular, Gwyneth and John Machin. I would like also to thank Julia Pickles for her help in keying some of the longer lists. Finally I must thank my mentors John Clark and David Skinner whose advice, criticism and support helped to see the book through to completion. I hope the finished work will prove to be helpful and add to the enjoyment of fellow crossword fanatics and other puzzle solvers.

G.C. - Oxford 1993.

Contents

Contents

Contents

Contents

African countries

3 & 4

Chad
Mali
Togo
UAR

5

Benin
Congo
Egypt
Gabon
Ghana
Kenya
Libya
Niger
Sudan
Zaïre

6

Angola

Gambia
Guinea
Malawi
Rwanda
Uganda
Zambia

7

Algeria
Burkina
Burundi
Comoros
Eritrea
Lesotho
Liberia
Mayotte
Morocco
Namibia
Nigeria
Réunion
Senegal

Somalia
Tunisia

8

Botswana
Cameroon
Djibouti
Ethiopia
St. Helena
Tanzania
Zimbabwe

9

Mauritius
Swaziland

10

Ivory Coast
Madagascar
Mauritania

Mozambique
Seychelles

11

Burkina Faso
Côte d'Ivoire
Saint Helena
Sierra Leone
South Africa

12

Guinea-Bissau

15 +

Cape Verde Islands
Central African
  Republic
Equatorial Guinea
Sao Tomé and
  Principé

Air and space travel

3	**4**			**5**		**6**
ace	bank	lift	wing	apron	crate	stall
bay	bump	loop	zoom	cabin	ditch	strut
fin	buzz	mach		cargo	drift	stunt
fly	crew	nose		chock	flaps	
gas	dive	prop		chord	glide	aerial
jet	dope	roll		climb	pitch	airbus
rev	drag	slip		Comet	plane	air car
UFO	flap	span		craft	prang	airman
yaw	hull	spar		crash	pylon	airway
	kite	spin			radar	basket
	land	tail			range	beacon
	lane	taxi			rigid	bomber
		trim			slots	
		wash			stage	

canard
cruise
drogue
fanjet
flight
gas-bag
George
glider
hangar
intake
launch
module
nose-up
ramjet
refuel
rocket
rudder
runway
yawing

7

aileron
airbase
aircrew
air flow
air lane
air lift
airline
airport
airraid
airship
aviator
ballast
balloon
biplane
bale out
bomb bay
capsule
ceiling
charter
chassis
chopper
clipper
cockpit
co-pilot

cowling
ejector
fairing
fighter
flyover
flypast
gondola
Halifax
Harrier
Heinkel
jump-jet
Junkers
landing
lift-off
Mae West
missile
Mustang
nacelle
nose-cap
pancake
payload
re-entry
ripcord
shuttle
sponson
Sputnik
tail fin
take-off
twin-jet
wingtip

8

aerofoil
aeronaut
aerostat
air brake
aircraft
airfield
air force
air frame
airliner
airplane
airscrew
airspace
airspeed

airstrip
airwoman
altitude
anhedral
approach
autogiro
autogyro
aviation
Beaufort
Blenheim
bomb-rack
Canberra
Concorde
corridor
dihedral
elevator
envelope
fuselage
grounded
gyrostat
heliport
in-flight
intercom
jet plane
joystick
Jumbo jet
Moonshot
Mosquito
non-rigid
nose cone
nosedive
nose down
pulse jet
rotodyne
seaplane
sideslip
spaceman
Spitfire
squadron
stopover
subsonic
tail boom
tail skid
tail unit
terminal

triplane
turbofan
turbojet
warplane
wind cone
wind sock
wing flap
Zeppelin

9

aerodrome
aeroplane
air intake
air pocket
airworthy
altimeter
amphibian
astrodome
astronaut
autopilot
cabin crew
cargo hold
cosmonaut
countdown
crash-land
delta wing
dirigible
Gladiator
gyroplane
Hurricane
jet bomber
Lancaster
launch pad
longerons
low-flying
mail plane
monocoque
monoplane
navigator
nosewheel
overshoot
parachute
power dive
propeller
rudder bar

sailplane
satellite
semi-rigid
spaceship
spacesuit
spacewalk
sweepback
Swordfish
tailplane
test pilot
Tiger Moth
touchdown
turboprop
twin-screw

10

aerobatics
aero engine
aeronautic
air control
air defence
air hostess
air steward
air support
air traffic
anemometer
balloonist
cantilever
cargo plane
dive bomber
flight deck
flight path
flight plan
flying-boat
gas-balloon
gas turbine
ground crew
helicopter
Hindenberg
hovercraft
hydroplane
jet fighter
landing run
mach number
outer space

robot plane
slipstream
solo flight
spacecraft
space probe
splashdown
stabilizer
stewardess
streamline
supersonic
test flight
Wellington

11

aeronautics
aerostatics
afterburner
blind flying
ejector seat
fire-balloon
flying speed
ground speed
heat barrier
heavy bomber
laminar flow
landing deck
landing gear
leading edge
loop the loop
Montgolfier
Moon landing
ornithopter
retro-rocket
sesquiplane
slotted wing
soft landing
space centre
stabilizers
strike plane
stunt flying
vapour trail

12

aerodynamics
air-sea rescue

arrester gear
arrester wire
belly landing
control tower
crash landing
ejection seat
fighter pilot
flying circus
flying saucer
freight-plane
jet propelled
landing light
landing speed
launching pad
maiden flight
night fighter
pressure suit
pursuit plane
radial engine
sound barrier
space capsule
space station
space vehicle
trailing edge

13

airworthiness
control column
cruising speed
forced landing
ground control
hot-air balloon
radiolocation
stalling speed
Stratocruiser
undercarriage

14 +

aircraft carrier
decompression
escape velocity
flying bedstead
heavier-than-air
lighter-than-air

looping the loop
Montgolfier balloon
passenger plane
semiretractable

space traveller
troop transport
undercarriage
weightlessness

American Indian tribes

2 & 3	5				
		Ponca	Guaymí	Toltec	Hidatsa
		Sarsi	Jivaro	Tucuna	Klamath
Fox	Acona	Sioux	Kayopo	Tupina	Kutchin
Gê	Adena	Slave	Kichai	Warrau	Kutenai
Ona	Arara	Taino	Laguna	Wintun	Koyukon
Uru	Aztec	Teton	Lenape	Witoto	Luiseno
Ute	Blood	Wappo	Lucayo	Yahgan	Mahican
	Caddo	Yagua	Mandan	Zamuco	Mapuche
	Campa	Yaqui	Mataco		Mohegan
4	Cañar	Yuchi	Micmac		Mohican
	Carib	Yunca	Mixtec	**7**	Naskapi
Arua	Chimu	Zoque	Mohave		Natchez
Cree	Chocó		Mohawk	Abenaki	Ojibway
Crow	Chono		Mojave	Arapaho	Orejone
Cuna	Creek	**6**	Munsee	Araucan	Payaguá
Erie	Guató		Navaho	Arikara	Puelche
Hare	Haidi	Abipón	Nootka	Atakapa	Quechua
Hopi	Huron	Abnaki	Oglala	Bannock	Shawnee
Hupa	Incas	Apache	Omagua	Beothuk	Sirionó
Inca	Kansa	Apinai	Oneida	Camacan	Tairona
Iowa	Karok	Arawak	Ostiak	Carrier	Tanaina
Lipe	Kaska	Atoara	Ottowa	Catawba	Timbira
Macú	Kiowa	Aymara	Paiute	Charrua	Timucua
Maya	Lenca	Aztecs	Papago	Chibcha	Tlingit
Moki	Lipan	Beaver	Panare	Chilcal	Tonkawa
Mojo	Maidu	Biloxi	Pawnee	Chinook	Waiguri
Mura	Mbaya	Bororo	Pequot	Chumash	Wichita
Pano	Miami	Calusa	Pericu	Choctaw	Wyandot
Pima	Modoc	Cariri	Piegan	Ciboney	Yankton
Pomo	Moqui	Cayapa	Pueblo	Cochimi	Yamasee
Sauk	Nahau	Cayapó	Quapaw	Coroado	Zapotec
Taos	Nazca	Cayuga	Salish	Dakotah	
Tupi	Olmec	Cayuse	Santee	Fuegian	
Yumi	Omaha	Chavin	Sarcee	Goajiro	**8**
Zuma	Osage	Conibo	Siwash	Gosiute	Aguarana
Zuñi	Otomi	Dakota	Seneca	Guaraní	Alacaluf
		Dogrib		Guayaná	

Amahuaca	Puebloan	Chipewyan	Chiviguano
Arikaree	Puelches	Conestoga	Coahuiltec
Barbacoa	Querandi	Flatheads	Gabrielino
Caingang	Quichuan	Guaranian	Gros Ventre
Cherokee	Quileute	Harasupai	Leni-Lenapé
Cheyenne	Quinault	Hoochinoo	Miccosukee
Chibchan	Seminole	Karankawa	Minnetaree
Chippewa	Sherente	Menominee	Montagnais
Colorado	Shoshone	Motilones	Nambicuara
Comanche	Shoshoni	Mundurucú	Patagonian
Delaware	Shushwap	Penobscot	Potawatomi
Diaguita	Sihasapa	Puelchean	Tarahumara
Diegueño	Silksika	Taulipang	
Illinois	Sisseton	Tehuelche	
Iroquois	Subtaino	Tsmishian	**11**
Jirajara	Tarascan	Tupinambá	
Kickapoo	Tutchone	Tuscarora	Narraganset
Klikitat	Yamamadi	Wampanoag	Susquehanna
Kootenai		Winnebago	Tupi-guaraní
Kwakiutl			Yellowknife
Malecite	**9**		
Maricopa		**10**	**12**
Menomini	Algonkian		
Missouri	Algonquin	Alacalufan	Pasamaquoddy
Mosquito	Apalachee	Algonquian	San
Muskogee	Ashluslay	Araucanian	Ildefonso
Nez Percé	Ashochimi	Assiniboin	
Onondaga	Blackfoot	Athabascan	**13**
Powhatan	Chickasaw	Bella Coola	
	Chilcotin	Chitimacha	Massachusetts

American presidents

4

Bush, George H.W.
Ford, Gerald R.
Polk, James K.
Taft, William H.

5

Adams, John & John Quincy
Grant, Ulysses S.
Hayes, Rutherford B.

Nixon, Richard M.
Tyler, John

6

Arthur,   Chester A.
Carter,   James E.
Hoover,   Herbert C.
Monroe,   James
Pierce,   Franklin
Reagan,   Ronald W.
Taylor,   Zachary

Truman, Harry S.
Wilson, Woodrow

7

Clinton, William J. (Bill)
Harding, Warren G.
Jackson, Andrew
Johnson, Andrew & Lyndon B.
Kennedy, John F.
Lincoln, Abraham
Madison, James

8

Buchanan, James
Coolidge, Calvin
Fillmore, Millard

Garfield, James A
Harrison, Benjamin &
  William H.
McKinley, William
Van Buren, Martin

9

Cleveland, Grover
Jefferson, Thomas
Roosevelt, Franklin D. &
  Theodore

10

Eisenhower, Dwight D.
Washington, George

American States
(including abbreviations and ZIP codes)

4

Iowa (Ia., Io)	IA
Ohio (O.)	OH
Utah (Ut.)	UT

5

Idaho (Id., Ida.)	ID
Maine (Me.)	ME
Texas (Tex.)	TX

6 letters

Alaska	AK
Hawaii	HI
Kansas (Kans.)	KA
Nevada (Nev.)	NV
Oregon (Ore., Oreg.)	OR

7 letters

Alabama (Ala.)	AL

Arizona (Ariz.)		AZ
Florida (Fla.)		FL
Georgia (Ga.)		GA
Indiana (Ind.)		IN
Montana (Mont.)		MT
New York (N.Y.)		NY
Vermont (Vt.)		VT
Wyoming (Wyo.)		WY

8

Arkansas	(Ark.)	AR
Colorado	(Colo.)	CO
Delaware	(Del.)	DE
Illinois	(Ill.)	IL
Kentucky	(Ken,Ky.)	KY
Maryland	(Md.)	MD
Michigan	(Mich.)	MI
Missouri	(Mo.)	MO
Nebraska	(Neb.,Nebr.)	NE
Oklahoma	(Okla.)	OK
Virginia	(Va.)	VA

9

Louisiana (La.)	LA
Minnesota (Minn.)	MN
New Jersey (N.J.)	NJ
New Mexico (N. M.,N.Mex.)	NM
Tennessee (Tenn.)	TN
Winconsin (Wis.)	WI

10

California (Cal.,Calif.)	CA
Washington (Wash.)	WA

11

Connecticut (Conn.)	CT
Mississippi (Miss.)	MS
North Dakota (N.D.,N.Dak)	ND

Rhode Island (R.I.)	RI
South Dakota (S.D.,S.Dak.)	SD

12

New Hampshire (N.H.)	NH
Pennsylvania (Pa,Penn.)	PA
West Virginia (W.Va.)	WV

13

Massachusetts (Mass)	MA
North Carolina (N.C)	NC
South Carolina (S.C)	SC

15 +

District of Columbia (D.C)	DC

Animal groups

3

gam (whales)
mob (kangaroos)
nye (pheasants)
pod (seals,
  whales,whiting)
rag (colts)

4

army (frogs)
bale (turtles)
bevy (larks,
  quails, swans)
cast (hawks)
cete (badgers)
down (hares)
dule (doves,
  turtles)

fall (woodcock)
gang (elk)
haul (fish)
herd (antelope,
  asses, buffalo,
  cattle, cranes,
  deer,
  elephants,
  giraffes,
  goats, oxen,
  pigs, sheep,
  swine)
hive (bees)
host (sparrows)
husk (hares)
knob (pochards,
  teal, toads,
  widgeon)
leap (leopards)
lepe (leopards)

loft (pigeons)
mute (hounds)
nest (mice,
  rabbits,wasps)
nide (pheasants)
pace (asses)
pack (grouse,
  hounds,hyenas,
  wolves)
rush (pochards)
rout (wolves)
sord (mallards)
sute (mallards,
  wildfowl)
team (draught
  animals,oxen,
  young ducks)
walk (snipe)
wing (plovers)

wisp (snipe)
yoke (oxen)

5

brood (chickens, hens)
catch (fish)
charm (finches)
cloud (gnats)
covey (grouse, partridges)
crash (rhinos)
drift (swine)
drove (cattle, oxen)
flock (geese, goats, pigeons, sheep)
flush (mallards)
grist (bees)
plump (waterfowl)
pride (lions)
sedge (bitterns, cranes, herons)
shoal (fish)
siege (cranes, herons)
skein (flying geese)
skulk (foxes)
sloth (bears)
smuck (jellyfish)
swarm (bees, flies)
tribe (goats)
troop (antelopes, kangaroos, monkeys)

watch (nightingales)
wedge (swans)

6

clutch (hens)
colony (ants, gulls, herons)
covert (coots)
desert (lapwings)
flight (doves, ducks, pigeons, swallows)
gaggle (geese)
kennel (hounds, raches)
kindle (kittens)
labour (moles)
litter (cubs, kittens, pigs, pups)
murder (crows)
muster (peafowl)
school (fish, porpoises, whales)
sleuth (bears)
spring (teal)
warren (rabbits)

7

badling (ducks)
draught (fish)
clamour (rooks or starlings)
clouder (cats)

clowder (cats)
cluster (cats)
company (widgeon)
dopping (sheldrake)
rookery (penguins, rooks, seals)
sounder (pigs)

8

building (rooks)
fesnying (ferrets)
paddling (ducks)
richesse (martens)
singular (boars)

9

badelynge (ducks)
mustering (storks)

10

chattering (choughs)
exaltation (larks)
shrewdness (apes)
unkindness (ravens)

11

murmuration (starlings)

12

congregation (plovers)

Architectural terms

3	die	4	apse	bell	fret
	eye		arch	dado	frog
bay	key	ambo	band	dais	fust
cap		anta	bead	dome	jamb

nave	ashlar	plinth	fluting	baluster
ogee	atrium	pulpit	gadroon	bartizan
pele	attick	quadra	galilee	basilica
peel	aumbry	regula	gallery	beak head
stoa	aumery	rococo	Grecian	buttress
	belfry	scapus	lacunar	caryatid
5	bonnet	screen	lantern	cimborio
	broach	scroll	lattice	cincture
aisle	canopy	sedile	lequear	crenelle
ambry	chevet	soffit	lunette	cresting
arris	column	Tuscan	narthex	cymatium
attic	corbel	trophy	nulling	diastyle
conge	corona	urella	obelisk	dipteral
crown	crenel	vestry	oratory	dog-tooth
crypt	cupola	volute	parvise	edge roll
Doric	dagger	wreath	portail	Egyptian
foils	dentil	xystus	portico	extrados
gable	diaper	zig-zag	postern	formeret
glyph	facade		pteroma	gargoyle
helix	fillet	**7**	redding	intrados
inlay	finial		regency	Jacobean
Ionic	flèche	annulet	reredos	keel arch
lobby	fresco	arch rib	rosette	keystone
newel	frieze	astylar	rotunda	lich gate
niche	gablet	balcony	roundel	lych gate
ogive	gazebo	baroque	scallop	miserere
ovolo	Gothic	bastion	Spanish	pavilion
Roman	guttae	boultin	systyle	pedestal
scape	heroic	butment	tessara	pediment
shaft	impost	calotte	tondino	pilaster
shank	lancet	capital	tracery	predella
socle	lesene	cavetto	transom	pulpitum
talon	lierne	chancel	trumeau	rocaille
tenia	lintel	chebron	zikurat	spandrel
torus	lintol	cornice		spandril
Tudor	loggia	crochet	**8**	spirelet
verge	louvre	crocket		Sumerian
	mantel	distyle	abutment	torching
6	metope	Eastern	acanthus	transept
	Minoan	echinus	astragal	triglyph
abacus	mutule	encarpa	aedicula	tympanum
access	Norman	entasis	apophyge	verandha
alcove	oculus	eustyle	arenated	vignette
almery	patera	festoon	astragal	voussoir
arcade	pillar	fleuron	atlantes	wainscot

zikkurat
ziggurat

9

acropolis
antefixae
anthemion
apex stone
arabesque
arch brick
archivolt
attic base
bird's
  beak
Byzantine
campanile
canephora
cartouche
castellum
caulicoli
cloisters
colonnade
Composite
decorated
dripstone
foliation
hexastyle
hypocaust

hypostyle
ingle nook
label stop
lacunaria
linenfold
mezzanine
mouldings
octastyle
Palladian
refectory
sgraffito
stanchion
strapwork
stylobate
trabeated
triforium
trilithon
vestibule
zoophorus

10

acroterion
abmulatory
araeostyle
architrave
baldachino
ball flower
balustrade

battlemen
caryatides
cinquefoil
colonnette
Corinthian
egg and dart
enrichment
hagioscope
Lady chapel
lancet arch
misericord
modillions
pietra dura
presbytery
pycnostyle
quatrefoil
Romanesque
rood screen
rose window
sexpartite
tetrastyle
trachelion

11

castellated
entablature
fan vaulting
harelip arch
leaded light

mantelpiece
mantelshelf
oriel window
rectilinear
Renaissance
reticulated

12

amphitheatre
blind tracery
cockle stairs
Early English
egg and tongue
lancet window
porte-cochère
superimposed
transitional

13

amphi-prostyle
Perpendicular

14

angular capital
flying buttress
hypotrachelion

Arthurian legend

(Kn = knight)

3

Amr
Cai   (Kn)
Cei   (Kn)
Kay   (Kn)

4

Anna
Bors   (Kn)
Bran
Bron
Drem

Erec   (Kn)
Loth
Lugh
Mark   (King
Menw
Urry   (Kn)

5

Annwn
Balan
Balin
Cabal
Clust

Damas
Ector   (Kn)
Eidyn
Enide
Gorre
Grail
Gwair
Gwynn

Hélie
Linet
Llwch
Lucan (Kn)
Mabon
Mador (Kn)
Olwen
Owain (Kn)
Troit
Urien (King)
Uther
Yvain (Kn)

6

Arthur
Avalon
Bedwyr (Kn)
Boarte (Kn)
Brisen
Cafall
Cedric
Elaine
Evrain (King)
Gareth (Kn)
Gawain (Kn)
Gildas
Helake
Helias
Lionel (Kn)
Logres
Lunete
Meliot (Kn)
Melwas
Merlin
Modred (Kn)
Morgan
Pelles (King)
Pisear (King)
Yseult

7

Accolon
Astolat

Brewnor
Caer Gai
Camelot
Camille
Camlann
Culhwch
Dinodan (Kn)
Escolat
Ettarde
Gaheris (Kn)
Galahad (Kn)
Galigan
Ganadin
Gorlois
Guiomar (Kn)
Gwythyr
Lamorak
Lyonors
Medraut
Morholt
Mordred (Kn)
Niniane
Niviene
Pelleas (Kn)
Pryderi
Prydwen
Tristan (Kn)
Viviane
Viviene
Ygraine

8

Afarnach
Agravain (Kn)
Amesbury
Avallach
Bedivere (Kn)
Bercilak
Brangane
Caerleon
Caer Wydr
Corbenic
Galahalt (Kn)
Hellawes

Lancelot (Kn)
Leodegan (King)
Morgause
Perceval
Rhiannon
Sangreal
Taliesin
Tintagel
Tristram (Kn)

9

Agravaine
Alexander (Kn)
Caer Siddi
Excalibur
Gornement
Grail King (The)
Gringolet
Guinevere
Guinglain (Kn)
Guingmars
Gwalchmei
Hermaunce (King)
Holy Grail (The)
Holy Lance (The)
La Pucelle
Launcelot (Kn)
Manawydan
Meleagant
Palug's Cat
Palomides (Kn)
Pellinore (King)
Trebuchet
Vortigern
Waste Land

10

Baudemagus (King)
Belle Garde
Black Witch (The)
Blanchflor
Caledfwlch
Creiddylad

Cup of Llwyr
Fisher King   (The)
Gwenhwyfar
Joyous Isle
Lost Forest
Maimed King   (The)
Rich Fisher
Round Table   (The)
Ysbadadden

11

City of Glass
Fair Unknown
Glastonbury
Grail Bearer   (The)
Grail Keeper   (The)
Green Chapel
Green Knight   (The)
Isle of Glass
Joyous Garde
Lady Laudine
Mabonagrain
Morgan le Fay
Perilous Bed
Twrch Trwyth

12

Caer Feddiwid
Golden Island
Isle of Apples
Isle of Avalon
Lady Lyonesse
Orgueilleuse
Perilous Ford

13

Blonde Esmerée
Drwst Iron Fist
Fairy Fortress
Glass Fortress

Isle of Maidens
Lady of the Lake   (The)
Loathly Damsel   (The)
Questing Beast   (The)
Siege Perilous
Weeping Castle
Yseult the Fair

14

Boar of Cornwall   (The)
Bran the Blessed
Castle Perilous
Esclados the Red
Mador de la Porte   (Kn)
Mound of Arberth
Perilous Forest
Queen of Denmark
Uther Pendragon

15 +

Alexander the Orphan   (Kn)
Battle of Camlann
Broceliande Forest
Castle of Evil Adventure
Castle of Maidens
Castle of Wonders
Cauldron of Diwrnach
Demon Cat of Lausanne   (The)
Drinking Horn of Gwlgawd
Echel Pierced Thigh
Fortress of Carousal
Harbin of the Mountain
King Mark of Cornwall
Knight with the Lion
Magic Cauldron of Annwn
Maiden of the White Hands
Table of Gwyddneu Long Leg
Valley of No Return
Waste City of Senaudon
Yseult of the White Hands

Artists

3

Arp
Apt
Cox
Baj
Bol
Dix
Dou
Egg
Fry
Fyt
Gay
Gow
Key
Lam
Lee
Low
Mor
May
Nay
Pot
Poy
Puy
Ryn
Vos
Wit

4

Adam
Ager
Agam
Ball
Bell
Bird
Bone
Both
Boyd
Burn
Bush
Carr

Caro
Cima
Cole
Colt
Cuyp
Dadd
Dali
Deas
Dick
Dine
Dodd
Doré
Dove
Duca
Dufy
Dyce
Dyck
Earl
East
Etty
Eves
Eyck
Faed
Falk
Fehr
Feke
Ford
Gabo
Gere
Gill
Goes
Gogh
Good
Gore
Goya
Graf
Gray
Gris
Gros
Guys
Hall
Hals

Hand
Hare
Hart
Heba
Hemy
Herp
Holl
Home
Hone
Hook
Huet
Hunt
Ives
Jack
Jorn
John
Judd
Juel
Kalf
Kane
Katz
Kaus
Kent
Kerr
King
Klee
Koch
Koen
Laer
Lamb
Lane
Lear
Leck
Lely
Lion
Long
Luks
Mack
Maes
Mara
Marc
Meit

Mena
Miró
Mola
Nash
Nast
Neer
Nost
Opie
Orsi
Owen
Page
Pane
Peto
Post
Pyne
Reid
Reni
Rich
Rizi
Rohe
Rops
Ross
Rush
Sage
Sant
Shaw
Shee
Shin
Sime
Sims
Smet
Soto
Spee
Swan
Tait
Todd
Toft
Tome
Tosi
Town
Troy
Tuke

Turo
Ubac
Uden
Uhde
Vien
Vita
Wade
Wain
Ward
Watt
Webb
Weir
West
Witz
Wols
Wood
Wren
Wyck
Zick
Zorn

5

Aalto
Abbey
Adams
Adler
Allan
Allen
Amiet
Amman
Andre
Ajlak
Arman
Appel
Auger
Avery
Bacon
Baily
Bakic
Balla
Banks

Barry
Barye
Bates
Beale
Beham
Bevin
Bezzi
Bigot
Birch
Blake
Blume
Boehm
Bolgi
Bosch
Bough
Breer
Brett
Brock
Brown
Bundy
Burra
Caffa
Carra
Cesar
Chase
Cione
Clark
Clint
Cohen
Cooke
Corot
Cossa
Costa
Cotes
Craig
Crane
Credi
Crome
Curry
Dalou
Danby
David

Davie
Davis
Degas
Denny
Devis
Dixon
Dolci
Dosse
Doyle
Drury
Dürer
Dulac
Dupré
Elias
Ensor
Ernst
Estes
Evans
Exter
Ferri
Finui
Flint
Foley
Freud
Frink
Frith
Frost
Fuger
Furse
Gaddi
Gallo
Gaudí
Gaunt
Genga
Gibbs
Giles
Golub
Gorky
Gotch
Goyen
Greco
Grant

Grosz	Mills	Rossi	Yanes	Calder	Foster
Gully	Milne	Ryder	Yeats	Callow	Fraser
Haden	Mochi	Ryman	Zoppo	Campin	French
Haghe	Moira	Sands		Carter	Fuller
Hayes	Monet	Saura		Casson	Fuseli
Healy	Moore	Scott	**6**	Chabot	Geddes
Heron	Muche	Segna		Claude	Gellée
Hicks	Munch	Short	Aachen	Clouet	Gérard
Holty	Myron	Siloe	Abbate	Clovie	Gerome
Hooch	Nebot	Sleap	Abbott	Colton	Gibson
Huber	Neefs	Small	Aikman	Conder	Gilman
Inman	Nervi	Smith	Albers	Cooper	Ginner
Innes	Nicol	Soane	Allori	Copley	Giotto
Itten	Noble	Soest	Antigo	Corbet	Girtin
Jacob	Nolde	Somer	Archer	Cotman	Glover
Jance	North	Speed	Arnold	Cowper	Goethe
Johns	Okada	Staël	Ashbee	Cozens	Gordon
Jones	Orley	Stark	Ashton	Currie	Graham
Keene	Orpen	Steen	Ayrton	Dahmen	Greuze
Keith	Oudry	Steer	Barker	Davies	Guardi
Kelly	Pajou	Stone	Barton	Dawson	Gulich
Kitja	Palma	Stott	Baskin	Deacon	Hacker
Klein	Pater	Studd	Bawden	Derain	Hanson
Klimt	Payne	Sully	Behnes	De Wint	Harral
Kolbe	Peale	Tacco	Benson	Dobson	Haydon
Kraft	Penny	Tassi	Benton	Dobell	Heckel
Kroll	Piper	Testa	Berman	Donner	Helion
Kurin	Plaas	Tobey	Bettes	Draper	Hilton
Laing	Platt	Tonks	Bewick	Du Bois	Holmes
Lance	Ponte	Towne	Biddle	Duccio	Hodges
Leech	Ponti	Udine	Birley	Dunbar	Hopper
Leger	Poole	Unwin	Bishop	Dunlop	Howard
Lemon	Prout	Uwins	Blanch	Eakins	Hudson
Le Vau	Proot	Vanni	Blythe	Elwell	Hughes
Lewis	Pryde	Velde	Bodley	Ellard	Hunter
Lippi	Pryse	Vivan	Boudin	Erlach	Ingles
Lotto	Puget	Vonet	Boxall	Eworth	Ingres
Lowry	Pugin	Watts	Braque	Ferber	Inness
Lucas	Pynas	Wells	Briggs	Ferren	Isabey
Manet	Rabin	White	Brough	Fildes	Ivanon
Maris	Redon	Wiens	Brunel	Finlay	Jagger
Mason	Ricci	Woods	Buchel	Fisher	Jarvis
Mauve	Riley	Wyatt	Burnet	Flavin	Jennys
Mense	Rodin	Wyeth	Burton	Floris	Joseph
Metso	Rooke	Wylie	Butler	Forbes	Kantor
			Bylert		

Kaprow	Nisbet	Saachi	Walker	Bellini
Kessel	Noland	Sadler	Waller	Bellows
Kettle	Obrist	Sandby	Wallis	Bennett
Keyser	Oliver	Sandys	Walton	Bercham
Knight	Olsson	Savery	Wardle	Bernard
Kramer	O'Neill	Scully	Warhol	Bernini
Kruger	Ostade	Seddon	Watson	Bianchi
Laroon	Paalen	Serres	Weekes	Bingham
Laszlo	Palmer	Seurat	Weenix	Boamyer
Latham	Panini	Signac	Weight	Boldini
Lavery	Parker	Sisley	Weyden	Bomberg
Lawson	Parton	Sluter	Wilkie	Bonnard
Leader	Paxton	Smirke	Wilson	Boshier
Lebrun	Pegram	Smythe	Wittel	Boucher
Ledoux	Pellan	Sodoma	Windus	Bramley
Legros	Penley	Spagna	Wright	Brauner
Le Nain	Pereda	Spence	Wyllie	Bridell
Le Witt	Perret	Stokes	Wynter	Brouwer
Leslie	Pettie	Storck	Yeames	Burlink
Linton	Pierce	Storey	Yvaral	Calvert
Lurcat	Pignon	Strang	Zenale	Camargo
Mabuse	Piombo	Strube	Zucchi	Cameron
McEvoy	Pimmer	Stuart		Campion
Manson	Pisano	Stubbs	**7**	Carraci
Marden	Potter	Tadema		Cellini
Marini	Powers	Tamayo	Acconci	Cennini
Martin	Predis	Tanguy	Aersten	Cézanne
Massys	Raffet	Tatlin	Alberti	Chagall
Merida	Ramsay	Tayler	Algardi	Chardin
Mesdac	Renoir	Taylor	Allston	Charles
Millet	Ribera	Thomas	Amigoni	Cheston
Miller	Riccio	Tissot	Andrews	Chirico
Monaco	Ridley	Titian	Appleby	Christo
Morley	Rimmer	Tocque	Aretino	Chryssa
Morone	Rivera	Troyon	Arundel	Cimabue
Morris	Rivers	Turner	Baldung	Clausen
Morrow	Robbia	Vacher	Balthos	Cockram
Müller	Robert	Valdes	Barlach	Cocteau
Murphy	Rogers	Van Ryn	Barocci	Collier
Murray	Romano	Varley	Bassano	Collins
Mytens	Romney	Vernet	Bateman	Connard
Neagle	Rothko	Verrio	Bazille	Corinth
Negret	Roualt	Vertue	Bearden	Cornell
Newman	Rubens	Vignon	Beechey	Cortona
Newton	Ruskin	Villon	Belcher	Courbet

Cranach	Goodwin	Klinger	Morrice	Rackham
Cundell	Gozzoli	Knapton	Mueller	Raeburn
Currier	Greaves	Kneller	Murillo	Raphael
Dalziel	Gregory	Knights	Nasmith	Rattner
Daniell	Grimmer	Kooning	Nattier	Resnick
Daumier	Gropius	Kossoff	Neumann	Reveron
Da Vinci	Guarini	Krasner	Noguchi	Richier
De Hooch	Guevara	La Fosse	O'Connor	Riviere
Deineka	Guthrie	Lambert	O'Gorman	Roberts
Dekkers	Haberle	Lancret	Olitzki	Rouault
Delvaux	Hackert	Lanteri	Onushto	Roussel
De Lazlo	Harding	Laurens	Orcagna	Russell
Dicksee	Hartley	Lemoyne	Orchard	Rustici
Diderot	Hartung	Lenbach	Osborne	Samaras
Dighton	Hayward	Lessore	Ordonez	Sanchez
Dorazio	Herbert	Levitan	Pacchia	Sargent
Douglas	Herring	Linnell	Pacheco	Schetky
Downman	Hillier	Llander	Parrish	Schiele
Duchamp	Hobbema	Lochner	Parsons	Sedgely
Edridge	Hockney	Lombard	Pasmore	Seghers
Edwards	Hodgkin	Lorenzo	Peacock	Seymour
El Greco	Hofland	Lucidel	Penrose	Shannon
Emanuel	Hofmann	Macbeth	Perreal	Shields
Epstein	Hogarth	Maccoli	Peruzzi	Sickert
Falcone	Hokusai	Maclise	Pevsner	Siddall
Ferrari	Holbein	Maderno	Phidias	Simpson
Flaxman	Holland	Maillol	Philips	Smetham
Fontana	Holroyd	Maistre	Phillip	Snyders
Fouquet	Hoppner	Mancini	Philpot	Solomon
Fox-Pitt	Hopwood	Mansart	Picabia	Spencer
Francia	Horsley	Maratti	Picasso	Stanley
Francke	Hoskins	Martini	Pickard	Stevens
Froment	Housman	Matisse	Pigalle	Stimmer
Furniss	Humphry	Meadows	Pinwell	Strozzi
Gabriel	Indiana	Memlinc	Pittoni	Tanning
Gallego	Isakson	Merritt	Polenus	Teniers
Garstin	Israels	Metcalf	Pollock	Tenniel
Gauguin	Jackson	Meunier	Pomeroy	Thirtle
Gertler	Jaggers	Michaux	Pourbus	Thomson
Gertlin	Jenkins	Millais	Poussin	Tibaldi
Gibbons	Jespers	Mitchel	Poynter	Tiepolo
Gifford	Johnson	Morales	Prinsep	Tiffany
Gilbert	Joulett	Morandi	Preston	Torelli
Gillray	Kallela	Morisot	Pucelle	Tunnard
Goodall	Kensett	Morland	Quellan	Uccello

Ugolino	Basissio	Desnoyer	Ironside	Nesfield
Utamaro	Bauchant	Deverell	Jacobsen	Nevinson
Utrillo	Beaumont	Dietrich	Jamesone	Niemeyer
Van Dyck	Beckmann	Domenico	Jan Steen	Oliveira
Van Eyck	Beerbohm	Dressler	John Opie	Overbesk
Van Gogh	Bellange	Dubuffet	Johnston	Ozenfant
Valadon	Bellotto	Dufresne	Jordaens	Palladio
Vaughan	Boccioni	Eastlake	Kaufmann	Papworth
Vecchio	Boffraud	Eggeling	Kaulbach	Paolozzi
Vellert	Boughton	Etchelle	Kienholz	Passmore
Vermeer	Brabazon	Evergood	Kirchner	Paul Nash
Vischer	Bramante	Falconet	Kokoshka	Pederson
von Elst	Brancusi	Fancelli	Kollwitz	Perugino
Vostell	Brangwyn	Ferguson	Kruseman	Phillips
Warburg	Brearley	Fielding	Lachaise	Pissarro
Watteau	Breitner	Flanagan	Landseer	Pomodoro
Webster	Bronzine	Fontaine	Lawrence	Pontormo
Westall	Brooking	Frampton	Leighton	Pynacker
Whiting	Breughel	Garofalo	Leonardo	Raimondi
Whitley	Caffière	Gerhaert	Logsdail	Redgrave
Wildens	Calderon	Ghiberti	Lombardo	Regnault
Woolner	Callcott	Gibbings	Lariondu	Reynolds
Wootton	Calthorp	Giordand	Macallum	Richmond
Wynants	Cappelle	Giovanni	Macquoid	Ricketts
Yunkers	Carducci	Goldberg	Magnelli	Robinson
Zadkins	Carracci	Gonzales	Magritte	Rockwell
Zoffany	Carrière	Gottlieb	Maitland	Romanino
Zuccaro	Chambers	Granacci	Mantegna	Rombouts
	Champney	Greenway	Marshall	Rossetti
8	Chandler	Grimaldi	Masaccio	Rousseau
	Chantrey	Grimshaw	Melville	Rugendas
Aaltonen	Christus	Hamilton	Melondez	Rushbury
Agostini	Colville	Hartwell	Millares	Saarinen
Albright	Cousteau	Hartigan	Mondrian	Salviati
Allinson	Crawford	Hepworth	Montalba	Sassetta
Amberger	Crawhall	Herkomer	Montanes	Scamozzi
Angelico	Creswick	Highmore	Montegna	Scheffer
Annesley	Crivelli	Hilliard	Mortimer	Schinkel
Annigoni	Darboven	Hitchens	Moynihan	Segonzac
Armitage	Daubigny	Hodgkins	Muirhead	Severini
Armstead	De Keyser	Holloway	Mulready	Simmonds
Atkinson	De Laszlo	Houghton	Munnings	Smithson
Augustin	Delaunay	Hultberg	Nadelman	Solimena
Aumonier	Del Prete	Ibbetson	Nanteuil	Spinello
Avercamp	Delville	Inchbold	Naviasky	Springer

Stanhope	Bickerton	Griffiths	Nicholson
Stothard	Biederman	Grünewald	Norhtcote
Streeter	Blackburn	Guido Reni	Oldenburg
Stringer	Blakelock	Halswelle	Oppenheim
Sullivan	Blanchard	Hatherell	Pechstein
Taiebaut	Bonington	Haussmann	Peselling
Terbosch	Botticini	Hawksmoor	Pettoruti
Tidemand	Boulicant	Henderson	Peverelli
Tinguely	Branwhite	Hitchcock	Pisanello
Topolski	Brustolon	Honthorst	Poliakoff
Tournier	Caldecott	Houbraken	Portinari
Turnbull	Caulfield	Hurlstone	Ravilious
Vanbrugh	Canaletto	Immendorf	Reinharot
Van Cleve	Cavallini	Jacobello	Rembrandt
Van Goyen	Collinson	Jawlensky	Remington
Van Steen	Colquhoon	Josephson	Romanello
Vasarely	Constable	Kandinsky	Roubillac
Verbeeck	Cornelius	Kauffmann	Salisbury
Vermeyen	Correggio	Kemp-Welch	Sansovino
Veronese	Courtauld	Kiprensky	Schafener
Vigeland	De Fresnov	Kokoschka	Schalcken
Vittoria	Delacroix	Kreighoff	Segantini
Vlaminck	Delaroche	Lancaster	Singleton
Vuillard	d'Erlanger	Lanfranco	Solrenson
Waterlow	Dominguez	La Thangue	Stanfield
Wheatley	Donaldson	Laurencin	Steenwyck
Whistler	Donatello	Lee-Hankey	Steinberg
Willcock	Elsheimer	Lightfoot	Stevenson
Williams	Everdiner	Llewellyn	Strudwick
Willinck	Fahlstrom	Lundquist	Telemaque
Woodward	Farington	Lundstrom	Thornhill
Zakharov	Feininger	MacDonald	Tischbein
Zurbarán	Fergusson	MacGregor	Trevisani
	Fernandez	MacKennal	Woodville
9	Flannagan	McLachlan	Velazquez
	Fragonard	McWhirter	Verrochio
Ackermann	Friedrich	Maleevich	Waterford
Alexander	Fromentin	Martineau	Whitcombe
Antonella	Gastineau	Maundrell	Yamaguchi
Appleyard	Generalic	Mazzolino	Yoshihara
Ardizzone	Géricault	Mestrovic	
Armstrong	Gillespie	Metzinger	**10**
Aston Webb	Giorgione	Mondriaan	
Baizerman	Greenhill	Mortenson	Alechinsky
Bakhinzen	Greenough	Multscher	Alma-Tadema
Beardsley			

Altichiero
Archipenko
Arcimsoldo
Baddelaire
Bandinelli
Bellegambi
Berrucuete
Blashfield
Botticelli
Bramantino
Breenbergh
Brockhurst
Burchfield
Burne-Jones
Carraciole
Caravaggio
Carmichael
Cattermole
Chasseriau
Courturier
Cruikshank
D'Arcangelo
Del Pacchia
Diebenkorn
di Giovanni
Eilshemius
Epiphanius
Everdingen
Fiddes-Watt
Finoguerra
Freundlich
Friedenson
Fulleylove
Giacometti
Glendening
Goncharova
Grandville
Guillaumin
Hammershoi
Heartfield
Hildebrand
Holman-Hunt
Huntingdon
Ipousteguy
Isenbrandt

Jan van Eyck
Kennington
La Brocquey
La Fresnaye
Lethbridge
Liebermann
Lienberger
Lorenzetti
Mackintosh
Macmonnies
Marcoussis
Meissonier
Meyer-Amden
Michelozzo
Modigliani
Monticelli
Ochtervelt
Orchardson
Padovanino
Passarotti
Pelligrini
Peppercorn
Pollaiuolo
Praxiteles
Procaccini
Richardson
Rowlandson
Saint-Aubin
Sanmicheli
Schonfeldt
Schneemann
Sebastiano
Shackleton
Siberechts
Somerville
Sutherland
Swynnerton
Tacuber-Arp
Tintoretto
Torrington
Trubetskuy
Van der Goes
Van der Meer
Van de Velde
Verrocchio

Verspronck
Waldmuller
Waterhouse
Wesselmann
Whittredge
Winstanley
Woollaston
Youngerman
Zuccarelli

11

Appolodorus
Beggarstaff
Cappogrossi
Chamberlain
Copley Heath
Craig-Martin
Della Robbia
Domenichino
Erhenstrahl
Fairweather
Falkenstein
Farquharson
Fra Angelico
Frothingham
Gheerhaerts
Ghirlandaio
Hondecoeter
Joos van Gent
Le Corbusier
Lloyd Wright
Lotherburg
Margaritone
Maso de Banco
Pickersgill
Poelenburgh
Polycleitus
Polykleitos
Prendergast
Rippingille
San Severino
Seisenegger
Somerscales
Terbrugghen

Thornycroft
Valkenborch
Van der Plaas
Van Ruisdael
Vereschagin

12

Beidermeiser
Brunelleschi
Carolusduran
Daring Hauser
Diaz de le Peña
Engelbrechsz
Fatin-Latour
Franciabigio
Gainsborough
Giunta Pisano
Grandma Moses
Huchtenburgh
Le Fauconnier
Lichtenstein
Loutherbourg
Marmigianino
Michelangelo
Muirhead-bone
Nanni di Ranco
Petroe-Vodkin
Rauschenberg
Rottenhammer
Sassoferrato
Schauffelein
Van der Weyden
Weissenbruch
Winterhalter
Witherington

13

Buenconsiglio
de Hondecoeter
Frankenthaler
Gallen Kallela
Heath Robinson
Hughes-Stanton

Middleton-Todd
Piero di Cosimo
Van Ochtervelt

Haynes-Williams
Riccidi Lorenzo
Schmidt Rutluff

Lawes Witteronge
Leonardo da Vinci
Pietro de Cortonia
Puvis de Chavannes
Rembrandt van Ryn
Theodoric of Prague
Theophanes the
 Greek
Toulouse-Lautrec
Van Huchenburgh
Vitale da Bologna

14

Andrea del Sarid
Bartold di Fredi
Della Francesca
de Loutherbourg
Ford Madox Brown
Gaudier-Brzeska

15 +

Arnold di Cambo
Augustino de Duccio
Baranoff Russine
Cornetille de Lyon
Giovanni da Milano
Giovanni di Bondone

Australian Prime Ministers

4

Cook, Sir J.
Holt, Harold
Page, Sir Earle
Reid, Sir G.

5

Bruce, Stanley M.
Forde, F.M.
Hawke, Robert

Lyons, Joseph A.

6

Barton, Sir Edmund
Curtin, John
Deakin, Alfred
Fadden, A.W.
Fisher, Andrew
Fraser, Malcolm
Gorton, J.G.
Hughes, William M.

McEwen, John
Watson, John

7

Chifley, J.B.
Keating, Paul
McMahon, William
Menzies, Sir Robert
Scullin, J.H.
Whitlam, Gough

Authors, philosophers, poets and playwrights

2 & 3	Gay	4	Ball	Bolt	Dahl
	Hay		Bana	Boye	Dons
Ady	Kyd	Agee	Baum	Buck	Dues
Aho	Lee	Alan	Beer	Bull	Du Fu
Arp	Paz	Amis	Benn	Cats	Eich
Ash	Poe	Asch	Blok	Cary	Folz
Dam	Sue	Ayer	Blox	Char	Ford
Fry	Vas	Ayme	Boll	Cruz	Frug

Fust	Roth	Ayres	Eliot	Kemal	Peele
Gide	Rowe	Barry	Elyot	Kesey	Peguy
Glyn	Ruiz	Barth	Ewald	Kidde	Pepys
Gray	Rung	Bates	Freud	Kinck	Perse
Grey	Saar	Bazin	Frost	Kraus	Piron
Hein	Sade	Beets	Gatti	Larra	Plath
Heym	Sa'Di	Behan	Genet	Leino	Plato
Hoel	Saki	Bello	Gogol	Lewis	Pliny
Hood	Sand	Belyl	Gorki	Locke	Pound
Hope	Shaw	Bembo	Gosse	Lodge	Powys
Hugo	Smaj	Benda	Gower	Logue	Prati
Hume	Snow	Benet	Grass	Lorca	Preti
Hunt	Soya	Berni	Green	Lowry	Prior
Ilie	Stub	Bette	Greig	Lucan	Pulci
Jens	Toth	Blake	Grimm	Lucas	Raabe
Kant	Tate	Bloem	Guidi	Macha	Raine
Kirk	Urfe	Bolto	Hacks	Marot	Ramuz
Kiss	Vega	Bojer	Halbe	Marsh	Reade
Koch	Vraz	Bowen	Halle	Marti	Rezac
Kock	Wain	Brant	Hardy	Mason	Ridja
Lamb	Ward	Broch	Harte	Matos	Rilke
Lang	Webb	Bunin	Hasek	Meyer	Rolfe
Lear	West	Burns	Hauff	Milne	Rozov
Lenz	Wood	Butor	Haugh	Monti	Sachs
Livy	Wren	Byron	Hegel	Moore	Sagan
Lobb	Wyss	Camus	Heine	Murry	Scene
Loos	Zola	Capek	Henry	Musil	Scott
Mann	Zech	Carew	Henty	Myers	Seton
Marx		Clare	Hertz	Nashe	Shute
Melo		Colum	Hesse	Nazor	Simms
Mill	**5**	Cople	Heyse	Novak	Simon
More		Cosie	Homer	Noyes	Smart
Muir	Abell	Craik	Hooft	Odets	Smith
Munk	Aboab	Crane	Hulme	O'Hara	Spark
Nash	Acton	Croce	Ibsen	Olsen	Staël
Nexo	Acuna	Dante	Imber	Opitz	Staff
Obey	Adams	Dario	Jahnn	Orczy	Stein
Oles	Aesop	Defoe	James	Orton	Storm
Ovid	Agnon	Deval	Jarry	Otway	Stowe
Perk	Ahlin	Donne	Jasik	Ouida	Svevo
Pope	Albee	Doyle	Jones	Paine	Swift
Read	Arany	Dumas	Joyce	Pan Gu	Synge
Renn	Arden	Duras	Kafka	Pater	Szabo
Rhys	Arnim	Dutch	Kaleb	Paton	Talev
Rode	Asnyk	Eeden	Keats	Peake	Tasso
	Auden				

Testi	Andric	Browne	Ekelof	Jonson	Muller
Thoor	Aprily	Bryant	Eluard	Jotuni	Munthe
Tieck	Aquino	Buchan	Empson	Jovine	Murger
Tompa	Aragon	Bunyan	Ennius	Kaiser	Murray
Tuwim	Archer	Burger	Evelyn	Kallas	Musset
Twain	Arnold	Burney	Falcao	Kalvos	Nechun
Tynan	Ascham	Butler	Fichte	Keller	Neruda
Tzara	Aseyeu	Caesar	Fouque	Kleist	Nemeth
Udall	Asimov	Camoes	Fowles	Kostic	Nerval
Urban	Aubrey	Capote	France	Kramer	Nesbit
Vadja	Austen	Carson	Frisch	Krieza	Njegos
Varro	Azorin	Castro	Fugard	Kumick	Norwid
Verde	Azuela	Cayrol	Fuller	Laclos	O'Brien
Verne	Balzac	Cavafy	Gaiser	Landor	O'Casey
Vidal	Barbey	Celine	Gibbon	Lanier	Olesha
Vigny	Barham	Celaya	Gibran	Lao-Tse	O'Neill
Virta	Barker	Celtis	Goethe	Larkin	Onerva
Waley	Barnes	Chekov	Grabbe	Larney	Orwell
Waugh	Baroja	Cibber	Graham	Lateur	Pagnal
Weiss	Barres	Clarke	Graves	Lawler	Parker
Wells	Barrie	Clough	Greene	Le Fanu	Pascal
White	Basile	Coffin	Grossi	Lefort	Pavese
Wilde	Baudri	Colman	Guitry	Leonov	Pereda
Wolfe	Bellay	Conrad	Habana	Lesage	Perron
Woolf	Belloc	Cooper	Hamsun	Lidman	Petofi
Wyatt	Bellow	Coppee	Harris	London	Picard
Yeats	Becque	Coward	Hebbel	Lowell	Pindar
Yonge	Ben-Ami	Cowley	Heller	Ludwig	Pinero
Zesen	Benson	Cowper	Hesiod	Lu Hsun	Pinter
Zeyer	Besant	Crabbe	Hierro	Lytton	Piozzi
Zorin	Bialik	Cretin	Hilton	Machen	Plomer
Zweig	Bierce	Cronin	Hobbes	Mailer	Porter
	Binyon	Curtis	Hoddis	Malory	Potter
6	Blyton	Daumal	Hojeda	Marino	Prados
	Bocage	Daniel	Holmes	Marner	Proust
Accius	Borges	Daudet	Horace	Mendes	Racine
Adamov	Borrow	Davies	Hudson	Mercer	Ramlar
Alcott	Brecht	Dehmel	Hughes	Millay	Ramsay
Aldana	Bremer	Dekker	Huxley	Miller	Ransom
Aldiss	Breton	de Sade	Illyes	Milton	Raynal
Aleman	Bridie	Donnay	Irving	Moberg	Reizen
Alfasi	Brieux	Dowson	Isaacs	Modena	Restif
Algren	Brontë	Dryden	Ivanov	Molnar	Reuter
Ambler	Brooke	Dunbar	Jammes	Morgan	Rhigas
Andres	Brophy	Durych	Jensen	Morike	Roland

Rowley	Vondel	Belleau	Corelli	Golding
Runyon	Wagner	Bellman	Crashaw	Grahame
Ruskin	Walden	Bennett	Creeley	Gresser
Samain	Waller	Bentham	da Ponte	Guarini
Sandel	Walser	Bentley	Deledda	Gunther
Sapper	Walton	Bergman	Delille	Haggard
Sappho	Warton	Bergson	Desnick	Hammett
Sardou	Werfel	Bernard	de Vigny	Hansson
Sartre	Wesker	Blunden	Dickens	Hartley
Savage	Wilder	Boiardo	Diderot	Hartman
Sayers	Wilson	Boileau	Dinesen	Hazlitt
Scribe	Wolker	Boreman	Dodgson	Heiberg
Seneca	Wotton	Boswell	Douglas	Hellman
Sereni	Wright	Bousono	Drabble	Herbert
Sidney	Yovkou	Boutens	Drayton	Hermans
Silone		Bo Zhu Yi	Dreiser	Herrick
Singer	**7**	Bradley	Duhamel	Heywood
Smiles		Brandao	Dunsany	Holberg
Sponde	Aakjeer	Bridges	Durrell	Hopkins
Stampa	Addison	Bronson	Ekelund	Housman
Steele	Aelfric	Buchner	Emerson	Huygens
Sterne	Aguilar	Burgess	Ercilla	Ibn Ezra
Stoker	Aksakov	Burnett	Eupolis	Iflland
Storey	Alarcon	Buzzati	Ferrier	Ionesco
Stramm	Alberti	Cadalso	Feuillet	Jeffers
Surrey	Alcaeus	Caedmon	Feydeau	Jimenez
Symons	Aldanov	Campana	Firbank	Jodelle
Tagore	Aldrich	Cao Chan	Flecker	Johnson
Talvio	Alegria	Carossa	Fleming	Juvenal
Tarsis	Aneirin	Carroll	Folengo	Kassack
Thomas	Anouilh	Cernuda	Fontane	Kastner
Toller	Aquinas	Centina	Forster	Kaufman
Torres	Arbuzon	Chamson	Foscolo	Kendall
Toulet	Aretino	Chapman	Freneau	Kerouac
Traven	Arghezi	Chaucer	Freytag	Kipling
Uhland	Ariosto	Chekhov	Froding	Kirshon
Elevic	Arrabal	Chenier	Gabirol	Klinger
Undset	Azevedo	Chu Yuan	Gallico	Knudsen
Updike	Babusse	Clauden	Garnier	Labiche
Uppdal	Balchin	Cleland	Garrett	Lardner
Valery	Baldwin	Cocteau	Gaskell	Layamon
Vesaas	Barbour	Cobbett	Gautier	Leacock
Vidric	Baretti	Colette	Gilbert	Le Carre
Villon	Beckett	Collins	Gippius	Lehmann
Virgil	Beddoes	Conetti	Gissing	Lessing

Lindsay	Prevert	Thomson	Bataille	Fielding
Lydgate	Pushkin	Thoreau	Beaumont	Figueroa
Machaut	Pynchon	Thurber	Beckford	Firdausi
McKenna	Queneau	Todorov	Beerbohm	Fischart
Malamud	Quental	Tolkein	Belinsky	Flaubert
Malraux	Radnoti	Tolstoy	Benchley	Fletcher
Manzoni	Ransome	Travers	Beranger	Fontaine
Marceau	Regnier	Trenyov	Berkeley	Fontanes
Marlowe	Reymont	Tristan	Bernanos	Forester
Marryat	Richler	Tutuola	Bertrand	Ginsberg
Marston	Rimbaud	Unamuno	Betjeman	Goncourt
Martial	Rolland	Ustinov	Bjornson	Gonzales
Martins	Romains	Vaughan	Bradbury	Gryphius
Marvell	Ronsard	Veldeke	Brancati	Heinesen
Masters	Rostand	Vicente	Brentano	Henryson
Maugham	Rousell	Volodin	Browning	Hochhuth
Mauriac	Russell	Wallace	Calderon	Hoffmman
Maurois	Rydberg	Walpole	Campbell	Holstein
Medrona	Sarment	Webster	Carducci	Huysmans
Mencken	Sassoon	Weinert	Carrillo	Imperial
Mercier	Scarron	Wharton	Castilho	Jacobsen
Merimée	Schaper	Whitman	Catullus	Kalidasa
Mishima	Seferis	Wieland	Chandler	Kavanagh
Mistral	Shaffer	Winkler	Chartier	Kingsley
Molière	Shapiro	Wittlin	Christie	Kirsanov
Montagu	Shelley	Yesenin	Claudian	Koestler
Montale	Simenon	Yavarov	Claussen	Kornilov
Moravia	Simonov		Congreve	Kotzebue
Morante	Sitwell		Conquest	Kualmann
Moretti	Siwertz	**8**	Constant	Laforgue
Murdoch	Skelton		Corbiere	Lagerlöf
Nabokov	Sosyura	Abulafia	Crompton	Langland
Naevius	Southey	Abu Nuwas	Cummings	Las Cases
Nagibin	Staring	Agricola	Cynewulf	La Taille
Naipaul	Soyinka	Anacreon	Dagerman	Lawrence
Neumann	Spencer	Anchieta	Davenant	Leibnitz
Novalis	Spender	Andersch	Day Lewis	Leopardi
Obaldia	Spenser	Andersen	De la Mare	Lehtonen
O'Connor	Spinoza	Anderson	De Musset	Leopardi
Osborne	Stevens	Annensky	Disraeli	Lockhart
Palacio	Surtees	Apuleius	Donleavy	Longinus
Patmore	Tacitus	Asturias	Du Bartas	Lovelace
Peacock	Tardieu	Atterbom	Elsschot	Macaulay
Piovene	Terence	Bandeira	Etherege	Macleish
Plautus	Thespis	Banville	Faulkner	Macneice
		Barbusse		

Majerova	Sillitoe	Aldington	Goncharov	O'Flaherty
Malherbe	Sinclair	Alexandre	Gottsched	Osterling
Mallarmé	Slowacki	Allingham	Greenwood	Ostrovsky
Manninen	Smollet	Angilbert	Guerrazzi	Parkinson
Marivauz	Spillane	Arbuthnot	Hauptmann	Pasternak
Marquand	Stendhal	Aristotle	Hawthorne	Perzynski
Melville	Stoppard	Berkowitz	Hemingway	Poliziano
Menander	Strachey	Bernardes	Hernandes	Pratolini
Meredith	Stricker	Bernstein	Herodotus	Pratchett
Michelet	Suckling	Bidermann	Highsmith	Priestley
Mirabeau	Su Dong Po	Blackmore	Holderlin	Pritchett
Mitchell	Taliesin	Blackwood	Immermann	Radcliffe
Mustapaa	Tansillo	Bobrowski	Isherwood	Rochester
Naogeorg	Tennyson	Boccaccio	Jefferies	Rodriguez
Nekrasov	Thompson	Borchardt	Jorgenson	Rosenhane
Nicolson	Timeneda	Bulatovie	Kisfaludy	Sackville
Overland	Tourneur	Burroughs	Klopstock	Schickele
Palgrave	Traherne	Cervantes	La Bruyere	Schreiner
Pasolini	Trilling	Cesarotti	La Fayette	Sebastian
Pearlman	Trollope	Charteris	Lamartine	Shenstone
Perrault	Tulsidas	Churchill	Lampedusa	Sholokhov
Petrarch	Turgenev	Ciminelli	Laurenyou	Slaveykov
Phaedrus	Tyutcher	Coleridge	Lermontov	Sodergran
Philemon	Ukrainka	Compaomor	Linklater	Sophocles
Pichette	Vailland	Corneille	Llewellyn	Steinbeck
Plutarch	Vanbrugh	Dabrowski	Lomonosov	Sternheim
Quintana	Verlaine	D'Annunzio	Lovecraft	Stevenson
Rabelais	Vennberg	de la	Lucretius	Sturluson
Radiguet	Villegas	Roche	Lundkuist	Suetonius
Rankovic	Voltaire	de Quincey	Mackenzie	Sumarokov
Rattigan	Voronsky	Descartes	Malaparte	Swinburne
Remarque	Vonnegut	Deschamps	Mansfield	Thackeray
Richards	Wedekind	Doolittle	Marinette	Theotokas
Rossetti	Welhaven	Dos Passos	Martineau	Trevelyan
Rousseau	Williams	Drachmann	Martinson	Tsvetaeva
Runeberg	Zapolska	Du Guillet	Masefield	Ungaretti
Salinger	Zamyatin	Du Maurier	Massinger	Velichkov
Sandburg	Zorilla	Eckermann	McCullers	Verhaeren
San Pedro		Edgeworth	Middleton	Vinokorov
Sarraute	**9**	Ehrenberg	Michaelis	Vittorini
Scaliger		Euripides	Monsarrat	Wergeland
Scheffel	Abravenel	Fridegard	Montaigne	Wildenvey
Schiller	Aeschylus	Froissart	Mutanabbi	Witkewicz
Shadwell	Ainsworth	Giraudoux	Nordstrom	Wodehouse
Sheridan	Akhmatova	Goldsmith	Nietzsche	Woestjine

Wycherley
Zhukovsky
Zimorovic
Zuckmayer

10

Achterberg
Albertinus
Alecsandri
Ballantyne
Baudelaire
Bilderdijk
Brassilach
Bregendahl
Campanella
Cavalcanti
Chatterjee
Chatterton
Chesterton
Clenfuegos
Colliander
Conan Doyle
Conscience
Courteline
Czechowiez
Dazai Osamu
de Beauvoir
Della Vale
Destouches
Dio Cassius
Dostoevsky
Drinkwater
Dürrenmatt
Ebrenstein
Fitzgerald
Fontanella
Galsworthy
Guinizelli
Hallgrimur
Heidenstam
Henningsen
Ignjatovic
Kasprovicz
Khlebnikov

La Fontaine
Lagerkvist
Lohenstein
Longfellow
Macdiarmid
Mandelstam
Maupassant
McGonagall
Metastasio
Mickiewicz
Obstfelder
Ostrovskii
Peyrefitte
Pirandello
Prevalakis
Propertius
Quintilian
Richardson
Rutherford
Saint-Simon
Schnitzler
Shevchenko
Spielhagen
Strindberg
Tannhauser
Tendryakou
Theocritus
Thucydides
Van Der Post
Vishnevsky
Wassermann
Williamson
Wordsworth
Zabolotsky
Zamfiresco

11

Ankerlarsen
Anzengruber
Apollinaire
Archilochus
Bacchylides
Beer-Hofman
Blessington

Bontempelli
Callimachus
Castiglione
Champfleury
de la Bruyère
Dostoyevski
Eichendorff
Friis Muller
Garcia Lorca
Grillparzer
Gyllenstein
Kazantazkis
Kochanowski
Lautréamont
Lo-Johansson
Maeterlinck
Matsuo Basho
Mayakovskii
Montherlant
Omar Khayyam
Palazzeschi
Perez Galdos
Pontoppidan
Shakespeare
Sienkiewicz
Stuckenberg
Superveille
Veselinovic
Valdivielso
Yevtushenko
Weyssenhoff

12

Aristophanes
Beaumarchais
Dahlistjerna
Ferlinghetti
Feuchtwanger
Gabrie y Galan
Hartzenbusch
Hofmannsthal
Lichtenstein
Lopez de Ayala
Martin Du Gard

Matthew Paris
Perez de Ayala
Robbe-Grillet
Saint-Exupery
Solzhenitsyn
Tocqueville
Viele-Griffin
Voznesenskii
Wittgenstein

13

Castelo Branco
Chateaubriand
Csokonai Vitez
Harishchandra
Marie de France
Montchristien
Paludan-Muller
Sep-Szarzynski
Tirso de Molina
Villchardouin
Zeami Motokiyo

14

Avarez Quintero
Brillat-Savarin
Compton-Burnett
Dafydd Ap Gwilym
Dante Alighieri
Droste-Hulshoff
Gongora y Argote
Grimmelshausen
Herrmann-Neisse
Jacopone da Todi
Leconte de Lisle
Lopez de Mendoza
Martinez Sierra
Ochlenschlager
Prévost
 de'exiles
Sully-Prudhomme
Tchernichowski
Wollstonecraft

Wollstonecroft
Velez de Guevara
Zorrilla y Moral

15

Alarcon y Mendoza
Bores D'Hauterive
Diodorus Siculus
Garcia Gutierrez
Granville Barker
Guittone D'arezzo
Kaden-Brandrowski
Pliny The Younger
Villiers de Lisle

16

Bosboom-Toussaint
Chretien de Troyes
Christine de Pison
Cyrano de Bergerac
Garcilas de la Vega
Hedenvind-Erksson
Kawabata Yasunari
Petronius Arbiter
Platen-Hallemunde
Rojas Villandrano

17 +

Andreas Capellanus
Apollonius of Rhodes
Benoit de Sainte-Maure
Bernardin de Saint-Pierre
Calderon de la Barca
Chikamatsu Monzaemon
Dionysius of Halicarnassus
Drummond of Hawthornden
Echegaray y Eizaguirre
Friederich von Hausen
Gottfried von Strassburg
Guillaume de Lorris
Heinrich von Melsson
Heinrich von Neustade
Heinrich von Witten Weller
Helinand de Fradmont
Kakinomoto Hitomaro
Sanchez de Badojoz
Tanizaki Jun-Ichiro
Thomas of Erceldoune
Ulrich von Lichenstein
Villiers de l'Isle-Adam
Walter of Chatillon
Walter von der Vogelweide
Ziegler und Kliphausen

Battles and sieges

3	Alma	Taku	Arras	El	Malta	Tagus
	Amoy	Troy	Basra	Teb	Marne	Texel
Kut	Caen	Yser	Blitz	Eylau	Meuse	Tours
Lys	Gaza	Zama	Boyne	Genoa	Miami	Valmy
Tet	Ivry		Bulge	Herat	Paris	Ypres
Ulm	Jena	**5**	Burma	Issus	Pusan	
	Laon		Cadiz	Kabul	Rhine	**6**
	Loos	Aisne	Cairo	Kandy	Sedan	
4	Maas	Alamo	Calvi	Lewes	Selby	Actium
	Mons	Alton	Crécy	Liege	Selle	Amiens
Acre	Nile	Anzio	Crete	Ligny	Shilo	Arbela
Aden	Rhur	Arcot	Delhi	Maida	Somme	Argaon
Agra						

Arnhem	Orthez	Cape Bon	Preston	Lake Erie
Assaye	Ostend	Cassino	St. Kitts	Lansdown
Atbara	Peking	Chalons	St. Lucia	Le Cateau
Bagdad	Pinkie	Chester	Salamis	Langside
Barnet	Plevna	Coimbra	Salerno	Mafeking
Bastia	Quebec	Colenso	Sobraon	Malakoff
Bataan	Rhodes	Concord	Solebay	Marathon
Berlin	Rivoli	Cordova	Taranto	Maubeuge
Burgos	Rocroi	Coronel	Trenton	Medellin
Busaco	Sadowa	Corunna	Vimiera	Messines
Calais	Saints	Dresden	Vitoria	Metaurus
Camden	Shiloh	Dunkirk	Wareham	Mohne Dam
Cannae	Tarifa	Edgecot		Montreal
Chusan	Tobago	Edghill		Navarino
Coruna	Tobruk	El Obeid	**8**	Nieuport
Dargai	Toulon	Evesham		Normandy
Delium	Towton	Falkirk	Antietam	Omdurman
Dieppe	Tudela	Flodden	Ardennes	Philippi
Dyrham	Tugela	Granada	Atlantic	Poitiers
Dunbar	Ushant	Gwalior	Bastille	Potidaea
Exeter	Verdun	Iwo Jima	Benfleet	Pretoria
Ferrol	Vienna	Jutland	Beresina	Przemysl
Guarda	Wagram	La Hogue	Blenheim	St. Albans
Gujrat	Warsaw	Leipzig	Bhurtpur	St. Mihiel
Havana		Lemberg	Borodino	St. Pierre
Hexham	**7**	Lepanto	Bosworth	Salsette
Isonzo		Leuthen	Brooklyn	Saratoga
Jattoo	Aboukir	Lucknow	Calcutta	Spion Kop
Jhansi	Abu Klea	Magdala	Carthage	Stirling
Lutzen	Alamein	Magenta	Cawnpore	Suvla Bay
Madras	Albuera	Marengo	Coral Sea	Syracuse
Madrid	Almansa	Matapan	Cowperis	Talavera
Majuba	Almeida	Megiddo	Culloden	Tenerife
Malaga	Antwerp	Minorca	Edgehill	Tiberias
Manila	Ashdown	Moselle	Edington	Toulouse
Mantua	Atlanta	Moskowa	Flanders	Valencia
Masada	Badajoz	Nations	Flushing	Waterloo
Midway	Baghdad	Newbury	Fontenoy	Yorktown
Mileto	Bapaume	Nivelle	Fort Erie	Zaragoza
Minden	Bautzen	Okinawa	Granicus	
Moscow	Bousaco	Orléans	Guernica	**9**
Nagpur	Brienne	Plassey	Hastings	
Narvik	Britain	Plataea	Hydaspes	Agincourt
Naseby	Bull Run	Ploesti	Inkerman	Aldershot
Oporto	Cambrai	Poltava	Kandahar	Algeciras
			Khartoum	

Ashingdon
Balaclava
Belle Isle
Caporetto
Chaeronea
Champagne
Charleroi
Ctesiphon
Dettingen
Eddington
El Alamein
Falklands
Festubert
Friedland
Gallipoli
Gaugamela
Gibraltar
Hyderabad
Kimberley
Ladysmith
Laing's Nek
Leningrad
Lexington
Leyte Gulf
Louisburg
Mauritius
Melagnano
Mobile Bay
Otterburn
Oudenarde
Pharsalus
Port Mahon
Ramillies
Rochester
Rodriguez
Saragossa
St. Quentin
St. Vincent
Salamanca
Sedgemoor
Solferino
Stormberg
Stromboli
Tarragona
Tourcoing

Trafalgar
Vicksburg
Vimy Ridge
Wakefield
Walcheren
Worcester
Zeebrugge

10

Adrianople
Ahmednagar
Alexandria
Appomattox
Austerlitz
Beachy Head
Brandywine
Brownstown
Brunanburh
Bunker Hill
Camperdown
Charleston
Chevy-chase
Chichester
Cold Harbor
Copenhagen
Corregidor
Dogger Bank
Fort George
Fort Hudson
Fort Sumter
Germantown
Gettysburg
Goose Green
Gravelotte
Guadeloupe
Heligoland
Imjin River
Kut-el-Amara
La Rochelle
Les Saintes
Malplaquet
Martinique
Montevideo
Montfaucon

New Orleans
Nördlingen
Paardeburg
Petersburg
Port Arthur
Porto Praya
Quatre Bras
River Plate
River Stour
Sevastopol
Shrewsbury
Solway Moss
Stalingrad
Tannenberg
Tel-el-Kebir
Tewkesbury
Tinchebray
Wilderness

11

Albuquerque
Bannockburn
Breitenfeld
Chattanooga
Chilianwala
Dardanelles
Dien Bien Phu
Fort Niagara
Guadalcanal
Halidon Hill
Hedgley Moor
Hohenlinden
Isandhlwana
Jameson Raid
Lostwithiel
Marston Moor
Pearl Harbor
Philiphaugh
Philippines
Pieter's Hill
Pondicherry
Prestonpans
Quiberon Bay
Rorke's Drift

Schoneveldt
Schweinfurt
Sheriffmuir
Thermoplyae
Ticonderoga
White Plains

12

Adwalton Moor
Belville Wood
Bloemfontein
Flodden Field
Gainsborough
Harper's Ferry
Homildon Hill
Maiden Castle
Northallerton
Radcot Bridge
Roundway Down
San Sebastian
Seringapatam
Trichinopoly
Turnham Green

13

Antietam Creek
Boroughbridge
Bosworth Field
Cape St.
   Vincent
Ciudad Rodrigo
Lake Champlain
Little Bighorn
Losecoat Field
Magersfontein
Messines Ridge
Neuve Chapelle
Neville's Cross
Passchendaele
Spanish Armada
Stow-on-the-
   Wold
White Mountain

29

14

Chalgrove Field
Constantinople
Cropredy Bridge
Fredericksburg
Mortimer's Cross

Stamford Bridge
Tsushima Strait

15 +

Battle of Britain
Brandywine River

Countisbury Hill
Falkland Islands
Guilford Court
  House
Heights of Abraham
Plains of Abraham

Bays (b), capes (c), channels (ch), firths (f), gulfs (g) and straits (s)

3 & 4

Aden	(g)	Hawke	(b)	Biscay	(b)	Bothnia	(g)
Bass	(s)	Kerch	(s)	Botany	(b)	Bristol	(b,ch)
Cod	(c)	Kutch	(g)	Cambay	(g)	Chidley	(c)
Cook	(s)	Lions	(g)	Colwyn	(b)	Corinth	(g)
East	(c)	Lorne	(f)	Danzig	(g)	Denmark	(s)
Horn	(c)	Maine	(g)	Dingle	(b)	Donegal	(b)
Luce	(b)	Menai	(s)	Dublin	(b)	Dornoch	(f)
Lyme	(b)	Moray	(f)	Hormuz	(s)	Dundalk	(b)
Oman	(g)	North	(c,ch)	Hudson	(b,s)	Dundrum	(b)
Race	(c)	Papua	(g)	Mannai	(g)	English	(ch)
Riga	(g)	Paria	(g)	Masira	(g)	Finland	(g)
Suez	(g)	Sable	(c)	Mexico	(g)	Florida	(s)
		Salem	(g)	Mounts	(b)	Formosa	(s)

5

		Scott	(c)	Naples	(g)	Foveaux	(s)
Aqaba	(g)	Sirte	(g)	Panama	(g)	Killala	(b)
Cabot	(s)	Start	(b)	Parita	(g)	Malacca	(s)
Cadiz	(g)	Tunis	(g)	Plenty	(b)	Persian	(g)
Clyde	(f)	Verde	(c)	Solway	(f)	Salerno	(g)
Corfu	(s)			St.Ives	(b)	Sandown	(b)
Davis	(s)			Tasman	(b)	Swansea	(b)
Dover	(s)	**6**		Tonkin	(g)	Taranto	(g)
Forth	(f)			Torbay	(b)	Totland	(b)
Fundy	(b)	Alaska	(g)			Trieste	(g)
Gabes	(g)	Anadyr	(g)			Trinity	(b)
Genoa	(g)	Baffin	(b)	**7**		Wigtown	(b)
		Bantry	(b)			Yucatan	(ch)
		Barrow	(b)	Aboukir	(b)		
		Beauly	(f)	Bigbury	(b)		
		Bering	(s)	Boothia	(g)		

8

Amundsen	(g)
Bideford	(b)
Blacksod	(b)
Campeche	(g)
Cardigan	(b)
Chiriqui	(g)
Colombia	(c)
Cromarty	(f)
Delaware	(b)
Farewell	(c)
Flamingo	(b)
Flattery	(c)
Good Hope	(c)
Hammamet	(g)
Hatteras	(c)
Honduras	(g)
Makassar	(s)
Martaban	(g)
Pentland	(f)
Quiberon	(b)
San Jorge	(g)

Sembilan	(s)
St. Bride's	(b)
Tremadoc	(b)
Valencia	(g)

9

Belle Isle	(s)
Capricorn	(ch)
Discovery	(b)
Frobisher	(b)
Gibraltar	(s)
Guayaquil	(g)
Liverpool	(b)
Mendocino	(c)
Morecambe	(b)
Mosquitos	(g)
Notre Dame	(b)
Placentia	(b)
St. Bridges	(b)
St. Vincent	(c)
Trafalgar	(c)
Trearddur	(b)

10

Bridgwater	(b)
Byam Martin	(ch)
Carmarthen	(b)
California	(g)
Conception	(b)
Coronation	(g)
Freshwater	(b)
St. Lawrence	(g)
Van Diemen	(g)

11

Carpentaria	(g)
Tehuantepec	(g)

12 +

Morrosquillo	(g)
Joseph Bonaparte	(g)

Biblical characters

2 & 3	4		5		
Asa	Abel	Ezra	Noah	Abner	Gaius
Buz	Adah	Heth	Onan	Abram	Gomer
Eli	Adam	Irad	Paul	Annas	Hagar
Eve	Ahab	Jael	Phut	Barak	Haman
Gad	Ahaz	Jehu	Ruth	Caleb	Hamor
God	Amos	Joab	Saul	Cyrus	Herod
Gog	Aner	Joel	Seba	Dagon	Hiram
Ham	Aser	John	Seth	David	Hosea
Huz	Baal	Jude	Shah	Dedan	Isaac
Job	Boaz	Leah	Shem	Demas	Jabel
Lot	Cain	Levi		Devil	Jacob
Og	Cush	Luke	**5**	Dinah	James
	Enos	Magi	Aaron	Elias	Jarod
	Esau	Mark	Abiah	Elihu	Javan
		Mary	Abihu	Enoch	Jeran
		Moab		Gaham	Jesse

Jesus	Apphra	Nahath	Gabriel	Caiaphas
Joash	Balaam	Nathan	Goliath	Ebenezer
Jonah	Belial	Nimrod	Havilah	Gamaliel
Joram	Bilhah	Philip	Ishmael	Habakkuk
Joses	Cainan	Pilate	Japheth	Herodius
Jubal	Canaan	Raamah	Jehovah	Hezekiah
Judah	Christ	Rachel	Jezebel	Immanuel
Judas	Daniel	Reuben	Jezreel	Isacchar
Laban	Darius	Reumah	Joiakim	Iscariot
Linus	Dismas	Rizpah	Keturah	Issachar
Lucas	Dorcas	Sabtah	Lazarus	Jephthah
Lydia	Elijah	Salome	Lucifer	Jeremiah
Madai	Elisha	Samson	Malachi	Jeraboam
Magog	Ephron	Samuel	Malchus	Jonathan
Mamre	Eschol	Shelah	Maneses	Josedech
Micah	Esther	Simeon	Matthew	Maccabee
Moses	Eunice	Sisera	Meshach	Manasseh
Nahor	Festus	Thomas	Michael	Matthias
Nahum	Gehazi	Uzziah	Mizraim	Mehujael
Naomi	Gideon	Yahweh	Obadiah	Mordecai
Ophir	Gilboa	Zillah	Ogarmah	Naphtali
Peter	Haggai	Zilpah	Pharoah	Nehemiah
Rahab	Hannah	Zimran	Philcol	Onesimus
Sarah	Isaiah	Zophar	Phineas	Philemon
Satan	Israel		Raphael	Potiphar
Sheba	Jairus	**7**	Rebekah	Rehoboam
Sihon	Jethro		Riphath	St. Dismas
Silas	Joseph	Abigail	Scechem	Sabtecha
Simon	Joshua	Abraham	Shallum	Sapphira
Tamar	Josiah	Absalom	Solomon	Shadrach
Tebah	Jotham	Ananias	Stephen	Zecharia
Tirus	Judith	Antipas	Timothy	Zedekiah
Titus	Kemuel	Apolyon	Zebedee	Zipporah
Tubal	Kittim	Azariah	Zebulon	
Uriah	Kohath	Bethual		**9**
Uriel	Lamech	Clement	**8**	
Zadok	Marcus	Cleopas		Abimelech
Zimri	Martha	Deborah	Abednego	Ahasuerus
	Milcar	Delilah	Abinadab	Barachias
6	Miriam	Didymus	Adonijah	Bathsheba
	Mizpah	Dodanim	Alphaeus	Boanerges
Abadon	Naamah	Eleazer	Archipus	Cornelius
Abijah	Naaman	Elkanah	Barabbas	Demetrius
Amalek	Naboth	Ephraim	Barnabas	Elisabeth
Andrew	Nahash	Ezekiel	Benjamin	Jehoiakim

Magdalene
Methusael
Nathanael
Nepthalim
Nicodemus
Sephamiah
Shealtiel
Thaddaeus
Tubal-Cain
Zacchaeus
Zachariah
Zacharias
Zephaniah

Mahalaleel
Theophilus
Virgin Mary

11

Aristarchus
Bartholomew
Jehoshaphat
Jesus Christ
Melchisedec
Melchizedek
Sennacherib

13

Judas Iscariot
Mary of Bethany
Mary Magdalene
Pontius Pilate

14

John the Baptist
Nebuchadnezzar

15 +

James's the Greater
John's the Evangelist
Joseph of Arimathea
Philip of Bethsaida
Philip the Evangelist
Simon the Caananite

10

Bartimaeus
Belshazzar
Holofernes
Methuselah

12

James the Less
Witch of Endor

Birds

2	owl	crow	kiwi	rhea	amsel	diver
	pau	dodo	knot	rook	annet	drake
ka	pen	dove	koel	ruff	argus	dunne
oo	pie	duck	kora	rype	biddy	dunny
	poe	erne	lark	shag	bongo	eagle
3	roc	eyas	loon	skua	booby	egret
	tit	fowl	lory	smee	bowet	eider
auk	tui	gawk	mina	smew	brant	finch
cob	wry	gowk	monk	swan	brent	frank
daw		guan	myna	taha	bucco	galah
emu		gull	nene	teal	capon	ganza
ern	**4**	hawk	nias	tern	chick	glede
hen		hern	nyas	tody	claik	goose
jay	barb	huia	nyas	weka	colin	grebe
kea	baya	huma	pauw	wren	crake	gripe
mao	bubo	ibis	pavo	xema	crane	harpy
maw	chat	jack	pern	yite	creak	henny
mew	cirl	kagu	pica		curre	heron
moa	cock	kaka	piet	**5**	daker	hobby
nun	coly	kite	poll		didus	homer
	coot		rail	agami		

imber	reeve	veery	coucal	keltis	pygarg
jager	robin	vireo	cuckoo	kiddow	queest
junco	rodge	virgo	culver	kondor	quelea
larus	rotch	wader	curlew	lanner	quezal
layer	rudge	wagel	cushat	leipoa	ratite
lowan	ryper	wavey	cygnet	linnet	redcap
loxia	sacre	whaup	cygnus	loriot	reeler
lyrie	saker	whilk	darter	magpie	roberd
macaw	sally	wonga	dipper	marrot	rocker
madge	sarus	yacou	dopper	martin	roller
maneh	sasia		drongo	menura	rotche
mavis	saury	**6**	ducker	merlin	ruddoc
merle	scape		duiker	merops	rumkin
minah	scarf	Adelie	dunlin	merula	runner
miner	scaup	aiglet	eaglet	missel	sappho
molly	scoby	aigret	einack	mistle	scaury
monal	scops	alcedo	elanet	monaul	scobby
murre	scout	alcyon	falcon	mopoke	scoter
mynah	scray	Amazon	fulmar	mot-mot	sea-bar
nandu	scull	ananas	galeen	musket	sea-cob
nelly	senex	ancona	gambet	nandoo	sea-hen
noddy	serin	argala	gander	nandow	sea-mew
ornis	shama	auklet	gannet	nestor	sea-pie
ortyx	sitta	avocet	garrot	nicker	serula
ousel	skite	avoset	gentoo	oriole	shrike
ouzel	snipe	bantam	godurt	osprey	shrite
owlet	solan	barbet	godwit	ouzlem	sicsac
oxeye	soree	bishop	gorhen	oxbird	simbil
paauw	spink	bonxie	goslet	parrot	siskin
pewet	squab	bowess	grakle	parson	smeath
pewit	stare	brahma	grouse	pastor	soland
picus	stilt	brolga	guinea	pavone	sorage
piper	stint	budgie	hacket	peahen	sparve
pipit	stork	buffel	hagden	peeper	strich
pitta	strix	bulbul	hareld	peewit	strick
poaka	swift	cagmag	hermit	pernis	sultan
poker	tarin	canary	hoazin	petrel	surrey
polly	terek	chough	hoopoe	phoebe	takahe
poult	tiddy	chukar	hoopoo	pigeon	tarsel
prion	topau	chukor	houdan	plover	tatler
purre	topet	citril	jabiru	poulet	tercel
quail	twite	cochin	jacana	pouter	tewhit
radge	umbre	condor	jaeger	powter	thrush
ralph	urile	corbie	jerkin	puffin	tirwit
raven	urubu	corvus	kakapo	pullet	tomtit

toucan
towhee
tringa
trogon
turaco
turbit
turkey
turner
turtle
tystie
waggel
weaver
whidah
whydah
wigeon
willet
witwal
xenops
yaffle
yaffil
ynambu
yucker
zicsac
zivola
zoozoo

7

antbird
apteryx
attagas
attagen
awl-bird
babbler
barn owl
bee-bird
bee-kite
bittern
blue-cap
blue-eye
blue jay
bluetit
boobook
buceros
bull-bat

bummalo
bunting
buphaga
bush-tit
bustard
butcher
buzzard
cackler
caponet
cariama
carvist
cat-bird
chewink
chicken
ciconia
coal tit
cob-swan
colibri
columba
corella
cotinga
courlan
courlin
courser
cow-bird
cracker
creeper
crombec
cropper
dididae
dorhawk
dorking
dottrel
doucher
dovekie
dovelet
dun-bird
dunnock
egg-bird
emu-wren
fantail
fen duck
fern owl
fig-bird
finfoot

fish owl
flapper
flicker
flusher
gadwall
gavilan
gobbler
gorcock
gorcrow
goshawk
gosling
grackle
grallae
graylag
greyhen
greylag
grey hen
grey owl
hacklet
halcyon
harfang
harrier
hatcher
hawk owl
hickway
hoatzin
horn owl
ice-bird
impeyan
jacamar
jacinth
jackass
jackdaw
jacksaw
jacobin
jashawk
jedcock
kamichi
kestrel
killdee
kinglet
lagopus
lapwing
laugher
lavrock

Leghorn
lentner
lich-owl
lorilet
mallard
manakin
manikin
marabou
maracan
martlet
may-bird
megamys
migrant
minivet
minorca
modwall
moorhen
motacil
moth-owl
mudlark
muggent
noctule
oilbird
ortolan
ostrich
oven-tit
pandion
partlet
peacock
peafowl
pelican
penguin
percher
peterel
phaeton
phoenix
pinnock
pintado
pintail
pinnock
pintado
pochard
poe-bird
poulard
poultry

poy-bird
puttock
quabird
quetzel
raddock
rainbow
rantock
ratitae
redhead
redpoll
redtail
redwing
robinet
rooster
rosella
rotchie
royston
ruddock
sakeret
sawbill
sawwhet
scammel
scooper
sea-bird
sea-crow
sea-dove
sea-duck
sea-fowl
seagull
sea-hawk
senegal
seriema
serinus
shorley
simargh
sirgang
skimmer
skylark
snow-owl
sparrow
squacco
staniel
stannel
stanyel
stumpie

sturnus	arapunga	cutwater	hornbill	penelope
sunbird	avadavat	dabchick	horseman	percolin
swallow	bald-coot	daker-hen	hula-bird	petchary
swimmer	bald ibis	dandy-hen	keskidee	pheasant
tandora	baldpate	didapper	killdeer	philomer
tanager	barnacle	dinornis	kingbird	pickerel
tarrock	bateleur	dipchick	king-crow	plungeon
tattler	beam-bird	dotterel	landrail	poorwill
tiercel	becafico	duck-hawk	langshan	popinjay
tinamou	bee-eater	duckling	lanneret	puffbird
tinamus	bell-bird	duckmole	laverock	pygmy owl
titlark	berghaan	dun-diver	lingbird	rainbird
titling	blackcap	eagle-owl	lorikeet	redshank
touraco	bluebird	estridge	lovebird	redstart
trochil	bluewing	falconet	lyrebird	reed-bird
tumbler	blue-wren	fauvette	mannikin	reedling
turakoo	boat-bill	fen-goose	man-of-war	reed-wren
vulture	boat-tail	fig-eater	maori hen	rice-bird
vulturn	bobolink	finnikin	marabout	rifleman
wagtail	bob-white	fire-bird	marsh-hen	ringbill
wapacut	bockelet	firetail	marsh tit	ring dove
warbler	bockeret	fish-hawk	megapode	ringtail
waxbill	brancher	flamingo	mire-crow	rock dove
waxwing	brevipen	forktail	mire-drum	rocketer
whooper	brown owl	gairfowl	moorcock	rubecula
widgeon	bush chat	gamebird	moorfowl	sage-cock
willock	bush lark	gamecock	moorgame	sand-bird
wimbrel	cage bird	gang-gang	more-pork	sand-cock
witlock	calandra	garefowl	morillon	sand-lark
witwall	calangay	garganey	murrelet	sarcelle
wood owl	call-bird	great tit	musk duck	scops owl
wren-tit	caneroma	greenlet	mute swan	screamer
wrybill	capuchin	grey teal	mynabird	scrub tit
wryneck	caracara	grosbeak	nestling	sea-eagle
wyandot	cardinal	guachero	nightjar	sea-quail
yeldrin	cargoose	hackbolt	night-owl	sea-raven
	churn owl	hangbird	notornis	sea-snipe
8	clot-bird	hangnest	nuthatch	sedge-hen
	cockatoo	hawfinch	ovenbird	shelduck
aasvogel	cock bird	hazel-hen	oxpecker	shoebill
accentor	cockerel	heath-hen	palm dove	shoveler
adjutant	coquimbo	hemipode	parakeet	silktail
aigrette	corn bird	hernshaw	paraquet	sittella
alcatras	curassow	hickwall	paroquet	snowbird
amadavad	cursores	hoactzin	peachick	snowy owl
amadavat				

songbird	zopilote	cock robin	heathcock	ptarmigan
songster		columbine	hen-driver	quachilto
starling	**9**	cormorant	heronshaw	razorbill
struthio		corncrake	hirundine	redbreast
swamp-hen	accipiter	crossbill	honey-bird	red grouse
swiftlet	albatross	currawong	horned owl	rhynchops
tanagers	abdorinha	dandy-cock	jack-snipe	riflebird
tantalus	ant-thrush	deinornis	Jenny wren	ring-ousel
tapaculo	autophagi	dicky bird	jerfalcon	rock-pipit
tawny owl	bald eagle	dowitcher	kittiwake	rosefinch
tell-tale	baldicoot	eagle-hawk	lint-white	rossignol
tercelet	baltimore	eider duck	little auk	sabrewing
thrasher	bean goose	field-duck	little owl	salangane
thresher	beccafico	fieldfare	log-runner	sandpiper
throstle	beefeater	field wren	lorrikeet	sapsucker
titmouse	bell-minah	fig parrot	malee hen	satin-bird
titterel	bergander	figpecker	mallemuck	scald-crow
tomnoddy	birgander	firecrest	mango bird	scratcher
toucanet	blackbird	fledgling	marshbird	scrub-bird
tragopan	black cock	flute-bird	merganser	scrubfowl
trembler	black duck	francolin	meropidan	scrub-wren
troupial	black game	friarbird	merulidan	sea-parrot
umbrette	black gull	fringilla	mire-snipe	secretary
water-hen	blackhead	frogmouth	moundbird	sedge-bird
wheatear	black swan	gallinazo	mousebird	sedge wren
whimbrel	blacktail	gallinule	mousehawk	shearbill
whinchat	black tern	gerfalcon	mud-sucker	sheldrake
whip-bird	blood-bird	gier-eagle	muscipaca	shitepoke
whistler	blue crane	glaucopis	natatores	shoveller
whitecap	bowerbird	goldcrest	night-fowl	shrike-tit
white-ear	brambling	goldeneye	night hawk	silver-eye
white-eye	broadbill	goldfinch	ossifraga	skunk-bird
wildfowl	brown hawk	goldspink	ossifrage	snake-bird
woodchat	bullfinch	goosander	owl-parrot	snow-finch
woodcock	buzzardet	grassbird	paradisea	snow goose
wood duck	campanero	grass wren	paraquito	sooty tern
wood ibis	cassowary	great skua	pardalote	solitaire
woodlark	cedar-bird	grey goose	parrakeet	spinebill
woodwale	cereopsis	grey heron	parroquet	spoonbill
wood-wren	chaffinch	grossbeak	partridge	stick-bird
wrannock	chatterer	guillemot	peregrine	stilt-bird
xanthura	chevalier	guinea hen	petaurist	stink-bird
yeldring	chickadee	gyrfalcon	phalarope	stock dove
yeldrock	chickling	hatchling	pied-goose	stonechat
yoldring	coal-mouse	heathbird	pine finch	stone-hawk
	cockatiel			

storm-bird	blue-bonnet	grey parrot	rock-hopper
swamp-hawk	bluebreast	grey plover	rock parrot
swartback	bluethroat	ground dove	rock pigeon
swordbill	boobook owl	ground lark	ruby-throat
talegalla	brent goose	ground robin	sacred ibis
tetraonid	bronze-wing	guinea fowl	saddleback
thickhead	budgerigar	gymnocitta	sage grouse
thick-knee	budgerygah	hammerhead	salpinctes
thornbill	bufflehead	harpy eagle	sanderling
tiercelet	burrow-duck	heath-poult	sand grouse
trochilus	bush-shrike	hen-harrier	sandmartin
trumpeter	butter-bird	herald duck	sassorolla
turkey-hen	butterbump	honeyeater	scoter duck
turnstone	canary bird	honeyguide	screech-owl
umber-bird	canvasback	hooded crow	sea-swallow
waterbird	Cape pigeon	jungle-fowl	shearwater
water-cock	chiffchaff	kingfisher	sickle-bill
waterfowl	chittagong	king parrot	silver gull
water-rail	common gull	kookaburra	solan goose
wedgebill	cow-bunting	magpie-lark	song-shrike
whale-head	crested tit	mallee bird	songthrush
wheat-bird	crow-shrike	mallee fowl	summer-duck
whiteface	demoiselle	maned goose	spirit-duck
whitehead	dickcissel	meadow-lark	stone-snipe
whitetail	didunculus	missel-bird	sun bittern
whitewing	dishwasher	mutton-bird	tailor-bird
widow-bird	diving duck	night heron	talegallus
willow tit	dollar-bird	night raven	tit-warbler
windhover	dung-hunter	nutcracker	tree-runner
woodspite	dusky minah	parson-bird	tropic bird
wyandotte	dusky robin	peewee-lark	turkey-cock
	ember goose	pettichaps	turtle dove
10	eurylaimus	pick-cheese	tyrant-bird
	fallow-chat	piping crow	water-ousel
aberdevine	fledgeling	prairie hen	water pipit
Andalusian	flycatcher	pratincole	wattle-bird
ant-catcher	fratercula	quaker-bird	weasel-coot
Arctic skua	goatmilker	racket-tail	weaverbird
Arctic tern	goatsucker	rafter-bird	whidah-bird
bearded tit	goldhammer	rain plover	whydah-bird
bell-magpie	gooney-bird	ramphastos	white brant
bird of prey	grassfinch	reed thrush	white egret
bishop bird	greenfinch	regent-bird	white stork
black stork	greenshank	ring-plover	willow wren
blight-bird	grey falcon	road runner	wonga-wonga

wood grouse
woodpecker
wood pigeon
wood-shrike
wood-thrush
yaffingale
yellow-bird
yellowlegs
zebra finch

11

Alpine swift
apostle bird
banded stilt
black falcon
black grouse
black martin
blackthroat
bonebreaker
bristle-bird
brush turkey
buffalo bird
bush-creeper
butcherbird
Canada goose
carrion crow
cattle egret
chanticleer
cirl bunting
cock-sparrow
conirostres
corn bunting
diamondbird
dragoon-bird
fairy martin
fallow finch
flock pigeon
frigate-bird
fruit pigeon
gallows-bird
game-chicken
gnatcatcher
gnat-snapper
golden eagle

grallatores
green linnet
grey wagtail
ground-robin
harrier-hawk
hazel grouse
herring gull
hooded robin
honey-sucker
house martin
hummingbird
Java sparrow
kestrel-hawk
king penguin
king vulture
lammergeier
lammergeyer
leatherhead
leptodactyl
lily-trotter
magpie-goose
meadow pipit
mockingbird
moor buzzard
mulga parrot
Muscovy duck
nightingale
Pacific gull
procellaria
pterodactyl
punchinello
purple finch
quail-thrush
querguedule
rainbow-bird
reed bunting
reed sparrow
reed warbler
rock warbler
scarlet ibis
scissorbill
scissortail
screech-hawk
scrub turkey
sea dotterel

sea-pheasant
shell-parrot
shrike-robin
singing bird
snow bunting
soldier-bird
sparrowhawk
stone curlew
stone falcon
stone plover
storm petrel
swallowtail
treecreeper
wallcreeper
weaver-finch
white stork
whitethroat
whooper swan
wood swallow
wood warbler
wren babbler
yellow robin

12

Adele penguin
Alpine chough
adjutant bird
bramble finch
bronze pigeon
burrowing owl
capercaillie
cardinal bird
cow blackbird
crested grebe
cuckoo-shrike
curvirostral
dabbling duck
dentirostres
drongo-cuckoo
drongo-shrike
elephant bird
Eskimo curlew
fairy penguin
fighting cock

fissirostres
flowerpecker
glaucous gull
golden oriole
golden plover
grass warbler
great bustard
greylag goose
ground cuckoo
ground pigeon
ground thrush
hedge sparrow
hedge warbler
homing pigeon
honey-buzzard
honeycreeper
house sparrow
lanner falcon
mandarin duck
man-of-war
  bird
mandarin duck
marsh harrier
marsh warbler
missel thrush
mistle thrush
mound-builder
mourning-dove
nutmeg-pigeon
painted quail
painted snipe
pallid cuckoo
peaceful dove
perching duck
pink cockatoo
Plymouth rock
razor-grinder
reed-pheasant
rifle warbler
sage-thrasher
sandwich tern
sapphire-wing
sedge warbler
serpent-eater
shoveler duck

shrike-thrush
stone-chatter
stormy petrel
stubble-goose
stubble-quail
swamp harrier
tachydromian
tiger-bittern
turbit-pigeon
turner pigeon
umbrella-bird
velvet-scoter
water wagtail
whippoorwill
white goshawk
willow grouse
yellowhammer

13

adjutant stork
American eagle
American robin
archaeopteryx
argus pheasant
Baltimore bird
barnacle goose
black cockatoo
boatswain-bird
brown thrasher
buff Orpington
carrier pigeon
chaparral cock
cock-of-the-rock
crested pigeon
crocodile bird
Egyptian goose
fantail pigeon
harlequin duck
Hawaiian goose
Iceland falcon
imperial eagle
little bunting
little bustard
long-tailed tit

mistletoe-bird
musk parrakeet
owlet-nightjar
oystercatcher
plantain-eater
red-wattle bird
rock partridge
rosella parrot
sandhill crane
screech-martin
screech-thrush
secretary bird
shell-parakeet
shining parrot
spidercatcher
stink-pheasant
swallow-shrike
tumbler pigeon
turkey-buzzard
whistling duck
white cockatoo
whooping crane
willow-warbler
wood-sandpiper
yellow bunting
yellow wagtail
zebra parakeet

14

babbling thrush
bearded vulture
bird of paradise
canvasback duck
Darwin's finches
diamond sparrow
double-bar finch
emperor penguin
golden pheasant
griffon vulture
horned screamer
king-lory parrot
long-tailed duck
long-tailed skua
Mank shearwater

mountain thrush
nankeen kestrel
oriental cuckoo
plains-wanderer
prairie chicken
rhinoceros bird
Rhode Island red
ring-tailed duck
robin redbreast
satin bowerbird
silver pheasant
sociable plover
spotted harrier
tawny frogmouth
welcome swallow
whistling eagle

15

American bittern
Baltimore oriole
Dartford warbler
fire-crested wren
gold-crested wren
laughing jackass
passenger pigeon
peacock-pheasant
peregrine falcon
pink-footed goose
spotted redshank
white-headed duck

16 +

American redstart
great crested grebe
great spotted woodpecker
ivory-billed woodpecker
lesser spotted
 woodpecker
spotted flycatcher
tyrant flycatcher
wandering albatross
white-fronted goose
yellow-headed blackbird

Birthstones

Note: Not all sources agree, so some months appear twice

4

opal (October)
ruby (July)

5

agate (June)
pearl (June)
topaz (November)

6

garnet (January)

7

diamond (April)
emerald (May)
peridot (August)

8

amethyst (February
sapphire (September)
sardonyx (August)

9

turquoise (December)

10

aquamarine (March)

Boats and ships
(including nautical terms)

2	gig	tug	comb	haul	mess	rope
	guy	USN	crew	haze	mine	rove
AB	HMS	USS	deck	hazy	mist	sail
PO	hoy	way	dhow	head	mole	salt
RM	jib	yaw	dive	helm	moor	scud
RN	jig		dock	hold	navy	ship
OS	kof		doni	hove	neap	sink
SS	lee	**4**	dory	hulk	oars	spar
	log		eddy	hull	peak	stay
	man	ahoy	fend	jack	poop	stem
3	MTB	alee	flag	jagt	port	surf
aak	aor	back	floe	junk	pram	swab
aft	ram	beam	flow	keel	prau	tack
ark	rig	beat	foam	knot	proa	tide
bay	RMS	bend	fore	land	prow	toss
bow	sea	bitt	furl	lead	punt	trim
cat	SOS	boom	gaff	leak	quay	veer
cay	sub	bows	gale	line	raft	wake
cog	tar	brig	gang	list	rail	warp
cox	TBD	bunk	grog	load	rake	wave
CPO	top	buoy	hand	luff	reef	wear
ebb	tow	calk	hank	mast	ride	wind
FOB	tub	calm	hard	mate	roll	wing
		capt.				

yawl	ferry	sheer	beacon	lugger	tender
yard	fleet	sheet	billow	marina	thwart
yarn	float	shell	bireme	marine	tiller
	fluke	shoal	boejer	marker	towage
5	fluyt	shore	bojort	maroon	trader
	foggy	siren	bonnet	mashwa	undock
aback	fusta	skeid	bridge	masted	unfurl
abaft	gauge	skiff	bunker	master	unlade
abeam	grave	sloop	caique	may day	unload
about	gusty	smack	canvas	mizzen	unship
afore	hatch	sound	careen	mutiny	vessel
after	haven	sprit	convoy	offing	voyage
ahead	hawse	steer	course	on deck	whaler
aloft	heads	stern	cruise	outfit	wherry
avast	hitch	storm	cutter	packet	zebeck
awash	hoist	swell	debark	paddle	
badan	jetty	thole	dinghy	patrol	**7**
balam	kayak	tidal	dromon	pay off	
balsa	kedge	tramp	dugout	pay out	aground
barge	ketch	U-boat	embark	pennon	athwart
beach	kevel	umiak	engine	piracy	bale out
belay	lay-to	watch	ensign	pirate	ballast
below	lay up	weigh	escort	raider	beached
bells	leaky	wharf	fathom	reefer	bearing
berth	liner	wheel	fender	rigged	beating
bight	misty	winch	flukes	rigger	boarder
bilge	naval	windy	fo'c's'le	rudder	bollard
block	oakum	wreck	funnel	sailor	bowline
board	ocean	xebec	galley	saloon	bow wave
brace	oiler	yacht	gromet	sampan	breaker
briny	orlop	zaruk	gunnel	sambuk	bulwark
cabin	pitch	zebec	hawser	sculls	bumboat
cable	prize		hooker	seaway	buoyage
canal	radar		hove-to	sheets	capsize
canoe	radio	**6**	inship	shroud	capstan
cargo	refit		jetsam	sinker	caracor
caulk	roads	aboard	jigger	slaver	caravel
chart	ropes	adrift	lading	splice	carrack
cleat	rower	afloat	lateen	squall	cast off
craft	royal	anchor	launch	stormy	catfall
davit	sally	armada	lay-off	strake	catwalk
depth	salvo	ashore	league	strand	channel
drift	sands	astern	leeway	stream	charter
E-boat	screw	baghla	Lloyd's	tackle	chebeck
eight	scull	barque	locker	tanker	clipper

coaling	gudgeon	monsoon	stowage	boatdeck
coaming	gunboat	moorage	tacking	boathook
coaster	gun-deck	mooring	tempest	bowsprit
cockpit	gun port	oarsman	tonnage	broach to
collier	gun room	old salt	top deck	bulkhead
compass	gunwale	on board	top mast	bulwarks
conning	hagboat	painter	topsail	buntline
coracle	halyard	pennant	topside	car ferry
corsair	harbour	pinnace	tornado	castaway
cruiser	harpoon	piragua	torpedo	caulking
currach	haul off	pirogue	towline	coasting
curragh	head off	polacca	towpath	cockboat
cyclone	headway	pontoon	towrope	corvette
deadeye	heave to	quarter	transom	crossing
deep-sea	horizon	rations	trawler	cruising
dismast	inboard	ratline	trireme	cutwater
dockage	iceberg	reefing	trysail	dead slow
drakkar	ice floe	ride out	tugboat	deckhand
draught	inboard	rigging	typhoon	derelict
dredger	inshore	rollers	unladen	ditty-bag
drifter	Jack Tar	rope-end	veering	ditty-box
dry dock	jib boom	rowboat	ward off	dockyard
ease off	keelage	rowlock	warping	dog watch
ebb tide	keelson	sailing	warship	doldrums
embargo	landing	salvage	whistle	downhaul
felucca	lanyard	sculler	wrecked	drifting
fishery	latches	scupper	wrecker	even keel
flotsam	leaking	scuttle	yardarm	faltboat
fog bank	lee side	sea lane		flagship
foghorn	lee tide	sea-legs	**8**	floating
foretop	leeward	sea room		flotilla
forward	lighter	seasick	ambatche	fogbound
founder	listing	seaward	anchored	foldboat
frigate	loading	set sail	at anchor	foot-rope
futtock	log book	sextant	backstay	foremast
galliot	lookout	shipper	backwash	forepeak
galleon	luffing	shrouds	baidarka	foresail
gangway	lugsail	sick bay	barbette	forestay
gimbals	man o' war	sinking	bargeman	free port
go about	mariner	skipper	barnacle	gaffsail
go below	marines	skysail	beam-ends	go aboard
gondola	marline	slipway	becalmed	go ashore
grapnel	minisub	spanker	berthage	gunsloop
graving	mistral	steamer	berthing	halliard
grommet	monitor	steward	binnacle	halyards

43

hatchway	mastless	squadron	chartroom	midstream
head into	messmate	standard	close haul	minefield
headwind	midships	stand off	cock-boat	minelayer
high seas	moorings	staysail	craftsman	mizzentop
high tide	mutineer	steerage	crosstree	motorboat
hornpipe	mutinous	sternway	crosswind	navigable
hull-down	nautical	stowaway	crow's	navigator
icebound	navigate	stranded	nest	orlop deck
ice-field	neap tide	submerge	Davy Jones	outrigger
Indiaman	outboard	surfboat	dead water	overboard
ironclad	paravane	tacking	deck cargo	periscope
jackstay	pattamar	taffrail	departure	pilot boat
jettison	pierhead	thole pin	destroyer	powerboat
jury mast	pilotage	tranship	discharge	press gang
keelhaul	poop deck	trimaran	disembark	privateer
keel over	porthole	unbuoyed	dress ship	prize crew
landfall	portside	under way	driftwood	quicksand
landmark	pump room	vanguard	Elmo's	red ensign
landsman	put about	wardroom	fire	revictual
landward	put to sea	waterman	ferryboat	riverboat
larboard	quarters	windlass	fire drill	roadstead
lead-line	reef knot	windward	flood tide	Royal Navy
leeboard	re-embark	wreckage	flying jib	rum runner
lee shore	sail loft	yachting	foreshore	sailcloth
lifebelt	sail room		foundered	seafaring
lifeboat	sail yard	**9**	freeboard	seaworthy
lifebuoy	salvable		freighter	semaphore
lifeline	salvager	admiralty	gangplank	shipboard
load line	sandbank	afterdeck	half-hitch	ship's
longboat	schooner	all aboard	hard aport	boat
long haul	scudding	alongside	high water	ship's
longship	scuppers	amidships	hoist sail	crew
low water	seaborne	anchorage	holystone	shipshape
magazine	sea chest	anchoring	houseboat	shipwreck
mailboat	seafarer	bargepole	house flag	shoreward
main boom	seagoing	below deck	hurricane	sick berth
main deck	shallows	bilge-keel	hydrofoil	sidelight
mainmast	sheer off	bilge pump	jack-staff	sou'wester
mainsail	ship ahoy	Blue Peter	jolly boat	speedboat
mainstay	shipmate	boat drill	kentledge	spindrift
main yard	ship oars	bomb ketch	lightship	spinnaker
make sail	shipping	broadside	lower deck	spritsail
man of war	showboat	canal boat	maelstrom	stanchion
maritime	sounding	captaincy	mainbrace	starboard
masthead	spy-glass	cargo boat	mainsheet	stateroom
		catamaran		

steamship	dockmaster	quarantine	debarkation
steersman	downstream	raking fire	depth charge
sternpost	drop anchor	reduce sail	dreadnought
stokehold	drop astern	rendezvous	echo-sounder
stromsail	engine room	rope ladder	embarkation
submarine	fathomless	rowing boat	escape hatch
tarpaulin	figurehead	rudderless	factory ship
telescope	fore-and-aft	rudder post	fishing boat
tide table	forecastle	seamanship	galley-slave
trade wind	full-rigged	ship broker	get under way
troopship	gaff-rigged	shipwright	go alongside
twin-screw	heavy-laden	slack water	graving dock
two-decker	high and dry	spring tide	ground-swell
upper deck	hovercraft	square-sail	harbour dues
waterline	ice-breaker	stern-board	hug the shore
whaleboat	Jolly Roger	sternsheet	keelhauling
whirlwind	jury-rigged	submariner	landing deck
yachtsman	jury rudder	take in sail	lifeboatman
	landlocked	tea clipper	make headway

10

	landlubber	tidal basin	merchantman
aboard ship	lateen sail	tidal river	middle watch
alongshore	lay a course	topgallant	minesweeper
anchor buoy	liberty-man	tea clipper	motor launch
banana boat	life jacket	unfathomed	naval rating
barkentine	lighterage	upperworks	paddle-wheel
batten down	lighthouse	water-borne	port of entry
battleship	marker buoy	waterspout	quarterdeck
Bermuda rig	martingale	watertight	quinquereme
bilge water	middle deck	wheel-house	racing eight
blue ensign	midshipman	windjammer	rangefinder
bluejacket	mizzen mast		riding light
breakwater	mizzen sail		sailing date
bootlegger	narrow boat	**11**	sailing ship
brigantine	navigating		searchlight
cargo space	navigation	abandon ship	seasickness
cast anchor	night watch	barquantine	sheet anchor
catch a crab	ocean-going	beachcomber	shipbreaker
charthouse	packetboat	belaying pin	ship's doctor
coal bunker	paddleboat	capital ship	ship's papers
crosstrees	pipe aboard	captainship	spring a leak
deadlights	port of call	centreboard	standing off
degaussing	powder room	close-hauled	steam launch
diving bell	prize money	cockleshell	steerage-way
diving suit	prisonship	compass card	stern-chaser
	quadrireme	compass rose	submersible
		contact mine	

supertanker
support ship
three-decker
three-master
thwartships
torpedo boat
torpedo tube
unballasted
unnavigable
waterlogged
weather ship
weather side
weigh anchor
white ensign

12

air-sea rescue
between-decks
bill of lading
breeches buoy
cabin cruiser
cable's-length
change course
clinker-built
collision mat
companionway
conning tower
displacement
East Indiaman
escort vessel
fishing fleet
floating dock
futtock-plate
ground tackle
hospital ship
Jacob's ladder
landing craft
liberty ship

line of battle
longshoreman
magnetic mine
maiden voyage
man overboard
marine engine
marline spike
merchant ship
minesweeping
nautical mile
navigability
outward-bound
Plimsoll line
privateering
recommission
ride at anchor
ship chandler
shipping lane
square-rigged
starboard bow
studding sail
tourist class
training ship
tramp steamer
transhipment
Trinity House
undercurrent
unfathomable
weatherglass
will-o'-the-wisp

13

battle cruiser
cat-o'-nine-tails
close quarters
container ship
dead reckoning
grappling iron

high-water mark
hurricane deck
life-preserver
naval dockyard
order of battle
paddle steamer
passenger ship
quartermaster
re-embarkation
royal dockyard
ship of the line
starboard beam

14

channel steamer
circumnavigate
compass bearing
disembarkation
letter of marque
Lloyd's Register
naval architect
powder magazine
prevailing wind
schooner-rigged
screw propeller
ship's carpenter
superstructure
topgallant mast

15 +

aircraft carrier
Davy Jones' locker
mariner's compass
motor torpedo boat
pocket battleship
through-deck
  cruiser

Books of the Bible

Old Testament

Genesis	Gen.	Ecclesiastes	Eccles.
Exodus	Exod.	Song of Solomon	S. of S.
Leviticus	Lev.	Isaiah	Isa.
Numbers	Num.	Jeremiah	Jer.
Deuteronomy	Deut.	Lamentations	Lam.
Joshua	Josh.	Ezekiel	Ezek.
Judges	Judg.	Daniel	Dan.
Ruth	Ruth	Hosea	Hos.
I. Samuel	I Sam.	Joel	Joel
II. Samuel	II Sa.	Amos	Amos
I. Kings	I Kgs.	Obadiah	Obad.
II. Kings	II Kgs.	Jonah	Jonah
I. Chronicles	I Chr.	Micah	Mic.
II. Chronicles	II Chr.	Nahum	Nahum
Ezra	Ezra	Habakkuk	Hab.
Nehemiah	Neh.	Zephaniah	Zeph.
Esther	Esther	Haggai	Hag.
Job	Job	Zechariah	Zech.
Psalms	Ps.	Malachi	Mal.
Proverbs	Prov.		

New Testament

Matthew	Matt.	I. Timothy	I Tim.
Mark	Mark	II. Timothy	II Tim.
Luke	Luke	Titus	Titus
John	John	Philemon	Philem.
The Acts	Acts	To the Hebrews	Heb.
The Romans	Rom.	Epistle of James	Jas.
I. Corinthians	I Cor.	I. Peter	I Pet.
II. Corinthians	II Cor.	II. Peter	II Pet.
Galatians	Gal.	I. John	I John
Ephesians	Eph.	II. John	II John
Philippians	Phil.	III. John	III John
Colossians	Col.	Jude	Jude
I. Thessalonains	I Thes.	Revelation	Rev.
II. Thessalonians	II Thes.		

Apocrypha

I. Esdras	I Esd.
II. Esdras	II Esd.
Tobit	Tobit
Judith	Judith
The Rest of Esther	Rest of Esth.
The Wisdom of Solomon	Wisd.
Ecclesiasticus	Ecclus.
Baruch, with the Epistle of Jeremiah	Baruch
The Song of the Three Holy Children	S. of III Ch.
The History of Susanna	Sus.
Bel and the Dragon	Bel & Dr.
The Prayer of Manasses	Pr. of Man.
I. Maccabees	I Macc.
II. Maccabees	II Macc.

Old Testament

3 & 4

Amos
Ezra
Job
Joel
Ruth

5

Hosea
Jonah
Kings
Micah

Nahum

6

Daniel
Esther
Exodus
Haggai
Isaiah
Joshua
Judges
Psalms
Samuel

7

Ezekiel
Genesis
Numbers
Obadiah
Malachi
Solomon

8

Habakkuk
Jeremiah

Nehemiah
Proverbs

9

Leviticus
Zechariah
Zephaniah

10

Chronicles

11

Deuteronomy

12

Ecclesiastes
Lamentations

13

Song of
Solomon

New Testament

4

Acts
John
Jude
Luke
Mark

5

James
Peter
Titus

6

Romans

7

Hebrews
Matthew
Timothy

8

Philemon

9

Ephesians
Galatians

10

Colossians
Revelation

11

Corinthians
Philippians

13

Thessalonians

Bottles and barrels

3

keg = 5-10 galls
nip = ¼ bottle
pin = 4 ½ galls
tun = 210 galls
vat = variable

4

baby = ⅛ bottle
back = variable
butt = 110 galls
cask = variable
pipe = 105 galls

6

barrel = 36 galls
bushel = 8 galls
carafe = variable
carboy = variable

firkin = 9 galls
magnum = 2 bottles

8

demijohn = variable
hogshead = 54 galls
Jeroboam = 4 bottles
puncheon = 72 galls
Rehaboam = 6 bottles

9

Balthazar = 16 bottles
kilderkin = 18 galls

10 +

double magnum = 4 bottles
Methuselah = 8 bottles
Nebuchadnezzar = 20 bottles
Salmanazar = 12 bottles

Boxing weights

9

flyweight

11

heavyweight
lightweight

12

bantamweight
middleweight

welterweight

13

cruiserweight
featherweight

14

light-flyweight
super-flyweight

15 +

light-heavyweight
light-middleweight
light-welterweight
super-bantamweight
super-
  featherweight
super-heavyweight
super-lightweight
super-middleweight
super-welterweight

British and Irish counties and regions

(including abbreviations, former county names and island areas of Scotland)

3 & 4

Avon
Ayr
Beds
Bute
Cork
Down
Fife
Kent
Leix
Mayo
Oxon
Ross
York

5

Angus
Banff
Berks
Bucks
Cambs
Cavan
Clare
Clwyd
Derby
Devon
Dyfed
Elgin
Essex
Flint
Gwent
Hants
Herts
Hunts
Kerry
Lancs
Louth
Meath
Moray
Nairn
Notts
Perth
Powys
Salop
Sligo
Wilts

6

Antrim
Argyll
Armagh
Border
Brecon
Carlow
Dorset
Dublin
Durham
Forfar
Galway
Lanark
London
Offaly
Orkney
Oxford
Radnor
Staffs
Surrey
Sussex
Tyrone

7

Bedford
Berwick
Central
Cumbria
Denbigh
Donegal
Gwynedd
Kildare
Kinross
Leitrim
Lincoln
Lothian
Norfolk
Peebles
Renfrew
Rutland
Selkirk
Suffolk
Tayside
Warwick
Wexford
Wicklow
Wigtown

8

Aberdeen
Anglesey
Ayrshire
Cardigan
Cheshire
Cornwall
Cromarty
Dumfries
Grampian
Hereford
Hertford
Highland
Kilkenny
Limerick
Longford
Monaghan
Monmouth
Pembroke
Roxburgh
Shetland
Somerset
Stafford
Stirling

9

Berkshire
Caithness
Cambridge
Cleveland
Connaught
Dunbarton
Edinburgh
Fermanagh
Fifeshire
Glamorgan
Hampshire
Inverness
Leicester
Merioneth
Middlesex
Northants
Roscommon
Tipperary
Waterford
Westmeath
Wiltshire
Worcester
Yorkshire

10

Banffshire
Buckingham
Caernarvon
Carmarthen
Cumberland
Derbyshire
East Sussex
Flintshire
Gloucester
Haddington
Humberside
Huntingdon
Kincardine
Lancashire
Linlithgow
Merseyside
Midlothian
Montgomery
Morayshire
Nottingham
Perthshire
Shropshire
Sutherland
West Sussex

11

Argyllshire
Clackmannan

Dorsetshire
East Lothian
Forfarshire
Isle of Wight
King's County
Lanarkshire
Londonderry
Northampton
Oxfordshire
Radnorshire
Strathclyde
Tyne and Wear
West Lothian
Westmorland

12

Bedfordshire
Berwickshire
Denbighshire
Kirkudbright
Lincolnshire
Mid Glamorgan
Queen's County
Renfrewshire

Rutlandshire
Warwickshire
Western Isles
West Midlands

13

Aberdeenshire
Cardiganshire
Dumfriesshire
Herefordshire
Hertfordshire
Monmouthshire
Pembrokeshire
Staffordshire
Stirlingshire
West Glamorgan
West Yorkshire

14

Brecknockshire
Cambridgeshire
Dunbartonshire
Glamorganshire

Inverness-shire
Leicestershire
Merionethshire
Northumberland
North Yorkshire
South Glamorgan
South Yorkshire
Worcestershire

15 +

Buckinghamshire
Caernarvonshire
Carmarthenshire
Clackmannanshire
Dumfries and
  Galloway
Gloucestershire
Huntingdonshire
Kircudbrightshire
Montgomeryshire
Northamptonshire
Nottinghamshire
Ross and Cromarty

British Prime Ministers

4

Bute, (Lord)
Eden, Sir Anthony
Grey, Lord
Peel, Sir Robert
Pitt, William

5

Derby, (Earl of)
Heath, Edward R.
Major, John
North, (Lord)

6

Attlee, Clement R.
Wilson, (J.) Harold

7

Asquith, Herbert H.
Baldwin, Stanley
Balfour, Arthur J.
Canning, George
Russell, Lord John

8

Aberdeen, (Earl of)
Bonar Law, Andrew
Disraeli Benjamin
Goderich, (Viscount)
Perceval, Spencer
Portland, (Duke of)
Rosebery, (Earl of)
Thatcher, Margaret H.

9

Addington, Henry
Callaghan, (L.) James

Churchill, Winston S.
Gladstone, William E.
Grenville, (Lord)
Liverpool, (Earl of)
MacDonald, (James) Ramsay
Macmillan, Harold
Melbourne, (Viscount)
Salisbury, (Marquess of)
Shelburne, Lord

10

Palmerston, (Viscount)

Rockingham, (Earl of)
Wellington, (Duke of)

11

Chamberlain, Neville
Douglas-Home, Sir Alec
Lloyd-George, David

12

Campbell-Bannerman, Sir
   Henry

Canadian Prime Ministers

4

King, William M.

5

Clark, Joseph

6

Abbott, Sir John
Borden, Sir Robert
Bowell, Sir
   Mackenzie

Tupper, Sir
   Charles
Turner, John

7

Bennett, Richard
   B.
Laurier, Sir
   Wilfrid
Meighen, Arthur
Pearson, Lester B.
Trudeau, Pierre E.

8

Thompson, Sir John
Mulroney, Brian

9

Macdonald, Sir John
Mackenzie, Alexander
St. Laurent, Louis S

11

Diefenbaker, John

Canadian provinces and territories

Provinces

Quebec
Alberta
Ontario
Manitoba

Nova Scotia
New Brunswick
Newfoundland
Saskatchewan

British Columbia
Prince Edward
   Island

Territories

Yukon Territory
Northwest Territories

Capital cities and towns

4

Aden
Apia
Bern
Bonn
Doha
Lima
Lome
Malé
Oslo
Rome
San'a
Suva
Vila

5

Accra
Agaña
Ajman
Alofi
Amman
Berne
Cairo
Dacca
Dakar
Dehli
Dhaka
Dubai
Hanoi
Kabul
Koror
Lagos
La Paz
Macao

Nauru
Paris
Praia
Quito
Rabat
Sana'a
Seoul
Sofia
Sucre
Tokyo
Tunis
Vaduz
Zomba

6

Ankara
Athens
Avarua
Bagdad
Bamako
Bangui
Banjul
Beirut
Belice
Belize
Bissau
Bogotá
Brunei
Dublin
Habana
Harare
Havana
Kigali
Kuwait
Lisbon

London
Luanda
Lusaka
Madrid
Majuro
Malabo
Manama
Manila
Maputo
Maseru
Masqat
Mexico
Monaco
Moroni
Moscow
Muscat
Nassau
Naimey
Noumea
Ottawa
Panama
Peking
Prague
Riyadh
Roseau
Saigon
Saipan
Taipei
Tarawa
Tehran
Thimbu
Thimpu
Tirana
Vienna
Warsaw

7

Abidjan
Algiers
Andorra
Baghdad
Bangkok
Beijing
Belfast
Caracas
Cardiff
Cayenne
Colombo
Conakry
Cotonou
Douglas
El Aaiun
Gangtok
Honiara
Jakarta
Kampala
Kolonia
Managua
Mata-Utu
Mbabane
Nairobi
Nicosia
Papeete
Rangoon
St. Denis
St. John's
San José
San Juan
Santiago
Sao Tomé
Sharjah

Stanley
Thimphu
Tripoli
Valetta
Vatican
Yaoundé

8

Abu Dhabi
Asunciòn
Belgrade
Belmopan
Brasilia
Brussels
Budapest
Canberra
Cape Town
Castries
Damascus
Djibouti
Freetown
Fujairah
Funafuti
Gaborone
Hamilton
Helsinki
Katmandu
Khartoum
Kingston
Kinshasa
Laayoune
Lilongwe
Monrovia
N'Djamena
New Delhi

Pago Pago
Plymouth
Pretoria
Road Town
St. Helier
St. Pierre
The Hague
Santiago
Valletta
Victoria
Windhoek

Mogadishu
Nuku'alofa
Phnom Penh
Port Louis
Porto Novo
Pyongyang
Reykjavik
St George's
Salisbury
San Marino
Singapore
Stockholm
The Valley
Thorshavn
Ulan Bator
Vientiane

Libreville
Luxembourg
Mamoundzou
Mexico City
Montevideo
Nouakchott
Oranjestad
Panama City
Paramaribo
Quezon City
Tananarive
Washington
Willemstad
Wellington

San Salvador
Santa Isabel
Tegucipalpa
Vatican City

12

Antananarivo
Luang Prabang
Port au Prince
Ras al-Khaimah
Santo Domingo
Umm al-Qaiwain

9

Amsterdam
Bucharest
Bujumbura
Edinburgh
Gaberones
Gibraltar
Grand Turk
Guatemala
Islamabad
Jamestown
Jerusalem
Kathmandu
Kingstown

10

Addis Ababa
Basse-Terre
Bridgetown
Copenhagen
East Berlin
Georgetown
George Town
Kuwait City

11

Brazzaville
Buenos Aires
Dar es Salaam
Kuala Lumpur
Monaco-ville
Ouagadougou
Port Moresby
Port of Spain
St. Peter Port

13

Guatemala City
Medina as-Shaab
Uaboe District

14

Andorra la Vella

15 +

Bandar Seri Begawan
Charlotte Amalie

Castles (British) and fortification

(including some fictional)

3	4		Roch	Burgh	Dover	Hurst
		Fast	Star	Carew	Drogo	Keiss
		Holt	Udny	Chirk	Duart	Keldy
Hay	Acre	Leod	York	Clare	Elcho	Knock
May	Bere	Maol		Coity	Ewloe	Leeds
Mey	Deal	Maud		Corfe	Flint	Lewes
Moy	Doon	Peel	**5**	Cowes	Fyvie	Lymne
Odo	Dore	Pool		Croft	Gylen	Mylor
Oer	Dote	Raby	Blair	Cutra	Hawen	Powis
	Drum	Rait	Borve	Donne	Hever	Riber
	Duns	Ring	Boyne			

Slane
Sween
Tenby
Zenda

6

Aboyne
Airlie
Auchen
Bodiam
Bolton
Brecon
Brodie
Brough
Builth
Cawdor
Conway
Cornet
Dudley
Duffus
Dundee
Dunure
Durham
Edzell
Exeter
Floors
Forter
Fraser
Glamis
Gordon
Gwrych
Gwydir
Hailes
Hoddom
Howard
Huntly
Kendal
Ludlow
Maiden
Midmar
Millom
Morton
Newark
Nunney

Ogmore
Oxford
Picton
Raglan
Raheen
Rowton
Spynie
Strame
Walmer
Walton
Yester

7

Adamant
Affleck
Alnwick
Appleby
Ardross
Arundel
Balloch
Barholm
Barnard
Beeston
Belvoir
Blarney
Braemar
Bramber
Bratton
Brodick
Cadbury
Caister
Cardiff
Chester
Cooling
Compton
Cowdray
Crathes
Culzean
Denbigh
Douglas
Dunluce
Dunskey
Dunster
Duntulm

Dynevor
Finavon
Guthrie
Harlech
Huntley
Kanturk
Kennedy
Kielder
Kilmory
Kinkell
Lincoln
Lochnaw
Lowther
Mingary
Narwick
Naworth
Newport
Niddrie
Norwich
Penrhyn
Penrice
Penrith
Rattray
Rossend
Ruthven
Saddell
St. Denis
St. Mawes
Seagate
Sizergh
Skipton
Stalker
Sudeley
Swansea
Taunton
Threave
Tilbury
Tutbury
Uisdein
Warwick
Wigmore
Windsor
Wressle

8

Aberdour
Amberley
Ardvreck
Ardmaddy
Balmoral
Balvenie
Bamburgh
Baynard's
Berkeley
Bothwell
Brougham
Bruckley
Burleigh
Campbell
Cardigan
Carlisle
Carsluth
Chepstow
Cigerran
Corgarff
Crawford
Crichton
Darnaway
Delgatie
Dirleton
Doubting
Dryslwyn
Drummond
Dunottar
Duntrune
Dunvegan
Finlarig
Goodrich
Hawarden
Helmsley
Hertford
Kidwelly
Kilchurn
Langwell
Maxstoke
Mountjoy
Muchalls
Neidpath

Nottland
Pembroke
Pevensey
Pitcaple
Pitsligo
Pittulie
Plymouth
Rhuddlan
Richmond
Rothesay
Roxburgh
St. Donats
Sandwich
Southsea
Stirling
Stokesay
Stormont
Sycharth
Tamworth
Thetford
Tintagel
Urquhart
Walworth
Yarnbury

9

Allington
Beaumaris
Blackness
Borthwick
Broughton
Cambridge
Cardoness
Carlswith
Caulfield
Cilgerran
Claypotts
Clitheroe
Comlongon
Craignish
Criccieth
Crookston
Dalhousie
Dalnaglar

Dinas Bran	Pickering	Pontefract	Ravenscraig
Donnamore	Powderham	Porchester	Scarborough
Drumminor	Restormel	Portsmouth	Tattershall
Dumbarton	Rochester	Rockingham	
Dundonald	St. Andrews	St. Briavels	**12**
Dunnottar	Scalloway	Sutherland	
Earlshall	Sherborne	Winchester	Berry Pomeroy
East Cowes	Skenfrith		Caerlaverock
Edinburgh	Tantallon	**11**	Carreg Cennen
Findlater	Tregennis		Castel Y Bere
Glasclune	Ulzieside	Abergavenny	Christchurch
Greystoke	Warkworth	Aberystwyth	Dunstanburgh
Haverford		Armathwaite	Eilean Donnan
Hedingham	**10**	Aughentaine	Fotheringhay
Hermitage		Carisbrooke	Fraoch Eilean
Keissimul	Auchindown	Carnasserie	Hertsmonceux
Kildrummy	Caernarfon	Castlecraig	Huntingtower
Kilkerran	Caerphilly	Chillingham	Inverallochy
Killochan	Carmarthen	Cockermouth	Kinlochaline
Kilracock	Colchester	Conisbrough	Tower of London
Kimbolton	Craigievar	Craignethan	
Lancaster	Donnington	Dolwyddelan	**13**
Lochleven	Fort George	Fort William	
Manorbier	Inverlochy	Framlingham	Kaim of Mathers
Middleham	Kenilworth	Harry Avery's	Kirkcudbright
Muncaster	Launceston	Lindisfarne	Smaitham Tower
Newcastle	Linlithgow	Llantrisant	
Old Slains	Lochindore	Llanstephan	**14**
Pembridge	Lough Cutra	Painscastle	
Pendennis	Okehampton	Ravensburgh	Ashby de la
			Zouche

Some technical terms

3 & 4	jamb	fosse	splay	clunch	oolite
	keep	gable	vault	course	plinth
cob	loop	joist		crenel	rubble
rib	moat	light	**6**	donjon	soffit
apse	pier	mural		dormer	squint
arch	rath	rewel	abacus	fillet	turret
bay	yett	oriel	arcade	fresco	
berm		pitch	ashlar	impost	**7**
bond	**5**	scarp	aumbry	lancet	
hall		shaft	bailey	louvre	bastion
hood	aisle	solar	batter	merlon	bratice

chamfer	bivalate	constable	drawbridge
chevron	buttress	crosswall	meutrieres
cornice	dogtooth	drum-tower	portcullis
curtain	dressing	embattled	quadrangle
gallery	drystone	embrasure	Romanesque
groined	foliated	freestone	weathering
mullion	footings	garderobe	
oratory	hillfort	half-shaft	**11**
parados	mangonel	nookshaft	
parapet	moulding	openjoint	castellated
piscina	nailhead	refectory	counterfort
postern	palisade	revetment	herringbone
rampart	pediment	roofridge	motte-bailey
ravelin	pilaster	shell-keep	rustication
saltire	pinnacle	trebuchet	
tracery	pitching	vitrified	**12 +**
transom	ring-work	wall-stair	
trefoil	voussoir		castellation
	wing-wall	**10**	counterscarp
8			forebuilding
	9	ambulatory	great chamber
barbican		battlement	multivallate
bartizan	castellan	diaper work	stringcourse
			machicolation

Cathedrals, abbeys and priories

Cathedrals

3 4, & 5	Durham	Norwich	Llandaff
	Exeter	St. Asaph	St. Albans
Ely	Oxford	St. Paul's	St. David's
Derby			St. Woolos
Elgin	**7**	**8**	
Ripon			**9**
Truro	Brechin	Aberdeen	
Wells	Bristol	Bradford	Blackburn
	Chester	Carlisle	Edinburgh
6	Dornoch	Coventry	Guildford
	Dunkeld	Dunblane	Leicester
Bangor	Glasgow	Hereford	Lichfield
Brecon	Lincoln	Kirkwall	Liverpool

Newcastle	Wakefield	Chelmsford	Minster
Rochester	Worcester	Gloucester	
St.		Manchester	**12**
Andrews	**10**	Portsmouth	
Salisbury		Winchester	Peterborough
Sheffield	Birmingham		
Southwark	Canterbury	**11**	**13**
Southwell	Chichester	York	Bury St. Edmunds

Abbeys and priories

3 & 4

Bath
Dale
Iona
Kyme
Usk

5

Blyth
Kelso
Selby
Swine
Tilty
Torre

6

Battle
Bayham
Binham
Bourne
Boxley
Bungay
Byland
Elstow
Ewenny
Hexham
Hurley
Ingham
Jarrow
Knaith

Lapley
Launde
Lenton
Margam
Milton
Owston
Pamber
Penmon
Pilton
Ramsey
Romsey
St. Bees
Whitby
Witham

7

Alnwick
Cartmel
Culross
Dunster
Leiston
Marrick
Melrose
Minster
Monkton
Paisley
Royston
Thorney
Tintern
Tutbury
Waltham
Worksop

Wroxall

8

Amesbury
Arbroath
Augustus
Beaulieu
Boxgrove
Cardigan
Chepstow
Chirbury
Croyland
Dalkeith
Dryburgh
Fairwell
Freiston
Glenluce
Holyrood
Jedburgh
Kidwelly
Merevale
Newstead
Nuneaton
Pershore
Rumburgh
St. Clears
Whithorn
Woodkirk

9

Abbey Dore

Beauchief
Blackmore
Brinkburn
Bromfield
Cranborne
Davington
Deerhurst
Haughmond
Kirkstall
Kirkstead
Lancaster
Lanercost
Newbattle
Old Malton
Prinknash
St. Germans
Sherborne
Stogursey
Stranraer
Up Holland
Weybourne
Wymondham

10

Ardchattan
Atherstone
Birkenhead
Blanchland
Dorchester
Dundrennan
Inchmahome
Lastingham

Leominster
LLangenith
Malmesbury
Monk's Kirby
Nun Monkton
Polesworth
Shrewsbury
Sweetheart
Tewkesbury
Thurgarton

11

Abergavenny
Bridlington
Canons Ashby
Carisbrooke
Crossraguel
Dunfermline
Glastonbury

Holm Cultram
West Malling
Westminster

12

Christchurch
Fort Augustus
Great Bricett
Great Malvern
Letheringham
Little Dunmow
Redlingfield

13

Cambuskenneth
Little Malvern
Monk Wearmouth

14

Bristol, St. James
Deeping St. James
Leonard Stanley
LLanbadarn Fawr
Hatfield Peverel
York, Holy Trinity
St. Michael's Mount

16

Breedon-on-the-
Hill
Hatfield Broad Oak
Little Coggeshall

Cheeses

4

blue
Brie
curd
Edam
tome

herve
leigh
molbo
murol
niolo
Swiss
tamie
toucy

5

banon
brick
caboc
comte
cream
danbo
Derby
Dutch
fetta
Gouda

6

asiago
bagnes
bondon
bresse
cantal
cachat
cantal
cendre
Dunlop
fourme

gapron
Gerome
halumi
hrasma
laruns
leiden
morven
olivet
rollot
salers
samsoe
sbrinz
surati
tilsit
venaco

7

bondard
boursin
brinzen

broccio
brocciu
brousse
brucciu
bryndza
cabecou
Cheddar
cottage
crowdie
dauphin
demi-sel
fontina
gaperon
Gruyère
jonchee
langres
levroux
limburg
livarot
macquée
mont-d'or

morbier
munster
mycella
nantais
picodon
pyramid
quargel
ricotta
sapsago
Stilton
vendôme

8

auvergne
Ayrshire
beaufort
beauvoir
bel paëse
bergkase
boulette

brickbat
chaource
Cheshire
Cotswold
edelpilz
emmental
epoisses
manchego
Parmesan
pecarino
pelardon
remoudou
rigottes
scamorze
taleggio
vacherin
valencay

9

appenzall

blue vinny
broodkass
Caithness
cambozola
Camembert
Chabichou
chevreton
emmenthal
excelsior
gambozola
gammelost
jarlsburg
la bouille
la gougère
Leicester
limburger
lymeswold
mâconnais
maroilles
mimolette
pave d'auge
port-salut
provolone
reblochon
roquefort
sage Derby

10

belle paese
Caerphilly
Danish blue
dolcelatte
Gloucester

gorgonzola
Lancashire
mozzarella
neufchatel
pithiviers
poivre d'ane
red Windsor
saingorlon
stracchino

11

carre de l'est
coeur de bray
coulommiers
croute rouge
katshkawalj
petit-suisse
pont-l'eveque
Saint Maurie
Saint Paulin
schabzieger
schlosskase
tête-de-moine
tome au raisin
triple cream
weisslacker
Wensleydale

12

bleu de bresse
blue Cheshire
caciocavallo

red Leicester
soumaintrain
tome de savoie

13

bleu d'auvergne
Saint-Nectaire
selles-sur-cher

14

bleu des causses
brillat-savarin
feuille de dreux
laguiole-aubrac
nantais dit cure
Saint-Florentine
Saint-Marcellin
trappistenkase

15 +

boulette d'avenes
bouton-de-culotte
chevrotin des aravi
crottin de chavigno
double Gloucester
pouligny-Saint-
 Pierre
rigotte de pelussin
valencay levroux
Westminster blue

Chemical elements
(alphabetical list, with symbols)

actinium	Ac	antimony	Sb	astatine	At
aluminium	Al	argon	Ar	barium	Ba
americium	Am	arsenic	As	berkelium	Bk

beryllium	Be	iridium	Ir	radon	Rn
bismuth	Bi	iron	Fe	rhenium	Re
boron	B	krypton	Kr	rhodium	Rh
bromine	Br	lanthanum	La	rubidium	Rb
cadmium	Cd	lawrencium	Lr	ruthenium	Ru
caesium	Cs	lead	Pb	rutherfordium	Rf
calcium	Ca	lithium	Li	samarium	Sm
californium	Cf	lutetium	Lu	scandium	Sc
carbon	C	magnesium	Mg	selenium	Se
cerium	Ce	manganese	Mn	silicon	Si
chlorine	Cl	mendelevium	Md	silver	Ag
chromium	Cr	mercury	Hg	sodium	Na
cobalt	Co	molybdenum	Mo	strontium	Sr
copper	Cu	neodymium	Nd	sulphur	S
curium	Cm	neon	Ne	tantalum	Ta
dysprosium	Dy	neptunium	Np	technetium	Tc
einsteinium	Es	nickel	Ni	tellurium	Te
erbium	Er	niobium	Nb	terbium	Tb
europium	Eu	nitrogen	N	thallium	Tl
fermium	Fm	nobelium	No	thorium	Th
fluorine	F	osmium	Os	thulium	Tm
francium	Fr	oxygen	O	tin	Sn
gadolinium	Gd	palladium	Pd	titanium	Ti
gallium	Ga	phosphorus	P	tungsten	W
germanium	Ge	platinum	Pt	uranium	U
gold	Au	plutonium	Pu	vanadium	V
hafnium	Hf	polonium	Po	xenon	Xe
hahnium	Ha	potassium	K	ytterbium	Yb
helium	He	praeseodymium	Pr	yttrium	Y
hydrogen	H	promethium	Pm	zinc	Zn
indium	In	protactinium	Pa	zirconium	Zr
iodine	I	radium	Ra		

3

tin

4

gold
iron
lead
zinc

5

argon
boron
radon
xenon

6

barium
carbon
cerium
cobalt
copper
curium
erbium
helium
iodine
nickel
osmium
oxygen
radium
silver
sodium

7

arsenic
bismuth
bromine
cadmium
caesium
calcium
fermium
gallium
hafnium
hahnium
holmium
iridium
krypton
lithium
mercury
niobium
rhenium
rhodium
silicon
sulphur
terbium
thorium
thulium
uranium
yttrium

8

actinium
antimony
astatine
chromium
europium
francium

hydrogen	**9**	strontium	**11**
lutetium		ytterbium	
nitrogen	aluminium	zirconium	californium
nobelium	americium		einsteinium
platinum	berkelium		mendelevium
polonium	beryllium	**10**	
rubidium	germanium	dysprosium	**12**
samarium	lanthanum	gadolinium	
scandium	magnesium	lawrencium	praseodymium
selenium	manganese	molybdenum	protactinium
tantalum	neodymium	phosphorus	
thallium	neptunium	promethium	**13**
titanium	palladium	technetium	
tungsten	potassium		rutherfordium
vanadium	ruthenium		

Chinese calendar

Rat	1924	1936	1948	1960	1972	1984
Ox	1925	1937	1949	1961	1973	1985
Tiger	1926	1938	1950	1962	1974	1986
Hare	1927	1939	1951	1963	1975	1987
Dragon	1928	1940	1952	1964	1976	1988
Snake	1929	1941	1953	1965	1977	1989
Horse	1930	1942	1954	1966	1978	1990
Sheep	1931	1943	1955	1967	1979	1991
Monkey	1932	1944	1956	1968	1980	1992
Fowl	1933	1945	1957	1969	1981	1993
Dog	1934	1946	1958	1970	1982	1994
Pig	1935	1947	1959	1971	1983	1995

Cinque Ports

3

Rye

5

Dover
Hythe

6

Romney

8

Hastings
Sandwich

10

Winchelsea

Cities and towns

3

Abo
Aix
Ava
Ayr
Ely
Fez
Pau
Rye
Ufa
Usk
Wem
Wye

4

Aden
Agra
Albi
Alva
Apia
Baku
Bala
Bâle
Bari
Barr
Bath
Bern
Bonn
Bray
Brno
Bude
Bury
Caen
Cali
Cobh
Cork
Deal
Diss
Doha

Duns
Elie
Eton
Gaza
Gera
Giza
Graz
Hilo
Holt
Homs
Hove
Hull
Hyde
Ince
Kano
Kiel
Kiev
Kirn
Kobe
Köln
Lamu
Leek
Lima
Linz
Looe
Lodz
Lome
Luta
Lvov
Lydd
Lyon
Male
Metz
Mold
Muff
Nice
Oban
Omsk
Oran
Oslo
Pécs

Pisa
Reno
Rhyl
Riga
Roma
Rome
Rona
Ross
Ryde
Sana
Shap
Sian
Stow
Suez
Suhl
Suva
Troy
Tyre
Vasa
Vigo
Waco
Ware
Wick
Yarm
York

5

Abuja
Aaiun
Accra
Ajmer
Akron
Alloa
Alofi
Alton
Alwar
Amman
Annan
Arhus
Arles

Arras
Aswan
Avaru
Ayton
Bacup
Balla
Banff
Basra
Basse
Basel
Basle
Berne
Blyth
Boise
Boyle
Bowen
Brest
Bronx
Brora
Bunaw
Butte
Cairo
Calne
Cadiz
Ceres
Chard
Cheam
Clare
Colne
Cowes
Crail
Crewe
Cupar
Cuzco
Dacca
Dakar
Delft
Delhi
Denny
Derby
Dijon

Doagh
Dover
Egham
Elgin
Ellon
Enugu
Epsom
Errol
Essen
Evian
Filey
Flint
Fowey
Frome
Gavle
Genoa
Galle
Ghent
Goole
Gorky
Gurst
Hague
Haifa
Halle
Hanoi
Hedon
Herat
Hythe
Izmir
Jaffa
Kabul
Kandy
Kazan
Keiss
Keith
Kells
Kelso
Koror
Kotah
Kyoto
Lagos

Lairg
La Paz
Largo
Larne
Leeds
Leigh
Leith
Lewes
Liege
Lille
Louth
Luton
Luxor
Lyons
Macon
Mâcon
Mainz
Malmo
March
Mecca
Miami
Milan
Minsk
Mosul
Nairn
Namur
Nancy
Natal
Neath
Nevin
Newry
Nimes
Olney
Omagh
Omaha
Osaka
Ostia
Otley
Ozark
Padua
Palma

Paria	Tulsa	Baroda	Carlow	Harare	Ludlow
Paris	Tunis	Barrow	Cashel	Harbin	Lurgan
Parma	Turin	Barton	Cassel	Harlow	Lusaka
Perth	Utica	Batley	Comrie	Havana	Lynton
Pinsk	Vaduz	Battle	Conway	Havant	Lytham
Poole	Varna	Bayeux	Cracow	Hawick	Madras
Poona	Vilna	Beauly	Cromer	Henley	Madrid
Posen	Visby	Bedale	Crieff	Hexham	Malabo
Praia	Wells	Beirut	Cullen	Hobart	Malaga
Pskov	Wigan	Belcoo	Dairen	Howrah	Maldon
Quito	Worms	Belize	Dallas	Huntly	Malton
Rabat	Wuhan	Belper	Danzig	Ibadan	Manama
Reims	Yalta	Beragh	Darwen	Ilford	Manila
Ripon	Yaren	Berber	Darwin	Ilkley	Maputo
Risca	Ypres	Bergen	Dayton	Imphal	Marlow
Rosas		Berlin	Denver	Indore	Margam
Rouen	**6**	Bhopal	Dieppe	Irvine	Masham
Rugby		Biggar	Dinant	Jaipur	Meerut
Salem	Aachen	Bilbao	Dodoma	Jarrow	Meknes
Salen	Abadan	Biloxi	Dollar	Jeddah	Mobile
Selby	Aboyne	Bissau	Dublin	Jhansi	Moffat
Selma	Agadir	Bochum	Dudley	Juarez	Morini
Seoul	Albany	Bodmin	Dunbar	Kanpur	Morley
Sidon	Aleppo	Bognor	Dundee	Kassel	Moscow
Siena	Alford	Bogotá	Dunlop	Kaunas	Moskva
Simla	Amalfi	Bolton	Dunnet	Kendal	Mukden
Sligo	Amiens	Bombay	Dunoon	Kigali	Munich
Sofia	Ancona	Bo'ness	Durban	Killin	Muscat
Split	Ankara	Bootle	Durham	Kohima	Mysore
Stoke	Anshan	Boston	Eccles	Krakow	Nagoya
Stone	Alston	Bourne	El Paso	Kuwait	Nagpur
Sucre	Antrim	Brecon	Epping	Lanark	Naples
Tampa	Arklow	Bremen	Erfurt	Lahore	Nantes
Tanta	Arnhem	Bruges	Eugene	Lauder	Napier
Tenby	Ashton	Bruton	Exeter	Leiden	Narvik
Thame	Athens	Buckie	Forfar	Le Mans	Naseby
Tokyo	Austin	Builth	Forres	Leslie	Nassau
Toome	Babani	Bungay	Fresno	Leyden	Nelson
Tours	Balboa	Burton	Fushun	Linton	Neston
Trent	Bamako	Buxton	Galatz	Lisbon	Newark
Trier	Bangor	Cairns	Galway	Lobito	Newent
Tring	Banjul	Calais	Geneva	London	Newlyn
Troon	Bantry	Callan	Gdansk	Luanda	Newton
Truro	Barnet	Cannes	Goring	Lubeck	Norham
Tulle	Barvas	Canton	Hanley	Lublin	Noumea

Oakham	Seaton	Wigton	Belfast	Clacton
Odense	Selsey	Wilton	Belfort	Clifton
Odessa	Settle	Wishaw	Benares	Clogher
Oldham	Shotts	Witham	Bendigo	Clonmel
Oporto	Shrule	Witney	Berwick	Colombo
Ossett	Skopje	Wooler	Bewdley	Coblenz
Ostend	Smyrna	Yarrow	Bexhill	Cologne
Ottawa	Snaith	Yeovil	Bickley	Conakry
Oundle	Soweto	Zagreb	Bilston	Concord
Oxford	Sparta	Zurich	Blarney	Cordoba
Peking	Strood		Bologna	Corinth
Penryn	Stroud	**7**	Boulder	Corunna
Peoria	Sutton		Bowmore	Cottbus
Pewsey	Sydney	Abilene	Braemar	Crawley
Pinner	Tabriz	Airdrie	Brandon	Croydon
Pilsen	Tacoma	Ajaccio	Brechin	Cumnock
Pladda	Taipei	Alençon	Breslau	Cwmbran
Potosi	Tarana	Algiers	Bristol	Datchet
Prague	Tetuan	Alma-Ata	Brixham	Dawlish
Pudsey	Tehran	Alnwick	Brodick	Denbigh
Puebla	Thebes	Anaheim	Bromley	Detroit
Quebec	Thirsk	Andover	Buffalo	Devizes
Quetta	Thorne	Antwerp	Burnham	Donetsk
Rampur	Thurso	Appleby	Burnley	Dongola
Ramsey	Tiflis	Arundel	Burslem	Dorking
Recife	Tirana	Ashford	Bushire	Douglas
Redcar	Tobruk	Athinai	Caistor	Dresden
Reggio	Toledo	Athlone	Calgary	Dundalk
Regina	Topeka	Atlanta	Canobie	Dundrum
Repton	Totnes	Avignon	Caracas	Dunedin
Rheims	Toulon	Aylsham	Carbury	Dunkeld
Ripley	Treves	Badajoz	Cardiff	Dunkirk
Riyadh	Tromso	Baghdad	Cargill	Dunster
Romney	Tsinan	Balloch	Carluke	Dursley
Romsey	Tucson	Bampton	Carrick	Elstree
Rosyth	Urbana	Banbury	Catford	Entebbe
Roseau	Verdun	Bandung	Cawston	Erzerum
Rothes	Venice	Bangkok	Cayenne	Esbjerg
Ruabon	Verona	Barking	Chatham	Estoril
Ruthin	Vienna	Bay City	Cheadle	Evanton
St. Ives	Walton	Bayonne	Cheddar	Everton
St. Malo	Warsaw	Beccles	Chesham	Evesham
St. Paul	Weston	Bedford	Chester	Exmouth
Santos	Whitby	Begawan	Chicago	Falkirk
Seaham	Widnes	Beijing	Chorley	Fareham

Farnham	Kilsyth	Munchen	Rostock	Tangier
Finedon	Kington	Mycenae	Royston	Taranto
Fintona	Kinross	Nairobi	Rugeley	Tarbert
Firenze	Kintyre	Nanking	Runcorn	Taunton
Fukuoka	Koblenz	Newbury	Saginaw	Tayport
Glasgow	Kolonia	Newport	St. Asaph	Tbilisi
Glossop	Kunming	New York	St. Louis	Tel Aviv
Godthab	Lanchow	Nicosia	St. Neots	Telford
Golspie	Lamlash	Norfolk	St. Johns	Tenbury
Gosport	La Plata	Norwich	Salerno	Tetbury
Gourock	Larbert	Oakland	Salford	Thaxted
Granada	Ledbury	Oldbury	Saltash	Tilbury
Granton	Leghorn	Orlando	Sandown	Toronto
Grimsby	Le Havre	Orleans	San José	Torquay
Gwalior	Leipzig	Ormesby	San Juan	Tranent
Halifax	Lemberg	Overton	San Remo	Trieste
Hamburg	Leyburn	Padstow	Santa Fe	Tripoli
Hanover	Limoges	Paisley	Sao Tomé	Twyford
Harwich	Lincoln	Palermo	Sapporo	Uppsala
Haworth	Lisburn	Palmyra	Saxelby	Utrecht
Helston	Livorno	Papeete	Seaford	Ventnor
Heywood	Lourdes	Peebles	Seattle	Vilnius
Hitchin	Lucknow	Penrith	Selkirk	Walsall
Hoboken	Lucerne	Phoenix	Setubal	Wantage
Honiara	Macduff	Piraeus	Seville	Wareham
Honiton	Madison	Pompeii	Shannon	Warwick
Hornsea	Maesteg	Portree	Shifnal	Watchet
Hornsey	Malines	Portsoy	Shipley	Watford
Horsham	Malvern	Potsdam	Shipton	Weobley
Houston	Managua	Poulton	Silloth	Wexford
Ipswich	Mansura	Prescot	Spandau	Wicklow
Irkutsk	Margate	Preston	Spilsby	Windsor
Isfahan	Mashhad	Rainham	Spokane	Winslow
Jackson	Massawa	Raleigh	Staines	Wisbeck
Jakarta	Masseru	Rangoon	Stanley	Worksop
Jodhpur	Mata-utu	Ravenna	Stilton	Wrexham
Kalinin	Matlock	Reading	Strathy	Yaounde
Kampala	Maybole	Redhill	Sudbury	Yakutsk
Karachi	Mbabane	Redruth	Sunbury	Yerevan
Kerkira	Melrose	Reigate	Swanage	Yonkers
Keswick	Memphis	Renfrew	Swansea	Youghal
Key West	Messina	Retford	Swindon	Zagazig
Kharkov	Modesto	Roanoke	Swinton	
Kildare	Mombasa	Romford	Taiyuan	
Kilmory	Morpeth	Rosario	Tallinn	

8

	Boulogne	Dingwall	Honolulu	Minehead
	Brackley	Djibouti	Holyhead	Moniaive
Aalesund	Bradford	Dortmund	Holywell	Monmouth
Aberavon	Brampton	Drogheda	Hunmanby	Monrovia
Aberdare	Brasilia	Dufftown	Ilkeston	Montreal
Aberdeen	Bridgend	Dumfries	Ismailia	Montrose
Abingdon	Bridport	Dunbeath	Istanbul	Monymusk
Abu Dhabi	Brighton	Dunblane	Jamalpur	Muirkirk
Acapulco	Brindisi	Dungiven	Jeantown	Murmansk
Adelaide	Brisbane	Earlston	Jedburgh	Nagasaki
Agartala	Bromyard	Ebbw Vale	Kandahar	Nantwich
Alfreton	Brooklyn	Egremont	Katmandu	Neilston
Alicante	Broseley	Eyemouth	Khartoum	Newburgh
Amesbury	Brussels	Fakenham	Keighley	New Delhi
Ampthill	Budapest	Falmouth	Kidwelly	New Mills
Amritsar	Burghead	Findhorn	Kilbride	Newhaven
Arbroath	Calcutta	Florence	Kilkenny	Novgorod
Armadale	Camborne	Fortrose	Kilrenny	Nuneaton
Arrochar	Canberra	Freetown	Kingston	Nurnburg
Asunción	Canisbay	Gisborne	Kinshasa	Oak Ridge
Augsburg	Canonbie	Glenluce	Kirkwall	Omdurman
Axbridge	Cape Town	Goteburg	Knighton	Ormskirk
Auckland	Cardigan	Grantham	La Guaira	Oswestry
Aycliffe	Carlisle	Grantown	Lambourn	Palo Alto
Bakewell	Castries	Grenoble	Lampeter	Pamplona
Ballarat	Caterham	Greenbay	Langholm	Pasadena
Ballater	Cawnpore	Greenlaw	Las Vegas	Pembroke
Ballybay	Chartres	Greenock	Lausanne	Penicuik
Banchory	Chepstow	Guilford	Lavenham	Penzance
Barmouth	Chertsey	Hadleigh	Lechlade	Pershore
Barnsley	Cheyenne	Hailsham	Leuchars	Peshawar
Barrhill	Columbus	Halstead	Limerick	Peterlee
Bathurst	Clevedon	Hamilton	Liskeard	Petworth
Bayreuth	Clontarf	Hannibal	Llanelly	Pevensey
Bedworth	Clovelly	Hartford	Llanrwst	Pitsligo
Belgrade	Coventry	Hastings	Loanhead	Plaistow
Benguela	Crediton	Hatfield	Longtown	Plymouth
Besançon	Creetown	Hay-on-Wye	Lynmouth	Pnom Penh
Beverley	Cromarty	Helsinki	Mafeking	Portrush
Biarritz	Damascus	Helmsley	Mannheim	Port Said
Bicester	Dalkeith	Hereford	Markinch	Portland
Bideford	Daventry	Herne Bay	Maryport	Pretoria
Blantyre	Dearborn	Hertford	Mandalay	Przemysl
Bolsover	Deptford	Hinckley	Maynoath	Pwllheli
Bordeaux	Dewsbury	Holbeach	Midhurst	Ramsgate

Redditch	Surabaja	Aberfoyle	Callander	Fairbanks
Rhayader	Surbiton	Agrigento	Cambridge	Faversham
Richmond	Swaffham	Ahmedabad	Carnarvon	Ferintosh
Ringwood	Syracuse	Aldeburgh	Carnforth	Festiniog
Rochdale	Takoradi	Aldershot	Carstairs	Fishguard
Rothbury	Talgarth	Allahabad	Cartagena	Fleetwood
Rothesay	Tamworth	Alresford	Champaign	Fort Wayne
St. Albans	Tangiers	Ambleside	Changchun	Fort Worth
St. Helens	Tashkent	Amsterdam	Charlotte	Frankfurt
St. Helier	The Hague	Anchorage	Cherbourg	Galveston
St. Pierre	Thetford	Annapolis	Cherkessk	Gateshead
St. Tropez	Thornaby	Ardrossan	Chesilton	Gibralter
Salonika	Tientsin	Arlington	Chihuahua	Godalming
Saltburn	Timbuktu	Ashbourne	Chingford	Gravesend
Salzburg	Tiverton	Ashburton	Chungking	Greenwich
San Diego	Toulouse	Astrakhan	Cleveland	Grinstead
Sandwich	Tredegar	Avonmouth	Clitheroe	Guildford
Santa Ana	Tregaron	Aylesbury	Coleraine	Guayaquil
Santiago	Trillick	Ballymena	Congleton	Harrogate
Sao Paulo	Trujillo	Ballymore	Connemara	Haslemere
Sarajevo	Tunstall	Baltimore	Constanza	Haverhill
Savannah	Uckfield	Banbridge	Cookstown	Hiroshima
Schwerin	Ullapool	Bangalore	Cranbrook	Hollywood
Sedbergh	Uxbridge	Barcelona	Crewkerne	Holmfirth
Shanghai	Valencia	Beaumaris	Criccieth	Hyderabad
Shanklin	Valletta	Beersheba	Cricklade	Ilchester
Shenyang	Varanasi	Belturbet	Cuckfield	Immingham
Shillong	Veracruz	Bethlehem	Darmstadt	Innsbruck
Shipston	Victoria	Blackburn	Dartmouth	Inveraray
Sidmouth	Wallasey	Blackburn	Des Moines	Inverness
Skegness	Wallsend	Blackpool	Devonport	Inverurie
Sleaford	Westbury	Blandford	Dolgellau	Islamabad
Smolensk	Winnipeg	Blisworth	Doncaster	Jamestown
Srinagar	Worthing	Bracadale	Donington	Jerusalem
Soissons	Yarmouth	Bracknell	Dordrecht	Johnstone
Sorrento	Yokohama	Braintree	Droitwich	Johnstown
Southend	Zanzibar	Brentwood	Dronfield	Kalamazoo
Spalding	Zaragoza	Brighouse	Dubrovnik	Karaganda
Stafford		Broughton	Dumbarton	Karlsruhe
Stamford	**9**	Brunswick	Dungannon	Kettering
Stanhope		Bucharest	Dunkerque	Killarney
Stockton	Abbeville	Buckhaven	Dunstable	Kimberley
Strabane	Aberaeron	Bushmills	Edinburgh	King's
Stratton	Aberdovey	Byzantium	Eindhoven	Lynn
Strichen	Aberfeldy	Cairntoul	Ellesmere	Kingstown

Kingswear
Kingussie
Kirkcaldy
Knutsford
Krivoi Rog
Kuibyshev
Ladysmith
Lambourn
Lancaster
Las Palmas
Leicester
Leningrad
Lexington
Lichfield
Liverpool
Ljubljana
Llandudno
Lochgelly
Lochinvar
Lockerbie
Long Beach
Longridge
Lowestoft
Lyme Regis
Lymington
Macau City
Magdeberg
Maidstone
Mansfield
Manhattan
Maracaibo
Marrakech
Marrakesh
Marseille
Mauchline
Melbourne
Middleton
Milwaukee
Mogadishu
Montauban
Monterrey
Morecombe
Nashville
Newcastle
New London

Newmarket
New Radnor
New Romney
Northwich
Nuremburg
Otterburn
Palembang
Panmunjon
Pembridge
Penistone
Penkridge
Penyghent
Perpignan
Peterhead
Phnom Penh
Pickering
Pitlochry
Pontypool
Portadown
Porthcawl
Port Louis
Portmadoc
Prestwick
Princeton
Rasharkin
Reykjavik
Riccarton
Rio Grande
Rochester
Ronaldsay
Roscommon
Rostrevor
Rotherham
Rotterdam
St. Andrews
St. Austell
St. Etienne
Salisbury
Saltcoats
Saltfleet
Samarkand
San Marino
Santander
Saragossa
Saskatoon

Sherborne
Singapore
Slamannan
Smethwick
Southport
Southwell
Southwold
Stavanger
Starcross
Stevenage
Stewarton
Stockholm
Stockport
Stokesley
Stourport
Stranraer
Stratford
Stuttgart
Sundsvall
Tarporley
Tavistock
Tenterden
Tipperary
Tobermory
Todmorden
Tonbridge
Toowoomba
Towcester
Trondheim
Tynemouth
Ulan Bator
Ulverston
Uppingham
Uttoxeter
Vadi Halfa
Vancouver
Vientiane
Volgograd
Wainfleet
Wakefield
Walvis Bay
Warkworth
Waterbury
Waterford
Welshpool

Weybridge
Wiesbaden
Wimbledon
Wincanton
Wokingham
Woodstock
Worcester
Wuppertal
Wymondham
Ypsilanti
Zeebrugge

10

Accrington
Addis Ababa
Alexandria
Altrincham
Anstruther
Ardrishaig
Atomic City
Auchinleck
Baden Baden
Bad Homburg
Ballantrae
Ballybofir
Ballyclare
Ballyhaise
Ballymoney
Barnstaple
Baton Rouge
Bedlington
Billericay
Birkenhead
Birmingham
Bratislava
Bridgnorth
Bridgwater
Broken Hill
Bromsgrove
Broxbourne
Buckingham
Caernarfon
Caernarvon
Canterbury

Carmarthen	Glenrothes	Linlithgow	Pontypridd
Carnoustie	Gloucester	Littleport	Portaferry
Carsphairn	Gothenburg	Little Rock	Port Arthur
Carshalton	Greensboro	Livingston	Portishead
Casablanca	Greenville	Llandovery	Portsmouth
Castelderg	Guantanamo	Llanfyllin	Port Talbot
Castelfinn	Halesworth	Llangadock	Presteigne
Castletown	Harrisburg	Llangollen	Providence
Chandigarh	Hartlepool	Llanidloes	Ravenglass
Charleston	Haslingden	Long Branch	Rawalpindi
Chelmsford	Heathfield	Los Angeles	Rutherglen
Cheltenham	Heidelberg	Lubumbashi	Sacramento
Chichester	Horncastle	Louisville	Saintfield
Chippenham	Hornchurch	Luxembourg	St. Leonards
Chittagong	Hungerford	Maidenhead	Saint Louis
Cincinatti	Hunstanton	Malmesbury	Saxmundham
Chulmleigh	Huntingdon	Manchester	Sevastapol
Coggeshall	Huntsville	Marseilles	Shepperton
Coatbridge	Ilfracombe	Mexborough	Sheringham
Colchester	Jamshedpur	Mexico City	Shrewsbury
Coldingham	Jersey City	Miami Beach	Simonstown
Coldstream	Johnshaven	Micheldean	Stalbridge
Copenhagen	Kalgoorlie	Middlewich	Stalingrad
Crickhowel	Kansas City	Mildenhall	Stonehaven
Cullompton	Kenilworth	Milnathort	Stonehouse
Cushenhall	Kilconnell	Monte Carlo	Stoneykirk
Dalbeattie	Kilcreggan	Montelimar	Strangford
Darjeeling	Killenaule	Montevideo	Strasbourg
Darlington	Kilmainham	Montgomery	Strathavon
Donaghadel	Kilmalcolm	Motherwell	Strathearn
Dorchester	Kilmarnock	Nailsworth	Stowmarket
Dukinfield	Kilwinning	New Bedford	Sunderland
Dusseldorf	Kincardine	New Orleans	Sverdlovsk
Eastbourne	Kingsbarns	Nottingham	Tanderagee
East Linton	Kirkmaiden	Okehampton	Teddington
East London	Kirriemuir	Palmerston	Teignmouth
Eccleshall	Kitakyushu	Pangbourne	Tewkesbury
Evansville	Konigsberg	Panama City	Thunder Bay
Ffestiniog	La Rochelle	Paramaribo	Torrington
Folkestone	Launceston	Patrington	Townsville
Fray Bentos	Leamington	Peacehaven	Trivandrum
Galashiels	Lennoxtown	Pernambuco	Trowbridge
Georgetown	Leominster	Pittenweem	Tweedmouth
Gillingham	Lesmahagow	Pittsburgh	Valparaiso
Glengariff	Libreville	Pontefract	Versailles

Walsingham
Warminster
Warrington
Washington
Wednesbury
Wellington
West Calder
Westward Ho
Whitchurch
Whitehaven
Whitstable
Whittlesey
Willemstad
Willenhall
Willington
Wilsontown
Winchelsea
Winchester
Windermere
Windlesham
Wirksworth
Withernsea
Woodbridge
Workington
Youngstown

11

Aberchirder
Abergavenny
Aberystwyth
Albuquerque
Antofagasta
Armentieres
Bahia Blanca
Ballycastle
Ballygawley
Ballymurphy
Balquhidder
Bannockburn
Basingstoke
Blairgowrie
Bognor Regis
Bournemouth
Brassaville

Bridlington
Builth Wells
Buenos Aires
Brandenburg
Bhubaneswar
Buntingford
Campbeltown
Carrickmore
Cedar Rapids
Charlestown
Chattanooga
Cleethorpes
Cockermouth
Crossmaglen
Cumbernauld
Dar-es-Salaam
Downpatrick
Draperstown
Dunfermline
Enniskillen
Fettercairn
Fort William
Fraserburgh
Fredericton
Glastonbury
Grahamstown
Grand Rapids
Guadalajara
Guisborough
Helensburgh
Haltwhistle
Hatherleigh
Helsingborg
High Wycombe
Ingatestone
Invergordon
Kaliningrad
Kuala Lumpar
Letterkenny
Llantrisant
Londonderry
Lossiemouth
Lostwithiel
Lutterworth
Mablethorpe

Machynlleth
Magherafelt
Manningtree
Market Rasen
Marlborough
Marl de Plata
Maxwelltown
Minneapolis
Montpellier
Much Wenlock
Musselburgh
New Brighton
Newport News
Newton Abbot
Northampton
Novosibirsk
Palm Springs
Petersfield
Port D'Allegre
Port Glasgow
Portglenone
Porto Alegre
Port of Spain
Port Patrick
Port Moresby
Port Stanley
Pultneytown
Rathfryland
Rawtenstall
Rockhampton
Saarbrucken
St. Peter Port
San Salvador
Scarborough
Shaftesbury
Sharpeville
Southampton
South Molton
Springfield
Stalybridge
Stourbridge
Tantanarive
Trincomalee
Vladivostok
Wallingford

Walthamstow
Whitechurch
Vatican City

12

Alice Springs
Atlantic City
Attleborough
Auchterarder
Barranquilla
Beverley Hills
Bexhill-on-Sea
Bloemfontein
Burnham-on-Sea
Castle Dawson
Chesterfield
Christchurch
Clacton-on-Sea
East Kilbride
Fayetteville
Five Mile Town
Fort Augustus
Forte-de-France
Gainsborough
Great Grimsby
Great Malvern
Huddersfield
Independence
Indianapolis
Inishtrahull
Innerleithen
Jacksonville
Johannesburg
Laurencekirk
Loughborough
Macclesfield
Milton Keynes
Niagara Falls
New Brunswick
Newton Abbott
North Berwick
North Sheilds
North Walsham
Oklahoma City

Peterborough
Philadelphia
Port-au-Prince
Poughkeepsie
Rio de Janeiro
St Petersburg
Salt Lake City
San Francisco
San Sebastian
Santa Barbara
Santo Domingo
Shoeburyness
South Shields
Stewartstown
Stoke-on-Trent
Strathpeffer
Tenbury Wells
Tillicoultry

13

Aix-la-Chapelle
Auchtermuchty
Barnard Castle
Berkhamstead
Belo Horizonte
Bishop's Castle
Boroughbridge
Brightlingsea
Brookeborough
Burton-on-Trent
Bury St Edmunds
Carrickfergus
Castle Douglas
Charlottetown
Dalmellington
East Grinstead
Godmanchester
Great Yarmouth
Guatemala City
Haverfordwest
Higham Ferrers
Inverkeithing
Inverkeithnie
Kidderminster

Kirkby Stephen
Kirkcubbright
Kirkintilloch
Knaresborough
Leamington Spa
Littlehampton
Lytham St Annes
Market Deeping
Market Drayton
Melton Mowbray
Middlesbrough
Merthyr Tydfil
Newark-on-Trent
Newton Stewart
Northallerton
Port Elizabeth
Saffron Walden
St Petersburgh
Shepton Mallet
Southend-on-Sea
Wolverhampton
Wootton Basset

14

Bishop Auckland
Bishops Waltham
Chipping Barnet
Chipping Norton
Constantinople
Fort Lauderdale
Grantown-on-Spey
Hemel Hempstead
Henley-on-Thames
Kirkby Lonsdale
Market Bosworth
Newtown Stewart
Poulton-le-Fylde
Stockton-on-Tees
Stony Stratford
Tunbridge Wells
Wellingborough

15 +

Ashton-under-Lyne

Barrow-in-Furness
Berwick-upon-Tweed
Bishop's Stortford
Burnham-on-Crouch
Burton-upon-Trent
Castle Donington
Claremont Ferrand
Colorado Springs
Kingstown-upon-Hull

Leighton Buzzard
Newcastle-on-Tyne
Santiago de Chile
Stratford-on-Avon
Stratford-upon-Avon
Sutton Coldfield
Welwyn Garden City
Weston-Super-Mare

Clergy and religious followers

2

DD
Fr
RR

3

Dom
Fra
nun
Rev.

4

abba
abbé
bapu
curé
dean
guru
imam
lama
mage
monk
Papa
Pope
sufi
yogi

5

abbot
bonze
canon
chela
clerk
druid
elder
fakir
frate
friar
hadji
magus
mahdi
minim
mufti
padre
prior
rabbi
sadhu
swami
vicar
yogin

6

abbess
beadle

bishop
cantor
clergy
cleric
curate
custos
datary
deacon
divine
doctor
eparch
exarch
Father
flamen
frater
hermit
lector
martyr
Mother
mullah
mystic
novice
nuncio
palmer
parson
pastor
priest
primus
reader

rector
scribe
server
sexton
sister
verger
votary
warden

7

acolyte
apostle
ascetic
brahman
brahmin
brother
caloyer
chanter
chorist
dervish
dignity
dominie
Holy Joe
hymnist
intoner
muezzin
ordinee
ostiary

pilgrim
Pontiff
prelate
primate
prophet
provost
recluse
sacrist
shriver
stylite
sub-dean

8

antipope
bacchant
beadsman
bedesman
brethren
canoness
canonist
cardinal
cenobite
chaplain
choirboy
choirman
choragus
co-bishop
Corybant

crucifer
ecclesia
eminence
exorcist
holiness
incenser
initiate
lay vicar
lectress
man of God
marabout
prioress
mathurin
minister
neophyte
ordainer
ordinand
ordinant
ordinary
organist
penitent
pontifex
preacher
prioress
Reverend
seminary
sidesman
sky-pilot
squarson
subprior
superior
thurifer
vicaress
vice-dean
votaress

9

anchoress
anchorite
archdruid
ayatollah
baccanite
bishopess
black monk

catechist
celebrant
cellarist
chantress
chorister
churchman
clergyman
coenobite
confessor
cordelier
Dalai Lama
deaconess
dignitary
grey friar
incumbent
lay reader
lay rector
lay sister
liturgist
mendicant
missioner
moderator
monsignor
novitiate
observant
officiant
Orangeman
patriarch
pillarist
postulant
precentor
predicant
prelatess
presbyter
priestess
recollect
rectoress
rural dean
sacristan
sextoness
shaveling
suc-cantor
sub-deacon
succentor
suffragan

theologer
vestryman

10

archbishop
archdeacon
archflamen
archpriest
beadswoman
bedeswoman
black friar
camerlengo
catechumen
cloisterer
conclavist
cloistress
covenanter
ecclesiast
enumerator
evangelist
high priest
lay brother
licentiate
limitarian
minor canon
missionary
prebendary
prolocutor
psalmodist
sanctifier
seminarian
seminarist
sermoniser
solemniser
sub-chanter
theologian
theologist
white friar

11

arch-
   prelate

churchwoman
class leader
clergywoman
commendator
consecrator
intercessor
internuncio
interventor
lord provost
monseigneur
Panchen Lama
papal legate
papal nuncio
parish clerk
precentress
probationer
sub-prioress
vicar-forane

12

canon regular
canon secular
churchwarden
ecclesiastic
low-churchman
metropolitan
parish priest
penitentiary
Prince-Bishop
Vicar-General

13

archimandrite
archpresbyter
church officer
high-churchman
high priestess
knight templar
local preacher
sister of mercy
spiritual peer
titular bishop

14

apostolic vicar
church organist
Devil's advocate

mother superior
parish minister
preaching friar
Reverend Mother
Superintendent

vicar-apostolic

15

suffragan bishop
whirling dervish

Colours

3

bay
dun
hue
jet
red
tan

4

anil
bice
blue
buff
cyan
dark
drab
ebon
écru
fawn
gold
gray
grey
iris
jade
kohl
lake
navy
noir
onyx
opal
pale
pied
pink

plum
puce
roan
rose
ruby
rust
sage
sand
vert
woad

5

amber
ashen
azure
beige
black
blond
brown
camel
cocoa
coral
cream
delft
flame
flesh
green
hazel
helio
henna
ivory
jaspé
khaki
light

lilac
livid
loden
maize
mauve
ocher
ochre
olive
peach
pearl
prune
rouge
ruddy
sable
sandy
sepia
shade
slate
snowy
stone
straw
taupe
tawny
topaz
umber
white

6

acajou
annato
archil
argent
auburn
bister

bistre
blonde
bronze
burnet
cerise
cherry
chroma
citron
claret
cobalt
copper
flaxen
garnet
golden
indigo
jasper
madder
maroon
motley
orange
orchil
oyster
pastel
pearly
purple
reseda
russet
sallow
salmon
sienna
silver
titian
violet
yellow

7

apricot
aureate
biscuit
caramel
carroty
carmine
chamois
citrine
crimson
cudbear
dark red
emerald
filbert
filemot
fuchsia
grizzle
heather
jacinth
jonquil
magenta
mottled
mustard
natural
neutral
old gold
old rose
piebald
red lead
ruby red
saffron
scarlet
sea blue
sky blue

tea rose
thistle
tile red

8

alizarin
amaranth
amethyst
ash blond
baby blue
baby pink
blood red
blue-grey
bordeaux
brunette
burgundy
chestnut
cinnamon
cyclamen
dark blue
dove grey
eau de nil
eggshell
grizzled
gun metal
hazel nut
hyacinth
iron grey
jet black
lavender
mahogany
mole grey
mulberry
navy blue
nut brown
off white
pale blue
pea green
pistache
poppy red
primrose
raw umber
red ochre
rose pink

sanguine
sapphire
saxe blue
sea green
spectrum
viridian
xanthein

9

alice blue
aubergine
azure blue
blue-black
blue-green
burnt lake
cadet blue
cadet grey
cameo pink
carnation
carnelian
champagne
cherry red
chocolate
chrome red
coal black
cochineal
dark green
dark brown
delph blue
duck green
dusky pink
Dutch blue
Dutch pink
flesh pink
green-blue
Indian red
jade green
leaf green
light blue
lily white
lime green
livid pink
madder red
moss green

mouse grey
Naples red
Nile green
olive drab
pale green
parchment
pearl grey
raspberry
raw sienna
royal blue
Saxon blue
slate grey
smoke grey
solferino
steel blue
tangerine
tomato red
turkey red
turquoise
verdigris
vermilion

10

acid yellow
apple green
aquamarine
Berlin blue
beryl green
burnt umber
brown ochre
café au lait
Chinese red
cobalt blue
congo brown
ensign blue
fiesta pink
flake white
French grey
French navy
grass green
green ochre
heliotrope
indigo blue
Irish green

ivory white
light green
liver brown
marine blue
olive brown
olive green
Oxford blue
Oxford grey
oyster pink
pale yellow
Paris green
Persian red
petrol blue
polychrome
powder blue
salmon pink
silver-grey
smoked grey
Spanish red
stone ochre
strawberry
terracotta
zenith blue

11

bottle green
brown madder
burnt almond
burnt orange
cardinal red
carmine lake
chrome green
chrome yellow
cinnamon red
cyanine blue
Dresden blue
forest green
horizon blue
hunting pink
Japanese red
lapis lazuli
lemon yellow
peacock blue
Persian blue

pomegranite
Prussian red
Russian jade
stone colour
straw colour
ultramarine
Venetian red
walnut brown
winter white
yellow ochre

12

air force blue
ball park blue
canary yellow
castilian red
Chinese white
chrome yellow
Egyptian blue
eggshell blue
electric blue
emerald green
golden yellow
hyacinth blue
lavender blue

Lincoln green
midnight blue
Naples yellow
pastel colour
pillar box red
Prussian blue
sapphire blue
solferino red
Spanish black
Spanish brown
Tyrian purple
Vandyke brown
verdant green
Wedgwood blue

13

bishop's purple
Cambridge blue
cadmium yellow
chestnut brown
mother-of-pearl
multicoloured
particoloured
pepper-and-salt
primary colour

Scheele's green
straw-coloured
sulphur yellow
tortoiseshell
turquoise blue
Tyrian purple

14

Brunswick black
Brunswick green
cornflower blue
heather mixture
imperial purple
periwinkle blue
pistachio green
platinum blonde
primrose yellow
strawberry roan
turquoise green

15 +

caledonian brown
chartreuse green
chartreuse yellow
secondary colour

Commonwealth countries

5

Ghana
India
Kenya
Malta
Nauru
Tonga

6

Belize
Brunei

Canada
Cyprus
Gambia
Guyana
Malawi
Tuvalu
Uganda
Zambia

7

Bahamas
Grenada
Jamaica

Lesotho
Nigeria
Vanuatu

8

Barbados
Botswana
Dominica
Kiribati
Malaysia
Maldives
Sri Lanka
Tanzania

Zimbabwe

9

Australia
Mauritius
Singapore
Swaziland

10

Bangladesh
New Zealand
Saint Lucia

Seychelles

11

Sierra Leone

12

Western Samoa

13

United
 Kingdom

14

Papua New Guinea
Solomon Islands

15 +

Antigua and Barbuda
Saint Christopher and Nevis
Saint Vincent and the Grenadines
Trinidad and Tobago

Composers and musicians

3	**5**				
		Gobbi	Webbe	Du Pres	Sankey
Bax	Alkan	Grieg	Weber	Dvorak	Schutz
Cui	Arrau	Grove	Weill	Enesco	Stefer
	Auber	Hallé	Widor	Flotow	Tallis
4	Auric	Haydn		Franck	Varese
	Baker	Henze	**6**	Galway	Wagner
Adam	Berio	Holst		Glinka	Walter
Arne	Bizet	Ibert	Arnold	Gounod	Walton
Bach	Bliss	Lehar	Barber	Gretry	Webern
Bart	Bloch	Liszt	Barnby	Groves	Wesley
Berg	Beohm	Locke	Bartok	Gruber	
Bing	Boult	Lully	Berlin	Halevy	**7**
Blow	Boyce	Melba	Bishop	Handel	
Bohm	Bream	Mehta	Boulez	Harris	Albeniz
Bolt	Bruch	Moffo	Brahms	Hawles	Allegri
Bull	Bulow	Moore	Bridge	Hotter	Antheil
Bush	Croft	Munch	Burney	Hummel	Arriaga
Butt	Davis	Ogdon	Busoni	Imbrie	Babbitt
Byrd	D'Indy	Parry	Callas	Jochum	Bantock
Cage	Dufay	Patti	Carter	Kirbye	Bartock
Cahn	Dukas	Pears	Caruso	Kodaly	Beecham
Doss	Dupré	Ravel	Casals	Krenek	Bellini
Goss	Dykes	Reger	Chopin	Lassus	Bennett
Hess	Elgar	Satie	Clarke	Ligeti	Berlioz
Ives	Evans	Sharp	Coates	Maazel	Borodin
Lalo	Falla	Smart	Cortot	Mahler	Brendel
Lill	Fauré	Solti	Cowell	Milnes	Britten
Lind	Field	Sousa	Curwen	Morley	Caballé
Monk	Freni	Spohr	Curzon	Mozart	Caccini
Nono	Friml	Stern	Davies	Porter	Campion
Orff	Gedda	Suppé	de Falk	Previn	Cavalli
Wolf	Gigli	Szell	Delius	Purday	Copland
Wood	Gluck	Teyte	Dibdin	Rameau	Corelli
		Verdi	Duparc	Rubbra	Debussy

Delibes
Domingo
Dowland
Farnaby
Ferrier
Gabriel
Galuppi
Gibbons
Giulini
Hammond
Hassler
Hofmann
Ireland
Janacek
Karajan
Kennedy
Kubelik
Lambert
Lehmann
Malcolm
Martinu
Mancini
Menotti
Menuhin
Milhaud
Monteux
Nicolai
Nielsen
Nikisch
Nilsson
Novello
Okeghem
Ormandy
Perotin
Poulenc
Puccini
Purcell
Redhead
Richter
Rodrigo
Rossini
Rouseel
Ruggles
Salieri
Sargent

Schuman
Smetana
Solomon
Stainer
Stamitz
Strauss
Tartini
Thibaud
Thomson
Tippett
Vivaldi
Warlock
Weelkes
Wellesz
Xenakis

8

Albinoni
Ansermet
Berkeley
Bjorling
Bruckner
Carreras
Chabrier
Chausson
Cimarosa
Clementi
Couperin
Dohnanyl
Flagstad
Gershwin
Gesualdo
Ghiaurov
Glazunov
Goossens
Grainger
Granados
Honegger
Horowitz
Kreisler
Maconchy
Marenzio
Mascagni
Massenet

Melchior
Messager
Messiaen
Milstein
Musgrave
Oistrakh
Paganini
Philidor
Phillips
Reinagle
Respighi
Schnabel
Schubert
Schumann
Scriabin
Sessions
Sibelius
Stanford
Sullivan
Taverner
Te Kanawa
Telemann
Teschner
Williams
Zabaleta

9

Addinsell
Ashkenazy
Balakirev
Barenboim
Beethoven
Bernstein
Boulanger
Buxtehude
Chaliapin
Cherubini
Christoff
Dolmetsch
Donizetti
Dunstable
Gauntlett
Hindemith
Hoddinott

Klemperer
Landowska
Mackerras
Malipiero
Meyerbeer
Offenbach
Pavarotti
Pergolesi
Prokofiev
Scarlatti
Stokowski
Tortelier
Toscanini

10

Barbirolli
Birtwistle
Boccherini
Galli-Curci
Los Angeles
Mengelberg
Monteverdi
Moszkowski
Mussorgski
Paderewski
Palestrina
Penderecki
Praetorius
Rawsthorne
Rubinstein
Saint-Saens
Sammartini
Schoenberg
Skalkottas
Stradivari
Stravinsky
Sutherland
Tetrazzini
Villa-Lobos
Wainwright

11

Charpentier

Furtwangler
Humperdinck
Leoncavallo
Leschetizky
Lloyd-Webber
Lutoslawski
Mendelssohn
Moussorgsky
Rachmaninov
Ravenscroft
Schwarzkopf
Stockhausen
Szymanowski
Tchaikovsky

Wolf-Ferrari

12

Dallapiccola
de Los Angeles
Guido d'Arezzo
Khachaturian
Koussevitsky
Rachmaninoff
Shostakovich

13

Rouget de l'Isle

Vassilievitch

14

Fischer-Dieskau
Jaques-Dalcroze
Josquin des Prez
Rimsky-Korsakov

15 +

Coleridge-Taylor
Strauss the Younger
Vaughan Williams

Constellations

3

Ara
Box
Cup
Fly
Fox
Leo
Net
Ram

4

Apus
Argo
Bull
Crab
Crow
Dove
Foal
Goat
Grus
Hare
Keel
Lion
Lynx

Lyra
Lyre
Pavo
Poop
Rule
Sail
Swan
Vela
Wolf

5

Altar
Aries
Arrow
Cetus
Clock
Crane
Draco
Eagle
Hydra
Indus
Lepus
Libra
Lupus
Mensa

Musca
Norma
Orion
Pyxis
River
Stern
Table
Twins
Virgo
Whale

6

Antila
Aquila
Archer
Auriga
Boötes
Caelum
Cancer
Carina
Corvus
Crater
Cygnus
Dorado
Dragon

Fishes
Fornax
Gemini
Hydrus
Indian
Lizard
Octans
Octant
Pictor
Pisces
Plough
Puppis
Scales
Scutum
Shield
Taurus
Toucan
Tucana
Virgin
Volans

7

Air pump
Balance
Centaur

Cepheus
Columba
Dolphin
Furnace
Giraffe
Lacerta
Lion cub
Painter
Peacock
Pegasus
Perseus
Phoenix
Sagitta
Serpens
Serpent
Sextans
Sextant
Unicorn

8

Aquarius
Circinus
Equuleus
Eridanus
Great dog

Hercules
Herdsman
Leo minor
Scorpion
Scorpius
Sculptor
Triangle

9

Andromeda
Big dipper
Centaurus
Chameleon
Compasses
Delphinus
Great bear
Little dog
Monoceros
Ophiuchus
Reticulum
Swordfish
Telescope
Ursa Major
Ursa Minor

Vulpecula

10

Canis Major
Canis Minor
Chamaeleon
Charioteer
Compass box
Flying fish
Horologium
Little bear
Microscope
Triangulum
Water snake

11

Capricornus
Cassiopeia
Hunting dogs
Little snake
Sagittarius
Telescopium
Water-bearer

12

Camelopardus
Microscopium

13 +

Berenice's hair
Bird of Paradise
Canes Venatici
Coma Berenices
Corona Australis
Corona Borealis
Crux Australis
Northern crown
Piscis Austrinus
Sculptor's chisel
Serpent bearer
Southern cross
Southern crown
Southern fish
Southern triangle
Triangulum
  Australe

Countries
(including names of former countries)

3

DDR
GDR
UAR
USA

4

Aden
Anam
Bali
Chad
Cuba

Eire
Fiji
Guam
Iran
Iraq
Java
Laos
Mali
Nejd
Niue
Oman
Peru
Siam
Togo

USSR

5

Annam
Aruba
Benin
Burma
Chile
China
Congo
Crete
Egypt
Fiume

Gabon
Ghana
Haiti
India
Italy
Japan
Kandy
Kenya
Khmer
Korea
Libya
Lydia
Macao
Malta

Natal
Nauru
Nepal
Niger
Palau
Papua
Qatar
Spain
Sudan
Syria
Tchad
Texas
Tibet
Timor

Tonga
Wales
Yemen
Zaïre

6

Angola
Arabia
Azores
Belice
Belize
Bhutan
Brazil

Brunei	Algeria	Nigeria	St. Helena
Canada	America	Prussia	Salvador
Ceylon	Andorra	Réunion	Sardinia
Cyprus	Antigua	Romania	Scotland
Epirus	Armenia	Rumania	Sri Lanka
Europe	Ashanti	St. Kitts	Tanzania
France	Assyria	St. Lucia	Tasmania
Gambia	Austria	Sao Tomé	Thailand
Greece	Bahamas	Sarawak	Togoland
Guinea	Bahrain	Senegal	Trinidad
Guyana	Bavaria	Somalia	Zanzibar
Hawaii	Belgium	Sumatra	Zimbabwe
Israel	Bermuda	Sumeria	Zululand
Johore	Bohemia	Surinam	
Jordan	Bolivia	Tartary	**9**
Kuwait	Britain	Tunisia	
Latvia	Burkina	Ukraine	Abyssinia
Malawi	Burundi	Uruguay	Argentina
Malaya	Comoros	Vanuatu	Argentine
Mexico	Corsica	Vatican	Australia
Monaco	Croatia	Vietnam	Babylonia
Muscat	Dahomey		Caledonia
Norway	Denmark		Cameroons
Panama	Ecuador	**8**	Costa Rica
Persia	England		Gibraltar
Poland	Eritrea	Anguilla	Greenland
Russia	Estonia	Barbados	Guatemala
Rwanda	Faeroes	Botswana	Hindustan
Serbia	Finland	Bulgaria	Indonesia
Servia	Formosa	Burgundy	Kampuchea
Sicily	Germany	Cambodia	Lithuania
Sikkim	Grenada	Cameroon	Luxemburg
Soudan	Holland	Colombia	Macedonia
Sweden	Hungary	Djibouti	Manchuria
Taiwan	Iceland	Dominica	Mauritius
Tobago	Ireland	Ethiopia	New Guinea
Turkey	Jamaica	Honduras	Nicaragua
Tuvalu	Lebanon	Hong Kong	Nyasaland
Ulster	Lesotho	Kiribati	Palestine
Uganda	Liberia	Malaysia	Patagonia
Urundi	Livonia	Maldives	Pondoland
Zambia	Macedon	Mongolia	San Marino
7	Mayotte	Pakistan	Singapore
	Morocco	Paraguay	Swaziland
Albania	Namibia	Portugal	Transvaal
		Rhodesia	Venezuela

10

Bangladesh
Basutoland
California
Cape Colony
Damaraland
Elba Island
El Salvador
Guadeloupe
Ivory Coast
Luxembourg
Madagascar
Martinique
Mauretania
Mauritania
Montenegro
Montserrat
Mozambique
New Zealand
North Korea
Puerto Rico
Seychelles
Shan States
Somaliland
South Korea
South Yemen
Tanganyika
Upper Volta
Yugoslavia

11

Afghanistan
Baluchistan
Cochin China
Cook Islands
Côte d'Ivoire
Dutch Guiana
East Germany
French Congo
Malay States
Mashonaland
Mesopotamia
Namaqualand

Netherlands
New Hebrides
Phillipines
Saudi Arabia
Sierra Leone
South Africa
Soviet Union
Switzerland
Transjordan
Vatican City
West Germany

12

Bechuanaland
Belgian Congo
Cocos Islands
Eastern Samoa
French Guiana
Great Britain
Guinea-Bissau
Liechenstein
Malta and Gozo
Matabeleland
New Caledonia
Newfoundland
North America
North Vietnam
Ruanda-Urundi
South Georgia
South Vietnam
United States
Western Samoa

13

Afars and Issas
Barbary States
Canary Islands
Cayman Islands
Comoro Islands
Faeroe Islands
Khmer Republic
Liechtenstein
Muscat and Oman

Norfolk Island
Trucial States
United Kingdom
Virgin Islands

14

Balearic Islands
Cape of Good Hope
Congo Free State
Czechoslovakia
Gilbert Islands
Irish Free State
Leeward Islands
Maldive Islands
Mariana Islands
Papua New Guinea
Pitcairn Island
Society Islands
Solomon Islands

15

Ascension Island
British Honduras
Caroline Islands
Christmas Island
Cyclades Islands
Dutch East Indies
Falkland Islands
French Polynesia
Holy Roman Empire
Marshall Islands
Northern Nigeria
Northern Ireland
Orange Free State
Southern Nigeria
South-West Africa

16 +

Antigua and Barbuda
Cape Verde Islands
Central African
  Republic

Congolese Republic
Dominican Republic
Equatorial New Guinea
Malagasy Republic
Martinique Island
Netherlands Antilles
Sao Tomé and Principe
St. Christopher and Nevis

St. Pierre and Miquelon
St. Vincent and the
  Grenadines
Trinidad and Tobago
Turks and Caicos Islands
United Arab Emirates
United Arab Republic
United States of America
Vatican City State

Dance
(including ballet terms)

3

act
arc
bob
bop
bug
dog
fly
gig
hay
hey
hop
jig
olé
pas
set
son
tap

4

ahir
ball
beat
bump
cana
clam
crab
drag
fado

fish
fris
frug
haka
hora
itch
jerk
jive
jota
juba
kolo
loop
piva
pogo
pony
reel
shag
slop
step
swim
Toby
trip
trot
turn
vira

5

baris
bebop
brawl

bulba
carol
conga
cueca
dansa
debka
disco
fling
galop
gavot
gigue
glide
gopak
grind
haloa
hopak
kummi
l'ag-ya
limbo
Lindy
loure
lundu
mambo
nazun
numba
okina
pavan
polka
poule
round
rueda

rumba
samba
sarba
shake
sibel
sibyl
skate
stomp
strut
tango
Ta-tao
trata
twirl
twist
valse
velal
volta
waltz

6

abuang
almain
amener
Apache
atinga
ballet
batuta
bolero
boogie

boston
bourée
branle
brante
calata
canary
cancan
canter
carole
cebell
cha-cha
chassé
contra
coupee
danzon
djoged
do-si-do
eixida
El Ocho
fading
figuer
friska
frisky
gangar
gienys
hustle
kick-up
jacara
jarabe
jarana
kagura

kalela
masque
maxina
maxixe
minuet
monkey
morris
pavane
pessah
pointe
polska
redowa
Reigen
Rogero
shimmy
spring
sousta
stroll
rirana
valeta
Watusi
Weller
yumari
zig-zag

7

ahidous
aparima
arnaout

baborak	landler	aurresku	kantikoy	bossa nova
ball pla	Languas	ballroom	lace step	boulanger
bambuco	La Rueda	balztanz	La Marche	breakaway
banjara	La Volta	Basilino	Lulu-Fado	break dance
batuque	llorona	big apple	mailehen	breakdown
beguine	madison	blue beat	merengue	bull-dance
bharang	maillot	boogaloo	mohobelo	camel walk
bourrée	maypole	bull-foot	moonwalk	cardadora
Cacucha	mazurka	bunny-hug	moresque	cha-cha-cha
canarie	measure	cabriole	mutchico	clog dance
canario	milonga	cachucha	nizzarda	cotillion
carioca	moresco	cakewalk	orchesis	Drehtanza
chicken	morisco	canacuas	oxdansen	eagle rock
cinq pas	muneira	Canaries	pachanga	Ecossaise
classic	old time	candiote	pantalon	elevation
Coranto	one-step	ceilidhe	pea straw	entrechant
courdant	pasillo	chaconne	pericote	Fanny bump
Csardas	pericon	charrada	race-ball	farandole
dos-a-dos	planxty	cinq pace	rigadoon	folk-dance
El Corte	polacca	coryphée	rigaudon	formation
El Passo	purpuri	courante	rutuburi	funky butt
estampe	ragtime	Dionysia	saraband	gallegada
farruca	romaika	egg-dance	skipping	gallopade
feather	roundel	ensemble	slow drag	hajdutanc
footing	routine	fallaway	stomping	hitch-hike
forlana	sardana	fan dance	tap-dance	horn dance
fouetté	satacek	fandango	tea-dance	horse trot
foxtrot	saunter	filly dog	telemark	jitterbug
furiant	shuffle	fishtail	Texas rag	kathakali
furlana	sikinik	fish walk	the walks	kolomejka
gavotte	tandava	flamenco	Trescone	Malaguena
geranos	tantara	flip-flop	Tsamikos	mistletoe
glocsen	traipse	galliard	waltzing	mokorotlo
gombeys	trenise	Guarjira	war dance	pas de deux
gondhal	twinkle	gymnaska		paso doble
goshiki	two-step	habanera		passepied
halling	wakamba	hand jive	**9**	Paul Jones
himinau	ziganka	hey-de-guy		pirouette
hoedown		hornpipe	allamande	polonaise
jabadao	**8**	huapango	arabesque	poussette
jon-nuke		hula-hula	bacchanal	promenade
knees-up	alegrias	hunt ball	baguettes	quadrille
lamento	a moleson	Irish jig	bailecito	quick-step
lambada	assemble	jazz roll	barn dance	renningen
lancers	attitude	Judy walk	Bauertanz	ring-dance

River Cree
rock 'n' roll
roundelay
sand-dance
sarabande
sateckova
saut major
Schwalmer
siciliana
siciliano
slow waltz
spot dance
stag-dance
step-dance
tamborito
tambourin
threesome
tripudium
troyanats
variation
Yale blues
zapateado

10

atnumokito
bandltantz
basse dance
baton dance
belly-dance
Bergamasca
bergeretta
Bonnie Kitty
carmagnole
castle walk
chaniotiko
charleston
cinque-pace
corroboree
demi-vuelta
epaulement
espringale
fackeltanz
farandoulo
furry dance

gay Gordons
grand march
haute dance
Havanagila
hokey-cokey
hully-gully
Kemp's jigge
Kibby dance
kyndaldans
Las Tijeras
lauterbach
locomotion
Monferrina
running set
masked ball
masquerade
orchestics
petronella
pigeon-wing
repertoire
roundabout
round dance
salterello
seguidilla
seven veils
Scotch reel
snake dance
Strathspey
strip tease
suruvakary
sword dance
tap-dancing
tarantella
thé dansant
torch-dance
trenchmore
turkey trot
tyrolienne
walk-around

11

antistrophe
babaroschka
black bottom
bumps-a-daisy

buzzard lope
contredanse
choreograph
circle dance
cracovienne
dansuringur
dinner-dance
discothèque
dithyrambos
figure-dance
floral dance
folk dancing
grizzly bear
kangaroo dip
Lambeth walk
lamb skinner
La Media Luna
Los Huapango
Los Negritos
monkey dance
Morris dance
Old Noll's Jig
palais glide
pamperruque
pas de basque
Passacaglia
pas redouble
pastourelle
Peggy Ramsey
performance
Quadernaria
rock and roll
rotary waltz
Royal Boston
schottische
semibradoras
shimmy-shake
slow foxtrot
square-dance
tewrdannckh
varsity drag
varsovienne

12

American spin

Bacchic dance
boogie-woogie
break dancing
Brechin Fancy
chassé-croisé
cheer-leading
chestnut tree
choreography
country dance
Court Masques
creux de vervi
damhsa nam boc
danse du salon
danse macabre
divertimento
double Boston
foursome reel
funky chicken
green garters
Hull's victory
Kalamationos
labanotation
mashed potato
mid-way rhythm
novelty dance
passy-measure
reel o'Tulloch
roulli-roilli
ruffty-tuffty
schuhplatter
Scottish reel
siebensprung
skating waltz
skirt-dancing
triple Boston

tripudation
Virginia reel
Yankee tangle

13

Admiral Nelson
baile con corte
Boston two-step
Church dancing
country dancing
double-shuffle
eightsome reel
ghillie callum
Hamilton house
Highland fling
Latin American
Mairi's wedding
Morris dancing
orchesography
palais de dance
Paseo con Golpe
pepper-is-black
Ronds de Jambes
Schwarzwalder
square dancing
Viennese waltz

14

babbity bowster
basic throwaway
country bumpkin
country dancing
Cumberland reel

Jack-in-the-green
milkmaid's dance
Mrs. Grant's Fancy
regel-quadrille
strip the willow
The Duke of Perth

15

ballroom dancing
Campbell's frolic
chasse à trois pas
cinderella-dance
college hornpipe
hesitation waltz
invitation waltz
military two-step
Roger de Coverley
sailor's hornpipe
sellinger's round
sequence dancing
soft-shoe shuffle
The White Cockade

16 +

All the flowers of the broom
Appalachian mountain dance
British Grenadiers
Circassian circle
Country and Western
Flowers of Edinburgh
Sir Roger de Coverley

Ballet terms

3	pas	demi	plié	tutu	avant	corps
		face	port	volé	barre	coupé
bas	4	haut	posé		battu	couru
cou		jeté	rond	5	beats	croix
dos	bras	levé	saut	arqué	brisé	début
lié	côté	pied	tour		collé	décor

élève
fondu
grand
jambe
ligne
passé
permé
petit
piqué
pivot
porté
poser
rosin
sauté
scène
serré
temps
tendu
terre
tombé

en l'air
entrée
épaulé
étendu
étoile
failli
flèche
gauche
glissé
jarret
marche
Maître
monter
ouvert
penché
pointé
relevé
retiré
stance
voyagé

retombé
seconde
sissone
soutenu
taqueté
turn out

équilibre
grotesque
hortensia
juponnage
limbering
marcheuse
pas de deux
pirouette
quatrième
raccourci
révérence
révoltade
troisième

8

assemblé
attitude
back bend
ballonné
batterie
cabriole
cagneaux
coryphée
courdone
couronne
danseuse
demi-plié
derrière
détourné
glissade
pistolet
première
renversé
serpette
spotting
stulchik
tonnelet
tournant

10

balançoire
changement
choreology
enlèvement
épaulement
port de bras
répétition
soubresaut
taquèterie

6

aplomb
à terre
attack
baissé
ballon
cambré
chainé
changé
chassé
croisé
cuisse
dedans
dégagé
dehors
dessus
détiré
devant
double
droite
écarté
effacé
élancé

7

allongé
arrière
arrondi
attaque
balance
comique
danseur
déboîté
déboulé
dessous
échappé
emboité
épaulée
étendre
fouetté
jarreté
leotard
maillot
marquer
posture
ramassé
répéter

11

contretemps
double tours
grand jettés
pas de basque
sur la pointe

9

arabesque
ballerina
ballabile
battement
cou de pied
cinquième
développé
élévation
entrechat
entrelace
enveloppé

12

choreography
danseur noble
enchainement
gargouillade

13

corps de ballet
demi-character

14

closed position
divertissement
grand battement
prima ballerina

15 +

autour de la salle
l'expression corporelle
régisseur-géneral

Deserts

4

Gila
Gobi
Kara
Thar

5

Dahna
Namib
Nafud
Nazca
Nefud
Negev
Olmos
Ordos
Sinai
Sturt

6

Arunta
Barren
Gibson

Indian
Kerman
Libyan
Mohave
Mojave
Nubian
Sahara
Somali
Syrian
Zirreh

7

Alashan
An Nafud
Arabian
Atacama
Eastern
Kara Kum
Morrope
Painted
Qara Qum
Sechura
Shamiya
Simpson

Sonoran

8

Colorado
Kalahari
Kyzyl Kum
Muyunkum
Vizcaino

9

Anatolian
Black Rock
Black Sand
Dasht-e-Lut
Dasht-i-Lut
Dzungaria
Great Salt
Mongolian
Turkestan

10

Australian

Bet-Pak-Dala
Great Sandy
Patagonian
Rub'al Khali
Takla Makan

11

Dasht-I-Kavir
Dasht-e-Kavir
Dasht-I-Margo
Dasht-e-Margo
Death Valley

13

Great Salt Lake
Great Victoria

14

Bolson De Mapimi

16

Turfan
Depression

Charles Dickens

Books by Charles Dickens

9

Chimes, The
Hard Times

10

Bleak House
Edwin Drood

11

Oliver Twist

12

Barnaby Rudge
Dombey and Son

Little Dorrit

13

Haunted Man, The
Mugby Junction
Sketches by Boz

14

No Thoroughfare
Pickwick Papers

15

Battle of Life, The
Christmas Carol, A
Mudfog Papers, The
Our Mutual Friend

16 +

Cricket on the Hearth, The
David Copperfield
George Silverman's
 Explanation
Great Expectations
Martin Chuzzlewit
Master Humphrey's Clock
Message From The Sea, A
Mrs. Lirriper's Legacy
Mrs. Lirriper's Lodgings
Nicholas Nickleby
Old Curiosity Shop, The
Poor Relation's Story, The
Tale of Two Cities, A
Uncommercial Traveller, The

Dickensian characters

2 & 3

Bet
Bob
Gay
Jip
Jo
Joe
Kit
Liz
Mat
Meg
Pip
Tim
Tom

4

Aged (The)
Anny
Bell
Bill
Bray
Bray (Miss)

Bung
Clem
Clem (Mrs.)
Cobb
Cute
Dick
Duff
Fang
Fern
Fips
Fogg
Gamp (Mrs.)
Grip
Grub
Hawk
Heep
Heep (Mrs.)
Hugh
Jane
Jink
John
Jowl
Jupe
Kags

Kate
Klem
Klem (Miss)
Knag
Knag (Miss)
Mann (Mrs.)
Mary
Nell
Muff
Nemo
Omer
Peak
Peel
Pell
Peps (Dr.)
Pott
Pott (Mrs.)
Prig
Pyke
Riah
Rosa
Rugg
Ruth
Slug

Slum
Tigg
Tope (Miss)
Veck
Wade
Wade (Miss)
Wegg

5

Agnes
Alice
Alick
Bates
Becky
Betsy
Bevan
Biddy
Bloss
Bloss (Mrs.)
Boxer
Brass
Brick
Brown

Caddy	Lorry	Trott	Butler
Carlo	Lupin	Tuggs	Buzfuz
Casby	Lupin (Mrs.)	Twist	Calton
Chick	Maggy	Venus	Carker
Chips	Marks	Wosky (Dr.)	Carton
Choke	Mercy		Cheggs
Clare	Miggs	**6**	Cherry
Crupp	Mills		Cherub
Crupp (Mrs.)	Minns	Alfred	Codlin
Daisy	Mitts (Mrs.)	Babley	Cooper
Diver	Molly	Badger	Corney
Drood	Monks	Badger (Mrs.)	Corney (Mrs.)
Dumps	Mould	Bagman	Cousin
Emily	Nancy	Bagnet	Craggs
Evans	Neddy	Bagnet (Mrs.)	Craggs (Mrs.)
Fagin	Noggs	Bailey	Cuttle
Filer	Pedro	Bamber	Dadson
Fixem	Perch	Bantam	Dadson (Mrs.)
Flite	Perch (Mrs.)	Barker	Danton
Giles	Pinch	Barkis	Darnay
Gills	Pluck	Barley	Dartle
Gowan	Price	Barney	Denham
Gowan (Mrs.)	Pross	Barton	Dennis
Grace	Quale	Beadle	Dodson
Green	Quilp	Bedwin	Dombey
Green (Mrs.)	Quilp (Mrs.)	Bedwin (Mrs.)	Dorrit
Gride	Rudge	Benton	Dounce
Grime	Rudge (Mrs.)	Bertha	Dowler
Grove	Sarah	Bitzer	Dowler (Mrs.)
Guppy	Scott	Boffin	Durden
Gwynn	Short	Bowley	Edkins
Hardy	Slurk	Briggs	Endell
Henry	Slyme	Briggs (Mrs.)	Fat Boy
Hicks	Smart	Bucket	Feeder
Jacob	Smike	(Inspector)	Folair
Janet	Sophy	Bucket (Mrs.)	Gaffer
Jenny	Squod	Budden	George
Jerry	Stagg	Budger	George (Mrs.)
Jinks	Sykes	Budger (Mrs.)	Gordon
Jones	Tibbs	Buffum	Graham
Jones (Mrs.)	Tipps (Mrs.)	Bulder	Grueby
Joram	Toots	Bulder (Mrs.)	Guster
Kenge	Tozer	Bumble	Harmon
Krook	Trabb	Bumple	Harris
Lobbs	Trent	Bunsby	Harris (Mrs.)

Hawdon	Pancks	Wardle
Helves	Parker	Wardle (Mrs.)
Hexham	Parker (Mrs.)	Waters
Higdon (Mrs.)	Parkle	Weller
Hilton	Pegler	Wilfer
Hobler	Pegler (Mrs.)	Wilfer (Mrs.)
Hominy (Mrs.)	Peploe	Willet
Hubble	Peploe (Mrs.)	Wilson
Hubble (Mrs.)	Perker	Winkle
Hunter	Phunky	Wugsby
Hunter (Mrs.)	Pipkin	Wugsby (Mrs.)
Hutley	Pirrip	
Jaques	Pocket	
Jarley	Pogram	**7**
Jarley (Mrs.)	Potter	
Jellby	Purday	Akerman
Jingle	Quinch (Mrs.)	Antonio
Johnny	Rachel	Bangham (Mrs.)
Lammle	Raddle	Barbara
Lammle (Mrs.)	Raddle (Mrs.)	Bardell
Lively	Redlaw	Bardell (Mrs.)
Lowten	Rigaud	Batters
Lumbey (Dr.)	Rogers	Bazzard
Magnus	Sapsea	Blimber (Dr.)
Marion	Sawyer	Blotton
Marley	Sleary	Bobster
Martha	Sloppy	Boldwig
Martin	Specks (Mrs.)	Britain
Marton	Strong (Dr.)	Brooker
Maylie	Stubbs	Browdie
Maylie (Mrs.)	Stubbs (Mrs.)	Bullamy
Merdle	Tapley	Charity
Merdle (Mrs.)	Tapley (Mrs.)	Charley
Miller	Tiffey	Chester
Milvey	Timson	Chiggie
Milvey (Mrs.)	Toodle	Chillip
Mivins	Tottle	Chivery
Moddle	Tupman	Chivery (Mrs.)
Morfin	Tupple	Chuffey
Mullet	Varden	Cleaver
Muzzel	Varden (Mrs.)	Clenham
Nathan	Vholes	Clenham (Mrs.)
Nipper	Vuffin	Crackit
Noakes	Walker	Creakle
Orlick	Warden	Creakle (Mrs.)
		Crewler

Crewler (Mrs.)
Dawkins
Dedlock
Defarge
Drummle
Dubbley
Durdles
Edmunds
Edmunds (Mrs.)
Estella
Evenson
Fleming
Gargery
Gargery (Mrs.)
Garland
Garland (Mrs.)
Gaspard
Gazingi
General
General (Mrs.)
Granger
Gridley
Grimwig
Grudden (Mrs.)
Grinder
Groffin
Heyling
Hopkins
Jackman
Jackson
Jaggers
Jeddler (Dr.)
Jellyby
Jellyby (Mrs.)
Jiniwin
Jiniwin (Mrs.)
Jinkins
Jobling (Dr.)
Jorkins
Kenwigs
Kenwigs (Mrs.)
Larkins
Lewsome
Loggins
Macklin

Macklin (Mrs.)
Mallard
Manette (Dr.)
Manners
Meagles
Meagles (Mrs.)
Mercury
Mowcher
Nadgeth
Neckett
Newcome
Nubbles
Nubbles (Mrs.)
Nupkins
O'Bleary
Overton
Parsons (Mrs.)
Pawkins
Peecher
Pipchin
Pipchin (Mrs.)
Plummer
Podsnap
Podsnap (Mrs.)
Nupkins (Mrs.)
Quinion
Redburn
Richard
Saggers (Mrs.)
Sampson
Scadder
Scrooge
Simpson
Skewton
Skewton (Mrs.)
Slammer (Dr.)
Slowboy
Slunkey
Smangle
Smauker
Snagsby
Snagsby (Mrs.)
Snawley
Snubbin
Snuffin

Sowerby (Mrs.)
Sparsit
Sparsit (Mrs.)
Spenlow
Squeers
Squeers (Mrs.)
Stryver
Sweeney (Mrs.)
Swidger
Swidger (Mrs.)
Taunton
Taunton (Mrs.)
'The Aged'
Tickler
'Tiny Tim'
Tippins
Todgers
Todgers (Mrs.)
Tom Cobb
Tomkins
Toughey
Trotter
Trundle
Wackles
Wackles (Mrs.)
Wemmick
Whimple
Whimple (Mrs.)
Whisker
Wickham
Wickham (Mrs.)
Wilkins
Wobbler

8

Ada Clare
Alphonse
Anderson (Mrs.)
Aunt Jane
Bachelor
Bagstock
Barnacle
Beckwith
Beverley

Blathers
Brandley
Brandley (Mrs.)
Bravassa
Brittles
Brownlow
Bull's Eye
Carstone
Chadband (Rev.)
Chadband (Mrs.)
Chitling
Claypole
Cleriker
Cluppins
Cluppins (Mrs.)
Craddock (Mrs.)
Cratchit
Cratchit (Mrs.)
Crummles
Crummles (Mrs.)
Crumpton
Cruncher
Cruncher (Mrs.)
Crushton
Dark Jack
Dingwall
Dingwall (Mrs.)
Diogenes
Fielding
Fielding (Mrs.)
Finching
Finching (Mrs.)
Fladdock
Flammell
Fledgeby
Flornish
Gamfield
Gashford
Gliddery
Gummidge (Mrs.)
Haredale
Harleigh
Havisham
Hortense
Humphrey

Jarndyce
Jem Grove
Jennings
John Owen
La Creevy
Langdale
Langford
Ledbrain
Ledbrook
Lenville
Limbkins
Littimer
Lobskini
Losberne
Magwitch
Micawber
Micawber (Mrs.)
Miss Bray
Miss Klem
Miss Knag
Miss Tope
Miss Wade
Nicholas
Nickleby
Nickleby (Mrs.)
Old Lobbs
Old Sally
Peggotty
Petowker
Pickwick
Plornish
Plornish (Mrs.)
Quickear
Robinson
Roger Cly
Sharpeye
Skettles
Skiffins
Skimpole
Slinkton
Smithers
Snitchey
Sparkins
Sparkler
Sparkler (Mrs.)

Stiggins (Rev.)
Tetterby
Tetterby (Mrs.)
Toby Veck
Tom Green
Tom Pinch
Tom Scott
Tom Smart
Traddles
Trotters
Trotwood
Uncle Tom
Westlock
Whiffers
Will Fern
Woolford

9

Amy Dorrit
Belvawney
Betsy Prig
Billickin (Mrs.)
Bill Sykes
Blackpool
Bob Sawyer
Bounderby
Bullfinch
Charlotte
Cheeryble
Chickweed
Chuckster
'Cleopatra'
Compeyson
Doctor Peps
Evremonde
Fleetwood
Flipfield
Flipfield (Mrs.)
Gattleton
Gradgrind (Mrs.)
Gregsbury
Grewgious
Harthouse
Headstone
Isaac List

Jem Hutley
Jem Groves
Joe Specks
Joe Willet
Kindheart
Leo Hunter
Lightwood
Lillyvick
'Lord Peter'
Malderton
Mantalini
Maplesone
Maplesome (Mrs.)
Markleham
Miss Flite
Miss Gwynn
Miss Miggs
Miss Mills
Miss Pross
Murdstone
Ned Dennis
Nell Trent
Oakun Head
Old Chuffy
Old Orlick
Pardiggle
Pardiggle (Mrs.)
Pecksniff
Phil Squod
Potterson
Riderhood
Ruth Pinch
Sam Weller
Sarah Gamp
Silas Wegg
Sludberry
Smallweed
Snodgrass
Spruggins
Swiveller
Tackleton
Tappertit
'The Bagman'
'The Cherub'
'The Fat Boy'

Tom Codlin
Towlinson
Uncle Bill
Uriah Heep
Veneering
Veneering (Mrs.)
Verisopht
Walter Gay
Wickfield
Will Marks
Wiltshire
Wisbottle
Witherden
Woodcourt
Wrayburne

10

Alice Brown
Aunt Martha
Ayresleigh
Banjo Jones
Betsy Clark
Bevis Marks
Bill Barker
Bill Barley
Bitherston
Chevy Slyme
Chuzzlewit
Crisparkle (Mrs.)
'Cymon' Tuggs
Dame Durden
Doctor Peps
Edwin Drood
Emma Porter
Flintwinch
Heathfield
Henry Gowan
'Honest John'
Jack Bamber
Jack Bunsby
Jack Maloon
Jack Martin
Jem Larkins
Jesse Hexam

Job Trotter
Joe Gargery
John Basard
John Carker
John Dounce
John Grueby
John Harman
John Jasper
John Willet
Jonas Mudge
Julia Mills
'Kit' Nubbles
Kittlebell
Knight Bell
Little Dick
Little Paul
MacStinger
MacStinger (Mrs.)
Maria Lobbs
Mark Tapley
Mary Graham
Minnie Omer
Miss Benton
Miss Cheggs
Miss Wilfer
Onewenever (Mrs.)
Parker Peps (Dr.)
Paul Dombey
Phil Parkes
Rosa Dartle
Rose Maylie
Rouncewell
Rouncewell (Mrs.)
Sally Brass
Sempronius
Signor Jupe
Simon Tuggs
Sliderskew
Sowerberry
Sowerberry (Mrs.)
Spottletoe
Spottletoe (Mrs.)
Stareleigh
  (Justice)
Steerforth

Steerforth (Mrs.)
Tony Weller
Turveydrop
Williamson
Williamson (Mrs.)
Wititterly

11

Abel Garland
Annie Strong (Mrs.)
Anthony Humm
Arthur Gride
Balderstone
Bella Wilfer
Betsey Quilp
Betty Higden (Mrs.)
Bob Cratchit
Cecilia Jupe
Charles Well
Copperfield
Copperfield (Mrs.)
Daniel Doyce
Daniel Quilp
Deputy 'Winks'
Doctor Payne
Doctor Wosky
Dodge Orlick
Dora Spenlow
Edith Dombey
Emily Wardle
Emma Peecher
Fanny Dombey
Fanny Dorrit
Frank Milvey (Rev.)
Gabriel Grub
'Game Chicken', The
Grandfather
Ham Peggotty
Harry Maylie
Horace Kinch
Jack Hopkins
Jack Redburn
Jacob Barton
James Carker

Jane Wackles
Jarvis Lorry
Jemima Evans
Jesse Hexham
John Browdie
John Chivery
John Dawkins
John Edmunds
John Evenson
John Jobling (Dr.)
John Podsnap
John Smauker
John Wemmock
Joseph Tuggs
Lady Clubber
Lady Dedlock
Lady Tippins
Linkinwater
Little Emily
Lizzie Hexam
Louisa Chick
Lucretia Fox
Lucy Crewler
Malta Bagnet
Mark Gilbert
Mary Heyling
Marchioness
Misses Brown
Miss Crewler
Miss Edwards
Miss Gazingi
Miss Larkins
Miss Mowcher
Miss Peecher
Miss Wackles
Monflathers
Newman Noggs
Oliver Twist
Peerybingle
Peerybingle (Mrs.)
Percy Noakes
Peter Magnus
Polly Toodle
  (Mrs.)
Pumblechook

Robin Toodle
Slackbridge
Snevellicci
Snevellicci (Mrs.)
Solomon Peel
Solomon Pell
Susan Nipper
Susan Weller
Sweedlepipe
'The Bachelor'
Tim Cratchit
Toby Crackit
Tom Chitling
Tony Jobling
Tracy Tupman
Tulkinghorn
Uncle George
Uncle Robert
Witherfield (Miss)
Young Bright

12

Abel Magwitch
Agnes Fleming
Alderman Cute
Alfred Jingle
Alfred Lammie
Amelia Martin
'Artful Dodger'
  The
Aunt Margaret
Barnaby Rudge
Bayham Badger
Bully Globson
Bully Stryver
Charles Tuggs
Charley Bates
Charley Hexam
Colonel Diver
Dick Datchery
Doctor Lumbey
Doctor Strong
Duke Humphrey
Edith Granger

Edward Cuttle
Edward Dorrit
Elijah Pogram
Emily Taunton
Emma Haredale
Emma Micawber
Esther Hawdon
Fanny Cleaver
Fanny Squeers
Feenix cousin
George Gordon
Grace Jeddler
Honeythunder
Horace Hunter
Jessie Jobson
Job Potterson
Joe, the 'Fat Boy'
John Anderson
John Jarndyce
John Westlock
Julia Manners
Kate Nickleby
Koeldwethout
Little Dorrit
Little Swills
Lord Barnacle
Lucie Manette
Madeline Bray
Major Pawkins
Martha Endell
Martha Varden (Mrs.)
Mary Fielding
Matilda Price
Mathew Bagnet
Milly Swidger
Miss Bravassa
Miss Havisham
Miss La Creevy
Miss Ledbrook
Miss Skiffins
Miss Willises
Miss Woolford
Montague Tigg
Mulberry Hawk
Noah Claypole

'Peepy' Jellyby
Philip Pirrip
Philip Quarll
Philip Redlaw
Prince Blabud
Sampson Brass
Samuel Briggs
Samuel Weller
Sarah Crewler
Solomon Daisy
Solomon Gills
Solomon Pross
Sophy Crewler
Stoney Briggs
Straudenheim
Sydney Carton
The Clergyman
The Vengeance
Thomas Sapsea
Tilly Slowboy
Tite Barnacle
Tom Flipfield
Tom Gradgrind
Tom Malderton
William Guppy

13

Alfred Tomkins
Anastasia Rugg
Arabella Allen
Arthur Clenham
Augustus Minns
Belinda Pocket
Belinda Waters
Benjamin Allen
Benjamin Stagg
Bertha Plummer
Betty Clubbins
 (Mrs.)
'Bob the Grinder'
Brook-Dingwall
Captain Bunsby
Captain Cuttle
Captain Dowler

Captain George
Captain Hawdon
Captain Purday
Captain Waters
Charles Darnay
Chárles Timson
Charley Hexham
Clara Peggotty
Colonel Bulder
Colonel Gordon
Daniel Grummer
Dick Swiveller
Doctor Blimber
Doctor Jeddler
Doctor Jobling
Doctor Manette
Doctor Slammer
Dodson and Fogg
Dorothy Dibble
 (Mrs.)
Edward Chester
Edward Plummer
Emily Peggotty
Emily Smithers
Ernest Defarge
Flora Finching
Gabriel Varden
General Conway
George Heyling
George Nupkins
George Sampson
George Swidger
Harriet Beadle
Harriet Carker
Herbert Pocket
Horace Crewler
 (Rev.)
Horatio Fizkin
Jane Murdstone
Jerry Cruncher
Joseph Overton
Judy Smallweed
Lavinia Wilfer
Lord Verisopht
Louisa Crewler

Madame Defarge
Maria Crumpton
Marion Jeddler
Martha Bardell
Mary Ann Raddle
Matthew Bagnet
Matthew Pocket
Melvin Twemlow
Michael Bumple
Michael Warden
Minnie Meagles
 (Mrs.)
Miss Belvawney
Miss Flipfield
Misses Crewler
Misses Kenwigs
Misses Wackles
Miss Lillerton
Miss Potterson
Miss Woodcourt
Mistress Alice
Peg Sliderskew
Philip Swidger
Professor Muff
Rachael Wardle
Ralph Nickleby
Richard Babley
Sally Flanders
Sally Tetterby
Samson Dribble
Samuel Slumkey
Samuel Wilkins
Septimus Hicks
Seth Pecksniff
Sophie Wackles
Thomas Groffin
Tumley Snuffim
Watkins Tottle
William Barker
William Dorrit

14

Abbey Potterson
Agnes Wickfield
Alexander Trott

Allen Woodcourt
Amelia Crumpton
Anthony Jeddler
Augustus Cooper
Augustus Moddle
Barnet Skettles
Bentley Drummle
Betsey Cluppins
Betsey Trotwood
Captain Boldwig
Caroline Jellby
Caroline Wilson
Cecilia Bobster
'Charlotta' Tuggs
Chickenstalker
Daniel Peggotty
'Dot' Peerybingle
Edward Sparkler
Edwin Cheeryble
Eugene Wrayburn
Florence Dombey
Francis Spenlow
Frank Cheeryble
Fam Grewgious
Honoria Dedlock
Isabella Wardle
Jefferson Brick
Johnny Tetterby
Lady Snuohanuph
Lavinia Spenlow
Master Humphery
Mercantile Jack
Mercy Pecksniff
'Merry' Pecksniff
Miss Julia Mills
Miss Monflather
Miss Twinkerton
Monsieur Rigaud
Nicodemus Dumps
Octavius Budden
Olympia Squires
Reginald Wilfer
Reuben Haredale
Roger Riderhood
Samuel Pickwick

Serjeant Buzfuz
Signor Lobskini
Simon Tappertit
Sir John Chester
Solphia Tetterby
'The Game Chicken'
Therese Defarge
Thomas Traddles
Tim Linkinwater
Toby Chuzzlewit
Watt Rouncewell
William Swidger
Woolwich Bagnet

15

Alexander Briggs
Alexander Budden
Alfred Mantalini
Anastasia Weedle
Benjamin Britain
Captain Murderer
Caroline Crewler
Caroline Jellyby
'Cherry' Pecksniff
Clarissa Spenlow
Clemency Newcome
Conkey Chickweed
Cornelia Blimber
David Copperfield
Doctor Mannette
'Dolphus Tetterby
Dora Copperfield
Ebenezer Scrooge
Edward Murdstone
Estella Havisham
Esther Summerson
Eugene Wrayburne
Frederick Dorrit
General Fladdock
Georgina Podsnap
Godfrey Nickleby
Hannibal Chollop
Henrietta Boffin
Henry Wititterly
Hon. Elijah Pogram

Horatio Sparkins
'Horatio St. Julien'
Inspector Bucket
James Steerforth
John Edward Nandy
John Peerybingle
Jonas Chuzzlewit
Josephine Sleary
Josiah Rounderby
Julia Wititterly
Lavinia Dingwall
Louisa Gradgrind
MacChoakumchild
Madame Mantalini
Margaret Crewler
Mary Peerybingle
Miss Snevellicci
Monsieur Defarge
Mrs. Joseph Porter
Nathaniel Pipkin
Nathaniel Winkle
Neville Landless
Nicodemus Boffin
Ninetta Crummles
Paul Sweedlepipe
Professor Mullet
Richard Carstone
Serjeant Snubbin
Sir Joseph Bowley
Sir Mulberry Hawk
Smallweed Family
Sophronia Sphynx
Teresa Malderton
'The Artful Dodger'
Vincent Crummles
Volumnia Dedlock
Wilkins Micawber
William Cleverly

16 +

Affery Flinchwinch (Mrs.)
Alexander Grazinglands
Alexander Mannette (Dr.)
Angelo Cyrus Bantam
Augustus Snodgrass

Bartholomew Smallweed
Bradley Headstone
Chancery prisoner, The
Charles St. Evremonde
Charlotte Neckett
Christopher Casby
Christopher Nubbles
Chuzzlewit Fawkes
Clara Copperfield
Clarence Barnacle
Doctor Honeythunder
Doctor Parker Peps
Doctor John Jobling
Ferdinand Barnacle
Geoffrey Haredale
George Chuzzlewit
George Rouncewell
Georgiana Podsnap
Giovanni Carlavero
Grandfather Smallweed
Grandmother Smallweed
Gregory Chuzzlewit
Hamilton Veneering
Henrietta Nupkins (Mrs.)
Henrietta Simmons
Indignation Cocker
Jeremiah Flintwinch
John Baptiste Cavalletto
Lady Honoria Dedlock
Lawrence Boythorne
Lieutenant Tappleton
Lieutenant Tartar
Lord George Gordon
Lucie St Evremonde
Luke Honeythunder (Dr.)
Mademoiselle Hortense
Marquis St Evremonde
Master Tommy Bardell
Monsieur Ernest Defarge
Monsieur The Face Maker
Monsieur Theophile Gabelle
Mortimer Lightwood
Nicholas Nickleby
Pleasant Riderhood
Prince Turveydrop

Septimus Crisparkle (Rev.)   Susannah Cleverly
Sir Leicester Dedlock   Theophile Gabelle (Monsieur)
Sir Thomas Clubber   The Ventriloquist (Monsieur)
Sophronia Akershem   Young John Chuvery

Dogs (breeds)

3 & 4

chow
peke
pug
puli

5

Akita
boxer
corgi
hound
husky
spitz

6

Afghan
basset
beagle
borzoi
briard
collie
Kuvasz
poodle
Saluki
setter
shelty

7

basenji
bulldog
griffon

harrier
lowchen
lurcher
Maltese
mastiff
pointer
Samoyed
shih-tzu
spaniel
terrier
whippet

8

Airedale
Alsatian
chow-chow
Doberman
elkhound
foxhound
keeshond
komondor
Labrador
Malinois
papillon
Sealyham
sheepdog

9

Chihuahua
dachshund
Dalmatian
deerhound
Dobermann

Great Dane
greyhound
Kerry blue
lhasa apso
Pekingese
red setter
retriever
St. Bernard
schnauzer
Tervueren
wolfhound

10

Bedlington
bloodhound
fox terrier
Jack Russel
otter hound
Pomeranian
Rottweiler
schipperke
Weimaraner
Welsh corgi

11

Afghan hound
basset hound
bichon frise
bull mastiff
bull terrier
Groenendael
Ibizan hound
Irish setter

rough collie
Skye terrier

12

border collie
cairn terrier
field spaniel
Finnish spitz
gazelle hound
Gordon setter
Irish terrier
Japanese Chin
Newfoundland
Pharoah hound
silky terrier
smooth collie
Welsh terrier

13

affenpinscher
bearded collie
border terrier
Boston terrier
cocker spaniel
Dandie Dinmont
Dutch barge dog
English setter
French bulldog
Hungarian puli
Japanese spitz
Siberian husky
Sussex spaniel

14

Chinese crested
Clumber spaniel
giant schnauzer
Irish wolfhound
Maltese terrier
Norfolk terrier
Norwich terrier
Tibetan spaniel
Tibetan terrier
Wheaten terrier

15 & 16

Airedale terrier
Alaskan Malamute
Brittany spaniel
Doberman pinscher
golden retriever
Hungarian Vizsla
Italian greyhound
Kerry blue terrier
Lakeland terrier
Mexican hairless
Norwegian buhund
Persian greyhound
Russian wolfhound
Scottish terrier
Sealyham terrier
Shetland sheepdog
springer spaniel
Swedish vallhund
Tosa fighting dog
Yorkshire terrier

17 & 18

American foxhound
American toy terrier
Australian cattle dog
Australian terrier
Bedlington terrier

Bernese mountain dog
Belgian shepherd dog
black and tan terrier
Bouvier des Flandres
Cardigan Welsh corgi
English toy spaniel
English toy terrier
German shepherd dog
griffon Bruxellois
Irish water spaniel
King Charles spaniel
Labrador retriever
large Munsterlander
Manchester terrier
Miniature pinscher
Old English sheepdog
Pembroke Welsh corgi
Pyrenean mountain dog
Rhodesian ridgeback

19 +

American cocker spaniel
American pit bull terrier
American Staffordshire
  terrier
American water spaniel
Australian silky terrier
Cavalier King Charles
  spaniel
Chesapeake Bay retriever
Curly-coated retriever
Dandie Dinmont terrier
English cocker spaniel
English springer spaniel
flat-coated retriever
German shorthaired pointer
German wirehaired pointer
miniature bull terrier
Staffordshire bull terrier
Welsh springer spaniel
West Highland white terrier
wirehaired pointing
  griffon

Domestic animals

3

ass
bay
cat
cow
cur
dam
dog
dun
ewe
hog
kid
nag
pet
pig
pup
ram
rex
rip
sow
teg
tom
tup

4

boar
bull
byre
calf
cavy
colt
duck
foal
fowl
gilt
grey
goat
hack
kine

jack
jade
lamb
Manx
mare
moke
mule
mutt
neat
plug
pony
roan
runt
sire
Soay
stot
stud
tike
tyke
urus
zebu

5

billy
bitch
bluey
brach
burro
chick
cuddy
Duroc
dogie
filly
goose
hinny
horse
hound
hutch
Jacob
jenny

Kerry
kitty
mount
nanny
pacer
Pekin
pooch
puppy
screw
sheep
shire
shoat
slink
steed
steer
swine
tabby
whelp

6

agouti
albino
Angora
bantam
barton
bayard
bovine
bronco
cattle
canine
chaser
cayuse
Dexter
donkey
entire
equine
Exmoor
farrow
feline
gerbil

gun-dog
heifer
hogget
hunter
hummel
jennet
Jersey
jumper
kitten
lap-dog
maiden
merino
onager
piglet
porker
rabbit
racker
ratter
roarer
ringer
sorrel
tomcat
wether

7

aurochs
Beveren
bighorn
bird-dog
bovidae
brachet
brindle
bullock
Burmese
caracul
catling
cattalo
charger
Cheviot
chicken

courser
equidae
gelding
gosling
hackney
hamster
harrier
hircune
jackass
karakul
Leghorn
Manx cat
mongrel
Muscovy
mustang
palfrey
Persian
piebald
pit pony
porcine
poultry
Red Poll
rosette
Siamese
sumpter
trotter

8

Ayrshire
cavicorn
chestnut
coach dog
Cotswold
dairy cow
Dartmoor
Devon rex
duckling
Friesian
Galloway
Guernsey

guide dog
Hereford
Herdwick
Highland
landrace
longhorn
maverick
pack mule
palomino
polo pony
ruminant
Shetland
skewbald
stallion
Tamworth
tortoise
war horse
watchdog
water dog
yearling

9

Angora cat
badger dog
billy goat
brood mare
buckhound
cart-horse
dray-horse
gazehound
grimalkin
guinea pig
Jersey cow
Judas goat
Kent Marsh
Kerry Hill
nanny goat
New Forest
Orpington
pack-horse
police dog
racehorse
Rough Fell
seal-point

shorthorn
Southdown
staghound
stud-horse
Swaledale
Wyandotte

10

Abyssinian
Angora goat
Barnvelder
bellwether
blue heeler
Burmese cat
chinchilla
Clun Forest
Clydesdale
coach-horse
Cornish rex
dapple grey
Dorset horn
Exmoor pony
free-marten
guinea fowl
hunting dog
Indian game
Maltese cat
lilac-point
Jacob sheep
Persian cat
saddleback
sausage dog
shaft-horse
shire horse
Siamese cat
South Devon
sucking pig
tabby-point
tracker dog

11

badger-hound

Belgian hare
blue Burmese
carriage dog
Cheshire cat
colourpoint
Dutch rabbit
dwarf rabbit
English game
Highland cow
Light Sussex
Romney Marsh
saddle-horse
silver tabby
sorrel horse
sumpter mule

12

Berkshire pig
Black Norfolk
Black Leghorn
Blue Imperial
brown Burmese
cashmere goat
Dartmoor pony
draught-horse
Flemish giant
Havana rabbit
Plymouth rock
Polish rabbit
quarter-horse
Suffolk sheep
sumpter horse
thoroughbred
water spaniel
White Leghorn
Yorkshire pig

13

Aberdeen Angus
Aylesbury duck
Beveren rabbit
Buff Orpington
carriage-horse

Cotswold sheep
English rabbit
golden hamster
Hampshire Down
khaki Campbell
Large black pig
Large white pig
New Forest pony
red Abyssinian
steeplechaser
tortoiseshell
Welsh mountain

14

blackface sheep
chocolate-point
Japanese rabbit
lop-eared rabbit
Rhode Island Red
Southdown sheep
strawberry roan
tortie-and-white

15 & 16

British Friesian
Copenhagen rabbit
Dorset Horn sheep
Himalayan rabbit
red-point Siamese
Shropshire sheep

17 +

blue-pointed
 Siamese
Border Leicester
 sheep
chocolate-pointed
 Siamese
English Leicester
 sheep
Gloucester Old
 Spot

```
lilac-pointed Siamese          Peruvian guinea-pig
Lincolnshire Curly-coat        Scottish blackface
Lincoln Red Shorthorn          seal-pointed Siamese
New Zealand White rabbit       Wensleydale longwool
```

Dress

3

aba
alb
bal
bat
bib
bra
cap
cop
fez
fur
hat
kit
lei
mac
obi
tam
tie
top

4

abba
agal
alba
apex
baju
barb
beck
belt
boot
benn
bota
busk
cape

clog
coat
cope
cote
cowl
cuff
daps
dido
duds
garb
gear
geta
gown
haik
hood
hose
izar
jama
képi
kilt
mask
maxi
midi
mini
mink
mitt
muff
mule
pump
robe
ruff
sari
sash
saya
shoe
slip

sock
spat
suit
tabi
toga
togs
topi
tutu
vamp
veil
vest
wrap

5

abnet
Acton
aegie
amice
ampyx
apron
arcan
armor
Ascot
Barbe
Barry
Benjy
beret
Blake
boina
boots
burka
busby
cabas
cappa
chale

chaps
choga
choli
cloak
clogs
clout
cordy
cotta
cotte
crest
crown
curch
cylas
cymar
Derby
dhoti
dicky
dress
ephod
fichu
frock
gansy
get-up
gilet
gippo
glove
habit
irham
jabot
jamah
jeans
jelab
jupon
lammy
Levis
lodeb

lungi
mitre
mitts
mufti
nappy
pagne
pagri
palla
pants
parka
pilch
pinny
pumps
sabot
scarf
shako
shawl
shift
shirt
skirt
smock
snood
spats
stock
stole
strip
tammy
tails
teddy
tiara
tongs
topee
toque
train
trews
tunic

V-neck
visor
vizor
weeds

6

abolla
almuce
anadem
analav
anklet
anorak
arctic
armlet
armour
artois
Balkan
banyan
barret
barvel
basque
bautta
beanie
beaver
bertha
bicorn
bietle
biggin
bikini
binder
bishop
blazer
bliaud
blouse
boater

bodice	corset	mitten	tucker	brimmer
bolero	cothum	mobcap	turban	broigne
bonnet	covert	moggan	tuxedo	bustier
bootee	cravat	muller	tweeds	burnous
bowler	diadem	nylons	ulster	busskin
bow tie	diaper	outfit	undies	calecon
boxers	dickey	Panama	uplift	calette
bracae	dirndl	patten	vampay	camorro
braces	dolman	peg-top	vestee	canezou
bragas	domino	peplos	waders	cape hat
braies	fuster	peplum	whites	capuche
breton	farcap	pileus	wimple	capulet
briefs	fedora	pinner	woolly	casaque
brogan	fillet	pirnie	Zouave	cassock
brogue	flares	poncho		casuals
buskin	gaiter	pop-sox	**7**	catskin
bustle	gansey	pugree		caubeen
burnie	garter	puttee	amictus	cerevis
caftan	gaucho	raglan	apparel	chainse
calash	girdle	reefer	arisard	chalwar
calcie	guimpe	ruffle	armband	chaplet
caliga	halter	sandal	baboosh	chemise
calpac	helmet	sarong	baldric	chevron
camail	hennin	serape	balteus	chimere
camisa	huipil	shimmy	bandana	chip hat
camise	jacket	shorts	bandeau	chlamys
capote	jelick	shroud	bandore	chopine
capuce	jerkin	slacks	Barbour	chou hat
caputi	jersey	smalls	barbute	chrisom
caraco	jubbah	sontag	baroque	chuddar
casque	jumper	square	bashlyk	chudder
castor	kabaya	step-in	basinet	clobber
causia	kaftan	sun hat	bavette	commode
cestus	kersey	sun top	bavolet	coronel
chadar	kimono	tabard	bedizen	coronet
chiton	kirtle	tamise	belcher	corsage
choker	kittel	tartan	berdash	cossack
cilice	lammie	thongs	beretta	costume
cimier	livery	tights	betsies	coxcomb
claque	loafer	tippet	biretta	crepida
cloche	lungee	top hat	blouson	crispin
cobcab	Magyar	topper	blucher	cuculla
cocket	mantee	trilby	bottine	cuirass
cornet	mantle	trunks	box cape	culotte
corona	Mantua	t-shirt	box coat	curchef

cutaway	pattern	wedgies	canotier	flimsies
dopatta	pelisse	wellies	cape coat	footwear
doublet	petasos	wing tie	capeline	galoshes
drawers	pierrot	woollen	capriole	gamashes
earmuff	pillbox	wrapper	capucine	gauntlet
epaulet	pluvial	xurqana	caputium	golf shoe
Eton cap	puggree	yashmak	carcanet	golf sock
fanchon	puttees	Y-fronts	cardigan	goloshes
fashion	pyjamas	zimarra	cardinal	Guernsey
filibet	raiment		Caroline	gumboots
flat cap	regalia		casaquin	gym shoes
flat hat	rompers	**8**	catercap	half-hose
foulard	rubbers	abbé cape	chandail	half slip
fur coat	sarafan	all-in-one	chaperon	headgear
gaiters	scogger	analabos	chaqueta	hipsters
garment	shalwar	antelope	charshaf	host coat
ghillie	silk hat	babouche	chasuble	hot pants
G-string	singlet	babushka	chausses	jackboot
gumboot	ski boot	baladran	chef's hat	judo coat
gumshoe	slip-ons	ball gown	chongsam	judo robe
gym shoe	slipper	Balmoral	cloth cap	jump suit
gym slip	slyders	bandanna	codpiece	kerchief
handbag	smicket	barbette	colobium	knickers
high-low	sneaker	basquine	copatain	knitwear
homburg	socklet	bathrobe	corselet	larrigan
hosiery	soutane	bearskin	couch hat	lala-lava
jodhpur	spencer	bed socks	coverall	leggings
klompen	sporran	benjamin	crew neck	lingerie
layette	stetson	biggonet	crush hat	liripipe
leotard	sultain	binnogue	cucullus	mantelet
loafers	sunsuit	black tie	culottes	mantilla
Mae West	surcoat	bloomers	dalmatic	moccasin
maillot	surtout	body coat	dance set	nightcap
manteau	sweater	body suit	dandy hat	negligée
montero	tank top	bombards	djellaba	nightcap
muffler	tea gown	boot-hose	dom pedro	oilskins
necktie	top boot	bottekin	dormeuse	opera hat
negligé	topcoat	breeches	duck-bill	overalls
nightie	traheen	Burberry	dunce cap	overcoat
olivers	tricorn	burgonet	dust coat	overshoe
overall	tunicle	burnoose	dutch cap	pantsuit
Oxfords	twinset	burnouse	earmuffs	parament
paletot	uniform	bycocket	Eton suit	peasecod
panties	veiling	cabasset	faldetta	peignoir
parasol	watteau	camisole	flannels	philibeg

pileolus
pinafore
plastron
platinum
plimsole
plimsoll
pullover
raincoat
sabotine
scapular
ski pants
skull-cap
slip-over
slippers
sneakers
snowshoe
sombrero
stocking
straw hat
sun dress
surplice
swimsuit
swimwear
tail coat
tailleur
tarboosh
toquette
trainers
trencher
tricorne
trousers
two-piece
white tie
woollens
woollies
zoot suit

9

afterwelt
alice band
alpargata
alpine hat
ankle boot
ankle sock

armilausa
baby-dolls
baby skirt
balaclava
balayeuse
ball dress
balmacaan
bambin hat
bandalier
bandoleer
beach wrap
beavertop
bed jacket
beegum hat
bell skirt
billicock
blousette
blue jeans
body linen
bourrelet
bowler hat
brassiere
broadbrim
brodequin
cabriolet
caparison
cape dress
cape stole
cartwheel
casentino
casquette
cassimere
chemiloon
chin-cloth
chivarras
cholo coat
coat dress
coat shirt
cocked hat
comforter
coolie hat
copataine
copintank
cornercap
cothurnus

court shoe
cowboy hat
creedmore
crinoline
dog collar
dominical
dress coat
dress shoe
dress suit
dungarees
epaulette
fleshings
flip-flops
forage cap
frock coat
full dress
gabardine
gaberdine
garibaldi
ghonnella
glengarry
greatcoat
headdress
headpiece
headscarf
helmet cap
high heels
hoop skirt
houri-coat
house-coat
hula skirt
jackboots
jockey cap
Juliet cap
kid gloves
knee socks
loincloth
long johns
macintosh
millinery
miniskirt
neckcloth
nightgown
night wear
outerwear

overdress
overshirt
overskirt
panama hat
pantaloon
pantelets
pantoffle
pantyhose
pea jacket
peaked cap
petticoat
pilot coat
plimsolls
plus fours
polonaise
polo shirt
Quaker hat
redingote
round neck
sack dress
sailor hat
sanbenito
school tie
separates
shaksheer
shellsuit
shintiyan
shovel hat
shower cap
shower hat
sloppy joe
slouch hat
snowshoes
sou'wester
stomacher
string tie
sunbonnet
surcingle
tent dress
thigh boot
trousseau
trunk-hose
undercoat
undergown
undervest

underwear
vestments
victorine
waistband
waistcoat
waist slip
watch coat
white coat
wide-awake
witch's hat
wyliecoat

10

Angelus cap
apron dress
apron tunic
baby bonnet
basic dress
bathing cap
beer jacket
bellboy cap
berrettino
bibi bonnet
bicycle bal
blouse coat
bobby socks
body-shaper
body-warmer
boiler suit
bosom shirt
boudoir cap
bridal gown
brigandine
brunch coat
bucket tops
bumper brim
bush jacket
button boot
calzoneras
canvas shoe
cape collar
cappa magna
carmagnole
cerveliere

chatelaine
chemisette
chignon cap
chouquette
clock-mutch
coolie coat
coqueluche
corps pique
cossack cap
cote-hardie
court shoes
couvre-chef
coverchief
covert coat
crepe soles
crosscloth
cummerbund
dance dress
deshabille
dinner suit
diploidian
douillette
drainpipes
dress plain
dress shirt
dress shoes
duffel coat
eclipse tie
espadrille
Eton collar
Eton jacket
Eugenie hat
fancy dress
fascinator
feather boa
flying suit
fore-and-aft
fustanella
garmenture
grass skirt
halter neck
harem skirt
hug-me-tight
jiffer coat
lederhosen

leghorn hat
liripipium
lounge suit
lumberjack
mackintosh
mess jacket
nightdress
nightshirt
opera cloak
overblouse
overgaiter
Oxford bags
Oxford gown
pantaloons
party dress
pettipants
picture hat
pith helmet
plastic mac
poke bonnet
pork pie hat
riding boot
riding-hood
sailor suit
service cap
showercoat
shirtwaist
slumber cap
smoking cap
sports coat
sport shirt
sportswear
sticharion
string vest
Sunday best
suspenders
sweat shirt
swirl skirt
three-piece
trench coat
underdress
underlinen
underpants
undershirt
underskirt

veldschoen
waterproof
windjammer
Windsor tie
wing collar

11

Alsatian bow
baby clothes
ballet dress
ballet shoes
bathing suit
battle dress
bellbottoms
bespoke suit
bib-and-brace
boiled shirt
bovver boots
boxer shorts
braçonnière
breechcloth
British warm
cancan dress
cavalier hat
chapeau bras
chapel de fer
circassiene
co-ordinates
corset cover
cowboy boots
dancing clog
deerstalker
dinner dress
dirndl skirt
drape jacket
empire skirt
espadrilles
evening gown
evening slip
evening wear
farthingale
flared skirt
formal dress
galligaskin

hand-me-downs
hobble skirt
hostess gown
houppelande
hunting boot
leisure suit
matinee coat
middy blouse
morning suit
mortar-board
neckerchief
overgarment
panty girdle
pencil skirt
Phrygian cap
puffa-jacket
rah-rah skirt
ready-to-wear
riding habit
rubber apron
running shoe
Russian boot
safari dress
sewing apron
shawl collar
snap-brim-hat
soup-and-fish
southwester
spatterdash
stocking cap
string glove
swagger coat
Tam-O'Shanter
tennis skirt
trouser suit
tunic blouse
Tyrolean hat
undergirdle
underthings
vagabond hat
walking shoe
wedding gown
wedding veil
wellingtons
widow's weeds

windbreaker
windcheater

12

Amish costume
Balkan blouse
balloon skirt
baseball boot
battle jacket
belly doublet
bloomer dress
body stocking
bomber jacket
business suit
camicia rossa
cami-knickers
cardigan suit
cartwheel hat
cavalier boot
chastity belt
chemise dress
chemise frock
chesterfield
chukker shirt
cigarette mit
collar and tie
college scarf
combinations
corset bodice
cottage cloak
crusader hood
dinner jacket
divided skirt
donkey jacket
dress clothes
dressing gown
Easter bonnet
English drape
evening dress
evening shoes
evening skirt
handkerchief
headkerchief
helmet bonnet

jockey shorts
knee-breeches
lounging robe
lumber jacket
manadrin coat
monkey jacket
morning dress
motoring viel
pedal pushers
penitentials
Quaker bonnet
roll-on girdle
safari jacket
sailor collar
Scotch bonnet
shirtwaister
sleeping coat
sleeping suit
smallclothes
stiletto heel
stovepipe hat
sweater dress
ten-gallon hat
tennis shorts
trouserettes
underclothes
undergarment
wide-awake hat
Zouave jacket

13

acrobatic shoe
apres-ski socks
Beefeater's hat
bellboy jacket
Bermuda shorts
circular skirt
coachman's coat
combing jacket
cottage bonnet
cropped jacket
culotte shorts
cut-away jacket
dressing saque

elevator shoes
football scarf
hacking jacket
Hawaiian skirt
liberty bodice
maternity wear
matinee jacket
Mother Hubbard
mourning dress
nofs ghonella
Norfolk jacket
nurse's uniform
peek-a-boo waist
period costume
pinafore dress
platform shoes
princess dress
puffball skirt
Sam Brown belt
school uniform
slingback shoe
smoking jacket
sports clothes
sugar-loaf suit
suspender-belt
teddybear coat
trunk-breeches
underclothing
winkle-pickers

14

afternoon dress

barefoot sandal
bathing costume
bicycle clip hat
cabbage-tree hat
cache-poussiere
camouflage suit
cardigan bodice
clerical collar
congress gaitor
continental hat
dressing jacket
dressmaker suit
Egyptian sandal
evening sweater
French knickers
knickerbockers
longline jacket
shooting jacket
straight-jacket
travelling suit

15

boudoir slippers
bridesmaid dress
brothel-creepers
Cardigan sweater
chapeau Francais
chemise à la reine
Chevalier bonnet
Christening robe

double-duty dress
envelope chemise
Fair Isle sweater
Gainsborough hat
Hungarian blouse
Montgomery beret
national costume
Wellington boots
wrap-around skirt

16 +

Ballerina costume
Bethlehem Headdress
butcher boy blouse
camel's hair shawl
Charlotte Corday cap
chemise a l'anglaise
Chesterfield coat
chicken skin glove
coal scuttle bonnet
Confirmation Dress
directoire knickers
Eisenhower jacket
Elbert Hubbard tie
foundation garment
going-away costume
Salvation Army bonnet
swaddling clothes
swallow-tailed coat
thermal underwear

Drinks and beverages

3		rum	arak	brut	Dawn	kava
	gin	rye	asti	Cape	dram	Kina
ale	HPW	sec	Auto	char	fizz	Kups
BDV	IPA	tea	Balm	coke	flip	kas
bub	KCB	Wow	Bass	cola	grog	Lily
cha	kir		beer	Cota	Hell	malt
Elk	nog	**4**	bock	Club	hock	marc
fix	pop		Bolo	Crow	Inca	mate
Flu	RAC	Ante	bols	Darb	Jo-jo	mead
	Roy					

mild	broth	morat	bitter	Hoopla
milk	bumbo	negus	Beadle	Hotcha
Moll	Byrrh	noyau	Bishop	Joburg
Navy	capri	Opera	Bombay	junora
mumm	chica	padra	boukha	Kicker
must	choum	Pansy	Bovril	kirsch
ouzo	cider	pekoe	branca	kummel
Peto	cocoa	perry	brandy	Ladies
Polo	congo	Pimms	Brazil	lambic
port	cream	Pinky	Bridal	Lerina
raki	Cuban	Plaza	Butler	liquor
reid	Cupid	plonk	bubbly	Lisbon
Rosé	cyser	punch	canary	London
sack	daisy	purre	Carrol	Malaga
sake	Dandy	quass	Caruso	Masdeu
saki	Davis	Royal	Casino	mastic
soda	Derby	Savoy	cassis	meliss
Soho	Diana	shrub	caudle	mescal
So-so	Dinah	sirop	chicha	Metaxa
sour	Dixie	sling	Choker	muscat
Star	Dream	smash	coffee	Nicado
stum	Duppy	stout	Cognac	noggin
tent	Ethel	tafia	Cooper	Old Pal
Ture	Fancy	Tango	Creole	oolong
wine	Fieth	toddy	Degree	orgeat
wort	Gypsy	tonic	Devil's	pastis
Yale	Hakam	Tuica	Dunlop	perkin
Zaza	H and H	vichy	egg-nog	Pernod
	Hasty	vodka	elixir	pimint
5	hooch	water	Empire	pontac
	hyson	winox	Fernet	porter
Abbey	Irish	Yeres	finkel	posset
Allen	irroy	Zamba	Floupe	poteen
anise	Jewel		Froupe	Presto
anram	julep	**6**	Gasper	ptisan
arack	kvass		Geneva	pulque
Araki	lagbi	Adonis	Gibson	qetsch
Aurum	lager	Alaska	Gilroy	Queens
ayala	Lasky	alegar	gimlet	rickey
Baron	lassi	Allies	Glider	Rob Roy
Biffy	Luigi	Angler	grappa	Saumur
Bijou	Mamie	arrack	Graves	Scotch
Blues	Melba	Bamboo	Guards	scubac
bohea	Melon	Bennet	Harry's	shandy
Bronx	mobby	Big Boy	Havana	sherry

Silver	Booster	low-wine	Sidecar	Bunny Hug
Snyder	boukhra	Jackson	sloe gin	Calvados
spirit	bourbon	Jeypack	spirits	Canadian
squash	Bulldog	Lawhill	Spokane	Cape Town
stingo	Cabaret	mace ale	Stinger	Chambery
Strega	Cachiry	Madeira	Sunrise	charneco
Striep	Campari	Malmsey	tea bags	China tea
Suisse	catawba	Manyann	Tempter	cider cup
Sunset	Cat's-eye	martini	tequila	ciderkin
swipes	Charles	Maurice	tintara	Claridge
Tavern	Chicago	Mayfair	twankay	Cliquot
tisane	Classic	Mexican	Twin Six	coca-cola
Trilby	cobbler	mint tea	vibrona	cocktail
Tuxedo	cordial	Morning	Vie Rose	Cornwell
Victor	Cordova	Newbury	Waldorf	daiquiri
Virgin	Culross	New Life	wassail	Diki-Diki
volnay	curacao	New York	Wembley	Drambuie
wherry	Deep Sea	Oh Henry	whiskey	Dubonnet
whisky	Dempsey	Oom Paul	Whisper	Earl Grey
	Devonia	pale ale	Whoopee	eau-de-vie
7	Diabalo	Perfect	Xanthia	espresso
	Doctor's	Perrier	Yolande	falernum
akvavit	Douglas	Pimento		Fairbank
alcamas	Douzico	pink gin	**8**	Fantasio
alcohol	dry wine	Pooh-Bah		Florence
ale-gill	Du Barry	Pomerol	absinthe	Fox River
Alfonso	Duchess	Pommard	Advocaat	fruit cup
alicant	Eclipse	pulchra	Affinity	gin and It
allasch	egg-flip	Putitan	anisette	gin-sling
Approve	escubac	Quakers	Apparency	green tea
aquavit	Falerno	Rainbow	Apple Car	Guinness
Astoria	Foxtrot	ratafia	apple tea	Habitant
Atta Boy	Gazette	Red Flag	aperitif	Handicap
Aviator	gimblet	red wine	Armangnac	Hawaiian
Bacardi	gin fizz	rickeys	Assam tea	Hercules
Bailey's	gin sour	Roc-a-Coe	Atom Bomb	Highball
Banjino	Glad Eye	sage tea	Aviation	Honolulu
Barbara	Guarozo	sambuca	Baracchs	Hollands
beef tea	Harvard	samshoo	bee's wing	Hoots Mon
bee wine	herb tea	sangria	beverage	Horlicks
Belmont	Hop Toad	schnaps	block tea	hot toddy
Bentley	Hot Deck	scrumpy	Blue Bird	hydromel
bitters	koumiss	seltzer	bock-beer	Jack Pine
Blanche	iced tea	Sevilla	brick tea	Jack Rose
Blenton	liqueur	sherbet	Brooklyn	King Cole

Kingston
Klondyke
Knock Out
lager top
Leap Frog
lemonade
limeade
Linstead
Lone Tree
Magnolia
Mah-Jongo
Martinez
Midnight
montilla
nightcap
Nick's Own
Night Car
oopak tea
Olivette
Oriental
Ovaltine
padra tea
Pall Mall
Palmetto
Paradise
pekoe tea
persicot
Peter Pan
Philomel
Planters
pilsener
Ping Pong
Pink Baby
Pink Lady
Pol Roger
Poop Deck
pouchong
prasites
prunelle
Pruneaux
punt y mes
ramboose
red biddy
red wines
roederer

root beer
ruby port
rum-punch
rum-shrub
sangaree
schnapps
Shamrock
sillabub
skim-milk
Snowball
souchong
Soul Kiss
sour milk
Spion Cop
Sunshine
Swizzles
syllabub
The Comet
Tia Maria
Tropical
Up-to-date
Valencia
Velocity
verjuice
vermouth
van de Ham
vin blanc
Which Way
Whiz Bang
wish-wash

9

Addington
Albertine
Alexander
Alice Mine
altar wine
angostura
Angel Face
Angel's Tip
Applejack
arquebuse
Artillery
aqua vitae

barley pop
Beautiful
Beaux Arts
Bee's Knees
Berry Wall
birch wine
bitter ale
bitter top
black beer
Blue Devil
Blue Train
Boomerang
brandewyn
Breakfast
Brunelle
Buck Jones
Buck's Fizz
Cablegram
Ceylon tea
chocolate
Cointreau
Commodore
Copa de Oro
cream soda
Cuba Libre
Deauville
Depth Bomb
De Rigueur
Diplomate
dry ginger
East India
elder wine
Eve's Apple
Eye Opener
Fairbanks
Falernian
framboise
Genevieve
ginger ale
ginger pop
Grape Vine
Grand Slam
grenadine
guignolet
Gun Cotton

Halls' wine
Harrovian
hermitage
Heidsieck
hippocras
Homestead
honey beer
Honeymoon
Indian tea
lager beer
limejuice
Lusitania
Manhattan
metheglin
milk punch
milkshake
Minnehaha
mint julep
mirabelle
Moonlight
Moonraker
moonshine
mulled ale
muscadine
oolong tea
orangeade
orange gin
Palm Beach
Pink Pearl
President
Quelle Vie
rice water
Rosington
Royal Mile
salutaris
San Martin
Scotch ale
Secrestat
Sensation
shandy gaff
slivovitz
small-beer
soda water
soft drink
South Side

still hock
sweet wine
sundowner
tarragona
tawny port
Tipperary
triple sec
Trocedero
whisky mac
White Baby
White Lady
White Lion
white port
white wine
Whizz Bang
Wincarnis
Union Jack

10

Abricotine
Angel's Kiss
Angel's Wing
angosturas
Archbishop
barley beer
barley wine
Biltong Dry
bitter beer
Blackthorn
Black Maria
black-strap
Blood Hound
Bloody Mary
Blue Monday
Bobby Burns
Bonnie Scot
Brain Storm
Broken Spur
Bush-Ranger
buttermilk
brou de noix
café-au-lait
calcavella
cappuccino

Charleston
chartreuse
Chorus Lady
clary-water
Clementine
Clover Club
camomile tea
coconut milk
constantia
Co-operation
Corn Popper
Coronation
crème de ciel
Crème Wette
Dolly O'Dare
dry martini
Earl Grey tea
Earthquake
Eddie Brown
Eton Blazer
Fairy Belle
Fascinator
Fifty-fifty
frontiniac
fruit juice
Gene Corrie
Gene Tunney
genevrette
ginger beer
ginger wine
Golden Dawn
Golden Gate
goldwasser
Green Briar
Hanky Panky
Hesitation
Horse's Neck
Jabberwock
Jack Kearns
Jamaica rum
Jimmy Blanc
Jockey Club
Journalist
lime squash
London Buck

malt liquor
malted milk
malt whiskey
mango mamba
maraschino
Merry Widow
mickey finn
Monte Carlo
Montpelier
Moselle cup
mulled wine
Munich beer
nettle beer
pale sherry
parsley tea
peppermint
Piccadilly
Pina Colada
Poet's Dream
raisin wine
Rolls Royce
Rum Collins
Sleepy Head
Tom Collins
rum and coke
rye whiskey
sack posset
shandygaff
soft drinks
spruce beer
still wines
Stone Fence
sweet wines
tanglefoot
Temptation
toast water
tonic water
twankey tea
usquebaugh
Vanderbilt
vichy water
Washington
whisky sour
white capri
white wines

Widow's Kiss

11

aguardiente
amontillado
apollinaris
apple brandy
barley broth
barleywater
Beachcomber
benedictine
Black Velvet
Bronx Silver
Bud's Special
Café de Paris
Chanticcleer
cider-brandy
citron water
Coopers Town
Courvoisier
cowslip wine
crème de moka
Depth Charge
dry monopole
Eagle's Dream
Fallen Angel
Fifth Avenue
Franken Jack
Froth Blower
Gloom Chaser
Gloom Raiser
Great Secret
Green Dragon
half and half
Hildebrande
Irish coffee
Irish whisky
John Collins
Johnnie Mack
Kiss-me-quick
lager shandy
Leave-it-to-
  me
lemon squash

Little Devil
Lord Suffolk
Loud Speaker
Millionaire
Mississippi
Modder River
montefiasco
mountain-dew
Moulin Rouge
orange-pekoe
peach brandy
Pat's special
Plymouth gin
potash water
pouchong tea
Quarter Deck
Rattlesnake
Screwdriver
Self-starter
Silver Bells
slivervitza
soda and milk
souchong tea
spring water
Swazi Freeze
tomato juice
Toby Special
Tom and Jerry
Third Degree
Thunder Clap
Trappistine
vintage wine
wassail bowl
Yellow Daisy

12

Barbary Coast
Bich's Special
bitter shandy
Block and Fall
Blood and Sand
Brandy Blazer
brandy coffee
Bronx Express

Cameron's Kick
cherry brandy
Church Parade
Churchwarden
crème de cacao
Crystal Bronx
Cyprus sherry
Desert Healer
dry ginger ale
Elephant's Ear
Fernet-Branca
Fine and Dandy
Fourth Degree
Gaelic coffee
gin and French
ginger brandy
Golden Ermine
Grand Marnier
hair of the dog
Hoffman House
Holland House
ice-cream soda
India pale ale
Irish whiskey
kirschwasser
Maiden's Blush
Malvern water
mineral water
Mule's Hind Leg
mulled claret
Old Fashioned
orange brandy
orange squash
peach bitters
Perrier-Jouet
Prince's Smile
red wine punch
Rhenish wines
sarsaparilla
Scotch whisky
seltzer water
Silver Streak
treacle water
Treble Chance
Wedding Belle

whisky and dry
white gin sour
Yankee Prince
Yellow Special

13

aerated waters
aperitif wines
apricot brandy
Barney Barnato
Barton Special
Bijou cocktail
Broadway Smile
Bronx cocktail
Champagne Buck
Champselysees
Cherry Blossom
Cherry Heering
Contrexeville
Corpse Reviver
crème-de-menthe
dandelion wine
Darjeeling tea
decaffeinated
Eau de Vie de Lie
Everything But
Fluffy Ruffles
ginger cordial
Golden Slipper
Grace's Delight
fortified wine
instant coffee
liqueur brandy
liqueur whisky
Knickerbocker
Maiden's Prayer
Mazato of Perou
orange bitters
Orange Blossom
pineapple fizz
pink champagne
Planters Punch
Prairie Oyster
seidlitz water
Seventh Heaven

sherry cobbler
sparkling hock
sparkling wine
Spring Feeling
Veuve Clicquot
vino ordinaire
whisky and soda
Yellow Rattler

14

Bacardi and coke
Bamboo cocktail
blended whiskey
champagne cider
champagne punch
Dam-the-weather
French vermouth
Johannisberger
Logan Princess
Lulu's Favourite
Lutkins Special
Newton's Special
Pink Peccadillo

Piper-Heidsieck
Rob Roy cocktail
sparkling wines
vermouth cassis
white wine punch

15

blackcurrant tea
Cascade cocktail
champagne cognac
champagne frappé
Duchess cocktail
Everybody's Irish
grapefruit juice
green chartreuse
Italian vermouth
Jersey Lightning
Martini-cocktail
Peychaud bitters
sacramental wine
Southern Comfort
tintara burgundy
Welcome Stranger

West Country mint

16 +

Amaretto di Saranno
American dry ginger
Between the Sheets
blackcurrant juice
Book-seller's Special
Chambery Quetsch of
  Alsace
Danziger Goldmasser
dandelion and burdock
decaffeinated coffee
drinking chocolate
granulated coffee
Green-eyed Monster
Harvey Wallbanger
Lapsang souchong tea
raspberry leaf tea
Schwarzwald Kirsh
  Wasser
Thunder and Lightning
whisky and American

Fabrics/materials

3

aba
abb
fur
net
PVC
rep

4

abba
baft
cony
drab
felt
gimp

gros
hide
jute
lace
lame
lawn
leno
mink
repp
silk
wool

5

abaya
baize
batik

braid
cloth
crape
crêpe
denim
drill
gauze
gunny
khaki
lacet
linen
lisle
lurex
mungo
ninon
nylon
orris

plaid
plush
rayon
sable
satin
serge
stuff
suede
surah
tabby
tamin
tasar
tulle
tweed
twill
tulle
voile

6

alpaca
angora
beaver
boucle
broche
burlap
byssus
calico
camlet
canvas
chintz
cotton
dacron
damask
dimity

dowlas
ermine
faille
fleece
foxfur
gurrah
hodden
jersey
Kendal
linsey
lustre
marmot
merino
mohair
moreen
muslin
poplin

ratine
samite
sateen
sendal
shoddy
soneri
tamine
tartan
ticken
tissue
toison
tusser
velour
velure
velvet
wincey
winsey

7

abb wool
acrilan
art-silk
baracan
batiste
brocade
buckram
cambric
chagrin
chamois
chiffon
cow-hide
crochet
delaine
doeskin
dornick
drabbet
drugget
ermelin
felting
flannel
foulard
fustian
galloon
genappe

gingham
grogram
guipure
hessian
holland
jaconet
leather
lockram
malines
matting
mechlin
minever
miniver
mockado
morocco
nacarat
nankeen
organza
orleans
orphrey
oil-silk
paisley
percale
pigskin
ratteen
sacking
scarlet
stammel
suiting
tabaret
tabinet
taffeta
taffety
tatting
ticking
tiffany
tussore
velours
vesting
worsted

8

barathea
barracan

baudekin
bayadere
bearskin
bobbinet
bonelace
brocatel
buckskin
Burberry
cashmere
chenille
corduroy
cordwain
cretonne
dagswain
deerskin
drabette
drilling
dungaree
florence
flox silk
gambroon
gossamer
homespun
jacquard
lambskin
moleskin
moquette
muslinet
musquash
nainsook
oilcloth
organdie
osnaburg
paduasoy
prunella
prunello
pure silk
sarcenet
sarsenet
sealskin
shagreen
shalloon
shantung
shot silk
spun silk

suedette
tabbinet
tapestry
tarlatan
Terylene
Thai silk
valentia
wool lace

9

astrakhan
baldachin
baldaquin
blond lace
bobbinnet
bombasine
bombazeen
bombazine
calamanco
camelhair
cassimere
cerecloth
Chantilly
Courtelle
crepoline
crinoline
floss silk
folk-weave
fur fabric
gaberdine
gabardine
georgette
grosgrain
haircloth
horsehair
huckaback
lambswool
levantine
moiré silk
organzine
paramatta
percaline
persienne
petersham

pina cloth
point lace
polyester
sackcloth
sailcloth
satinette
sharkskin
sheepskin
silk serge
snakeskin
spun rayon
tarpaulin
towelling
veloutine
velveteen

10

angora wool
Balbriggan
beaverteen
Berlin wool
blanketing
bobbin-lace
broadcloth
brocatelle
cassinette
chinchilla
corded silk
florentine
grass cloth
hodden-grey
hodden-gray
Irish linen
jersey silk
jersey wool
kerseymere
khaki drill
khaki serge
mackintosh
mock velvet
mousseline
needlecord
parramatta
pillow-lace

pilot cloth
rabbitskin
seersucker
thrown-silk
tussah silk
tusseh silk
tusser-silk
winceyette

11

cheesecloth
flannelette
Harris tweed
Honiton lace
Kendal cloth
leatherette
leopardskin

Mechlin lace
nettle-cloth
Persian lamb
stockinette
torchon lace
tussore silk
watered silk

12

cavalry twill
crêpe-de-chine
double jersey
gros de Naples
Indian cotton
Mechlin black
moire antique
moire taffeta
Welsh flannel

13

Chantilly lace
crocodile skin
linsey-woolsey
patent leather
Russia leather
uncut moquette

14

artificial silk
Morocco leather

15 +

broderie anglaise
mousseline-de-soie
mousseline-de-
   laine

Fairies, devils, ghosts, nymphs, etc.

3	pixy	dwarf	pixie	faunus	sprite
	Puck	Eblis	Satan	goblin	tangie
elf	Rahu	faery	spook	hobbit	Thetis
fay	soul	fairy	troll	hyades	Thoosa
imp	trow	fauni		ifreet	wraith
Mab		fetch	**6**	jinnee	
nix	**5**	fiend		kelpie	**7**
Pan		genie	Acheri	kobold	
	alfar	genii	Aegena	Laurin	Alastor
4	afrit	ghost	afreet	Lilith	Asteria
	angel	ghoul	Azazel	Merope	banshee
bogy	Ariel	gnome	Befana	nereid	brownie
drow	bogey	guelf	Calyce	nicker	Clymene
Echo	Bucca	kelpy	cherub	Oberon	Coronis
geni	demon	lutin	Clytie	Oenone	Galatea
jinn	devil	naiad	Cobweb	piskey	gremlin
Loki	dryad	nymph	Cyrene	Rhodas	Gytrash
Moth	duppi	oread	Daphne	Scylla	knocker
peri	duppy	pisky	Egeria	shades	lemures

Manitou
Morgana
Morgane
oceanid
Old Nick
phantom
sandman
Setebos
shedeem
spectre
Titania
Titivil

8

Alberich
Arethusa
Asmodeus
Barbason
bogeyman
Castalia
Cymodoce
Echenais
Eurydice
lubrican
mazikeen
Morgaine

Penelope
Periboca
phantasm
psammead
Queen Mab
Rübezahl
spriggan

9

adamastor
archangel
archfiend
Beelzebub
dockalfar
ectoplasm
hamadryad
hobgoblin
lubberkin
Mauthe Dog
nain rouge
oceanides
Parabanou
phantasma
pigwidgin
pigwiggen

white lady

10

apparition
archimagus
cacodaemon
cluricaune
demogorgon
ghibbeline
leprechaun
May Mollock
Morganetta
Tinkerbell
Tutivillus
tooth fairy
tylwyth teg

11

Fata Morgana
Morgan le Fay
Mustardseed
poltergeist

12

Jack o' the Bowl

La Dame Abonde
little people
Morgue la Fay
Phynnodderee
Peaseblossom
Wayland Smith

13

astral spirits
Cock Lane ghost
Lady of the Lake
Mother Shipton
Sampford ghost

14

La Dame d'Aprigny
Le Cheval Bayard
Mephistopheles
Stockwell ghost

15 +

Prince of Darkness
Robin Goodfellow
Rumplestiltskin
White lady of Avenel

Faiths and religions

3

Jew
Zen

4

Ainu
Babi
Copt
Jain
Sikh

Sufi
Yogi

5

Arian
Bahai
Deism
Deist
Druid
Fakir
Hadji

Hindu
Islam
Shiah
Sunni

6

Babism
Babist
Dipper
Dopper
Dunker

Essene
Hebrew
Jesuit
Jewess
Levite
Marist
Moonie
Mormon
Moslem
Muslim
Mystic
Papist

Parsee
Quaker
Ranter
Shaker
Shiite
Shinto
Taoism
Taoist
Theism
Theist
Voodoo
Wahabi

Zealot

7

Abelian
Abelite
Adamite
Ajivika
Amarite
Ascetic
Atheism
Atheist

Baalite
Bahaism
Bahaist
Baptist
Beghard
Brahman
Brahmin
Cluniac
Convert
Gentile
Gnostic
Heathen
Heretic
Infidel
Jacobin
Jainism
Judaism
Judaist
Lamaism
Lamaist
Lateran
Limiter
Lollard
Mahdist
Mahdist
Maurist
Mormons
Paulian
Puritan
Quakery
Saracen
Sceptic
Seceder
Shakers
Sikhism
Sivaite
Sunnite
Templar
Wahabis
Zionism
Zionist

8

Agnostic

Anglican
Apostasy
Apostate
Arianism
Armenian
Believer
Buddhism
Buddhist
Capuchin
Catholic
Disciple
Ditheism
Ditheist
Donatism
Donatist
Druidism
Druidess
Erastian
Essenism
Follower
Hinduism
Huguenot
Humanism
Humanist
Ignatian
Incenser
Islamite
Lutheran
Mahdiism
Mahdiist
Maronite
Minorite
Nazarene
Nazarite
Pharisee
Reformer
Sadducee
Salesian
Satanist
Shafiite
Talapoin
Totemism
Totemist
Trappist
Ursuline

Wahabite
Wesleyan

9

Abstinent
Adventist
Ambrosian
Augustine
Bacchanal
Balaamite
Buchanite
Calvinism
Calvinist
Carmelite
Christian
Dissenter
Dominican
Gospeller
Hebrewess
Jansenism
Jansenist
Lutherism
Lutherist
Methodism
Methodist
Mithraism
Mithraist
Mussalman
Mussulman
Mysticism
Occultism
Occultist
Orangeman
Oratorian
Pamtheism
Pantheist
Parseeism
Quakeress
Quakerism
Rabbinist
Rabbinite
Reformism
Reformist
Sectarian

Shamanism
Shamanist
Shintoism
Shintoist
Simeonite
Unitarian
Wyclifite

10

Abrahamite
Albigenses
Anabaptism
Anabaptist
Basilidean
Bernardine
Brahmanism
Brigittine
Carthusian
Church Army
Church-goer
Cistercian
Conformism
Conformist
Covenanter
Evangelism
Evangelist
Franciscan
Gilbertine
Gnosticism
Jeronymite
Limitarian
Lollardism
Mohammedan
Monotheism
Monotheist
Polytheism
Polytheist
Protestant
Puritanism
Revivalism
Revivalist
Schismatic
Secularism
Secularist

Unbeliever
Worshipper
Wycliffite

11

Abecedarian
Agnosticism
Albigensian
Anglicanism
Arminianism
Augustinian
Benedictine
Catabaptist
Catholicism
Devotionist
Disbeliever
Erastianism
Hospitaller
Lutheranism
Neo-Catholic
Old Catholic
Orthodox Jew
Plymouthism
Rastafarian
Rosicrucian
Sabbatarian
Tetratheism
Tetratheist
Theosophism
Theosophist
Trinitarian
Wesleyanism

Zen Buddhism
Zen Buddhist
Zoroastrian

12

Christianity
Confucianism
Confucianist
Episcopalian
Hot Gospeller
Neo-Christian
Paedobaptist
Presbyterian
Salvationism
Salvationist
Sectarianism
Unitarianism

13

Anglo-Catholic
Greek Orthodox
Mohammedanism
Nonconformism
Nonconformist
Protestantism
Redemptionist
Reform Judaism
Roman Catholic
Salvation Army
Scripturalist
Sun-worshipper

Zarathustrian

14

Congregational
Fire-worshipper
Fundamentalism
Fundamentalist
Latter-Day Saint
Sacramentalist
Uniformitarian

15 +

Anthroposophism
Anthroposophist
Antipaedobaptist
Christian Science
Christadelphian
Congregationalism
Conservative Judaism
Crypto-Christian
Devil-worshipper
Episcopalianism
Jehovah's Witness
Orthodox Judaism
Plymouth Brother
Plymouth Brethren
Presbyterianism
Roman Catholicism
Second-Adventist
Seventh-Day Adventist
Society of Friends

Famous pairings

Abraham and Isaac
Achemon and Basalas
Achilles and the Tortoise
Acis and Galatea
Adam and Eve
Sir John ALCOCK and Arthur
  Whitten BROWN
Ray ALLEN and LORD CHARLES

Alpheus and Arethusa
Amadis and Oriana
Amos and Andy
Ananias and Sapphira
Amis et Amiles
Amys and Amylion
Androcles and the Lion
Anthony and Cleopatra

Fred ASTAIRE and Ginger ROGERS
Lucille BALL and Desi ARNAZ
Daniel BARENBOIM and Jaqueline DU PRÉ
Barlaam and Josaphat
Phineas BARNUM and James BAILEY
Batman and Robin
Beauty and the Beast
BEERY, Noah and Wallace
Bennet and Williams
Bill and Ben
BONNIE Parker and CLYDE Barrow
Bernard BRADEN and Barbara KELLY
Brahma and Sarasvati
Peter BROUGH and Archie ANDREWS
Buddha and the Boar
Guy BURGESS and Donald MACLEAN
William BURKE and William HARE
George BURNS and Gracie ALLEN
Richard BURTON and Elizabeth TAYLOR
Butch Casssidy and the Sundance Kid
Cain and Abel
Calisto and Arcas
Leon CALMETTE and Camille GUERIN
Tommy CANNON and Bobby BALL
Castor and Pollux
Cephalus and Pocris
Dr Hawley Harvey CRIPPEN and Ethel LE NEVE
Bing CROSBY and Bob HOPE
Robinson CRUSOE and MAN FRIDAY
CURIE, Marie and Pierre
Gottlieb DAIMLER and Karl BENZ
Damon and Pythias
Dante and Beatrice
Daphnis and Chloe
Darby and Joan
David and Goliath
David and Jonathan

Diana and Artemis
Dido and Aeneas
EDWARD VIII and Mrs. Wallis SIMPSON
Esau and Jacob
EVERLEY BROTHERS, Don and Phil
Douglas FAIRBANKS and Mary PICKFORD
Ferrex and Porrex
Michael FLANDERS and Donald SWANN
Flotsam and Jetsam
Dawn FRENCH and Jennifer SAUNDERS
Gert and Daisy
Sir William GILBERT and Sir Arthur SULLIVAN
Gog and Magog
Gareth HALE and Norman PACE
Hansel and Gretel
Harlequin and Columbine
Bill HARLEY and Walter DAVIDSON
Tony HATCH and Jackie TRENT
Heathcliff and Catherine
Helen of Troy and Paris
Heloïse and Abelard
Hengist and Horsa
Hero and Leander
Hiawatha and Minnehaha
Sir Edmund HILLARY and Sherpa TENZING
Myra HINDLEY and Ian BRADY
Dame Evadne HINGE and Dr Hilda BRACKET
Adolf HITLER and Eva BRAUN
Sherlock HOLMES and Dr WATSON
Isis and Osiris
Jack and Jill
Dr JEKYLL and Mr HYDE
Jewell and Warriss
Teddy JOHNSON and Pearl CARR
KRAY TWINS, Ronald and Reginald
KROGER, Peter and Helen

Lady and the Tramp
Lancelot and Guinevere
Stanley LAUREL and Oliver HARDY
Layton and Johnson
John LENNON and Paul MCCARTNEY
Sid LITTLE and Eddie LARGE
Andrew LLOYD WEBBER and Tim RICE
LOUIS XVI and MARIE ANTOINETTE
Ben LYON and Bebe DANIELS
Victor MACLAGEN and Marie DRESSLER
Mary and Martha
Mary and Joseph
MARY Queen of Scots and Henry DARNLEY
Jessie MATTHEWS and Sonie HALE
Mickey and Minnie Mouse
Jim MOLLISON and Amy JOHNSON
MONTGOLFIER, Joseph and Jacques Etiene
Eric MORECAMBE and Ernie WISE
MURRAY, John and Nora
Napoleon and Joséphine
Naughton and Gold
Lord Horatio NELSON and Lady Emma HAMILTON
Nervo and Knox
Oberon and Titania
Orpheus and Eurydice
Owl and the Pussycat
PANKHURST, Emily and Sylvia
Paola and Francesca
Pat and Mick
PEARSON, Bob and Alf
Perseus and Andromeda
Peter and the Wolf
Peter Pan and Wendy
Peters and Lee
Philemon and Baucis

Pinky and Perky
Popeye and Olive Oyl
Punch and Judy
Pyramus and Thisbe
Quasimodo and Esmeralda
Don QUIXOTE and SANCHO PANZA
Rawicz and Landauer
Ethel REVNELL and Gracie WEST
Richard RODGERS and Oscar HAMMERSTEIN
Robin Hood and Maid Marian
ROMEO Montague and JULIET Capulet
Romulus and Remus
Charles ROLLS and Sir (Frederick) Henry ROYCE
Ruth and Naomi
St.George and the dragon
Samson and Delilah
Ira SANKEY and Dwight MOODY
Scylla and Charybdis
Shiva and Kali
Paul SIMON and Art GARFUNKEL
Mel SMITH and Griff Rhys JONES
Sooty and Sweep
Sir Henry STANLEY and David LIVINGSTONE
Tarzan and Jane
Tom and Jerry
Tortoise and the Hare
Jayne TORVILLE and Christopher DEAN
Tristan and Isolda
Troilus and Cressida
Tweedledum and Tweedledee
TWO RONNIES, Corbett and Barker
Vishnu and Lakshmi
Walrus and the Carpenter
WATERS, Elsie and Doris
WESLEY, John and Charles
WINTERS, Mike and Bernie
WRIGHT, Orville and Wilbur
Yin and Yang
Anne ZEIGLER and Webster BOOTH

First names

Female names

2	Kay	Aimé	Enid	Kate	Noll	5
	Kit	Alba	Erna	Katy	Nora	
Di	Kim	Alex	Esme	Kaye	Olga	Abbey
Em	Lea	Ally	Etta	Lala	Oona	Abbie
Jo	Lee	Alma	Etty	Leah	Pola	Adela
Vi	Liz	Alys	Evie	Lena	Poll	Adele
	Lot	Anna	Fifi	Lila	Prue	Aggie
3	Lou	Anne	Floy	Lily	Puss	Agnes
	Lyn	Anny	Beck	Lina	Rena	Ailie
Ada	Mae	Avis	Gaby	Lisa	Rene	Ailsa
Amy	Mai	Baba	Gage	Lita	Rita	Aimée
Ann	May	Babs	Gail	Liza	Rosa	Alice
Ava	Meg	Bebe	Gene	Lois	Rose	Aline
Bab	Nan	Beck	Gert	Lola	Rosy	Allie
Bea	Net	Bell	Gill	Lucy	Ruby	Altha
Bee	Pam	Bess	Gina	Lulu	Ruth	Amata
Bel	Pat	Beth	Gola	Lynn	Sara	Angel
Bet	Peg	Cara	Gwen	Mags	Sita	Anita
Dol	Pen	Caré	Gwyn	Maie	Spry	Annie
Dot	Pip	Cely	Hebe	Mana	Suky	Annis
Deb	Pru	Ciss	Hope	Mary	Susy	Annot
Eda	Ray	Clea	Ilse	Maud	Syme	April
Ena	Rio	Cleo	Ines	Megs	Tess	Arbel
Eva	Sal	Cora	Inez	Meta	Thea	Arden
Eve	Sis	Cory	Iona	Mimi	Tina	Avice
Fay	Sue	Dawn	Ione	Mima	Toni	Avril
Flo	Tam	Dido	Iris	Mina	Trix	Barbi
Gay	Toy	Dodo	Irma	Moll	Vera	Barby
Han	Una	Doll	Isla	Mona	Vida	Becky
Hat	Val	Dora	Isma	Muff	Viki	Bella
Ida	Viv	Edie	Ivey	Muir	Vita	Belle
Ina	Win	Edna	Jade	Myra	Viva	Berta
Isa	Yda	Edye	Jane	Nell	Zara	Beryl
Ivy	Zia	Ella	Jean	Nena	Zena	Bessy
Iza	Zoë	Elma	Jess	Neva	Zita	Betsy
Jan		Elsa	Jill	Niki	Zora	Betty
Jem	4	Else	Joan	Nina		Biddy
Jen		Emma	Judy	Nino		Bobby
Joy	Aggy	Emmy	June	Nita		Budie

Buena	Ellen	Janny	Màiri	Pansy	Vicki
Bunty	Ellie	Jayne	Mamie	Patsy	Vicky
Carla	Elsie	Jenny	Manie	Patty	Viola
Carly	Emily	Jesse	Manon	Paula	Vivie
Carol	Emmie	Jessy	Marge	Pearl	Wanda
Carré	Erica	Jilly	Maria	Peggy	Wendy
Caryl	Essie	Joann	Marie	Penny	Zeeta
Casey	Ethel	Josie	Matty	Phebe	Zelia
Cathy	Ettie	Joyce	Maude	Pippa	
Celia	Faith	Julia	Mavis	Pixie	**6**
Chloe	Fanny	Julie	Meave	Polly	
Chris	Feona	Karen	Megan	Poppy	Agatha
Chune	Filia	Karin	Mercy	Queen	Aileen
Cilla	Fiona	Katey	Merle	Rahel	Airlie
Circe	Fleur	Kathy	Meryl	Renée	Alexia
Cissy	Flora	Katie	Merry	Rhoda	Alicia
Clair	Freda	Kelly	Milly	Rhona	Alison
Clara	Gabie	Kerry	Minna	Robin	Almond
Clare	Gemma	Kitty	Mitzi	Rosie	Althea
Coral	Gerda	Laila	Moira	Sadie	Amabel
Corin	Gerty	Laura	Molly	Sally	Amanda
Daisy	Ginny	Leigh	Morag	Sandy	Amalia
Debby	Gipsy	Leila	Morna	Sarah	Amelia
Delia	Grace	Letty	Moyra	Sasie	Amélie
Della	Greer	Libby	Myrle	Shona	Anabel
Denes	Greta	Lilia	Myrna	Sonia	Andrea
Diana	Gussy	Lilly	Mysie	Susan	Angela
Diane	Hatty	Linda	Nance	Susie	Anthea
Dilys	Hazel	Lindy	Nancy	Sybil	Armyne
Dinah	Helen	Lizzy	Nanny	Tania	Astrid
Dodie	Helga	Lolly	Naomi	Tanya	Athene
Dolly	Henny	Lorna	Nelly	Tanis	Audrey
Donie	Hetty	Lotta	Nessa	Tatum	Aurora
Donna	Hilda	Lotty	Nesta	Teify	Averil
Dorah	Honor	Louie	Netta	Terka	Awdrey
Doris	Hulda	Lucia	Netty	Terri	Azelle
Dreda	Hylda	Lydia	Ninie	Tessa	Babbie
Dulce	Idina	Lynne	Ninny	Thora	Barbie
Edith	Innes	Lynda	Ninon	Tilly	Baubie
Effie	Irene	Mabel	Niobe	Tracy	Beatie
Eilsa	Isbel	Madge	Nolly	Trudy	Beatty
Elena	Isold	Maeve	Norah	Urith	Benita
Elfie	Janet	Magda	Norma	Venis	Bertha
Elise	Janey	Maggy	Olive	Venus	Berthe
Eliza	Janie	Maida	Olwen	Vesta	Bessie

Bettie	Elinor	Isabel	Marian	Poppet	Tracey
Bianca	Eloisa	Ishbel	Marion	Poppie	Tricia
Bibbie	Eloïse	Isobel	Marnie	Popsie	Trixie
Biddie	Elspet	Isolda	Martha	Portia	Trudie
Billie	Elvira	Isolde	Mattie	Rachel	Ulrica
Binnie	Emilia	Jackie	Maxine	Ramona	Ursula
Birdie	Emilie	Jacoba	Melita	Raquel	Verity
Blanca	Esther	Janice	Mercia	Regina	Verona
Blanch	Eunice	Jeanie	Merial	Renata	Violet
Blanka	Evadne	Jeanne	Mignon	Renira	Vivian
Blaise	Evelyn	Jemima	Millie	Richie	Vivien
Bobbie	Eyleen	Jennie	Mimosa	Robina	Vyvyen
Brenda	Fannie	Jessie	Minnie	Rosana	Willow
Bridie	Fatima	Joanna	Miriam	Rosina	Winnie
Brigid	Felice	Joanne	Mollie	Rowena	Yvette
Bryony	Flavia	Judith	Monica	Roxana	Yvonne
Carmen	Frieda	Juliet	Morwen	Sabina	
Carole	Galena	Kathie	Moulie	Sabine	
Carrie	Gerrie	Kirsty	Muriel	Salome	**7**
Cathie	Gertie	Kittie	Murtle	Sandra	
Cecile	Gleana	Lalage	Myrtle	Sappho	Abigail
Cecily	Gladys	Lallie	Nadine	Seabel	Adeline
Celina	Glenda	Lassie	Nancie	Selina	Adriana
Charis	Gloria	Leonie	Nellie	Seonad	Alberta
Cherry	Godiva	Lesley	Nelsie	Serena	Alethea
Cicely	Gracie	Lettie	Nessie	Sharon	Alfrida
Cissie	Greeba	Levina	Nettie	Sheena	Ameline
Claire	Gretel	Lilian	Nicola	Sheila	Ankaret
Connie	Gussie	Lilias	Nicole	Sicele	Annabel
Daphne	Gwenda	Lillah	Noelle	Silvia	Annaple
Davina	Gwynne	Lillie	Noreen	Simone	Annette
Debbie	Hannah	Lizzie	Odette	Sophia	Anstice
Denise	Hattie	Lolita	Olivia	Sophie	Antonia
Dianne	Hedwig	Lorina	Oonagh	Stella	Antonie
Dorcas	Helena	Lottie	Oriana	Sybell	Ariadne
Doreen	Hester	Louisa	Paddie	Sylvia	Asenath
Dorice	Hilary	Louise	Pamela	Tamsin	Athenia
Dulcie	Honora	Lucile	Parnel	Teresa	Augusta
Editha	Honour	Maggie	Pattie	Terrie	Aurelia
Edwina	Ianthe	Maimie	Pegeen	Tertia	Aveline
Edythe	Ileana	Maisie	Peggie	Tessie	Babette
Eileen	Imelda	Marcia	Pernel	Thalia	Barbara
Eirene	Imogen	Marcie	Persis	Thecla	Barbary
Elaine	Ingrid	Margie	Petula	Thelma	Beatrix
Elgiva	Ioanna	Margot	Phoebe	Tootie	Belinda
					Bettina

Beverly	Estella	Jillian	Miranda	Theresa	Collette
Blanche	Estelle	Jocelyn	Modesty	Therese	Consuelo
Blodwen	Etienne	Johanna	Myfanwy	Titania	Cordelia
Blossom	Eudoxia	Juanita	Natalia	Tootles	Cornelia
Brigida	Eugenia	Juliana	Natalie	Valerie	Cressida
Bridget	Eugenie	Justine	Natasha	Valetta	Danielle
Bronwen	Eulalia	Kathryn	Nigella	Vanessa	Dominica
Camilla	Evaline	Katrina	Ninette	Venetia	Dorothea
Candida	Eveleen	Katrine	Octavia	Winsome	Dorothie
Carolyn	Eveline	Kirstie	Ophelia	Yolande	Drusilla
Cecilia	Fayette	Lavinia	Ottilia	Zirphie	Dulcinia
Celeste	Felicia	Leoline	Ottilie		Eleanora
Charity	Fenella	Leonora	Palmyra	**8**	Eleanore
Cherrie	Feodora	Letitia	Pandora		Elfriede
Chloris	Fidelia	Lettice	Paulina	Adelaide	Ellaline
Chrissy	Florrie	Lillian	Pauline	Adrienne	Emmanuel
Clarice	Flossie	Lillias	Perdita	Albertha	Emmeline
Claudia	Frances	Linette	Phillis	Amabelle	Ethelind
Colette	Francie	Lisbeth	Phyllis	Angelica	Euphemia
Colleen	Frankie	Lizbeth	Queenie	Angelina	Evelinda
Coralie	Georgia	Lorinda	Rachael	Angeline	Everalda
Corinne	Georgie	Lucilla	Rachele	Angharad	Faustina
Corinna	Gertrud	Lucille	Rebecca	Arabella	Faustine
Crystal	Gillian	Lucinda	Rebekah	Araminta	Felicity
Cynthia	Giselle	Lucrece	Rhodena	Atalanta	Filomena
Damozel	Gladden	Mabelle	Ricarda	Beatrice	Florence
Deborah	Gwennie	Mafalda	Roberta	Berenice	Francine
Deirdre	Gwyneth	Margery	Rosabel	Beverley	Georgina
Delysia	Gwynnie	Marilyn	Rosalie	Camilla	Germaine
Désirée	Harriet	Marjery	Rosella	Carlotta	Gertrude
Diamond	Heather	Marjory	Rosetta	Carolina	Gretchen
Dolores	Hellena	Marlene	Rosette	Carolina	Griselda
Dorinda	Heloïse	Martina	Roxanne	Caroline	Grizelda
Dorothe	Honoria	Martine	Sabrina	Catalina	Grizelle
Dorothy	Horatia	Matilda	Shambra	Caterina	Gwynneth
Dorrice	Hypatia	Maudlin	Shelagh	Cathleen	Harriett
Dulcima	Isadora	Maureen	Shirley	Catriona	Hermione
Eleanor	Isidora	Melanie	Sidonia	Chrissie	Hortense
Elfreda	Janetta	Melissa	Siobhan	Christie	Hyacinth
Elfrida	Janette	Michele	Susanna	Chrystal	Immanuel
Ellenor	Janitha	Mildred	Susanne	Clemency	Isabella
Ellinor	Jasmine	Minella	Suzanne	Claribel	Jacobina
Elspeth	Jeannie	Minerva	Sybilla	Clarinda	Jamesina
Emerald	Jenifer	Mirabel	Tabitha	Clarissa	Jeanette
Emiline	Jessica	Miralda	Tatania	Clotilde	Jennifer

Jeromina	Penelope	Ambrosine	Guinevere	Theodosia
Joceline	Petronel	Anastasia	Gwendolyn	Thomasina
Julianna	Philippa	Annabelle	Gwenllian	Valentina
Julietta	Primrose	Annabella	Harriette	Veronique
Juliette	Prudence	Britannia	Henrietta	Winefride
Katerina	Prunella	Cassandra	Henriette	
Katharin	Raymonde	Catharine	Hildegard	**10**
Kathleen	Rebeccah	Catherine	Hortensia	
Kimberly	Reinagle	Celestine	Hyacinthe	Alessandra
Kirsteen	Reinelde	Charlotte	Iphigenia	Antoinette
Laburnum	Rosalind	Christian	Jacquetta	Bernadette
Laetitia	Rosaline	Christina	Jaqueline	Christabel
Lauretta	Rosamond	Christine	Jessamine	Christiana
Laurinda	Rosamund	Clarenora	Josephine	Christobel
Lavender	Roseanna	Cleopatra	Kathailin	Cinderella
Lorraine	Roseanne	Clothilde	Katharina	Clementina
Lucretia	Rosemary	Columbine	Katharine	Clementine
Madeline	Samantha	Constance	Katherine	Constantia
Magdalen	Sapphire	Corisande	Kimberley	Desiderata
Marcella	Seabelle	Desdemona	Madeleine	Ermentrude
Marcelle	Scarlett	Eglantine	Magdalena	Ethelwynne
Margaret	Sheelagh	Elisabeth	Magdalene	Evangelina
Marianne	Susannah	Elizabeth	Maraquita	Evangeline
Marietta	Tallulah	Ermengard	Margarete	Fredericka
Mariette	Theodora	Ernestine	Margarita	Gwendoline
Marigold	Theresia	Esmeralda	Melisande	Hildegarde
Marjorie	Veronica	Esperance	Millicent	Irmentrude
Marvella	Victoria	Ethelinda	Mirabelle	Jacqueline
Mathilda	Violetta	Francesca	Nicolette	Margaretta
Meredith	Virginia	Françoise	Pepronill	Margherita
Michelle	Vivienne	Franziska	Pierrette	Marguerite
Mireille	Vourneen	Frederica	Priscilla	Petronella
Morwenna	Winifred	Gabrielle	Rosabella	Philippina
Murielle		Georgiana	Rosabelle	Wilhelmina
Nathalie	**9**	Georgette	Rosaritta	
Nathanie		Genevieve	Rosemarie	**11**
Patience	Albertine	Geraldine	Seraphina	
Patricia	Alexandra	Guglielma	Stephanie	Alexandrina

Male names

2	Ed	Si	Ade	Art	Cec	Dai
	Hu		Air	Asa	Cis	Dan
Ad	Jo	**3**	Alf	Baz	Col	Del
Al	Mo		Ali	Ben	Con	Den
Cy	Os	Abe	Arn	Bob	Cyr	Des

Dob	Lix	Zak	Cass	Esra	Jago	Moss
Dod	Lob		Cedd	Euan	Jean	Muir
Don	Lou	**4**	Ciro	Evan	Jeff	Neal
Dud	Luk		Chad	Ewan	Jess	Neil
Eck	Lyn	Abel	Chas	Ewen	Jock	Nero
Edd	Mac	Abie	Clem	Eyre	Joel	Nial
Eli	Mat	Able	Clim	Ezra	Joey	Nick
Ely	Max	Adam	Cole	Ferd	John	Noah
Ern	Nat	Adda	Colm	Finn	José	Noel
Emo	Ned	Agar	Conn	Fitz	Josh	Norm
Gay	Nob	Alan	Curt	Flem	Juan	Ogle
Gib	Nye	Albe	Cyro	Fran	Jude	Olaf
Gil	Pan	Aldo	Dahl	Fred	Jule	Orme
Gus	Pat	Alec	Dave	Frey	Karl	Ossy
Guy	Pip	Alex	Davy	Fulk	Kaye	Otho
Hal	Rab	Algy	Deio	Gabe	Keir	Otis
Ham	Rae	Ally	Dewi	Gary	Kemp	Otto
Hew	Ray	Alon	Dick	Gene	Kent	Owen
Hob	Red	Alun	Diot	Gide	Kiki	Ozzy
Huw	Reg	Alva	Dirk	Glen	King	Page
Ian	Rex	Amos	Doug	Glyn	Kuno	Paul
Ike	Ric	Andy	Drew	Goth	Kunz	Pedr
Ing	Rob	Arch	Duda	Greg	Kurt	Penn
Ira	Rog	Arne	Duff	Gwyn	Kyle	Pepe
Ivo	Rod	Arno	Duke	Hank	Lamy	Pery
Jan	Ron	Arny	Earl	Hans	Lars	Pete
Jay	Roy	Arty	Ecky	Herb	Lacy	Phil
Jem	Ruy	Axel	Eddy	Hope	Leon	Pung
Jim	Sam	Bald	Edie	Hugh	Leri	Rafe
Job	Sid	Barn	Eden	Hugo	Lexy	Raff
Joe	Sim	Bart	Edom	Hume	Liam	René
Jon	Sly	Bate	Elie	Hyam	Llew	Rhys
Jos	Stu	Beau	Elis	Iago	Loel	Rich
Kai	Syd	Bede	Elmo	Iain	Luke	Rick
Kay	Ted	Bedo	Elye	Ifan	Lyle	Riou
Ken	Tel	Bert	Elon	Ifor	Lynd	Rolf
Kid	Tim	Bill	Emil	Igor	Lyon	Roly
Kit	Tom	Boyd	Enog	Ikey	Marc	Rory
Lam	Val	Bram	Eoin	Ioan	Mark	Ross
Lee	Vic	Buck	Eral	Iohn	Matt	Rudy
Len	Viv	Burt	Eric	Ivan	Merv	Ryan
Leo	Vin	Bury	Erie	Ives	Mick	Saul
Les	Wat	Cain	Eros	Ivor	Mike	Sean
Lew	Wal	Carl	Esau	Jack	Milo	Seth
Lex	Zac	Cary	Esme	Jake	Mort	Sion

First names

Sior	Algie	Benet	Colin	Eamon	Gabey	Jacky
Stan	Alick	Benji	Colum	Earle	Gaius	Jacob
Stew	Allan	Benjy	Conal	Ebert	Garin	Jaime
Tavy	Allen	Benny	Conan	Eckie	Garry	James
Theo	Allin	Beppo	Corny	Ector	Garth	Jamie
Toby	Almer	Bermy	Cosmo	Eddie	Gavin	Jared
Todd	Aloys	Berno	Count	Edgar	Gawen	Jason
Tony	Alred	Berty	Craig	Edred	Geoff	Jemmy
Trev	Alroy	Bevis	Cyril	Edwin	Gerry	Jerry
Vane	Alves	Billy	Cyrus	Edwyn	Gidie	Jesse
Vere	Alvin	Bjorn	Dacre	Eille	Giles	Jesus
Walt	Alwin	Blake	Dadoo	Eirik	Glyde	Jevan
Wilf	Alwyn	Bobby	Dakin	Eldon	Glynn	Jewel
Will	Amand	Booth	Damon	Eliab	Gowin	Jimmy
Wing	Ambie	Boris	Dandy	Elias	Govan	Johan
Winn	Amias	Brian	Danny	Eliot	Grant	Jolin
Wray	Amiot	Brien	Darby	Ellis	Gregg	Jonah
Wynn	Amyas	Bruce	Darch	Elmer	Guido	Jonas
Yule	Andie	Bruno	Darcy	Elsye	Gyles	Jonaz
Yuri	André	Bryan	D'arcy	Elvis	Hagen	Jonty
Yves	Angus	Bunny	Daryl	Elwyn	Harry	Joyce
Yvon	Anson	Cadog	David	Emery	Haden	Jozef
Zack	Anton	Cairn	Davit	Emlyn	Hebel	Judah
Zeke	Archy	Caius	Davie	Emory	Heinz	Judas
	Ariel	Caleb	Denis	Emrys	Henri	Jules
5	Artie	Candy	Denny	Emile	Henry	Keith
	Artur	Carew	Denri	Eneas	Herne	Kenny
Aaron	Askew	Carlo	Denys	Enoch	Heron	Kevin
Abdul	Athol	Carne	Derby	Eneys	Hiram	Klaus
Abner	Aubyn	Carol	Derek	Ernie	Hodge	Kuros
Abram	Augie	Cecil	Deric	Ernst	Homer	Lance
Adolf	Aurel	Ceese	Derry	Errol	Humph	Lanty
Aesop	Avere	Celyn	Deryk	Euric	Hyman	Larry
Ailin	Avery	César	Dickë	Evans	Hymie	Leigh
Airay	Aymar	Chris	Dicky	Ewart	Hyram	Lenny
Alain	Aymie	Chuck	Diego	Eyles	Ianto	Lewie
Alawn	Baden	Clair	Doddy	Felix	Idris	Lewin
Alban	Barny	Clare	Dodge	Floyd	Iltyd	Lewis
Albat	Barry	Clark	Dolph	Franc	Inigo	Lexie
Albin	Barty	Claud	Donal	Frank	Innes	Lisle
Albyn	Basie	Claus	Donny	Franz	Isaac	Llelo
Aldis	Basil	Cliff	Dylan	Frith	Ivone	Lloyd
Aldus	Basty	Clive	Drake	Fritz	Ivory	Lluyd
Aleck	Batty	Clyde	Drogo	Gabay	Izaak	Loren
Alfie	Beaty	Colet	Dusty	Gabby	Jabez	Louie

Louis	Ollie	Ronny	Wally	Arthur	Caspar	Deryck
Lucan	Oprin	Rowan	Wayne	Arturo	Cedric	Dickey
Lucas	Oriel	Rowly	Willi	Ashley	Cenred	Dickie
Luigi	Orpen	Royce	Willy	Aubert	Cenydd	Dickon
Lysle	Orson	Rufus	Wolfe	Aubrey	Cerdic	Dobbin
Lynch	Oscar	Rurik	Wyatt	August	Cesare	Dominy
Madoc	Osmon	Ryder	Wylie	Austen	Charly	Donald
Major	Osric	Sammy	Wynne	Austin	Chilla	Dougal
Manny	Oswin	Sandy	Wyvil	Averil	Chippy	Dryden
Manus	Owain	Saxon	Yorke	Awstin	Cicero	Dudley
Marco	Ozzie	Scott		Aylmer	Clarry	Dugald
Marty	Pablo	Serge	**6**	Aylwin	Clarus	Duggie
Massy	Paolo	Shane		Balbus	Claude	Duncan
Matty	Paddy	Shaun	Adolph	Baldie	Clovis	Dundus
Mavor	Paget	Shawn	Adolfo	Baliol	Colley	Dunlop
Mayor	Paton	Silas	Adrian	Barney	Connie	Dustin
Merry	Pedro	Simon	Aeneas	Baston	Connor	Dwight
Meyer	Pelan	Speed	Alaric	Baxter	Conrad	Eamonn
Miall	Perce	Speke	Albany	Bedwyr	Conway	Earley
Micah	Percy	Spike	Albert	Benett	Corney	Eddard
Micky	Perry	Starr	Albery	Benito	Crease	Edmond
Miles	Peter	Steve	Albion	Benjie	Crusoe	Edmund
Mitch	Phene	Storm	Aldous	Bennet	Cuddie	Eduard
Monte	Piers	Tabor	Aldred	Bennie	Curran	Edward
Monty	Power	Taffy	Alexis	Benoît	Dafydd	Egbert
Moray	Punch	Tandy	Alfons	Berend	Dallas	Eggert
Morty	Ralph	Teddy	Alfred	Berney	Damian	Eilian
Moses	Ramon	Terry	Alleyn	Bernie	Dandie	Eldred
Moshe	Randy	Titus	Alston	Bertie	Daniel	Elfrid
Moule	Raoul	Timmy	Amilek	Billee	Danill	Elijah
Mungo	Remis	Tobie	Anders	Billie	Danilo	Elisha
Murdo	Renée	Tobin	Andrea	Blosse	Donnie	Ellick
Myles	Ricky	Tolly	Andrés	Bobbie	Dansil	Elliot
Myrie	Rider	Tommy	Andrew	Bossil	Darren	Ernest
Nahum	Robin	Trant	Angelo	Braham	Darryl	Erroll
Nanty	Roddy	Tubby	Anselm	Briton	Deakin	Ervine
Neddy	Roden	Tudor	Anthin	Brodie	Decius	Esmond
Neill	Rodge	Ulick	Anthon	Brutus	Declan	Eugene
Niall	Roger	Ulric	Antony	Bryden	Dekker	Evelyn
Nicky	Ralph	Uriah	Archer	Bulwer	Demian	Fabian
Nicco	Rollo	Usher	Archie	Caesar	Dennis	Fabius
Nicol	Rolly	Vijay	Armand	Calvin	Denzil	Felton
Nigel	Rolph	Vince	Arnaud	Camile	Derick	Ferdie
Odden	Romeo	Vinny	Arnaut	Canice	Dermot	Fergie
Olave	Romer	Wahab	Arnold	Carlos	Derric	Fergus

Fingal	Hamlet	Jacopo	Linnel	Murphy	Ranald	Shafto
Finlay	Hamlyn	Jairus	Lionel	Murray	Randal	Shamus
Forbes	Harold	Janion	Loftus	Nainby	Randle	Sholto
Franck	Harrel	Japhet	Lowrie	Nairne	Ranson	Sidney
Franco	Harris	Jaques	Lucian	Napier	Raphel	Sigurd
Franko	Harrow	Jarvis	Lucien	Nathan	Rasmus	Sigrid
Freddy	Harvey	Jasper	Lucius	Nelson	Rastus	Simeon
Fyodor	Hayden	Jeremy	Ludwig	Neddie	Ratsey	Simons
Gareth	Haydon	Jerome	Lupton	Nevile	Rawden	Sinbad
Garnet	Hector	Jervis	Luther	Nevill	Rayner	Square
Garret	Hedley	Jessie	Lyonel	Nikita	Reggie	Squire
Garvey	Heintz	Jeston	Macsen	Nickel	Rendle	Stepan
Gaspar	Helier	Jethro	Magnus	Nicolo	Reuben	Steven
Gaston	Henric	Jockey	Maidoc	Nicols	Rhodes	Stevyn
Gawain	Henryk	Johann	Malise	Ninian	Rhodri	Stiven
George	Henzel	Johnny	Mansel	Norman	Ricard	Stuart
Georgy	Herbie	Joseph	Manuel	Norris	Richie	Sydney
Gerald	Herman	Joshua	Marcel	Norton	Ringan	Symkyn
Gerard	Hervey	Josiah	Marcus	Nowell	Rippin	Symond
Gerold	Hilary	Julian	Marius	Oberon	Robbie	Talbot
Gerrie	Hilton	Julien	Marten	Olafur	Robert	Teodor
Gervas	Hinton	Julius	Martel	Oliver	Roddie	Thaddy
Gibbie	Hobart	Jollan	Marten	Onslow	Rodger	Thomas
Gideon	Hobbie	Jolyon	Martin	Orazio	Rodney	Tizard
Gilbee	Holman	Julyan	Marvin	Osbert	Roland	Tobias
Girard	Horace	Justin	Mattus	Osborn	Ronald	Trefor
Giulio	Howard	Justus	Mauris	Osmond	Ronnie	Trevor
Godric	Howell	Kaspar	Melvin	Oswald	Rowley	Vashon
Godwin	Hubert	Kersey	Melvyn	Padrig	Rowlie	Verney
Gonvil	Hubard	Kester	Merlin	Pascoe	Royden	Vernon
Gordon	Huberd	Kirwan	Merrik	Pelham	Rudolf	Vicary
Graeme	Hughie	Konrad	Mervyn	Pepito	Rupert	Victor
Graham	Hunter	Kunzel	Meurig	Percie	Russel	Viktor
Gregan	Hylton	Laddie	Mickie	Perkin	Samson	Vinnie
Gregor	Ignace	Lamley	Mickey	Petros	Samuel	Virgil
Grizel	Inglis	Larrie	Miguel	Philip	Sancho	Vivian
Grogan	Ingram	Launce	Millis	Pierre	Sander	Vyvian
Gunner	Irvine	Lauren	Milton	Pietro	Sandro	Wallis
Gunter	Irving	Laurie	Minden	Poldie	Saurin	Walter
Gussie	Isaiah	Lawrie	Montie	Powell	Sawnie	Warner
Gustof	Isidor	Lawley	Morgan	Prince	Seamas	Warren
Gustus	Israel	Lemuel	Moritz	Rabbie	Seamus	Watkin
Gwilym	Jackey	Lennie	Morris	Rafael	Sefton	Wesley
Hallam	Jackie	Leslie	Morvyn	Ramage	Selwyn	Wilbur
Hamish	Jacomb	Lester	Mostyn	Ramsay	Seumas	Willem

Willie	Barclay	Connell	Fielder	Ibrahim	Nicolas
Willis	Barnaby	Conrade	Fithian	Ingleby	Niccolo
Wilmot	Barnard	Crispin	Fitzroy	Jackson	Nicolai
Winnie	Bartley	Crispus	Francis	Jacques	Obadiah
Wolsey	Bartram	Cuthred	Frankie	Jaffray	Olivier
Xavier	Beaufoi	Cynebil	Freddie	Jalland	Orlando
Yehudi	Bennett	Cyriack	Fredric	Jeffrey	Orpheus
Yorick	Bernard	Cyprian	Gabriel	Jerrard	Orville
	Bertram	Dalison	Galahad	Joachim	Osborne

7

	Berwald	Dalziel	Gaspard	Johnnie	Paladin
	Boswell	Dandini	Geoffry	Jocelyn	Padraic
Abraham	Brandon	Deiniol	Geordie	Justice	Patrick
Absalom	Brendan	Delancy	Georgie	Kasimir	Peredur
Ackroyd	Brennan	Denison	Geraint	Kenneth	Perseus
Adolphe	Buckler	Denzill	Gerallt	Knyvett	Pheroze
Ainslie	Burnard	Derrick	Gerhard	Lachlan	Phillip
Aladdin	Calvert	Desmond	Gerhold	Lambart	Philpot
Alberic	Cameron	Diarmid	Gervais	Lambard	Phineas
Alberto	Caradoc	Diarmit	Gervase	Lambert	Pierrot
Alexius	Carlton	Diggory	Gilbert	Lazarus	Placido
Alfonso	Carlyon	Dillwyn	Gilmour	Leander	Quentin
Alister	Carolus	Domingo	Giacomo	Lennard	Quintin
Alleyne	Casimir	Dominic	Gladwyn	Leonard	Quintus
Almeric	Catesby	Dominyk	Gloster	Leopold	Randall
Alphege	Cedrych	Donovan	Godfrey	Lindsay	Ranulph
Alsager	Cennydd	Douglas	Goronwy	Lindsey	Raphael
Amadeus	Charles	Downing	Grahame	Lorenzo	Raymond
Ambrose	Charley	Drystan	Gregory	Lorimer	Raymund
Anatole	Charlie	Duerdin	Gunther	Lucifer	Redvers
Andries	Charlot	Dunstan	Gustave	Luciano	Reynard
Andreas	Chawner	Eardley	Gwythyr	Ludovic	Reynold
Aneirin	Chester	Edouard	Gwillym	Madison	Rhicert
Aneurin	Chewton	Eleazar	Hadrian	Malachi	Ricardo
Anthony	Chollie	Elphege	Halbert	Malcolm	Richard
Antoine	Christy	Emanuel	Hartley	Matthew	Rinaldo
Antonio	Claudie	Emilius	Herbert	Maurice	Rodbert
Arnauld	Claudio	Ephraim	Hermann	Maxwell	Roderic
Artemas	Clayton	Erasmus	Hewlett	Maynard	Rodolph
Artemus	Clement	Erastus	Hilaire	Merrick	Rodrigo
Auberon	Clemmie	Etienne	Hilarie	Michael	Romulus
Auguste	Clinton	Eustace	Hildred	Mogador	Ronayne
Auveray	Coemgen	Everard	Horatio	Montagu	Roussel
Baptist	Collwyn	Ezekiel	Humbert	Morcant	Rowland
Baldwin	Columba	Faraday	Humphry	Murdoch	Rudolph
Balfour	Compton	Faulder	Iachimo	Neville	Rudyard

Russell	Wyndham	Bertrand	Franklin	Lutwyche
Rutland	Ximenes	Boudewyn	Frederic	Maddison
Sergius	Ystffan	Brenainn	Gabriele	Maitland
Seymour	Zachary	Campbell	Geoffrey	Marshall
Shachel	Zebedee	Carleton	Geoffroy	Martival
Sheldon		Champion	Geronimo	Matthias
Sigmund	**8**	Chauncey	Giovanni	Melchior
Silvius		Charnock	Greville	Meredith
Sylvius	Achilles	Charlton	Griffith	Meredydd
Solomon	Adalbert	Cheyenny	Guiseppe	Montague
Spencer	Adolphus	Chretien	Gulliver	Morrison
Spenser	Agostino	Christie	Gustavus	Mortimer
Stanley	Alasdair	Clarence	Hamilton	Nehemiah
Steffan	Alastair	Claudius	Hannibal	Nicholas
Stephan	Albrecht	Clementi	Harcourt	Nicolaus
Stenson	Aleister	Clements	Harrison	Octavius
Stephen	Algernon	Clifford	Havelock	Odysseus
Steuart	Alisdair	Clotaire	Heinrich	Oliphant
Stewart	Alistair	Conbelin	Herbrand	Ormiston
Tebaldo	Allister	Conradin	Hercules	Oughtred
Terence	Aloysius	Constans	Hereward	Parsifal
Tertius	Alphonse	Constant	Hezekiah	Parzifal
Theodor	Alphonso	Crauford	Horatius	Paulinus
Thorold	Annesley	Crawford	Humphrey	Perceval
Timothy	Antonius	Crispian	Ignatius	Percival
Trenham	Aristide	Cuthbert	Immanuel	Peterkin
Tristan	Augustin	Dederick	Ingenuel	Philemon
Ughtred	Augustus	Diarmaid	Ingelram	Philippe
Ulysses	Aurelius	Diarmuid	Jeremiah	Raffaelo
Umberto	Balliser	Diarmuit	Jonathan	Randolph
Vaughan	Bancroft	Diederik	Joscelin	Randulph
Vauncey	Banister	Dietrich	Joscelyn	Reginald
Vincent	Bardolph	Dominick	Josephus	Robinson
Vittore	Barnabas	Drustens	Kingsley	Roderick
Wallace	Bartlemy	Ebenezer	Lancelot	Rhisiart
Walther	Baudouin	Eberhard	Laurence	Ruaraidh
Wariner	Beaumont	Emmanuel	Lavallin	Sandford
Warwick	Bedivere	Ethelred	Lawrance	Scoltock
Westley	Belgrave	Faithful	Lawrence	Secundus
Wilfred	Benedick	Farquhar	Leonardo	Septimus
Wilfrid	Benedict	Fernando	Leonhard	Sherlock
Wilhelm	Benjamin	Fitzhugh	Leonidas	Siegmund
William	Bernardi	Florizel	Llewelyn	Silvanus
Wilkins	Bernardo	Fluellen	Llywelyn	Sinclair
Winston	Bernhard	François	Lothario	Somerset

Spensley	Aristotle	Glanville	Valentino	Sacheverel
Stafford	Armstrong	Gottfried	Vincentio	Somerville
Stephano	Athelstan	Granville	Wenceslas	Stanislaus
Stiobhan	Augustine	Grenville	Wilbraham	Theodosius
Sylvanus	Baldewyne	Hazledine	Zachariah	Theophilus
Tearlach	Balthasar	Honoratus	Zacharias	Tyrrhenian
Thaddeus	Balthazar	Jefferson	Zechariah	Washington
Theobald	Bartimeus	Josceline		Willoughby
Theodore	Beauchamp	Juscelino	**10**	
Trelawny	Benedetto	Llewellyn		**11**
Tristram	Caratacos	Lucretius	Alessandro	
Valdimar	Christian	Mackenzie	Alaksandus	Bartholomew
Vladimir	Christmas	Marmaduke	Alisaundre	Bartolommeo
Wolseley	Constable	Martineau	Athanasius	Benedictine
Zedekiah	Cornelius	Nathaniel	Athelstane	Christopher
	Courtenay	Nicodemus	Augustulus	Charlemagne
9	Courteney	Outhwaite	Barrington	Constantine
	Crispinus	Peregrine	Barthelémy	Constantius
Abernethy	Cristobal	Rodriguez	Bartolomeu	Cruickshank
Abimeleck	Creighton	Rupprecht	Belshazzar	Fitzherbert
Alaistair	Cymbeline	Sackville	Caractacus	Fitzpatrick
Alejandro	Demetrius	Sebastian	Carmichael	Ravenscroft
Alexander	Dionysius	Sébastien	Cecilianus	Skeffington
Alexandre	Donalbian	Siegfried	Christiern	
Alisander	Elshender	Sigismund	Crispinian	**12**
Allardyce	Ethelbert	Silvester	Cristoforo	
Almosnino	Ferdinand	Stephanos	Eustachius	Chesterfield
Alphonsus	Fortescue	Sylvester	Haliburton	
Alysandyr	Francesco	Stanislas	Hildebrand	**13**
Antoninus	Francisco	Thaddaeus	Llewhellin	
Arbuthnot	Frederick	Theodoric	Maximilian	Cristopheros
Archibald	Friedrich	Valentine	Montgomery	
Arcibaldo	Gascoigne		Pierrepont	

Fish

3	ide	carp	drum	moor	pout	tope
	ray	char	goby	opah	rudd	tuna
bib		chub	grig	orfe	ruff	
cod	**4**	chum	hake	parr	scad	**5**
dab		coho	jack	peal	scup	
eel	bass	cusk	kelt	pike	shad	bleak
gar	blay	dace	ling	pogy	sild	bream
hag	brit	dory	luce	pope	sole	brill

charr	**6**	saurel	gourami	sea wolf
cisco		sea bat	grouper	silurid
cobia	alevin	sea dog	grunion	skipper
coley	anabas	sea fox	grunter	snapper
cuddy	barbel	sea hog	gudgeon	sockeye
danio	beluga	sea pig	gurnard	sterlet
elver	blenny	shanny	gwyniad	sunfish
fluke	bonito	shiner	haddock	teleost
grunt	bowfin	sucker	hagfish	tiddler
gummy	burbot	tailor	halibut	topknot
guppy	callop	tarpon	herring	torpedo
lance	caplin	tautog	hogfish	vendace
loach	conger	turbot	houting	walleye
manta	cottus	weever	ice fish	whiting
molly	darter	wirrah	jewfish	
moray	dentex	wrasse	kahawai	
musky	dorado	zander	kokanee	**8**
perch	gadoid		lampern	
pogge	ganoid	**7**	lamprey	albacore
porgy	grilse		mahseer	billfish
powan	groper	alewife	mooneye	boarfish
roach	gunnel	anchovy	morwong	bullhead
ruffe	gurnet	batfish	mudfish	blowfish
saury	kipper	bloater	oarfish	bluefish
scrod	launce	blue cod	oldwife	bluegill
sepia	marlin	bummalo	pandora	bonefish
sewin	megrim	capelin	pigfish	brisling
shark	milter	catfish	pinfish	bullhead
skate	minnow	cavalla	piranha	cave fish
smelt	mudcat	cavally	pollack	characin
smolt	mud eel	cichlid	pollock	coalfish
smout	mullet	clupeid	pomfret	dealfish
smowt	muskie	codfish	pompano	devil ray
snoek	plaice	codling	quinnat	dragonet
snook	pollan	cowfish	ratfish	drumfish
sprat	puffer	croaker	rat-tail	eagle ray
tench	red cod	crucian	redfish	filefish
tetra	redeye	dipnoan	rock cod	flatfish
toady	redfin	dogfish	sand dab	flathead
torsk	remora	eelpout	sand eel	flounder
trout	robalo	escolar	sardine	frogfish
tunny	runner	fantail	sawfish	gamefish
witch	saithe	finnock	sculpin	gilthead
	salmon	garfish	sea bass	goatfish
	sauger	garpike	sea pike	goldfish
				grayling

jackfish
John Dory
kingfish
lemon fish
lionfish
lumpfish
lungfish
mackerel
manta ray
menhaden
monkfish
moonfish
moray eel
nannygai
numbfish
pickerel
pilchard
pipefish
red porgy
red tetra
rockfish
rockling
rosefish
sailfish
salmonid
sea bream
sea devil
sea-horse
sea purse
sea raven
sea perch
sea robin
sea trout
skipjack
sparling
stingray
sturgeon
suckfish
swamp eel
tarwhine
teraglin
toadfish
weakfish
wolf-fish

9

angelfish
barracuda
black bass
blackfish
black moor
blindfish
blue shark
bull trout
clingfish
conger eel
coral fish
devilfish
Dover sole
glassfish
globefish
goldfinny
goldsinny
goosefish
greenbone
greenling
grenadier
houndfish
killifish
latimeria
lemon sole
murray cod
pearlfish
pike perch
pilot fish
porbeagle
razor fish
red mullet
red salmon
scaldfish
schnapper
selachian
sheatfish
snipefish
solenette
spearfish
stargazer
stockfish
stone bass

stonefish
surfperch
surmullet
swordfish
swordtail
thornback
threadfin
topminnow
trunkfish
whitebait
whitefish
wobbegong
wreckfish
zebra fish

10

angel shark
angler fish
archer fish
bitterling
Bombay duck
brook trout
brown trout
candlefish
carpet shark
coelacanth
damselfish
dragonfish
fingerling
flame tetra
flying fish
ghost shark
great skate
grey mullet
groundling
guitar fish
lancet fish
lumpsucker
midshipman
mirror carp
mossbunker
mudskipper
needlefish
nurse shark

paddlefish
parrot fish
pink salmon
red grouper
red snapper
ribbonfish
rock salmon
rock turbot
sand launce
sea poacher
shovelhead
shovelnose
silverfish
silverside
squeteague
tiger shark
whale shark
white shark
yellowtail

11

bellows fish
Dolly Varden
electric eel
electric ray
golden perch
hippocampus
lake herring
lantern fish
leatherskin
lepidosiren
lophobranch
Moorish idol
muskellunge
plectognath
salmon trout
sea scorpion
stickleback
surgeonfish
swallowfish
triggerfish
whitingpout

12

basking shark
fatherlasher
fighting fish
four-eyed fish
miller's thumb
mouthbrooder
paradise fish
rainbow trout
requiem shark
river lamprey
sea porcupine
scorpion fish
silver salmon

walleyed pike

13

climbing perch
horse mackerel
finnan haddock
flying gurnard
labyrinth fish
leatherjacket
mackerel shark
porcupine fish
snake mackerel
sockeye salmon
thresher shark

14 +

Australian
  salmon
great white shark
hammerhead shark
king of the
  herrings
shovelhead shark
Spanish mackerel
wheel animalcule

Flowers

3 & 4

acer
aloe
arum
balm
bixa
flag
geum
ilex
iris
ivy
ixia
lily
ling
may
meum
musa
musk
olea
poa
pink
rapa
rhus
rosa
rose

ruta
sium
thea
ulex
whin
zea

5

abies
abrus
agave
algae
anona
areca
aspic
aster
avens
briza
butea
calla
camas
canna
carex
carya
chara

daisy
dwale
erica
glaux
gowan
hosta
larix
ledum
lemna
linum
lotus
lupin
malva
melia
morus
mucor
musci
naias
orris
oryza
ox-eye
oxlip
panax
pansy
peony
phlox

picea
pinus
piper
poker
poppy
pyrus
rheum
ribes
rubia
rubus
rumen
sabal
salix
sedum
stipa
stock
tansy
taxus
thuja
tilia
tsuga
tuber
tulip
typha
ulmas
urena

usnea
vetch
vinca
viola
vitex
vitis
xyris
yucca
yulan
zamia

6

abroma
acacia
acorus
alhagi
alisma
alpine
amomum
arabis
aralia
arnica
aucuba
betula
bryony

cactus
caltha
camass
carapa
carica
cassia
cedrus
celtis
cereus
cicuta
cistus
clover
clusia
cnicus
cosmos
costus
crocus
croton
dahlia
daphne
datura
derris
elaeis
elodea
empusa
gnetum

hedera	sundew	dionaea	nemesia	zostera
henbit	sylvia	dog rose	nigella	**8**
hypnum	thrift	drosera	nopalea	
iberis	tulipa	epacris	opuntia	abutilon
isatis	urtica	ephedra	osmunda	acanthus
kalmia	violet	erodium	panicum	achillea
kerria	viscum	eugenia	papaver	ageratum
laurus	yarrow	figwort	petunia	amaranth
lucuma	zinnia	filices	phallus	angelica
lupine		freesia	picotee	anthemis
madder	**7**	frogbit	populus	arum lily
mallow		fuchsia	primula	asphodel
mimosa	aconite	fumaria	pythium	aubretia
myrica	althaea	gazania	quercus	auricula
myrtus	alyssum	genista	ragwort	bedstraw
nerine	anchusa	gentian	rambler	bignonia
nerium	anemone	gerbera	rampion	bindweed
nostoc	arachis	godetia	rhamnus	bird's eye
nuphar	arbutus	honesty	ricinus	bluebell
orchid	banksia	hordeum	robinia	calamint
orchis	bartsia	ipomoea	ruellia	camellia
oxalis	begonia	isoetes	saffron	catchfly
paigle	boletus	jacinth	salsola	centaury
peziza	bugloss	jasmine	scandix	clematis
phleum	burdock	jonquil	scirpus	corn lily
protea	bursera	juglans	sea-pink	crowfoot
pteris	calluna	kingcup	senecio	cyclamen
punica	campion	lactuca	sequoia	daffodil
pyrola	catalpa	lantana	skimmia	dianthus
raphia	cat's ear	lobelia	solanum	dicentra
reseda	cedrela	logania	sonchus	dog-brier
rocket	chelone	lychnis	sorghum	dropwort
riccia	clarkia	lythrum	spiraea	erigeron
ruscus	corylus	manihot	statice	fleabane
sagina	corypha	maranta	syringa	foxglove
salvia	cowslip	may lily	tagetes	gardenia
sapium	cudweed	melilot	tamarix	geranium
sapota	curcuma	melissa	tea rose	gladioli
scilla	cyathea	milfoil	thistle	gloriosa
sesame	cyperus	mimulus	trefoil	gloxinia
seseli	cytisus	monilia	tritoma	harebell
silene	day lily	moringa	verbena	hawkweed
smilax	deutzia	mullein	vervain	helenium
squill	digynia	musales	xylopia	hepatica
styrax	dioecia	nelumbo	zizania	hibiscus

hyacinth
ice plant
japonica
knapweed
larkspur
lavatera
lent lily
marigold
martagon
milkwort
moss rose
musk rose
myosotis
phacelia
phormium
plumbago
pond lily
primrose
rockrose
sandwort
scabious
skullcap
snowdrop
soapwort
starwort
sweet pea
tigridia
toadflax
trillium
tuberose
valerian
veronica
viscaria
wild rose
wood sage
xanthium

9

Aaron's rod
achimenes
amaryllis
bear's foot
bee orchid
buttercup

calendula
candytuft
campanula
candytuft
carnation
celandine
chamomile
cherry-pie
chickweed
China rose
cineraria
clove pink
cockscomb
colchicum
colt's foot
columbine
coreopsis
corn poppy
cotyledon
dandelion
digitalis
dog violet
edelweiss
eglantine
gladiolus
golden rod
hellebore
hollyhock
impatiens
jessamine
kniphofia
mayflower
narcissus
nemophila
pimpernel
pyrethrum
saxifrage
sea rocket
snowflake
spearwort
speedwell
stonecrop
sunflower
tiger lily
twayblade

wake robin
waterlily
wolf's-bane

10

agapanthus
amaranthus
aspidistra
belladonna
bellflower
bluebottle
burnet rose
busy lizzie
China aster
cinquefoil
coquelicot
compositae
corn cockle
cornflower
cranesbill
cuckoopint
damask rose
deadnettle
delphinium
Dutch tulip
Easter lily
field poppy
fritillary
fox and cubs
gaillardia
goat's beard
goldilocks
gypsophila
heart's-ease
helianthus
heliotrope
immortelle
lady orchid
lady's smock
marguerite
mignonette
nasturtium
nightshade
opium poppy

oxeye daisy
passiflora
periwinkle
poached egg
poinsettia
polyanthus
potentilla
ranunculus
red campion
rose mallow
sarracenia
snake's head
snapdragon
stitchwort
storksbill
wallflower
Welsh poppy
willowherb
windflower
wood sorrel
yellow wort

11

antirrhinum
bell heather
bitter-cress
black medick
bouncing Bet
cabbage rose
calceolaria
convolvulus
cotoneaster
eschschozia
everlasting
fig marigold
forget-me-not
gentianella
gilliflower
gillyflower
globeflower
helichrysum
helleborine
honeysuckle
kidney vetch

love-in-a-mist
London pride
loosestrife
meadowsweet
Parma violet
pelargonium
ragged robin
rambler rose
red-hot poker
St. John's wort
schizanthus
stephanotis
sweet cicely
tiger flower
wood anemone

pasque flower
pitcher plant
prickly poppy
salpiglossis
snow in summer
Solomon's seal
sweet william
Turk's cap lily
weasel's snout
venus flytrap
virgin's bower
wild hyacinth

13

African violet
bleeding heart
butter-and-eggs
cherry blossom
Christmas rose
chrysanthemum
creeping Jenny
grape hyacinth
huntsman's horn
Joseph and Mary
ladies' fingers
marsh marigold
meadow saffron
orange blossom
passion flower
soldier orchid
townhall clock
traveller's joy
trumpet flower
water hyacinth

14

bladder campion
Canterbury bell
cardinal flower
creeping Jennie
creeping Myrtle
jack-by-the-hedge
lords-and-ladies
love-in-idleness
military orchid
shepherd's purse

15 +

batchelor's buttons
bats-in-the-belfry
blood-drop emlets
bristly ox-tongue
butterfly orchid
creeping Charlie
deadly nightshade
Duke of Argyll's tea-
    plant
evening primrose
love-lies-bleeding
lily of the valley
Michaelmas daisy
mother-in-law's tongue
poor man's weatherglass
scarlet pimpernel
shepherd's weatherglass
star of Bethlehem
woody nightshade

12

adder's tongue
alpine flower
apple blossom
autumn crocus
bacon and eggs
corn marigold
cuckoo flower
fool's parsley
huntsman's cup
Iceland poppy
Jacob's ladder
lady's slipper
monkey flower
monkey orchid
morning glory
old man's beard

Food and cooking

3	egg	leg	soy	bean	cate	dhal
	fat	nan	wok	beef	chop	dill
bap	fig	nut		blin	chow	dine
bun	fry	oil	**4**	boil	clod	dish
cru	ham	pie		bran	crab	duck
dip	ice	rib	anna	butt	crib	duff
ear	jam	roe	bake	cake	curd	fare

fish	snow	diane	poach	batter	fumado
flan	sopa	dough	prawn	biffin	gammon
fool	soup	dulse	prune	blintz	gateau
fowl	stew	fancy	pulse	brains	gaufre
game	suet	feast	purée	braise	grease
ghee	taco	filet	quail	breast	greens
grub	tart	flank	reine	brunch	grouse
hand	tuna	flour	roast	burger	haggis
hare	veal	fruit	rojak	buffet	haunch
hash	whey	fudge	russe	butter	hot dog
herb	wing	gigot	salad	canapé	hot-pot
hock	yolk	glace	salmi	casein	hummus
jowl	zest	glaze	salmi	catsup	jujube
Kiev		goose	sauce	chilli	jumble
junk	**5**	gravy	sauté	caviar	junket
lamb		grill	scone	cheese	kernel
lard	à demi	gruel	scrag	cockle	kidney
lean	aspic	gumbo	shank	coddle	kipper
loaf	bacon	halva	skirt	collar	leaven
loin	baste	heart	snack	collop	lights
lung	belly	honey	spice	comfit	mornay
malt	blade	humus	steak	congee	mousse
mash	blini	icing	steam	cookie	muffin
meal	bombe	jelly	stock	corner	mussel
meat	boned	joint	sugar	cornet	mutton
menu	brawn	juice	sushi	creole	noodle
milk	bread	kebab	sweet	crisps	nougat
neck	brose	kofta	syrup	croute	noyeau
olio	broth	liver	taffy	crumbs	nut oil
olla	brulé	lunch	T bone	cutlet	oliver
pâté	bully	manna	toast	dainty	omelet
peel	candy	matzo	torte	dinner	oxtail
pork	capon	melba	tripe	dragée	paella
puff	cheek	mince	verte	eclair	panada
raan	chips	mocha	viand	eggnog	parkin
rare	chuck	offal	vichy	entrée	passer
rice	condé	pasta	wafer	etuver	pastry
rock	cream	pasty	yeast	faggot	perkin
roll	crêpe	patty		fillet	pickle
roux	crown	pecan	**6**	finnan	picnic
rump	cruet	pilaf		flambé	pilaff
rusk	crumb	pilau	alaska	flitch	pillau
sago	crust	pilaw	alecha	fodder	poeler
salt	curds	pirog	almond	fondue	polony
shin	curry	pizza	barder	frappé	posset
			banger		

	7	custard	oatmeal	sirloin
potage		dariole	pabulum	soubise
potato	albumen	dartois	panache	soufflé
quiche	anchovy	deep fry	pancake	soupçon
rabbit	back rib	dessert	parboil	starter
ragout	banbury	egg yolk	parfait	stir-fry
raisin	bannock	epicure	pavlova	strudel
rasher	banquet	essence	pickles	succado
relish	Bath bun	fancies	pigs fry	sucrose
rolled	beef tea	fig cake	pikelet	sultana
romano	best end	fig roll	pilaffe	supreme
royale	biltong	fondant	pimento	tapioca
saddle	biryani	foo yung	piquant	tartlet
salami	biscuit	fore end	plum jam	tatties
salmon	blossom	fritter	plum pie	teacake
samosa	borscht	galette	poisson	terrine
scouse	bouilli	game pie	popcorn	top side
sea-pie	brioche	garnish	popover	treacle
shrimp	brisket	gelatin	pork pie	trotter
simmer	broiler	giblets	potargo	truffle
simnel	brownie	glucose	pottage	vanilla
sorbet	calipee	gnocchi	poultry	venison
sowens	candies	goulash	praline	veloute
sponge	caramel	gourmet	pretzel	vinegar
spread	carvery	gratine	pudding	wing rib
spring	catchup	gristle	ramekin	yoghurt
sundae	caviare	high tea	rarebit	york ham
supper	chapati	hoummos	ratafia	yule log
sweets	charqui	houmous	ravioli	
tamale	chicken	jam roll	rice bun	**8**
tamara	chowder	jam tart	risotto	
tamari	chutney	ketchup	rissole	aigrette
tariff	cobbler	knuckle	rossini	à la carte
tiffin	cobloaf	lardoon	roulade	à la creme
tit-bit	compote	lasagne	rum baba	amandine
toffee	cookies	lichees	sabayon	ambrosia
tongue	corn cob	lobster	samosas	aperitif
top rib	cracker	lozenge	sapsago	apple jam
trifle	crouton	matzoon	sardine	apple pie
turbot	crumble	matzoth	sausage	au gratin
turkey	crumpet	meat pie	saveloy	barbeque
umbles	cuisine	mustard	savoury	barvadis
viande	cup cake	niçoise	scallop	bath chap
viands	currant	noodles	seafood	béchamel
waffle	cushion	oat cake	sherbet	beignets
yogurt				

biscotin
bouchées
bouillon
bun fight
chapatti
chasseur
chop suey
chow mein
cinnamon
clambake
coleslaw
concasse
confetti
conserve
consommé
coq au vin
couscous
cracknel
cream bun
cross bun
croutons
crudités
dainties
date roll
dauphine
déjeuner
delicacy
doughnut
dressing
dripping
duchesse
duckling
dumpling
egg white
en croûte
ensalada
escalope
escargot
fish cake
fishmeal
flan case
flapjack
flamande
fleorons
flummery

foie gras
fore hock
frosting
fruit pie
frumenty
gazpacho
gelatine
gourmand
grand-duc
gratiner
hardbake
hardtack
hotchpot
hung beef
ice cream
iced cake
jambalay
jam butty
Julienne
kedgeree
licorice
loblolly
loin chop
lollipop
luncheon
lyonaise
macaroni
macaroon
marinade
marinate
marzipan
meatball
meat loaf
meat roll
meringue
meunière
mince pie
molasses
moussaka
mushroom
noisette
olive oil
omelette
pastrami
pemmican

pheasant
pilchard
plum cake
plum duff
pope's eye
poppadom
poppadum
porridge
pot au feu
pot roast
preserve
quenelle
racahout
raisinée
ravigote
rice cake
rock cake
rock salt
rollmops
roly poly
rye bread
salad oil
salpicon
salt beef
salt fish
salt junk
salt pork
sandwich
scrag end
scramble
seedcake
semolina
shoulder
side dish
skim-milk
slapjack
smorbrod
soda cake
soy sauce
spare rib
squab pie
steak pie
stockpot
stuffing
syllabub

tamarind
tipsy cod
tea break
tortilla
trotters
turnover
undercut
viaticum
victuals
vindaloo
water ice
wishbone
white-pot
yoghourt
Zwieback

9

aitchbone
a la turque
allumette
angel cake
antipasto
appetizer
apple tart
arrowroot
bara brith
barmbrack
barquette
bean feast
bearnaise
beaugency
beefsteak
blanching
bolognese
boucherie
bratwurst
breakfast
brochette
bridecake
bully beef
butter pat
canneloni
cassareep
casserole

cassonade
cassoulet
chantilly
charlotte
chatillon
cheese dip
chip butty
chipolata
chocolate
chump-chop
club steak
cochineal
colcannon
cornflour
comfiture
condiment
corn bread
corn salad
crackling
cream cake
cream horn
cream puff
croissant
croquette
croustade
dark bread
delmonico
drop scone
drumstick
Easter egg
enchilada
entremets
fish-paste
forcemeat
fricassee
fruit cake
fruit flan
fruit tart
galantine
Genoa cake
giblet pie
gravy soup
hamburger
hard sauce
hatelette

honeycomb
humble pie
Irish stew
italienne
layer cake
left-overs
lemon curd
liquorice
liver pâté
loafsugar
lobscouse
macedoine
madeleine
marchpane
margarine
marinière
marmalade
meat-paste
medallion
middle cut
mincemeat
mint sauce
mutton ham
mutton pie
onion soup
partridge
petit four
pigeon pie
pistachio
potato pie
pot pourri
pound cake
preserves
princesse
raised pie
ravigotte
rechauffe
red pepper
remoulade
rice paper
rump steak
sally lunn
schnitzel
scotch egg
seasoning

shellfish
shortcake
small hock
soda bread
soda scone
sour cream
sourdough
spaghetti
spare ribs
spit roast
spun sugar
stirabout
succotash
sugarloaf
sugar-lump
sugar-plum
sweet corn
sweetmeat
swiss roll
tipsy cake
tournedos
vegetable
vol-au-vent
Welsh cake
wet nellie
wheatgerm
white meat
wholemeal
wild honey

10

apple sauce
baked beans
Bath oliver
bill of fare
blanquette
beefburger
bêche-de-mer
beef olives
bercy sauce
blancmange
blanquette
blue cheese
boiled cake

bolognaise
Bombay duck
bonne femme
bosh butter
bourgeoise
brandy-snap
breadcrumb
bread sauce
bread stick
breadstuff
bridescake
brown bread
brown sugar
buttermilk
candy floss
cannelloni
caper sauce
capillaire
carrot cake
chaud-froid
cheesecake
Chelsea bun
comestible
confection
cooking fat
cooking oil
cordon bleu
corned beef
cornflakes
corroboree
cottage pie
cream slice
cromesquis
currant bun
curry sauce
custard pie
delicacies
dill pickle
double loin
Dundee cake
Eccles cake
eggs mornay
fig pudding
flank steak
florentine

frangipane
French cake
French loaf
fresh cream
fricandeau
fruit salad
garlic salt
gaufrettes
giblet soup
ginger cake
gingernuts
ginger-snap
girdle cake
grape sugar
green salad
ground rice
guava jelly
hickory nut
hodge-podge
honey crisp
hotch-potch
ice pudding
icing sugar
indian corn
jardinière
jelly cream
jugged hare
knackwurst
knockwurst
lamb cutlet
laver bread
liverwurst
maple syrup
marble cake
marrow bone
mayonnaise
Melba toast
middle neck
mimosa eggs
minced meat
minestrone
mixed grill
mock turtle
mutton chop
onion sauce

oxtail soup
panzanella
parisienne
parmentier
pastry case
pâtisserie
peach melba
pepper cake
peppermint
piccalilli
pickled egg
plat du jour
poached egg
potted fish
potted meat
printanier
provençale
pudding pie
puff pastry
raisin loaf
rhubarb pie
rolled oats
rotisserie
round steak
royal icing
saccharine
salmagundi
salt butter
sauerkraut
shallow fry
shirred egg
shish kebab
shortbread
shortcrust
silverside
simnel cake
smorrebrod
sour pickle
spatchcock
sponge cake
steak diane
stewed meat
stroganoff
stuffed egg
sucking pig

sugar candy
sugar mouse
sweetbread
tea biscuit
temse bread
tenderloin
tikka kebab
tinned food
tomato soup
turtle soup
vermicelli
Vienna loaf
Vienna roll
water gruel
water icing
white bread
white sauce
zabaglione

11

almond icing
almond paste
baked alaska
banana split
Banbury cake
barley sugar
bashed neeps
black butter
black pepper
bonne bouche
bourguignon
braised beef
brandy sauce
brandy snaps
breadcrumbs
bread sticks
bridge rolls
burnt almond
carbonnades
cassava cake
cassoulette
caster sugar
cheese board
cheese sauce

Chester cake
chiffon cake
chilli sauce
choux pastry
clam chowder
clove pepper
cock-a-leekie
corn fritter
cottage loaf
cream cheese
curry powder
custard tart
devilled egg
double cream
dressed crab
Eve's pudding
fillet steak
fish fingers
flank mutton
frankfurter
French bread
French toast
gammon steak
gingerbread
golden syrup
green pepper
green turtle
griddle cake
ground spice
Hollandaise
hors d'oeuvre
hot cross bun
iron rations
jam turnover
jellied eels
loaf of bread
madras curry
Madeira cake
marshmallow
meat biscuit
meat pudding
medlar jelly
milk pudding
minute steak
montpensier

napolitaine
olla podrida
oyster patty
parson's nose
pig's trotter
plum pudding
porterhouse
potato crisp
potato salad
pressed beef
raisin bread
ratatouille
rice biscuit
rice pudding
roast potato
sago pudding
sauerbraten
sausage meat
sausage roll
scotch broth
ship biscuit
short pastry
side of bacon
singin' hinny
single cream
skimmed milk
sliced bread
smörgåsbord
spotted Dick
staff of life
stewed fruit
suet pudding
sweet almond
sweet pepper
sweet pickle
tagliatelle
toffee apple
tomato sauce
tossed salad
treacle tart
vichyssoise
Vienna steak
wedding cake
Welsh mutton
Welsh rabbit

wheaten loaf
white potato
wine biscuit
windsor soup
zabagilione

12

afternoon tea
apple fritter
apple strudel
bakewell tart
baking powder
birthday cake
bitter almond
black pudding
bouquet garni
bouquetierre
brandy butter
bread pudding
brewer's yeast
burnt almonds
butterscotch
caraway seeds
cheeseburger
cheese straws
chilli pepper
chip potatoes
chitterlings
cinnamon ball
clotted cream
club sandwich
cockieleekie
Cornish pasty
corn-on-the-cob
cream cracker
crème caramel
crêpe suzette
crust of bread
curds and whey
custard sauce
Danish pastry
duck a l'orange
dunmow flitch
fillet of sole

finnan haddie
flamenco eggs
French pastry
grated cheese
ground almond
ground ginger
ground pepper
guarana-bread
Hamburg steak
hasty pudding
haute cuisine
ice cream cone
jacket potato
Julienne soup
liver sausage
lobster patty
luncheon-meat
maid of honour
maitre d' hotel
millefueille
mulligatawny
nutmeg butter
parsley sauce
peanut butter
pease pudding
pickled onion
planked steak
plum porridge
profiteroles
pumpernickel
Russian salad
salted peanut
scampi fritti
scrambled egg
shepherd's pie
sherry trifle
ship's biscuit
sirloin steak
smoked salmon
sponge finger
steak pudding
streaky bacon
stuffed heart
sweet and sour
tabasco sauce

taramasalata
tartare sauce
tripe de roche
vegetable oil
vichy carrots
Waldorf salad
water biscuit
Welsh rarebit
whipped cream

13

apple dumpling
barbecue sauce
béchamel sauce
bouillabaisse
chateaubriand
cheese biscuit
chili con carne
Christmas cake
condensed milk
confectionery
custard-coffin
custard powder
devilled sauce
finnan haddock
flitch of bacon
French mustard
fruit cocktail
German sausage
gigot de mouton
ginger pudding
guard of honour
lemon meringue
lobster bisque
mess of potage
milk chocolate
millefeuilles
minced collops
Neopolitan ice
Oxford sausage

pease porridge
pickled walnut
prawn cocktail
rasher of bacon
salad dressing
scotch collops
scrambled eggs
sirloin of beef
smoked sausage
sole veronique
soused herring
sponge pudding
strawberry jam
summer pudding
toad in the hole
veal-and-ham pie

14

almond hardbake
apple charlotte
bearnaise sauce
beef stroganoff
bologna sausage
cabinet pudding
Canterbury lamb
caramel custard
charlotte russe
chilli con carne
college pudding
cranberry sauce
evaporated milk
French dressing
gooseberry fool
haunch of mutton
ice cream sundae
macaroni cheese
mashed potatoes
mock-turtle soup
paté de foie gras
pickled herring

plain chocolate
pontefract cake
quiche Lorraine
remoulade sauce
saddle of mutton
tapioca pudding
toasted teacake
treacle pudding
Turkish delight
upside-down cake
Victoria sponge
Worcester sauce
wholemeal bread

15

bakewell pudding
beef bourguignon
black-cap pudding
bubble and squeak
chicken Maryland
chilli con carne
chocolate eclair
devilled kidneys
haunch of venison
ploughman's lunch
semi-skimmed milk
Spanish omelette
Wiener schnitzel

15 +

angels on horseback
christmas pudding
devils on horseback
duchesse potatoes
horseradish sauce
Lancashire hotpot
lobster thermidor
wedding breakfast
Yorkshire pudding

French Revolutionary Calendar

6

Nivôse – snow (Dec 22 – Jan 20)

7

Floréal – flowers (April 21 – May 20)

Ventôse – wind (Feb 20 – March 21)

8

Brumaire – mist (Oct 23 – Nov 21)

Fervidor – heat (July 20 – Aug 18)

Frimaire – frost (Nov 22 – Dec 21)

Germinal – buds (March 22 – April 20)

Messidor – harvest (June 20 – July 19)

Pluviôse – rain (Jan 21 – Feb 19)

Prairial – meadows (May 21 – June 19)

9

Fructidor – fruit (Aug 19 – Sept 22)

Thermidor – heat (July 20 – Aug 18)

11

Vendémiaire – vintage (Sept 23 – Oct 22)

Fruit, nuts and vegetables

3	cole	soya	Dancy	mooli	6	cashew
	Czar	spud	drupe	morel		celery
ber	date	taro	Dwarf	Navel	Alfred	cherry
cob	eddo	ugli	eddoe	navew	almond	chives
cos	Gala		Galia	olive	ananas	citron
fig	Hass	5	grape	onion	Aromel	cob nut
haw	kale		guava	orach	babaco	Comice
hip	kiwi	apple	habal	peach	Bogota	cowpea
pea	leek	Ariel	Jaffa	pecan	Bolero	daikon
yam	lime	betel	Lavan	prune	Bounty	damson
	mung	Bobbi	lemon	pulse	Breton	durian
4	Ogen	carob	lichi	Royal	banana	endive
	okra	chard	mâche	savoy	batata	Elruge
bean	neep	chive	maize	swede	bhindi	feijoa
beet	pear	choko	mango	Topaz	Brandt	fennel
Beth	plum	colza	melon	tuber	carrot	frijol
chou		cress				

Fuerte	**7**	pitanga	cole-wort	Valencia
garlic		pumpkin	Concorde	Victoria
greens	Almeria	rampion	cucumber	Williams
Italia	apricot	rhubarb	dewberry	zucchini
jicama	Atemoya	rose hip	eggplant	**9**
jujube	avocado	salsify	eschalot	
kiwano	Baldwin	satsuma	Ettinger	actinidia
kumera	Ben More	seakale	Fava bean	aduki bean
kumara	bok choy	Seville	Heritage	artichoke
lablab	bramble	shallot	honeydew	Asian pear
legume	Bramley	skirret	hazelnut	asparagus
lentil	brinjal	snow pea	ivory nut	aubergine
lichee	Bullace	soursop	jakfruit	beech mast
longan	cabbage	Spartan	java plum	Ben Lomond
loquat	cardoon	spinach	Jonathon	blaeberry
lychee	Cascade	Sturmer	kohlrabi	blueberry
manioc	cassava	sultana	leaf beet	Bobbi bean
marrow	celtuce	sweetie	lima bean	Bountiful
medlar	chayote	tangelo	Lord Derby	brazil nut
murphy	chicory	witloof	lima-bean	breadroot
Muscat	coconut	yam bean	mandarin	broad bean
nettle	collard	**8**	McIntosh	Brunswick
orange	costard		may apple	butternut
papaya	Crispin	Alicante	minneola	calabrese
pawpaw	cymling	Alphonse	mulberry	cantaloup
peanut	currant	baby corn	mung bean	carambola
pepper	dasheen	beetroot	mushroom	cashew nut
pomelo	Delight	Ben Nevis	oleaster	Charlotte
potato	Domanil	Ben Sarek	patty pan	Chasselas
quince	Edwards	betel nut	pearmain	Cherimoya
radish	filbert	bilberry	pecan nut	coco de mer
raisin	gherkin	Bluecrop	Pentland	corn salad
rocket	Iceberg	borecole	physalis	courgette
Romano	Gorella	brassica	pimentos	crab apple
runner	Grandee	broccoli	Quetsche	cranberry
sorrel	haricot	Burbanks	rambutan	crookneck
sprout	hubbard	calabash	Red flame	curly kale
squash	kumquat	capsicum	rutabaga	dandelion
Temple	lettuce	Careless	scallion	Discovery
tomato	limetta	celeriac	shaddock	Durondeau
turnip	Morello	Champion	soya bean	Dwarf bean
walnut	Oak-leaf	Cherokee	split pea	Dwarf corn
	Pandora	chestnut	Starking	Earliblue
	parsnip	chickpea	sweetsop	garden pea
	pimento	Cocktail	tamarind	green bean

greengage
Grenadier
groundnut
horse bean
Indian fig
jackfruit
kiwi fruit
kolocassi
Little gem
love apple
macedoine
mangetout
Maris bard
melanzane
Mirabelle
naseberry
nectarine
new potato
Ortanique
persimmon
petit pois
pigeon pea
pineapple
pistachio
plantains
radicchio
raspberry
red banana
red pepper
rock melon
Salad bowl
Santa Rosa
sapodilla
September
star apple
star fruit
sweetcorn
tamarillo
tangerine
winged pea

10

Alexandria
Amsden June
bean shoots

beansprout
Bellegarde
blackberry
black grape
Black satin
Black tokay
blueberry
breadfruit
butterball
butter bean
canteloupe
Charantais
Cherry plum
cider apple
clementine
cloudberry
Conference
cos lettuce
Duke of York
elderberry
French bean
Giant prune
gooseberry
grapefruit
Indian corn
Indian lime
Indian plum
Italian red
kidney bean
King Edward
Kirke's blue
lemon guava
loganberry
Lollo Rosso
mangosteen
Maris piper
plum tomato
red cabbage
red chicory
redcurrant
Roma tomato
runner bean
salad cress
scorzonera
strawberry

string bean
sugar apple
sweet lemon
Swiss chard
tree tomato
watercress
water melon
white grape

11

acorn squash
Ashton cross
Autumn bliss
bean sprouts
bitter gourd
black radish
Black reward
Black velvet
blood orange
Breton onion
boysenberry
Brown Turkey
cactus fruit
cauliflower
Charles Ross
Chinese leaf
curly endive
cup mushroom
Early laxton
Early rivers
Granny Smith
green pepper
haricot bean
haricot vert
horned melon
horseradish
huckleberry
Jaffa orange
Lady's finger
Lloyd George
navel orange
pomegranate
oyster plant
prickly pear
Pershore egg

Redgauntlet
scarlet-bean
seakale beet
Sharon fruit
spinach beet
spring onion
sweet fennel
sweet manioc
sweet pepper
sweet potato
Webb's wonder
white pepper
whortleberry
wild spinach
winter cress

12

Arthur Turner
asparagus pea
Bartlett pear
Beauty of Bath
Bedford giant
blackcurrant
black salsify
Boskoop giant
Bullock tomato
Chasselas d'Or
cherry tomato
Chestnut brown
chilli pepper
Chinese apple
Chinese chard
christophene
corn-on-the-cob
cooking apple
custard apple
dessert apple
Early sulphur
flat mushroom
French sorrel
green shallot
ground cherry
Hottentot fig
Japanese plum
lady's fingers

lamb's lettuce
mangel-wurzel
marrowfat pea
marrow squash
Newton wonder
Pantagruella
passion fruit
pea aubergine
savoy cabbage
Red delicious
Savoy cabbage
Scotch bonnet
Spanish onion
spider endive
spring greens
sugar snap pea
summer squash
Victoria plum
white cabbage
white currant
whortleberry
winter squash
yellow pepper

13

asparagus tips
blackeyed bean
Black Hamburgh
black mulberry
Bullock's heart
Byrnes apricot
Cambridge gage
Caribbean lime
celery cabbage
Compact Stella
cooking banana
custard marrow
dessert banana
double coconut
Early Victoria
Golden Everest
Good King Henry
ladies' fingers
Morello cherry

pe-tsai cabbage
pickling onion
prairie-turnip
ridge cucumber
Ross de Treviso
Rossa di Verona
sapodilla plum
scarlet runner
Spanish radish
spring cabbage
Surinam cherry
Swedish turnip
Thai aubergine
turnip cabbage
Tydeman's early
water chestnut

14

American mother
Annie Elizabeth
Batavian endive
Beurre superfin
Blenheim orange
Brusells sprout
button mushroom
cabbage lettuce
Cape gooseberry
chicorée frisée
Chinese lantern
Conference pear
Egremont russet
English spinach
Florence fennel
French Imperial
globe artichoke
iceberg lettuce
Jamaican banana
Japanese medlar
Laxton's superb
Madagascar bean
Malling promise
mercury spinach
oyster mushroom
pineapple guava
pink grapefruit

Royal sovereign
sprue asparagus
stinging nettle
stringless bean

15 +

Alpine strawberry
American watercress
Ashmead's kernel
asparagus lettuce
Baron Solemacher
beafsteak tomato
Belle de Fontenay
Beurre d'Amanlis
Bigarreau Napoleon
Bourjasotte grise
Bramley's seedling
Buckland sweetwater
Californian seedless
Cambridge favourite
Cambridge vigour
Chinese artichoke
Chinese gooseberry
Cox's orange pippin
Denniston's superb
Doyenne du Comice
Ellison's orange
Feuille de Chêne
Florentine fennel
forced radicchio
Golden delicious
Italian broccoli
Jerusalem artichoke
Marjorie's seedling
Miller's seedling
miniature red cabbage
New Zealand spinach
Oak-leaf lettuce
Packham's triumph
perpetual spinach
purple granadilla
spaghetti squash
spaghetti marrow
strawberry guava
strawberry tomato

summer cauliflower
sweet granadilla
turnip-rooted celery
vegetable marrow
vegetable oyster

Whinham's industry
William's Bon Chretien
winter cauliflower
Worcester pearmain
Yellow pear tomato

Gardening (general)

3

bed
bud
eye
hoe
pip
pot
pot
sap
sow

4

acid
axil
bole
bulb
burr
bush
cane
cone
corm
crop
curd
cyme
damp
fern
fork
gall
haft
herb
hose
keel
lawn

leaf
lime
loam
lobe
mist
moss
node
peat
pest
posy
rake
ring
root
sand
seed
slug
soil
spur
stem
tray
tree
trug
twig
vine
weed
wilt
wood

5

acute
algae
aphid
berry
besom

bloom
bough
bract
calyx
clamp
clone
crest
crock
crown
drawn
drupe
flora
frame
frond
fruit
genus
graft
grass
haulm
hardy
humus
light
mould
mulch
ovary
ovate
ovule
petal
plant
pulse
sandy
scent
scion
scree
sepal

shade
shoot
shrub
snail
spade
spike
spray
sprig
stalk
stool
style
tepal
tilth
tuber
tunic
trunk
truss
umbel
virus
whorl

6

alpine
annual
anther
blanch
branch
bulbil
calcar
callus
canopy
catkin
cloche
column

cordon
corona
corymb
dibble
dibber
flower
floret
fungus
gravel
heel in
hybrid
in leaf
leader
leaves
legume
linear
maiden
manure
mildew
mutant
nectar
nodule
oblong
obtuse
offset
pedate
pistil
pollen
potash
pruner
raceme
raffia
roller
rugate
rugose

rugous
runner
shears
shovel
spadix
spathe
stamen
stigma
stolon
strain
strike
sucker
throat
timber
trowel
wreath

7

baccate
bearded
blossom
bolting
bouquet
budding
bulb fly
bulb rot
cambium
capsule
climber
compost
conifer
cordate
corolla
corm rot
creeper
crenate
damp off
dentate
die back
disease
dormant
dry area
epicarp
exposed

falcate
fertile
foliage
forcing
friable
full sun
genetic
globose
habitat
harvest
hirsute
incided
leaflet
obovate
palmate
panicle
pedicel
pedicle
peltate
perfume
petiole
picotee
pinnate
plicate
potting
pyramid
radical
radicle
rhizome
rockery
root rot
root run
rosette
runners
sapwood
seed box
seed pod
sessile
spatula
species
staking
stem rot
sterile
storing
taproot

tendril
topiary
variety
weeping

8

acid soil
aeration
alkaline
axillary
biennial
bleeding
blooming
bone meal
botanist
botryose
botrytis
brassica
bud burst
bulb mite
club root
cropping
crucifer
cultivar
diaspore
digitate
Dutch hoe
earthing
elliptic
endocarp
espalier
filament
florigen
follicle
fragrant
fumigate
glabrate
glabrous
glaucous
greenery
greenfly
grafting
humidity
leaf fall

leaf spot
moisture
mutation
notching
parasite
peduncle
perianth
pericarp
petaloid
pinch out
planting
poor soil
pot group
rainfall
reniform
rich soil
scandent
scree bed
seedling
serrated
standard
stellate
systemic
terminal
thinning
tomentum
truncate
tuber rot
whitefly
windfall

9

acid-lover
acuminate
arboretum
bipinnate
biternate
bulb aphid
calcicole
calcifuge
catch-crop
chlorosis
cold frame
columella

cotyledon
cultivate
deciduous
decompose
decumbent
digitated
evergreen
feathered
fimbriate
flowerage
flowering
flowerpot
fragrance
fungicide
grey mould
half-hardy
half shade
harden off
herbarium
inorganic
intercrop
internode
involucre
landscape
lawn mower
leaf mould
leafy gall
lime-hater
orbucular
perennial
pollinate
pot pourri
pubescent
remontant
repellant
rock plant
rootstock
saggitate
secateurs
sheltered
shrubbery
spatulate
sprinkler
sprouting
strobilus

succulent
temperate
terrarium
tomentose
tulip fire
unisexual
varieties
variegated
weedkiller
wind-borne
window box

10

basal shoot
botryoidal
common name
fan-trained
calcareous
calceiform
chlorophyl
compositae
coriaceous
damping off
decomposed
greenhouse
fasciation
flore pleno
floribunda
flower head
foliar feed
herbacious
involucrum
jardinière
lanceolate
leguminous
lignotuber
monocarpic
monoecious
ornamental
pebble tray
perfoliate
pinnatifid
procumbent
propagated

reticulate
rhizome rot
sooty mould
spathulate
springtime
sub-shrubby
summertime
trifoliate
tripartite
viviparous
wild flower

11

aerial root
air humidity
campanulate
caterpillar
chlorophyll
contractile
dead-heading
dense growth
everlasting
family group
flowerheads
frost pocket
germination
ground cover
ground flora
infestation
inflorescent
insecticide
leaf-climber
leaf-cutting
leaf-sweeper
neutral soil
performance
pinching out
pollination
propagation
scale insect
self-fertile
self-sterile
severe frost
shade-loving

stem-cutting
tip layering
top dressing
ventilation
waterlogged

12

aquatic plant
black root rot
bottle garden
clematis wilt
garden centre
half-standard
hardening off
horticulture
indoor garden
oblanceolate
walled garden

13

country flower
dormant period
fertilization
growing pwriod
hanging basket
hedge trimming
lateral branch
monocotyledon
night-blooming
peach leaf curl
powdery mildew
resting period
shade tolerant
specimen plant
transpiration
transplanting

14

aquarium plants
classification
direct sunlight
floral envelope

fructification
mild conditions
photosynthesis
potting compost
rooting compound

15 +

botanical gardens
cross pollination
exposed position

ground-cover plant
low-growing plant
seasonal changes
sheltered position
soil composition
water frequently

Gemstones

3 & 4

jade
jet
onyx
opal
ruby
sard

6

garnet
jasper
quartz
spinel
zircon

7

citrine
diamond
emerald
peridot
sardine

5

agate
balas
beryl
lapis
pearl
topaz

8

amethyst

sapphire
sardonyx
sunstone

9

balas ruby
cairngorm
carnelian
cornelian
malachite
moonstone
turquoise

10

aquamarine
aventurine
bloodstone

chalcedony
chrysolite
false topaz
heliotrope
rose quartz
serpentine
tourmaline

11

chrysoberyl
chrysoprase
lapis lazuli
smoky quartz

13

oriental topaz

Giants

3 & 4

Gog
Irus
ogre
Otus
Rhea
Ymir

5

Agres
Argus
Atlas
Balan
Cacus
Coeus
Crius
Hydra
Magog

Orion
Theia
Titan

6

Cottus
Cronus
ogress
Pallas
Phoebe

Tethys
Themis

7

Antaeus
Brontes
Cyclops
Despair
Goliath
Iapetos

Oceanus

8

behemoth
Bellerus
Briareus
colossus
Cormoran
Ferragus
giantess

Hyperion
Orgoglio
Steropes
Titaness
Typhoeus

Fierabras
Gargantua
leviathan
Mnemosyne

11

Blunderbore

15 +

giants of Brobdingnag
Harbin of the
  Mountain
Morgante Maggiore

9

Colbronde
Enceladus
Ephialtes

10

Alifafaron
Pantagruel
Polyphemus
Ysbadadden

Gods and goddesses

2 & 3	Re	Here	Tane	Frigg	6
	Seb	Iris	Thor	Hodur	
Aah	Set	Isis	Upis	Horus	Aeolus
Anu	Shu	Jove	Yama	Hymen	Amen-
Ate	Sol	Juno	Zeus	Imana	Ra
Bel	Tiu	Kali		Indra	Anubis
Bes	Tyr	Kama		Irene	Apollo
Dis		Kami	**5**	Iruva	Aquilo
Don		Leza		Janus	Athene
Ea	**4**	Loki	Aegir	lares	Auster
Eir		Luba	Aesir	Momus	Aurora
Eos	Agni	Luna	Ammon	Mwari	Balder
Ge	Amor	Maat	Atlas	Nanna	Boreas
Geb	Amun	Maia	Belus	Neheh	Brahma
Hel	Apis	Mars	Bragi	Njord	Brigit
Hor	Ares	Mont	Ceres	Norns	Caurus
Io	Aten	Mors	Chaos	Orcus	Cronos
Jok	Atua	Nabu	Comus	Pluto	Cronus
lar	Ba'al	Nebo	Cupid	Rangi	Cybele
Lug	Brag	Nike	Dagda	Shiva	Daimon
Mut	deva	Odin	Dagon	Theoi	Faunus
Nox	Diva	Papa	Diana	Thoth	Freyja
Nut	Enyo	Ptah	disir	Tyche	Frigga
Nyx	Eris	Rama	Donar	Vanir	Furies
Ops	Eros	Rhea	durga	Venus	Graces
Oro	Frey	Seth	Euros	Vesta	Hathor
Pan	Gaea	Shay	Fates	Vidar	Hecate
Pax	Hari	Sita	Flora	Wodan	Helios
Ra	Hebe	Siva	Freya	Wotan	Hermes
	Hera		Freyr		

Heroes	Typhon	penates	**9**
Hestia	Upuaut	Pheobus	
Hother	Vishnu	Priapus	Apeliotes
Hygiea	Vulcan	Proteus	Aphrodite
Hypnos	Vishnu	Ruhanga	Asclepius
Ishtar		Sekhmet	Cernunnos
Kaikas		Shamash	Dipankara
Kronos	**7**	Silenus	Discordia
Marduk	Abraxas	Victory	Tetoinnan
Mexitl	Africus		
Mextli	Alastor	**8**	**10**
Mithra	Artemis		
Modimo	Bacchus	Amitabha	Akal Purakh
Moloch	Bellona	Bubastis	Dii Majores
Moirai	Berchta	Charites	Dii Minores
Nereus	Demeter	Dionysos	Hephaestus
Njorth	Forseti	Dionysus	Hephaistos
Nzambi	Fortuna	Favonius	Juggernaut
Orisha	Heimdal	Ganymede	Persephone
Osiris	Ishvara	Juventas	Prometheus
Pallas	Jupiter	Mahadevi	Proserpine
Parcae	Katonda	Morpheus	
Phenix	Kon-Tiki	Ometeotl	**11 +**
Plutus	Krishna	Poseidon	
Renpet	Lakshmi	Quirinus	Agathodaemon
Saturn	Masalai	Silvanus	Aesculapius
Selene	Mercury	Tangaroa	Bodhisattva
Shaiva	Minerva	Terminus	Huitzilopochtli
Shakti	Mithras	Thanatos	Pallas Athene
Skiron	Mulunga	Zephyrus	Phoebus Apollo
Somnus	Nemesis	Victoria	Quetzalcoatl
Tlaloc	Neptune	Zephyrus	Scamandius
Tellus	Oceanus		Tezcatlipoca
Tefnut	Parvata		Tuatha de Danaan

Greek alphabet

2	**3**	rho	iota	delta	**6**	omicron
		tau	zeta	gamma		upsilon
mu	chi			kappa	lambda	
nu	eta			omega	**7**	
pi	phi	**4**	**5**	sigma		
xi	psi	beta	alpha	theta	epsilon	

Heavenly bodies

2 & 3

Io
Sun

4

belt
coma
Faye
halo
Juno
Leda
limb
Moon
nova
pole
Rhea
Ross
star
Vega
Wolf

5

Algol
Ariel
Biela
Carme
Ceres
comet
Cygni
Deneb
Dione
Elara
Encke
epact
epoch
flare
giant
Hamal
Hyads

Janus
Kopff
lunar
Metis
Mimas
nadir
orbit
phase
Rigel
Sirus
solar
space
Spica
Thebe
Titan
umbra
Vesta

6

Adhara
albedo
Altair
Ananke
apogee
astral
aurora
binary
bolide
Castor
Charon
colure
corona
crater
Crucis
Europa
Deimos
galaxy
Halley
Huyten
Hyades
Icarus

lunary
Lyrids
meteor
nebula
Nereid
Oberon
Olbers
parsec
Phobos
Phoebe
planet
Plough
Pollux
pulsar
quasar
Shaula
Sinope
Sirius
sphere
sundog
syzygy
Tethys
Triton
Tuttle
Ursids
zenith
zodiac

7

Antares
apogean
auroral
azimuth
Bennett
Canopus
Capella
cluster
cometic
Cygnids
D'Arrest
Dog Star

eclipse
equator
equinox
gibbous
Iapetus
Lalande
Leonids
metonic
Milalia
Miranda
mock sun
nebulae
new moon
perigee
Polaris
Procyon
radiant
Regulus
sextile
spectra
sputnik
stellar
sunspot
synodic
Tau Ceti
Taurids
transit
Titania
Umbriel
Vaisala

8

Achernar
Adrastea
aerolite
almagest
Alpherat
Amalthea
aphelion
Arcturus
asterism

asteroid
Barnard's
Borrelly
Callisto
Centauri
Cepheids
cometary
daylight
ecliptic
epicycle
evection
fireball
full moon
Ganymede
Geminids
Hyperion
Kapteyn's
Kohoutek
latitude
Lodestar
lunarium
lunation
Lysithea
meridian
meteoric
Milky Way
nutation
parallax
Pasiphae
penumbra
perigeal
perigean
Orionids
Perseids
Pleiades
Pole Star
quartile
quintile
red giant
red shift
sidereal
solstice

spectrum
spheroid
stardust
stellary
sublunar
universe
variable
Westphal
zodiacal

satellite
solar wind
star-gazer
starlight
starshine
sublunary
supernova
synodical
telescope

siderolite
solar flare
solar month
supergiant
terminator
trajectory
white dwarf

sidereal time
solar eclipse
spiral galaxy
stratosphere
synodic month
total eclipse
Van Allen belt
variable star

11

conjunction
declination
Epsilon Indi
falling star
Gegenschein
giant planet
last quarter
minor planet
neutron star
occultation
photosphere
observatory
planetarium
Quadrantids
solar system
stratopause
terrestrial
uranography

9

aerolitic
Aldebaran
astrology
astronomy
Ballatrix
black hole
canicular
celestial
Comas Sola
cosmogony
cosmology
Crommelin
elevation
Enceladus
epicyclic
firmament
Fomalhaut
giant star
hour angle
light-year
longitude
lunar year
magnitude
meteorite
meteoroid
moonquake
moonshine
parhelion
planetary
planetoid
Red Planet
reflector
refractor

10

abberation
altazimuth
asteroidal
astrologer
astrometry
astronomer
astronomic
Australids
Betelgeuse
binary star
cosmic dust
cosmic rays
Crab nebula
depression
double star
earthshine
elongation
evectional
hour circle
lunar month
lunar probe
meteoritic
Ophiuchids
opposition
outer space
perihelion
Phoenicids
precession
prominence
quadrature
refraction
retrograde
selenology

12

astrogeology
astronomical
astrophysics
Capricornids
chromosphere
eccentricity
Halley's comet
interstellar
lunar eclipse
lunar rainbow
meteor shower
perturbation
selenography
shooting star

13

Alpha Centauri
celestial body
celestial pole
constellation
polar zenithal
sidereal month
zodiacal light

14

annular eclipse
astronavigation
celestial globe
interplanetary
partial eclipse
radio astronomy
radio telescope
right ascension
summer solstice
supergiant star
vertical circle
winter solstice

15

armillary sphere
celestial bodies
celestial sphere
eclipsing binary
equinoctial year
Fraunhoffer lines
oblique zenithal
Proxima Centauri

16 +

astronomical unit
astronomical year
azimuthal projection
Cassegrainian telescope
celestial guidance
celestial latitude
celestial longitude
celestial mechanics
equatorial telescope
equatorial zenithal
Newtonian telescope
zenithal projection
zodiacal constellation

Henry VIII's wives

Anne Boleyn (or Bullen)
Jane Seymour
Anne of Cleves
Catherine Parr
Catherine Howard
Katherine of Aragon

Note: The spelling of Katherine seems to be in dispute. Katharine and Catharine are suggested alternatives to the ones above.

Herbs and spices

3 & 4

balm
bay
dill
mace
mint
race
rue
sage

5

agave
anise
basil
caper
chive
clove
cumin
curry
senna
tansy

thyme

6

bennet
borage
burnet
chilli
cicely
fennel
garlic
ginger
hyssop
lovage
nutmeg
pepper
savory
sesame
sorrel

7

aniseed

bay leaf
caraway
cayenne
chervil
comfrey
mustard
oregano
paprika
parsley
pimento
saffron
Tabasco
vanilla

8

allspice
angelica
bergamot
camomile
capsicum
cinnamon
costmary

marjoram
rosemary
tarragon
turmeric
woodruff

9

chamomile
coriander
fenugreek
spearmint

10

mixed spice
pennyroyal
peppermint
rubbed sage

11

black pepper
curry powder
fines herbes
garam masala
herb of grace
pot marigold
salad burnet
sweet cicely
white pepper

12

bouquet garni
chilli powder

13

cayenne powder
sweet woodruff

Hobbies and pastimes

3

ace
art
bed
bet
bid
box
cup
cut
die
DIY
leg
loo
man
nap
oxo
peg
pig
pip
pit
rob
run
see

4

ball
bank
bone
brag
card
chip
club
coup
crib
deal
deck
dice
draw
faro

game
hand
home
jack
jink
king
ludo
mace
mate
move
noir
pack
pair
paix
pass
pawn
play
pool
pope
rook
skat
snap
solo
spin
stud
suit
trio
vint

5

après
banco
bango
batik
bingo
block
bluff
bower
capot
carré

check
chess
clubs
demon
deuce
divan
dummy
flush
grand
halma
heart
injun
inlay
joker
kitty
knave
knock
mitre
monte
motif
mould
nappa
passe
pay me
picot
plait
point
poker
print
punch
queen
quint
resin
rouge
royal
rules
rummy
score
scram
sheaf
skive

spade
stake
stamp
stick
stock
stops
straw
talon
taper
tarot
teeth
thong
trace
trade
trick
trump
twist
wager
weave
wheel
whist
widow

6

attack
banker
barter
basket
batten
bergen
bishop
bobbin
bonsai
boodle
boston
bridge
candle
canvas
casino
castle

cat-hop
cement
cinema
cotton
crowns
dabber
design
donkey
double
écarté
euchre
fan tan
figure
firing
floral
flower
frieze
fumage
fusing
gambit
gamble
go-bang
go boom
honour
impair
kaolin
knaves
knight
manque
marble
marker
milieu
milton
minoru
misère
misery
mobile
mosaic
needle
oil ink

paroli
pebble
piquet
plaque
punter
quinto
quinze
raffia
reading
red dog
refait
renege
revoke
ribbon
roller
rubber
rushes
scraps
screen
sewing
silica
sphere
spiral
sponge
staple
stitch
strand
stuzka
sultan
tallow
tassel
thread
treble
veneer
waxing
yablon

7

à cheval
alumina

aquaria
art deco
auction
beeswax
bézique
binding
blucher
bouquet
brisque
brulage
burnish
canasta
carding
cassino
casting
collage
colonel
conkers
conleur
counter
crochet
cookery
defence
diamond
discard
doublet
encarte
end-game
engrave
en plein
en prise
etching
feather
flat bar
forfeit
hessian
imprint
impress
inverse
j'adoube
jackpot
lacquer
leather
lozenge
keep fit

macramé
marbles
misdeal
old maid
order up
origami
partner
pattern
peep nap
penalty
picture
plaster
pontoon
pottery
propose
pysanky
red suit
reversi
rolling
sandown
scorper
sequins
seven up
shuffle
sleeper
spinado
stencil
tarocco
tatting
topiary
treadle
twining
varnish
vingt-un
weaving
whister
wood cut

8

aerobics
all fours
all fives
antiqued
appliqué

assemble
baccarat
bead work
bevelled
blown egg
cachette
cane work
castling
charcoal
commerce
cribbage
croupier
dead ball
decolage
decorate
dernière
dominoes
douzaine
draughts
dry point
embossed
flat knot
fretwork
full hand
fuse wire
gin rummy
gouge nib
heraldry
imperial
intrigue
knitting
knotting
Irish loo
linoleum
matadore
material
merelles
Michigan
Napoleon
no-trumps
open slam
painting
partager
patience
penuchle

picot bar
pinch pot
pinochle
polignac
Pope Joan
première
puppetry
pyramids
quilting
quatorze
roll-call
roulette
saw frame
scissors
Scrabble
sequence
shanghai
shell-out
skinball
spinning
staining
straight
smocking
spray-gun
tailleur
tapestry
template
tourneur
transfer
tweezers
vignette
windmill
woodwork
vinamold

9

abondance
arabesque
astrology
astronomy
bagatelle
balsa wood
berry knot
black jack

black suit
burnisher
cardboard
champleve
checkmate
cloisonné
coiled pot
court card
curl grain
découpage
double run
dowelling
draw poker
dummy hand
engraving
en passant
forty-five
gardening
genealogy
grand coup
grand slam
gum-arabic
half-hitch
hardboard
hem stitch
horse race
index card
indian ink
jewellery
lampshade
left bower
marquetry
matrimony
modelling
monte bank
newmarket
old sledge
overtrick
pair-royal
palmistry
patch work
pelmanism
philately
photogram
planisher

poker work
rug making
sculpture
shell work
solitaire
solo whist
spoil five
sprigging
stalemate
stud poker
stoneware
straw work
thirty-one
thrown pot
top stitch
vingt-et-un
wavy grain
web stitch
wood block
ziginette
zinc plate

10

arabic cage
backgammon
back stitch
basketwork
bearing off
bee-keeping
beer-making
black maria
bone folder
cat-showing
chess board
cotton wool
craft knife
crêpe paper
crosswords
decoration
dog-showing
double paix
drawing pin
embroidery
enamelling

fly-fishing
Genoese bar
heartsette
kalabriasz
kite flying
kite making
lace making
lansquenet
little slam
long stitch
metal frame
needlework
open misère
paintbrush
paix-paroli
plasticine
preference
pyrography
quint royal
rice stitch
right bower
sebastopol
spot hearts
spread slam
stop the bus
sweepstake
tent stitch
travellers
treble paix
turpentine
undertrick
upholstery
Wellington
whip stitch
willow reed
wine making

11

archaeology
arrangement
bark rubbing
basse taille
bell ringing
blind hookey

book binding
butt veneers
calligraphy
campanology
carbon paper
card-playing
catch the ten
chain stitch
chemin-de-fer
Chinese knot
confederacy
copper plate
coral stitch
cross stitch
crochet hook
crotch grain
dressmaking
earthenware
five hundred
five card loo
gutta-percha
German whist
grand spread
Greek hearts
jeux de règle
joker hearts
knotted lace
leather work
lepidoptery
lino cutting
my ship sails
papier colle
papier mâché
parrafin wax
photography
picture card
plique-a-jour
poster paint
purchase nap
quilt-making
racing demon
red and black
rubber mould
sand carving
sand picture

satin stitch
Scotch whist
short stitch
slippery Sam
speculation
stencilling
tamping tool
tissue paper
twill stitch
vintage cars

12

auction pitch
beach combing
bird watching
branch stitch
brass rubbing
calabrasella
candle making
card dominoes
carte blanche
chef-de-partie
corkscrew bar
cutting board
diamond point
domino hearts
faggot stitch
florist's wire
flower garden
flower making
French boston
glass etching
gouache paint
hoggenheimer
Japanese knot
Josephine knot
ladder stitch
little spread
Miss Milligan
mosaic stitch
parallel bars
parish stitch
petit chevaux
piccolissimo

rouge-et-noir
royal cassino
sand bottling
sand pictures
seven card nap
shadow stitch
shove-ha'penny
slip trailing
slobberhannes
spade cassino
stanley knife
three card loo
tie-and-dyeing
tracing paper
transversale
tropical fish
ventriloquism
well dressing
zig-zag stitch

13

auction bridge
basket weaving
blanket stitch
bulls and bears
call ace euchre
Chinese fan tan
clock patience
cribbage board
double bézique
egg decorating
feather stitch
giant patience
happy families
highest bidder
jigsaw puzzles
Kentucky derby
knockout whist
lattice stitch
misère ouverte
modelling clay
model railways
old man's bundle
outline stitch

poker patience
ranter-go-round
rawhide hammer
rolling stones
royal marriage
round the clock
single bézique
spray adhesive
straight flush
straight grain
the cannon game
three card brag
train spotting
Turkish stitch
water divining

14

Austrian tarock
baccarat banque
ball on the watch
cake decorating
California Jack
card put and take
coin collecting
common marriage
contract bridge
diagonal stitch
egg decorating
enamel painting
flower pressing
French knitting
hairpin crochet
metal detecting
nine men's morris
paper sculpture
pebble painting
pigeon fancying
plaster of Paris
railroad euchre
rubicon bézique
six deck bézique
snip snap snorem
three-stake brag
Trivial Pursuit

15 +

abondance declarée
amateur dramatics
auction forty-five
auction pinochle
autograph hunting
ballroom dancing
beggar my neighbour
butterfly collecting
corn-dolly making
double pair-royal
ducks and drakes
duplicate bridge
eight deck bézique
florentine stitch
flower arranging
foundation leader
hand-bell ringing
herringbone stitch
hurricane candle
interlocking grain
Japanese bézique
Japanese flower cards
jewellery making
lampshade making
lazy daisy stitch
pin and thread work
pressing flowers
quadruple bézique
royal draw cassino
Scottish dancing
serpent poker patience
shell collecting
single-stake brag
snakes and ladders
stamp collecting
traction engines
trente-et-quarante

Horses and ponies

3

Cob
Don
Jaf

4

Arab
Barb
Fell
Polo

5

Alter
Batak
Dales
Fjord
Haiti
Huzul

Jomud
Konik
Lokai
Minho
Orlov
Pinto
Shire
Timor
Toric
Waler
Welsh

6

Albino
Basuto
Breton
Brumby
Dülmen
Exmoor
Fulani

Morgan
Nonius
Peneia
Pindos
Poznan
Skyros
Tarpan
Viatka

7

Comtois
Costeno
Criollo
Crioulo
Furioso
Gotland
Hackney
Jutland
Kirghiz
Llanero

Marwari
Masuren
Mustang
Noriker
Pechora
Sokólsk
Sorraia
Trotter

8

Ardennes
Budjonny
Camargue
Dartmoor
Galiceño
Highland
Holstein
Kabardin
Karabair
Karabakh

Lusitano
Palomino
Polo pony
Shetland
Turkmene
Turkoman

9

Achal-Teké
Anglo-Arab
Appaloosa
Calabrese
Campolino
Connemara
Groningen
Haflinger
Haiti pony
Kladruber
Knabstrup
Kustanair

Morochuco
New Forest
Oldenburg
Percheron
Pinzgauer
Poitevine
Schleswig
Trakehner

Lipizzaner
Mangalarga
Peneia pony
Pindos pony
Sandalwood
Skyros pony
Shagya Arab
Tchenarani

Spotted Horse
Strelets Arab
Suffolk Punch
thoroughbred

13

Frederiksborg
Welsh mountain

10

Andalusian
Assateague
Avelignese
Carthusian
Clydesdale
Darashoori
Einsiedler
Frieberger
Gelderland
Hanoverian
Kathiawari

11

Anglo-Norman
Chicoteague
Chinese pony
Sable Island
Trait du Nord
Wurttemberg

15 +

Canadian Cutting Horse
Döle-Gudsbrandsdal
Kentucky Sadsler
Missouri Fox Trotting
   Horse
Pony of the Americas
Seine Inférieure
Tennessee Walking Horse

12

Cleveland Bay
Quarter Horse

Insects, arachnids, worms and snails

3	gnat	borer	6	cicala	lackey
---	goat	cimex	---	cimbex	lappet
ant	grub	comma	acarid	coccid	larvae
bee	hawk	culex	ant cow	coccus	locust
bot	lice	drone	bedbug	cocoon	looper
bug	mite	egger	bee fly	copper	maggot
dor	moth	emmet	beetle	dayfly	magpie
fly	pupa	flies	botfly	dobson	mantid
nit	puss	fluke	breeze	earwig	mantis
pug	tick	imago	burnet	elater	maybug
	wasp	larva	caddis	ermine	mayfly
		louse	chafer	gadfly	midget
4		midge	chegre	herald	nereis
	5	nymph	chigoe	hopper	palolo
cleg		sedge	chinch	hornet	red ant
flea	aphid	tiger	cicada	jigger	redbug
frit	aphis				

Insects, arachnids, worms and snails

sawfly
scarab
slater
sow bug
sphinx
spider
Thrips
tineid
tsetse
vespid
weevil
worker

7

annelid
ant lion
araneae
army ant
bagworm
bee moth
blowfly
carabid
cestoid
chalcid
chigger
cricket
culicid
cutworm
daphnia
drinker
dung fly
emerald
epizoon
firefly
fire ant
frit fly
frogfly
gallfly
goldbug
grannon
hexapod
June bug
katydid
lace bug

monarch
peacock
phasmid
pill bug
pinworm
pismire
pug moth
pyralid
ragworm
ringlet
rotifer
sandfly
skipper
spinner
syrphid
termite
trumpet
vespine
wax moth
wood ant

8

acaridan
alder fly
apterous
arachnid
army worm
black ant
blackfly
bollworm
caseworm
Colorado
cranefly
curculio
December
dipteran
ephemera
firebrat
flatworm
flesh fly
fruit fly
gall mite
gall wasp
glow-worm

goat moth
greenfly
hairworm
hawk moth
helminth
honey bee
hookworm
horntail
horsefly
housefly
inchworm
itch mite
lacewing
ladybird
longhorn
meal moth
mealy bug
mealworm
milkweed
milliped
mosquito
muckworm
multiped
myriapod
oak egger
parasite
puss moth
queen bee
ramshorn
sand flea
sand wasp
scorpion
sheep ked
silkworm
slave ant
slow worm
stonefly
subimago
tapeworm
tubeworm
water-bug
wheel bug
white ant
whitefly
wireworm

woodlice
wood mite
wood moth
wood wasp
woodworm

9

amazon ant
anopheles
arachnoid
bee beetle
blindworm
brandling
brimstone
bumble bee
butterfly
caddis fly
capsid bug
carpet bug
centipede
chaetopod
chinch bug
chrysalis
clavicorn
cochineal
cockroach
cornborer
crab louse
damselfly
dermestid
dragonfly
driver ant
egger moth
ephemerid
flour mite
flour moth
flower bug
flying ant
funnel-web
gall midge
ghost moth
gipsy moth
ground bug
holly blue

hornet fly
ichneumon
lac insect
leaf miner
longicorn
millipede
multipede
orange-tip
red spider
pea weevil
peripatus
plume moth
pond snail
robber fly
roundworm
saltatory
saucer bug
sheep tick
squash bug
swift moth
tarantula
thysanura
tiger moth
trematode
tsetse fly
tzetze fly
wall brown
warble fly
water flea
wax insect
whirligig
willowfly
woodborer
woodlouse
worker ant
worker bee
xylophaga

10

antler moth
antlion fly
bark beetle
bean weevil
bird spider

168

black widow
bluebottle
boll weevil
bombardier
burnet moth
cabbage bug
cabbage fly
canker worm
carpet moth
chalcid fly
cheese mite
chironomid
cluster fly
cockchafer
codlin moth
coleoptera
death's head
death watch
digger wasp
drosophila
dung beetle
flea beetle
fritillary
frog hopper
gatekeeper
gold beetle
grey dagger
grove snail
Guinea worm
hairstreak
harvestman
hemipteran
hessian fly
jigger flea
June beetle
kitten moth
lackey moth
lantern fly
lappet moth
leaf beetle
leaf hopper
leaf roller
looper moth
neuroptera
orthoptera

palmer worm
phylloxera
plant louse
pond skater
pond sponge
pupiparous
red admiral
ribbonworm
Roman snail
rosechafer
rose beetle
rove beetle
saltigrade
sand hopper
scarabaeus
silverfish
soldier ant
Spanish fly
spider mite
springtail
stag beetle
thysanuran
tree hopper
turnip moth
vinegar fly
vine weevil
water louse
winter moth
wolf spider
woolly bear
xylophagan

11

angle shades
apple maggot
assassin bug
August thorn
bacon beetle
bagworm moth
black arches
black beetle
bristletail
buffalo gnat
cabbage moth

cabbage worm
canatharides
caterpillar
clothes moth
codling moth
coleopteran
corn-ear worm
drinker moth
emperor moth
flour weavil
garden tiger
grasshopper
greenbottle
harvest mite
harvest tick
hymenoptera
Lepidoptera
meadow brown
mole cricket
money spider
painted lady
pharoah's ant
scale insect
scorpion fly
Scotch argus
snout beetle
stick insect
swallowtail
tetrapteran
tiger beetle
trichoptera
tussock moth
water skater
water spider
woolly aphid
zebra spider

12

book scorpion
cabbage white
carpenter bee
carpet beetle
cecropia moth
chafer beetle

cinnabar moth
diadem spider
diving beetle
feather louse
goldtail moth
ground beetle
harlequin bug
heart and dart
hellgrammite
ichneumon fly
lightning bug
marbled white
museum beetle
peach blossom
pirate spider
poplar kitten
rhynchophore
scarab beetle
speckled wood
trumpet snail
vapourer moth
walking stick
water boatman
water strider
white admiral

carpenter moth
cheese skipper
daddy-longlegs
false scorpion
goliath beetle
honeycomb moth
ichneumon wasp
jumping-spider
leafcutter ant
leafcutter bee
leatherjacket
measuring worm
mother-of-pearl
pied shieldbug
pill millipede
praying mantis
purple emperor
ramshorn snail
redback spider
red spider mite
tortoiseshell
water measurer
water scorpion

Hercules beetle
purse-web spider
trap-door spider

15

furniture beetle
grizzled skipper
heath potter wasp
hummingbird hawk
whirligig beetle
yellow longicorn

16 +

bloody-nosed beetle
bombardier beetle
cabbage white butterfly
Camberwell beauty
churchyard beetle
deathwatch beetle
devil's coach-horse
funnel-web spider
giant peacock moth
Jenkin's spire shell
jumping plant louse
long-horned beetle
oriental cockroach
robin's pincushion
spider-hunting wasp
water stick insect

14

cabbage-root fly
Colorado beetle
comma butterfly
death's head moth

13

blister beetle
browntail moth

International car codes

Aden	ADN	Bahrain	BRN	Burma	BUR
Afghanistan	AGF	Bangladesh	BD	Burundi	RU
Albania	AL	Barbados	BDS	Cameroon	RFC
Alderney	GBA	Belgium	B	Canada	CDN
Algeria	DY	Belize	BH	Central African	
Andorra	AND	Benin	DY	Republic	RCA
Argentina	RA	Botswana	RB	Chile	RCH
Australia	AUS	Brazil	BR	China	TJ
Austria	A	Brunei	BRU	Colombia	CO
Bahamas	BS	Bulgaria	BG	Congo	RCB

Country	Code	Country	Code	Country	Code
Costa Rica	CR	Jersey	GBJ	Romania	RO
Côte d'Ivoire	CI	Jordan	HKJ	Rwanda	RWA
Cuba	C	Kenya	EAK	St. Lucia	WL
Cyprus	CY	Kuwait	KWT	St. Vincent and	
Czechoslovakia		Laos	LAO	the Grenadines	
	CS	Lebanon	RL		WV
Denmark	D	Lesotho	LS	Samoa	WS
Dominica	WD	Liberia	LB	San Marino	RSM
Dominican Rep.		Libya	LAR	Senegal	SN
	DOM	Liechtenstein		Seychelles	SY
East Germany	DDR		FL	Sierra Leone	WAL
Egypt	ET	Luxembourg	L	Singapore	SGP
El Salvador	ES	Madagascar	RM	South Africa	ZA
Ethiopia	ETH	Malawi	MW	South Korea	ROK
Faroe Islands	FR	Malaysia	MAL	Spain	E
Fiji	FDI	Mali	RMM	Sri Lanka	CL
Finland	SF	Malta	M	Suriname	SME
France	F	Mauritania	RIM	Sweden	S
Gambia	WAG	Mauritius	MS	Swaziland	SD
Ghana	GH	Mexico	MEX	Switzerland	CH
Gibraltar	GBZ	Monaco	MC	Syria	SYR
Granada	WG	Morocco	MA	Tanzania	EAT
Great Britain	GB	Namibia	SWA	Taiwan	RC
Greece	GR	Netherlands	NL	Thailand	T
Guatemala	GCA	Netherlands		Togo	TG
Guernsey	GBG	Antilles	NA	Trinidad and	
Guyana	GUY	New Zealand	NZ	Tobago	TT
Haiti	RH	Nicaragua	NIC	Tunisia	TN
Hongkong	HK	Niger	RN	Turkey	TR
Hungary	H	Nigeria	WAN	Uganda	EAU
Iceland	IS	Norway	N	Uruguay	ROU
India	IND	Pakistan	PAK	USA	USA
Indonesia	RI	Panama	PA	USSR	SU
Iran	IR	Papua New Guinea		Vatican City	V
Iraq	IRQ		PNG	Vietnam	VN
Ireland	IRL	Paraguay	PY	West Germany	D
Isle of Man	GBM	Peru	PE	Yugoslavia	YU
Israel	IL	Philippines	RP	Venezuela	YV
Italy	I	Poland	PL	Zaïre	ZRE
Jamaica	JA	Portugal	P	Zambia	Z
Japan	J	Qatar	QA	Zimbabwe	ZW

Islands

> *(Where Island, Islands, Isles or Isle of is a normal part of the name, it is usually indicated in brackets as I., Is., or I. of)*

2 & 3

Adi
Bay (Is.)
Bua
Ely (I. of)
Eve
Ewe
Hoy
Kei (Is.)
Man (I. of)
May (I. of)
Neb
Rat (Is.)
Ré
Red
Roa
Rum
Yap
Zea

4

Adam
Amoy
Aran (I. of)
Arru (Is.)
Bali
Bear (I.)
Bere
Bird (I.)
Buru
Bute
Calf (I.)
Cebu
Ceos
Coll
Cook (Is.)

Cuba
Dago
Dogs (I. of)
Eday
Edge
Eigg
Elba
Fair (I.)
Farn (Is.)
Faro
Fiji
Fohr
Goat (I.)
Gozo
Guam
Gugh
Hall (Is.)
Herm
High (I.)
Holy (I.)
Idra
Iona
Java
Jura
Long (I.)
Milo
Moen
Mona
Muck
Mull (I. of)
Noss
Oahu
Omey
Osea (I.)
Rhum
Rona
Saba
Sark
Scio

Skye
Sulu (Is.)
Sylt
Syra
Swan (I.)
Tory
Uist
Ulva
Unst
Yell
Yezo
Zebu

5

Abaco
Aland (Is.)
Albay
Arran
Banca
Banda
Banks
Barra
Barry
Bonin (Is.)
Caldy
Canna
Capri
Ceram
Chios
Clare
Cocos (Is.)
Corfu
Corvo
Crete
Dabaz
Delos
Devon
Disco

Disko
Eagle (I.)
Ellis
Farne (Is.)
Fayal
Ferro
Foula
Funen
Goree
Gozzo
Grain (I. of)
Haiti
Hart's (I.)
Hatia
Hondo
Hydra
Ibiza
Inyak
Islay
Ivica
Lewis
Leyte
Lissa
Lobos (Is.)
Lundy (I.)
Luzon
Malta
Matsu
Melos
Milos
Nauru
Naxos
Nevis
Ormuz
Panay
Papua
Paros
Parry (Is.)

Paxoi	Candia	Marajo	Ameland
Pearl (Is.)	Canary (Is.)	Marken	Andaman (Is.)
Pelew (Is.)	Canvey (I.)	Negros	Antigua
Pemba	Cayman (Is.)	Oleron	Bahamas
Perim	Ceylon	Orkney (Is.)	Bahrain
Pines (I. of)	Cerigo	Patmos	Balleny (Is.)
Pinos	Cherso	Penang	Bardsey
Rhode (I.)	Chiloe	Philae	Barents
Rugen	Chusan	Pomona	Behring (Is.)
Sable (I.)	Comoro (Is.)	Puffin (I.)	Bermuda
Samar	Crozet (Is.)	Quemoy	Bernera
Samoa	Cyprus	Ramsey	British (Is.)
Samos	Dursey	Rhodes	Bourbon
Skyro	Easter (I.)	Robben	Cabrera
Spice (Is.)	Ellice (Is.)	Rottum	Capraja
Sunda (Is.)	Euboea	St. John	Caprera
Texel	Flores	St. Paul	Celebes
Timor	Gilolo	Samsoe	Channel (Is.)
Tiree	Gomera	Sangir (Is.)	Chatham (Is.)
Tonga	Hainan	Savage (I.)	Chincha (Is.)
Turk's (I.)	Harris	Scarba	Corisco
Voorn	Hawaii	Scilly (Is.)	Corsica
Whale (I.)	Honshu	Sicily	Cumbrae
Wight (I. of)	Imbros	Staffa	Curaçao
Zante	Inagua	Staten (I.)	Curzola
	Ionian (Is.)	Stroma	Dampier (Is.)
6	Ischia	Tahiti	Dinding (Is.)
	Ithaca	Taiwan	Diomede (Is.)
Achill	Iturup	Thanet (I. of)	Domingo
Aegina	Jaluit	Tholen	Faeroes
Albany	Jersey	Tobago	Falster
Anamba (Is.)	Jethou	Tresco	Fanning
Andros	Kishni	Trömso	Fehmeru
Azores	Kodiak	Tubuai (Is.)	Flannan (Is.)
Baffin (I.)	Kurile (Is.)	Tuvalu	Formosa
Banana (Is.)	Kyushu	Ushant	Frisian (Is.)
Bissao	Labuan	Vaigen	Gambier (Is.)
Borkum	Lambay	Virgin (Is.)	Gilbert (Is.)
Borneo	Lemnos	Walney	Gotland
Bounty (Is.)	Lerins (Is.)		Grenada
Brazza	Lesbos	**7**	Hayling (I.)
Bryher	Limmos		Iceland
Burray	Lipari (Is.)	Aegades (Is.)	Ireland
Caicos (Is.)	Lombok	Aeolian (Is.)	Jamaica
Calamo	Madura	Amboina	Johanna

Kamaran
Kandava
Keeling (Is.)
Kolonev
Laaland
Leeward (Is.)
Liakhov (Is.)
Lofoten (Is.)
Loyalty (Is.)
Madeira
Mageroe
Majorca
Maldive (Is.)
Massowa
Mayotte
Menorca
Mindoro
Minicoy
Minorca
Molokai
Molucca (Is.)
Mombasa
Mykonos
Nicobar (Is.)
Norfolk (I.)
Nossi Be
Okinawa
Orkneys
Palawan
Phoenix (I.)
Portsea (I.)
Princes (Is.)
Purbeck (I. of)
Rathlin
Reunion
Roanoke
Rockall
Rotumah
St. Agnes
St. Kilda
St. Kitts
St. Lucia
St. Marie
Salamis
Sao Tomé

Sheppy (I. of)
Sherbro
Shikoku
Society (Is.)
Socotra
Solomon (Is.)
Stewart (I.)
Sumatra
Sumbawa
Tenedos
Ternate
Tokelau (Is.)
Tortola
Tortuga
Tuamotu
Watling (I.)
Whalsay
Wrangel

8

Alderney
Aleutian (Is.)
Amirante (Is.)
Andamans
Anglesey
Antilles
Auklands (Is.)
Balearic (Is.)
Barbados
Berneray
Billiton
Bissagos (Is.)
Bornholm
Brownsea
Campbell
Canaries
Caribbee (Is.)
Caroline (Is.)
Colonsay
Copeland (Is.)
Cyclades (Is.)
Desertas
Desirade
Dominica
Fair Isle

Falkland (Is.)
Flat Holm
Flinders
Foulness
Friendly (Is.)
Furneaux (Is.)
Guernsey
Hebrides
Hokkaido
Hong Kong
Inchcolm
Jan Mayen
Kangaroo (Is.)
Kermadec (Is.)
Kiribati
Krakatoa
Ladrones
Leucadia
Lord Howe (Is.)
Magdalen (Is.)
Malagasy
Maldives
Malicolo
Mallorca
Manihiki (Is.)
Marianne (Is.)
Marshall (Is.)
Melville
Mindanao
Miquelon
Mitylene
Moluccas
Otaheite
Pitcairn (Is.)
Portland (I. of)
Pribilov (Is.)
Quelpart
Rothesay
St. Helena
St. Martin
St. Thomas
Sakhalin
Salsette
Sandwich (Is.)
Sardinia

Scillies
Somerset
Sri Lanka
Shetland (Is.)
Starbuck
Sulawesi
Sverdrup
Tasmania
Tenerife
Thousand (Is.)
Thursday (I.)
Tortugas (Is.)
Trinidad
Unalaska
Valancia
Valentia
Victoria
Viti-Levu
Vlieland
Windward (Is.)
Zanzibar

9

Admiralty (Is.)
Aleutians
Anticosti
Arranmore
Ascension
Australia
Belle Isle
Beverland
Calf of Man
Cape Verde (Is.)
Cerigotto
Christmas (I.)
Dordrecht
Elephanta
Eleuthera
Ellesmere
Erromanga
Falklands
Galapagos (Is.)
Greenland
Halmahera
Inchkeith

Inishturk
Isle of Man
Isle of May
Lampedusa
Langeland
Manhattan (I.)
Margarita
Marquesas (Is.)
Marshalls
Mauritius
Nantucket
Negropont
New Guinea
Norderney
North Uist
Porto Rico
Raratonga
Rodrigues
Saghalien
Saint John
St. Martin's
St. Michael
St. Nicholas
Saint Paul
St. Vincent
Santa Cruz
Santorini
Scarpanto
Shetlands
Singapore
South Uist
Steep Holm
Stromboli
Teneriffe
Timor Laut (Is.)
Vancouver
Vanua Levu
Walcheren
Wellesley (Is.)

10

Ailsa Craig
Bay Islands
Calamianes

Cape Barren (I.)
Cape Breton (I.)
Cephalonia
Dirk Hartog (I.)
Fernando Po
Formentara
Fortune Bay (I.)
Friendlies
Grenadines
Guadeloupe
Heligoland
Hispaniola
Inchgarvie
Isle of Dogs
Isle of Skye
Isle of Mull
Kuria Muria (Is.)
Laccadives
Long Island
Madagascar
Manitoulin
Martinique
Montserrat
New Britain
New Ireland
New Siberia
New Zealand
North Devon
Nova Zembla
Philippine (Is.)
Puerto Rico
Ronaldshay
Saint Agnes
Saint Kilda
Saint Kitts
Saint Lucia
Saint Marie
Sandalwood (I.)
Seychelles
Skerryvore
West Indies

11

Axel Heiberg

Dirk Hartogs
Grand Canary
Guadalcanal
Isle of Pines
Isle of Wight
Isola Grossa
Lindisfarne
Mascarenene (Is.)
Monte Cristo
New Hebrides
North Island
Pantellaria
Philippines
Rhode Island
Saint Helena
Saint Martin
Saint Thomas
Scilly Isles
Southampton
South Island
Spitsbergen

Easter Island
Great Britain
Great Cumbrae
Inaccessible (I.)
Isle of Thanet
Mariagalante
Melville Land
New Caledonia
Newfoundland
Novaya Zemlya
Prince Albert
Prince Edward (I.)
Puffin Island
Saint Michael
Saint Martin's
Saint Nicolas
Saint Vincent
South Georgia
Staten (I.)

Norfolk Island
North East Land
Prince Charles
Prince of Wales
 (I.)
Prince Patrick
St. Bartholomew
St. Christopher
Santa Catalina
Stewart Island

14

Isle of Portland
Queen Elizabeth
South Shetlands
Tierra del Fuego
Tristan da Cunha

15 +

Martha's Vineyard
Prince Edward
 Island
Van Dieman's Land
West Spitsbergen

12

Baffin Island
Bougainville
British Isles

13

Isle of Purpeck
Isle of Sheppey
Juan Fernandez
Kerguelen Land
Little Cumbrae

Labours of Hercules

Slay the Nemean lion.
Kill the Lernean hydra.
Catch and retain the Arcadian stag.
Destroy the Erymanthian boar.
Cleanse the Augean stables.
Drive off the cannibal birds of Lake Stymphalis.
Capture the Cretan bull.
Catch the mares of the Thracian Diomedes.
Get possession of the girdle of Hippolyta, Queen of the
 Amazons.
Capture the oxen of the monster Geryon.
Obtain the golden apples of the Hesperides.
Bring Cerberus from the infernal regions.

Lakes, lochs, loughs and waterfalls

Lakes, lochs and loughs

3	5	6		8
			Wanaka	
Ard	Abaya	Albert	Zaysan	Balkhash
Awe	Allen	Arkaig		Beysehir
Eil	Baker	Assynt		Chiemsee
Ewe	Broom	Austin	**7**	Colville
Key	Etive	Baykal		Coniston
Ree	Foyle	Chilka	Abitibi	Dongting
Tay	Frome	Chilko	Balaton	Gairdner
Tuz	Garda	Corrib	Blanch	Grasmere
Van	Garry	Edward	Chapela	Issyk Kul
Zug	Great	Geneva	Dead Sea	Maggiore
	Huron	George	Derwent	Manitoba
4	Kasba	Kariba	Dubawnt	Mazurian
	Kyoga	Ladoga	Egridir	Menindee
Aral	Leane	Khanka	Fannich	Michigan
Chad	Leman	Linnhe	Galilee	Neusiedl
Bala	Leven	Lomond	Idi Amin	Reindeer
Como	Lochy	Lop Nor	Katrine	Salt Lake
Conn	Loyne	Lugano	Koko Nor	Stefanie
Derg	Maree	Mackay	Leopold	Superior
Earn	Minto	Malawi	Lucerne	Titicaca
Erie	Mjosa	Mobutu	Managua	Tonle Sap
Erne	Moore	Nasser	Nipigon	Tung-T'ing
Eyre	Mweru	Natron	Nonacho	Victoria
Fyne	Neagh	Oneida	Nu Jiang	Wakatipu
Holy	Nyasa	Peipus	Ontario	Winnipeg
Kivu	Onega	Poyang	Qinghai	
Long	Poopo	Rudolf	Quesnel	**9**
Mask	Rainy	St. Jean	Rannoch	
Nemi	Rayne	Saimaa	St.	Argentino
Ness	Sevan	Shasta	Clair	Athabasca
Ryan	Shiel	Simcoe	Sheelin	Bangweulu
Tana	Taupo	Te Anu	Swilley	Champlain
Utah	Trout	Vanern	Torrens	Chudskoye
	Urmia	Viedma	Turkana	Constance
	Volta	Vyrnwy	Wannsee	Ennerdale

Faguibine
Great Bear
Great Salt
Mai Ndombe
Maracaibo
Neuchâtel
Nicaragua
Nipissing
Thirlmere
Trasimene

Ullswater
Wastwater
Wollaston

10 +

Buttermere
Coniston Water
Connewarre
Cabora Bassa

Derwent Water
Great Slave
Haogoundou
Ijsselmeer
Lake of the Woods
Okeechobee
Rydal water
Serpentine
Tanganyika
Windermere
Winnipegosis

Waterfalls and cataracts

5

Angel
Cedar
Della
Glass
Sioux

6

Boyoma
Foyers
Guayra
Iguaca
Ribbon
Rogart
Tugela

7

Glomach
Measach
Niagara
Roraima
Stanley
Swallow
Utigard

8

Cuquenan
Gavarnie
Hamilton
Iroquois
Kabalega

Kukenaam
Takkakaw
Victoria
Yosemite

9

Angrabies
Churchill
Invershin
Linn of Dee

10

Salto Angel
Skjeggedal
Sutherland

Wollomombi

11

Mardalsfoss
Mongefossen
Powerscourt

12 +

Caldron Snout
Eas Coul Aulin
Great Kamarang
Khone Cataracts
Pistyll Rhaeadr
Tyssestrengane

Land transport

2 & 3	BMX	FWD	rev	axle	dome
	BSA	gig	rod	Benz	drag
AA	bus	hub	van	bike	dray
AC	cab	JAP	VW	body	Fiat
AJS	cam	jet		boot	Ford
cc	car	key	**4**	bush	frog
bhp	fan	pas		cart	gear
BMW	fly	RAC	auto	coil	hack

halt	Honda	dennet	sleigh	chassis
horn	knock	dickey	snocat	Citroën
hump	lorry	diesel	stroke	cutting
jeep	Metro	dodgem	Subaru	Daimler
lock	moped	doolie	surrey	dog-cart
loco	motor	driver	Suzuki	Douglas
mini	palki	drosky	tandem	droshky
pram	pulka	dynamo	tanker	ejector
Saab	sedan	engine	tappet	exhaust
shay	servo	fiacre	tender	express
skis	shaft	filter	torque	fan belt
sled	spike	flange	tourer	Ferrari
sump	sulky	funnel	Toyota	firebox
tank	tonga	ganger	tricar	fireman
taxi	track	gasket	troika	flivver
tram	train	go-cart	Trojan	flyover
trap	trike	go-kart	tuning	foreman
tube	truck	Hansom	tunnel	gearbox
tyre	turbo	hearse	waggon	growler
wain	valve	Hiundi	weasel	hackney
	Volvo	hot-rod	whisky	hard-top
5	wagon	hub cap		hay wain
	wheel	Humber	**7**	Hillman
Alvis		hurdle		learner
araba	**6**	Indian	Amilcar	licence
Ariel		Jaguar	amtrack	Lincoln
block	Austin	jalopy	autobus	log book
bogie	banger	jaunty	autocar	mail van
brake	Bantam	jitnry	ballast	minibus
buggy	Beetle	kit car	battery	minicab
brake	Berlin	Lancia	bearing	Mustang
Buick	big end	landau	Bentley	omnibus
chain	boiler	limber	bicycle	Packard
chair	bonnet	litter	bob-sled	pannier
choke	bowser	maglev	britska	Peugeot
coach	bridge	Model T	britzka	phaeton
coupé	Brough	Morris	browser	pillion
crank	buffer	Norton	Bugatti	Porsche
crate	buffet	pedals	caboose	Pullman
cycle	bumper	piston	caleche	Raleigh
dandy	calash	points	caravan	road map
Essex	chaise	porter	cariole	road tax
float	clutch	Proton	caroche	scooter
grate	damper	saloon	cat's eye	shunter
guard	Datsun	sledge	chariot	sidecar

skidpan
sleeper
station
taxi cab
tilbury
tonneau
Trabant
trailer
tractor
trailer
tramcar
Transit
Triumph
trolley
tumbril
two-door
viaduct
voiture
whiskey
whistle

8

autobahn
barouche
bearings
brake pad
brake van
britzska
Brougham
bulkhead
cable car
cabriole
Cadillac
calliper
camshaft
carriage
carriole
catenary
clarence
corridor
coupling
crank pin
curricle
cylinder

dipstick
dustcart
flywheel
footrest
four-door
fuel pump
goods van
handcart
high ride
horse bus
horse cab
ice-yacht
ignition
injector
junction
Kawasaki
kick-down
knocking
live axle
manifold
Mercedes
monorail
motor car
motorist
motor van
motorway
old crock
open road
overtake
pavement
platform
pony cart
push-bike
radiator
reverser
rickshaw
roadster
rotor arm
runabout
selector
silencer
small end
smokebox
sociable
staff car

stanhope
steam car
steering
stock car
terminus
throttle
track rod
toboggan
tricycle
unicycle
Vauxhaul
victoria

9

air filter
ambulance
Alfa Romeo
bandwagon
bath chair
blast pipe
boat train
bobsleigh
brake shoe
britschka
bubblecar
buckboard
buffet car
cabriolet
charabanc
composite
condenser
conductor
crosshead
crossover
diligence
dining car
dipswitch
disc brake
Dormobile
drum brake
estate car
foot brake
footplate
funicular

gear lever
gear stick
generator
goods shed
goods yard
guards van
half shaft
hand brake
hatchback
landaulet
Land Rover
limousine
mail coach
milk float
monocycle
motorbike
overdrive
palanquin
piston rod
police car
prop shaft
racing car
regulator
saddlebag
saloon car
sand yacht
side valve
signal box
signalman
spark plug
sports car
street car
Tin Lizzie
T-junction
trunk road
turntable
two-seater
two-stroke
underseal
Velocette
wagonette
wheelbase
wheelspin

10

access road
alternator
Austin mini
automobile
Black Maria
boneshaker
brake fluid
buffer beam
buffer stop
broad gauge
cattle dock
conveyance
crankshaft
donkey cart
drive shaft
embankment
engine shed
fire engine
footbridge
four-in-hand
four-seater
four-stroke
glass coach
goods train
hackney cab
handlebars
hobby horse
horsepower
jinricksha
Lamborgini
Lanchester
Land Rover
locomotive
lubricator
mobile home
motor coach
motorcycle
Oldsmobile
paddywagon
pedal cycle
piston ring
post chaise
private car
rattletrap

removal van
rev counter
Rolls Royce
roundabout
roundhouse
safety belt
sedan chair
snowplough
spare wheel
speed limit
stagecoach
state coach
Studebaker
suspension
tachograph
tachometer
thermostat
tip-up lorry
trolleybus
trolley-car
two-wheeler
understeer
valve chest
velocipede
Volkswagen
wheelbrace
wheelchair
windscreen
wing mirror

11

accelerator
anti-roll bar
Aston Martin
Austin Rover
bullock cart
caravanette
carburettor
caterpillar
compression
convertible
delivery van
diesel train
distributor

driving test
four-wheeler
ground frame
gun carriage
jaunting car
jinrickshaw
landaulette
luggage rack
oil pressure
petrol gauge
quadricycle
racing cycle
safety valve
sleeping car
steam engine
steam roller
superheater
synchromesh
three-in-hand
tipper lorry
transporter
vacuum gauge
waiting room
water column
water trough
wheeltapper

12

booking clerk
coach and four
covered wagon
cylinder head
diesel engine
differential
double-decker
driving wheel
express train
freight train
furniture van
gypsy caravan
horse and cart
loading gauge
motorcyclist
motor scooter

motor vehicle
mountain bike
pantechnicon
perambulator
petrol engine
Puffing Billy
railway train
registration
single-decker
sparking plug
station wagon
supercharger
three-wheeler
ticket office
transmission
turbocharger

power steering
rack-and-pinion
restaurant car
shock absorber
shooting brake
slave cylinder
spark ignition
station master

14 +

automatic transmission
compression ignition
crown wheel and pinion
four-wheel drive
Hackney carriage
Harley Davidson
horseless carriage
independent suspension
marshalling yard
off-road vehicle
passenger train
petrol ignition
power-assisted steering
prairie schooner
revolution counter
traction engine
underground train

13

connecting rod
cooling system
electric train
fuel injection
governess cart
level crossing
overhead valve
penny-farthing

Languages and nationalities/ races

2 & 3	Giz	Kru	Shi	4	Bali
	Gur	Kui	Suk		Balt
Bat	Hun	Kwa	Tiv	Agni	Bant
Edo	Ibo	Lao	Twi	Ainu	Beja
Ewe	Ido	Luo	Vai	Akan	Bena
Fon	Ijo	Min	Wa	Ambo	Bete
Fur	Ila	Mon	Wu	Arab	Bini
Ga	Iru	Neo	Yao	Avar	Bisa
Gin	Jew	Rom		Baga	Bodo

Boer	Manx	Acoli	Gauls	Lunda	Sioux
Brit	Maya	Adeni	Gbari	Malay	Sotho
Bubi	Mede	Afars	Gipsy	Mande	Sudra
Celt	Meru	Aleut	Gissi	Maori	Suomi
Chad	Moor	Angle	Gondi	Masai	Swazi
Copt	Moxu	Anuak	Grebo	Mende	Swede
Cree	Naga	Arabs	Greek	Metis	Swiss
dago	Nama	Aryan	Griff	Mogul	Tamil
Dane	Norn	Asian	Gujar	Mossi	Tatar
Dyak	Nuba	Attic	Gumbo	Munda	Temne
Ebon	Nuer	Aztec	gypsy	Myall	Tigré
Efik	Nupe	Bamum	Hadza	Nandi	Tonga
Erse	Nyao	Bantu	Hausa	Naron	Turki
Fang	Pali	Bassa	Hindi	Negro	Tussi
Finn	Pedi	Batak	Hindu	Ngala	Tutsi
Fula	Pict	Baule	Husky	Ngoni	Uzbeg
Gael	Pole	Bemba	idiom	Nguni	Uzbek
Garo	Riff	Benga	Idoma	Nguru	Vedda
Gaul	Russ	Berta	Indic	Nisei	Venda
Ge'ez	Sard	Bhili	Inuit	Nkore	Vlach
Gogo	Scot	Black	Ionic	Norse	Welsh
Gond	Sena	Bulom	Iraqi	Nyong	Wolof
Goth	Serb	Bussi	Iraqu	Nyoro	Xhosa
Grig	Shan	Carib	Irish	Omani	Yakut
Guro	Sikh	Chaga	Kadai	Oriya	Yupik
Haya	Slav	Chewa	Kafir	Osage	Zande
Hima	Sobo	Chopi	Kamla	Oscan	
Hova	Sorb	Creek	Karen	Punic	
Hutu	Susu	Croat	Kazak	Pygmy	**6**
Igbo	Teso	Cuban	Khasi	rayah	
Impi	Thai	Cymry	Khmer	Roman	Acholi
Inca	Tswa	Czech	Kissi	Romic	Aeolic
Jute	Tupi	Dayak	Koine	Ronga	Afghan
Kelt	Turk	Dinka	Kongo	Rundi	Almain
Kroo	Urdu	Dogon	Kuo-Yu	Sabra	Alpine
Kurd	Wend	Doric	Ladin	Sakai	Altaic
Lala	Yako	Druse	Lamba	Sango	Amazon
Lapp	Yank	Dutch	Lango	Saudi	Andean
Lari	Zend	Dyold	Latin	Saxon	Angoni
Lett	Zulu	Dyula	Lenge	Scots	Apache
Loma	Zuni	Fante	limey	Shilh	Arabic
Lozi		Fanti	lingo	Shona	Arawak
Luba	**5**	Frank	Lomwe	Sican	Argive
Mali		Galla	lubra	Sikel	Ascian
Mano	Abuna	Ganda	Lulua	Sinic	Aussie
					Aymara

Bakota	Hamite	Nordic	Sindhi	Angevin
Balega	Hebrew	Norman	Slavic	Angolan
Baltic	Herero	Novial	Slovak	Arabian
Baoule	Ibibio	Nsenga	Somali	Aramaic
Basque	Indian	Nubian	Soviet	Aramean
Basuto	Inupik	Nyanja	Sukuma	Armoric
Bateke	Ionian	Ojibwa	Syriac	Ashanti
Bayaka	Italic	Ostman	Syrian	Asiatic
Belgae	Jewess	Ostyak	Telegu	Avestan
Berber	Jewish	Paduan	Telugu	Avestic
Bihari	Judaic	Pahari	Teuton	Baganda
Bokmal	Kabyle	Pakeha	Theban	Bagirmi
Brahui	Kaffir	Papuan	Thonga	Bakweii
Breton	Kanuri	Pariah	Tlokwa	Balanta
Briton	Kenyan	Parian	Tongan	Balochi
Bulgar	Kikuyu	Parsee	tongue	Bambara
Cantii	Korean	Pathan	Trojan	Bangala
Canuck	Kpelle	patois	Tsonga	Bapende
Celtic	Kpessi	Pawnee	Tswana	Barotse
Chagga	Kpwesi	Persic	Tuareg	Barundi
Chokwe	Kurukh	pidgin	Tungus	Basonge
Coptic	Ladino	Pueblo	Turkic	Batonka
Creole	Levite	Polish	Tuscan	Batutsi
Cretan	Libyan	Pushto	Tyrian	Bedouin
Cymric	Lumbwa	Pushtu	Ugrian	Belgian
Danish	Luvale	Rajput	Vaisya	Bengali
Dorian	Lydian	Rolong	Vandal	Berbers
Eskimo	Magyar	Romaic	Veddah	Bisayan
Fijian	Manchu	Romany	Viking	British
Franks	Median	Rwanda	Votyak	Brython
French	Mestee	Ryukyu	Warega	Bunduka
Fulani	Micmac	Sabine	Yankee	Burmese
Gadhel	Minoan	Salian	Yemeni	Bushman
Gaelic	Mohawk	Sambaa	Yoruba	Cairene
Gallic	Mongol	Samian	Zenaga	Catalan
Gascon	Murozi	Samiot	Zouave	Chaldee
Gentoo	native	Samoan		Chechen
German	Navaho	Saxons	**7**	Chilean
Gitana	Navajo	Scotch		Chinese
Gitano	Ndonga	Semite	Acadian	Chinook
Gothic	Nepali	Seneca	Achaean	Choctaw
Grikwa	Nesiot	Senufo	Aeolian	Cockney
Griqua	Ngbaka	Sérère	African	Cornish
Gullah	Ngombe	Shelta	Amerind	Cypriot
Gurkha	Ngwato	Sherpa	Amharic	Dagomba

Dalicad	Lugbara	Ruthene	Zantiot	Deerfoot
dialect	Maduran	Rwandan	zingaro	Delphian
Dorians	Malayan	Samburu		Devonian
English	Malinke	Samiote	**8**	dog Latin
Finnish	Maltese	Samnite		Dutchman
Fleming	Mandyak	Samoyed	Abderite	Egyptian
Flemish	Mantuan	Sandawe	Akkadian	Ephesian
Frisian	Manxman	Santali	Albanian	Estonian
Gambian	Marathi	Saracen	Algerian	Ethiopic
Gaulish	Mashona	Semitic	Algerine	Etruscan
Genoese	Mestizo	Senussi	Alsatian	Eurasian
Grecian	Mexican	Serbian	American	European
Griquas	Moabite	Shawnee	Andorran	Fanariot
Guarani	Mohican	Shilluk	Antiguan	Filipino
Haitian	Mongols	Siamese	Armenian	Frankish
Harijan	Moorish	Sienese	Assamese	Gadhelic
Hamitic	Mordvin	Slovene	Assyrian	Galilean
Hebraic	Morisco	Songhai	Athenian	Gallican
Hellene	Mozareb	Sorbian	Austrian	Georgian
Hessian	Mulatto	Spanish	Balinese	Germanic
Hittite	Nahuatl	Spartan	Batavian	Ghanaian
Iberian	Namaqua	Swahili	Bavarian	Guernsey
Ilocano	Nauruan	Swedish	Bergdama	Gujariti
Iranian	Ndebele	Switzer	Bermudan	Guyanese
Ishmael	Negress	Tagalog	Biscayan	Hawaiian
Ismaili	Ngbandi	Tartars	Boeotian	Hellenic
Israeli	Nilotes	Tibetan	Bohemian	Helvetic
Italian	Nilotic	Tigrina	Bolivian	Hittites
Judaean	Nynorsk	Tsigane	Bulgaric	Honduran
Kalmuck	Osmanli	Turkana	Bushongo	Illyrian
Kannada	Ottoman	Turkish	Cambrian	indigene
Karanga	Pahlavi	Ugandan	Canadian	Irishman
Kennick	Palaung	Umbrian	Cathayan	Iroquois
Khoisan	Paphian	Umbubdu	Chaldaic	islander
Kirghiz	Pehlevi	Valapuk	Chaldean	Jamaican
Kurdish	Persian	Vandals	Chamarro	Japanese
Kuwaiti	Prakrit	Vaudois	Cherokee	Javanese
Laotian	Punjabi	Veddoid	clansman	Jugoslav
Laotien	Pythian	Venetic	Congoese	Kanarese
Lappish	Quashee	Walloon	Corsican	Kashmiri
Latvian	Quechua	Watutsi	Cossacks	Kimbundu
Lettish	redskin	Wendish	Cumbrian	Kingwana
Lingala	Riffian	Yiddish	Cushitic	Kipsigis
Llanero	Romance	Zaïrese	Cyreniac	Kolarian
Lombard	Russian	Zambian	Dalesman	Kuki-Chin

Kukuruku	Polabian		Hanseatic
Kwanyama	Polonian	**9**	Hebridian
language	Prussian		Hesperian
Lebanese	Pyrenean	Abkhasian	Hibernian
Levanter	Rabbinic	aborigine	High Dutch
Liberian	Romanian	Afrikaans	Himyarite
Londoner	Romansch	Afrikaner	Hollander
Low Latin	Rumanian	Afro-Asian	Hottentot
Maeonian	Sanskrit	Algonquin	Hungarian
Mahratta	Savoyard	Anatolian	Icelander
Makassar	Scandian	Argentine	Icelandic
Malagash	Scotsman	Armorican	Israelite
Malagasy	Scottish	Atrebates	Jordanian
Malawian	Scythian	Barbadian	Kabardian
Mameluco	Seminole	Bengalese	Kannarese
Mamprusi	shagroon	Bratoslav	Kgalagedi
Mandaean	Sicilian	Barbadian	Landsmaal
Mandarin	Silesian	Bergamask	langue d'oc
Mandingo	Slavonic	Blackfoot	Laplander
Mandinka	Spaniard	Brazilian	Late Latin
Matabele	Spartans	Brigantes	Longobard
Memphian	Sudanese	Britisher	Low German
Milesian	Sumerian	Bulgarian	lowlander
Moravian	Sybarite	Byzantine	Malayalam
Moroccan	Tahitian	Cambodian	Malaysian
Moru-Madi	Tallensi	Cantonese	Manxwoman
national	Teucrian	Caribbean	Mauritian
Nazarene	Teutonic	Castilian	Mongolian
Neo-Latin	Tunisian	Caucasian	Mongoloid
Nepalese	Turanian	Ceylonese	Muscovite
Nigerian	Turkoman	Char-Nile	Nabataean
Norseman	Tyrolean	Cheremiss	Nepaulese
Nuba-Fula	Tyrolese	Cimmerian	New Yorker
Nyamwesi	Tyrrhene	Colombian	Norwegian
Old Norse	Ukranian	Congolese	Ostrogoth
Old Saxon	Vandalic	Damascene	Pakistani
Orcadian	Venetian	Dravidian	Parthians
Oriental	Viennese	Easterner	Pekingese
paleface	Visigoth	Englander	Periscian
Parisian	Volscian	Esperanto	plainsman
Parthian	Warragal	Esquimaux	Provencal
Pekinese	Welshman	Ethiopian	Red Indian
Pelasgic	Yugoslav	Finlander	Rhodesian
Peruvian		Frenchman	Roumanian
Phrygian		Galwegian	Ruthenian
		Grenadian	

Sabellian
Samaritan
Sardinian
Sassenach
Scotchman
Sere Mundu
Sinhalese
Slavonian
Slovenian
Springbok
Sri Lankan
Stagirite
Sundanese
Taiwanese
Tangerine
Tanzanian
Tasmanian
Tocharian
tribesman
Ukrainian
Ulotrichi
Ulsterman
Uruguayan
Varangian
Westerner
West Saxon
Zanzibari

10

aboriginal
Abyssinian
Afrikander
Algonquian
Amerindian
Andalusian
Anglo-Saxon
Australian
Autochthon
Babylonian
Bathlaping
Caledonian
Circassian
clanswoman
Cornishman

Costa Rican
countryman
Devanagari
East Indian
Ecuadorian
Englishman
Eurafrican
Finno-Ugric
Florentine
Glaswegian
Guatemalan
Hanoverian
High German
Highlander
Hindustani
Hottentots
Indonesian
Irishwoman
Ishmaelite
Israelitic
journalese
Karamojong
langue d'oil
Lithuanian
mainlander
Melanesian
Mingrelian
Monegasque
Neapolitan
Nicaraguan
Nicobarese
Niger-Congo
Northerner
Occidental
Old English
Ostrogoths
Panamanian
Paraguayan
Parisienne
Patagonian
Philippine
Philistine
Phillipian
Phoenician
Polynesian

Pomeranian
Portuguese
Rajasthani
Scillonian
Scotswoman
Senegalese
Serbo-Croat
Shetlander
Singhalese
Southerner
Thailander
townswoman
tramontane
Tridentine
Tyrrhenian
Venezuelan
vernacular
Vietnamese
Welshwoman
West Indian
woodlander
Zimbabwean

11

Afro-Asiatic
Anglo-Indian
Argentinian
Azerbaijani
Bangarwanda
Bangladeshi
Belorussian
continental
Frenchwoman
Greenlander
Indo-Hittite
Indo-Iranian
Lancastrian
marshlander
Mauretanian
Micronesian
Middle Latin
Modern Latin
Old Prussian
pakeha Maori

Palestinian
Scots Gaelic
Sino-Tibetan
transmontane
tribeswoman
Trinidadian
Ulsterwoman
Westphalian
Yugoslavian

12

Afro-American
Australasian
basic English
Byelorussian
Cornishwoman
countrywoman
Czechoslovak
dead language
Englishwoman
Eiro-American
frontiersman
Gibraltarian
Indo-European
King's English
lingua franca
Lunda-Bajokwe
Moru-Mangbetu
mother tongue
Netherlander
New Englander
New Zealander
Norman French
Northumbrian
Plattdeutsch
Pre-Dravidian
Saudi-Arabian
Scandinavian
Tibeto-Burman
Yorkshireman

13

Anglo-American

Knickerbocker
Oxford English
Peloponnesian
Philadelphian
pidgin English
Queen's English

Rhaeto-Romanic
Serbo-Croatian

14

American Indian
French Canadian

15

Czechoslovakian
North Countryman
received English
standard English

Male and female animals

Male animals

3

cob (swan)
dog (coyote, dog, wolf)
fox (fox)
ram (impala, sheep)
tom (bobcat, cat, cougar)
tup (sheep)

4

boar (badger, bear, pig,
  weasel)
buck (antelope, hare,
  kangaroo, rabbit, rat)
bull (buffalo, camel,
  cattle, eland, elephant,
  giraffe, hartebeest,
  moose, oxen, rhinoceros,
  seal, walrus, whale)
cock (birds, crab, fish,
  lobster)
jack (ass, donkey, ferret)
lion (lion)
sire (dog, horse)
stag (caribou, deer,
  turkey)

5

billy (goat)
drake (duck)
steer (cattle, oxen)
tiger (tiger)

6

gander (goose)

7

bullock (cattle, oxen)
jackass (ass, donkey)
leopard (leopard)
peacock (peafowl)

8

stallion (horse, zebra)

9

billygoat (goat)

Female animals

3

dam (dog, horse)

doe (antelope, caribou,
  deer, ferret, hare,
  kangaroo, rabbit, rat)

cow (buffalo, camel, cattle,
  eland, elephant, giraffe,
  hartebeest, moose, oxen,
  rhinoceros, seal, walrus,
  weasel, whale)
ewe (impala, sheep)
hen (birds, crab, fish,
  lobster)
pen (swan)
sow (badger, bear, pig)

4

duck (duck)
gill (ferret)
hind (deer)
jill (ferret)

5

bitch (coyote, dog, wolf)
brach (hunting dog)

goose (goose)
jenny (ass, donkey)
nanny (goat)
queen (cat)
reeve (ruff, sandpiper)
vixen (fox)

6

peahen (peafowl)

7

lioness (bobcat, cougar, lion)
tigress (tiger)

9

nannygoat (goat)

10

leopardess (leopard)

Mammals
(including whales, sealions, etc.)

2 & 3	ox	hart	puma	5	fossa
	pig	hind	saki		gayal
ape	rat	ibex	seal	addax	genet
ai	tod	joey	stag	bison	goral
bat	yak	kudu	tahr	bongo	hippo
cat		lion	tehr	camel	horse
doe	**4**	lynx	thar	civet	hyena
dog		mink	titi	coati	hyrax
elk	bear	mole	unua	coney	izard
fox	boar	mona	ursa	coypu	kiang
gam	buck	musk	vole	daman	koala
gnu	bull	oont	wolf	dhole	kulan
hob	cony	oryx	zebu	dingo	lemur
hog	deer	paca		drill	liger
kob	gaur	pard		eland	llama
orc	hare	pika		fitch	loris

moose	coluga	red fox	fur seal	sirenia
mouse	cougar	reebok	gazelle	sun bear
okapi	coyote	rhesus	gemsbok	tamarin
orang	cuscus	rodent	giraffe	tarsier
otter	dassie	sambar	glutton	tigress
ounce	desman	sambur	gorilla	vampire
panda	dik-dik	sea cow	grampus	vulpine
pi-dog	dog fox	serval	grey fox	wallaby
pongo	du gong	simian	grysbok	warthog
potto	duiker	tarpan	guanaco	water ox
rasse	duyker	teledu	guereza	wild ass
ratel	ermine	tenrec	hunuman	wild cat
rhino	feline	ursine	keitloa	wood rat
sable	fennec	vermin	lemming	
saiga	ferret	vervet	leonine	**8**
sasin	fox bat	vicuna	leopard	
serow	gibbon	walrus	leveret	aardvark
shrew	gopher	wapiti	linsang	aardwolf
skunk	grison	weasel	lioness	anteater
sloth	grivet	wild ox	macaque	antelope
stoat	guenon	wombat	manatee	babirusa
takin	howler		markhor	bactrian
tapir	hyaena	**7**	meerkat	black rat
tiger	impala		mole rat	blue buck
whale	jackal	ant bear	mouflon	brown rat
zebra	jaguar	bear cat	muntjac	bushbaby
zibet	jerboa	blaubok	muskrat	bush buck
	kit fox	blesbol	mustang	bontebok
6	koodoo	blue fox	narwhal	boschbok
	langur	brocket	opossum	burramys
agouti	lupine	buffalo	pack rat	cachalot
alpaca	margay	bushpig	panther	capuchin
angora	marmot	caracal	peccary	capybara
aoudad	marten	caribou	polecat	carcajou
argali	monkey	cervine	primate	chigetai
aye-aye	musk ox	cetacea	pricket	chipmunk
baboon	nilgai	chamois	raccoon	civet cat
badger	numbat	cheetah	red deer	dormouse
baleen	ocelot	colobus	roebuck	duckbill
beaver	possum	dolphin	roe deer	edentate
beluga	pie-dog	echidna	rorqual	elephant
bharal	pye-dog	finback	sapajou	fin whale
burhel	quagga	fitchet	sea calf	fruit bat
bobcat	rabbit	fitchen	sea-lion	grey wolf
chacma	racoon	foumart	siamang	harp seal

hedgehog
hedgepig
humpback
Irish elk
kangaroo
kinkajou
kolinsky
leoparine
mandrill
mangabey
markhoor
marmoset
mongoose
monk seal
moufflon
mule deer
musquash
omnivore
pangolin
pinniped
platypus
porpoise
predator
reindeer
sea otter
sei whale
serotine
squirrel
steinbok
swift fox
tamandua
ungulate
viscacha
wanderoo
water rat
wharf rat
whistler
white fox
wild boar
wild goat

9

arctic fox
armadillo

bandicoot
binturong
black bear
black buck
blacktail
blue whale
brown bear
carnivore
catamount
chickaree
deer mouse
desert rat
dromedary
dziggetai
flying fox
groundhog
herbivore
hog badger
honey bear
ichneumon
koala bear
March hare
marsupial
menagerie
monotreme
mouldwarp
mouse deer
orang-utan
pachyderm
palm civet
pariah dog
phalanger
polar bear
porcupine
pronghorn
quadruped
razorback
scavenger
shrew mole
silver fox
sloth bear
swamp hare
springbok
tree shrew
waterbuck

water vole
white bear
wolverine
woodchuck
youngling

10

angwantibo
Barbary ape
black whale
bottlenose
camelopard
chevrotain
chimpanzee
cottontail
desert lynx
fallow deer
field mouse
giant panda
hartebeest
honey mouse
hooded seal
jackrabbit
jaguarundi
Kodiak bear
leopardess
mona monkey
native bear
ottershrew
pantheress
pine marten
pouched rat
prairie dog
raccoon dog
rhinoceros
right whale
river horse
saki monkey
shrewmouse
sperm whale
spring buck
spring hare
timber wolf
vampire bat

vertebrate
white whale
wildebeest

11

Cape buffalo
barking deer
douroucouli
flying lemur
grizzly bear
ground sloth
honey badger
honey sucker
horned horse
kangaroo rat
killer whale
mountain cat
orang-outang
pipistrelle
plantigrade
pocket mouse
prairie wolf
red squirrel
sea elephant
snow leopard
stone marten
swamp rabbit
white ermine
wishtonwish

12

bonnet monkey
Cashmere goat
cinnamon bear
elephant seal
ferret badger
goat antelope
grampus whale
grey squirrel
harvest mouse
hippopotamus
horse-shoe bat
howler monkey

jumping mouse
klipspringer
mountain goat
mountain lion
pocket gopher
rhesus monkey
snowshoe hare
spider monkey
tree kangaroo
ursine monkey
Virginia deer
water buffalo
woolly monkey

giant anteater
man of the woods
rogue elephant
scaly anteater
spiny anteater
star-nosed mole
Tasmanian wolf

snowshoe rabbit
spectacled bear
Tasmanian devil

15 +

African elephant
Chinese water deer
duck-billed platypus
mountain viscacha
mountain chinchilla
prairie squirrel
Przewalski's horse
proboscis monkey
pygmy hippopotamus
Thomson's gazelle
white rhinoceros

13

Chapman's zebra

14

banded anteater
flying squirrel
ground squirrel
Indian elephant
New World monkey
Old World monkey
Père David's deer

Measurements and units

2	nm	rad	hide	yard	lumen
	ns	rod	hour		*metre
cg	oz	ton	inch	**5**	minim
cm	yd	tun	kilo		neper
dl			knot	cable	ounce
dm			link	carat	perch
dr	**3**	**4**	mile	chain	point
el			mole	cubit	poise
em	amp	acre	nail	curie	pound
en	are	bale	peck	cusec	quart
ft	bit	barn	phon	farad	quire
gr	BTU	bolt	phot	fermi	stere
hl	cal	byte	pica	gerah	stone
in	cwt	cord	pint	guage	tesla
kg	dal	cran	pole	grain	therm
km	dam	dram	ream	gross	tithe
lb	dwt	dyne	rood	gauss	tonne
mg	ell	feet	slug	grain	weber
mi	erg	foot	span	henry	
mm	lux	gill	torr	hertz	**6**
mt	mho	gram	troy	joule	
MV	mil	gray	volt	karat	ampère
MW	nit	hand	watt	*litre	bushel
	ohm	hank			

candle
cental
cupful
decare
degree
denier
drachm
fathom
firkin
gallon
gramme
kelvin
league
megohm
micron
minute
net ton
newton
octane
parsec
pascal
radian
second
shekel
stokes

gilbert
hectare
kiloton
lambert
long ton
maxwell
megabit
megaton
oersted
poundal
quarter
quintal
röntgen
scruple
sea mile
siemens
sievert
tonnage

7

Calorie
calorie
candela
coulomb
decibel
dioptre
diopter
faraday
furlong

8

angstrom
chaldron
imperial
kilobyte
kilogram
kilovolt
kilowatt
megabyte
megavolt
megawatt
millibar
roentgen
short ton
spoonful
watt-hour

9

becquerel
board foot
centigram
cubic foot
cubic inch
cubic yard
decalitre
decimetre
foot-pound
hectogram
kilocycle
kilohertz
light-year
megacycle
metric ton
microgram
milligram
nanometre
ounce troy
pound troy
steradium
troy ounce
troy pound

10

barleycorn
centilitre
centimetre
cubic metre
fluid ounce
freight ton
hectolitre
hectometre
horsepower

kilogramme
microfarad
millilitre
millimetre
nanosecond
rutherford
square acre
square foot
square inch
square mile
square yard

11

avoirdupois
gram calorie
hectogramme
kilocalorie
metric tonne
microsecond
milligramme
millimicron
millisecond
pennyweight
register ton
shipping ton

12 +

displacement ton
hundredweight
kilogramme calorie
kilowatt-hour
measurement ton
nautical mile
ounce apothecaries
short
   hundredweight
square kilometre

*(*The spelling of **litre** and **metre** is **liter** and **meter** in America and should be taken into consideration when using a word with these elements.)*

Medical terms

2	TPR	oral	D and C	shunt	ataxia
	TSH	otic	death	sleep	autism
id	wax	ovum	donor	sling	barium
IQ	wen	pain	enema	spasm	bedpan
ME		pica	ether	spore	benign
MS		pill	faint	sprue	biopsy
TB	**4**	pulp	fever	stoma	bougie
VD		rest	fibre	stone	bruise
	ache	rash	fluke	stria	bunion
3	acid	scab	flush	swoon	by-pass
	acne	scar	focus	sweat	callus
AID	agar	sore	fugue	taste	cancer
AIH	ague	stye	graft	taxis	caries
ALS	AIDS	swab	gripe	tests	chorea
bug	aura	weal	hives	tinea	climax
cap	bile	wind	ileus	tonic	clinic
CAT	bite	X-ray	laser	tonus	coccus
CPR	boil	yaws	leech	toxin	coitus
ECT	bubo		locum	truss	comedo
ECG	burn		lupus	twins	condom
EEG	cast	**5**	mania	ulcer	coryza
ego	case		moron	urine	costal
ENT	clot	acute	mucus	venom	cowpox
ESP	coil	angst	mumps	virus	crisis
fit	cold	assay	myope	worms	crutch
flu	coma	ataxy	nurse	wound	dengue
FSH	corn	atopy	opium		distal
HRT	cure	aural	palsy		doctor
ion	cyst	bends	phial	**6**	dorsal
IUD	diet	birth	piles		douche
NMR	dose	blood	polio	albino	dropsy
NSU	drip	brace	polyp	alexia	eczema
PKU	drug	bulla	pulse	alkali	elixir
PMS	duct	bursa	renal	amnion	emesis
PMT	dumb	chill	rheum	amoeba	emetic
pox	germ	chyle	rigor	angina	enamel
pus	gout	chyme	scald	anoxia	energy
REM	heal	clone	scurf	anuria	eunuch
sex	host	colic	sebum	apathy	fascia
STD	iron	cough	serum	apnoea	favism
tic	lint	cramp	shock	asthma	fester
	mole	croup		asylum	

fibrin	otitis	trauma	bubonic	flutter
flatus	oxygen	tremor	bulimia	forceps
fungus	period	trepan	cadaver	glasses
fusion	phenol	tumour	caesium	gumboil
gargle	phlegm	typhus	caliper	grommet
gluten	phobia	unwell	cannula	hare lip
goitre	physic	vector	capsule	healing
grippe	pimple	zygote	cardiac	healthy
growth	plague		carrier	hearing
healer	plaque	**7**	CAT scan	hormone
health	poison		catarrh	hospice
hernia	pollen	abscess	cautery	hygeine
heroin	potion	acetone	chancre	icterus
herpes	powder	acidity	chiasma	inquest
hiccup	psyche	adenoma	choking	insulin
hunger	Q fever	adipose	cholera	invalid
incest	quinsy	agnosia	choline	in vitro
infirm	rabies	ailment	chorion	itching
injury	radium	allergy	chronic	keratin
intern	reflex	amalgam	cocaine	lanolin
iodine	remedy	amentia	colitis	lozenge
iritis	saline	anatomy	colloid	leprosy
jet lag	saliva	ammonia	complex	linctus
kaolin	scurvy	amnesia	coroner	lockjaw
labour	senses	anaemia	culture	lumbago
lanugo	sepsis	angioma	cupping	malaise
laxity	sheath	anodyne	curette	malaria
lesion	sister	anosmia	dentine	massage
libido	splint	antacid	dentist	measles
lipoma	sprain	anthrax	dietary	meiosis
lochia	sputum	antigen	dioptre	melaena
lumbar	squint	anxiety	disease	melasma
lunacy	stapes	aphasia	embolus	microbe
malady	stitch	aphonia	emotion	midwife
matron	strain	asepsis	empyema	mitosis
medium	stress	aspirin	endemic	mixture
megrim	stroke	atrophy	ethanol	morphia
memory	stupor	autopsy	eupepsy	myalgia
murmur	tablet	balance	exudate	mycosis
mutism	tetany	bandage	fatigue	neonate
myopia	thrush	bedsore	fibroid	nostrum
naevus	tissue	blister	filling	obesity
nausea	torpor	booster	fissure	oculist
oedema	toxoid	boracic	fistula	oestrus
opiate	trance	bow legs	flexion	operate

organic	symptom	apoplexy	cyanosis	flooding
osmosis	syncope	Asian flu	cystitis	fluoride
panacea	syringe	asphyxia	dandruff	focusing
Pap test	systole	atheroma	deaf-mute	formalin
paresis	talipes	atropine	deafness	fracture
patient	tension	bacillus	debility	freckles
peptide	tetanus	backache	deformed	furuncle
persona	theatre	bacteria	delirium	ganglion
pessary	the Pill	baldness	delivery	gangrene
pink eye	torsion	beriberi	delusion	genetics
placebo	toxemia	bifocals	dementia	genotype
plaster	typhoid	bioassay	dentures	glaucoma
posture	urology	black eye	diabetes	grand mal
potency	vaccine	blackout	diagnose	handicap
puberty	variola	bleeding	dialysis	hangnail
purpura	ventral	blue baby	diastole	hangover
pustule	verruca	blushing	diplopia	hay fever
pyrexia	vertigo	botulism	diuretic	headache
quinine	vesicle	bursitis	dreaming	heat bump
recover	viscera	caduceus	dressing	heat rash
regimen	vitamin	caffeine	drowning	heredity
relapse	wasting	calamine	dwarfism	hospital
rickets	weaning	calculus	dyslexia	hot flush
rosacea	whitlow	calliper	dyspnoea	hygienic
roseola	wry neck	carotene	efferent	hypnosis
rubella	yawning	cataract	effusion	hysteria
rubeola		catheter	embolism	illusion
rupture	**8**	cephalic	epidemic	immunity
sarcoma		chloasma	epidural	impacted
scabies	ablation	chlorine	epilepsy	impetigo
section	abortion	cicatrix	erection	incision
seizure	abrasion	claw foot	ergotism	inflamed
sibling	acidosis	claw hand	eruption	infusion
sick bay	adenitis	clinical	erythema	inhalant
snoring	adhesion	clotting	etiology	insanity
spastic	alkaloid	clubbing	eugenics	insomnia
sterile	allergen	club foot	euphoria	instinct
styptic	alopecia	coenzyme	exanthem	intersex
stutter	analysis	cold sore	excision	irritant
stammer	androgen	collapse	face lift	jaundice
suicide	aneurysm	coloboma	fainting	kala-azar
sunburn	anorexia	compound	filament	knee-jerk
surgeon	antibody	cortisol	first aid	kyphosis
surgery	antidote	crepitus	fixation	lameness
sutures	aperient	cross-eye	flat foot	laudanum

laxative
lecithin
lethargy
ligature
liniment
lobotomy
lordosis
marasmus
mastitis
medicine
melanoma
menarche
methanol
migraine
moribund
morphine
mutation
myelitis
narcotic
necrosis
neoplasm
neuritis
neurosis
nicotine
nocturia
occlusal
ointment
oncology
optician
orchitis
osteitis
otoscope
pandemic
paranoia
parasite
parietal
paroxysm
pathogen
pellagra
petit mal
phimosis
pleurisy
polyuria
poultice
priapism

prolapse
proximal
pruritus
reaction
recovery
relaxant
rest-cure
rhinitis
ringworm

sanitary
scanning
schizoid
sciatica
sedation
sedative
senility
shingles
sickness
skin test
smallpox
sneezing
speculum
stenosis
steroids
stitches
superego
surgical
swelling
syndrome
syphilis
systemic
tapeworm
teething
terminal
test meal
thrombin
thrombus
tincture
tinnitus
toxaemia
traction
vagotomy
virilism
virology
virulent

vitiligo
vomiting
vulvitis
wheezing
xanthoma
zoonosis

9

achalasia
acidaemia
addiction
adrenalin
aetiology
alkalosis
alleviate
allopathy
amino acid
anabolism
anaerobic
analgesia
analgesic
anamnesis
androgyny
angiogram
angiology
ankylosis
anorectic
antenatal
antiserum
antitoxin
antivenin
antivenom
arthritis
aspirator
autoclave
autograft
autolysis
bacterium
bad breath
bedridden
birth rate
birthmark
blackhead
bland diet

blindness
blind spot
blood bank
blood clot
blood test
body odour
bone graft
breathing
Caesarean
carbuncle
carcinoma
catalepsy
catharsis
cathartic
causalgia
cauterise
chalazion
chancroid
chilblain
chiropody
Chlamydia
cirrhosis
cognition
colostomy
colostrum
commensal
contagion
contusion
cordotomy
cortisone
crab louse
cretinism
curvature
cytopenia
deformity
dentition
diagnosis
diaphragm
diarrhoea
diathermy
dietician
dietetics
digestion
digitalis
disinfect

dislocate
dizziness
drug abuse
dysentery
dyspepsia
dystrophy
echovirus
eclampsia
ectomorph
emollient
emphysema
endomorph
endoscope
enteritis
epileptic
epistaxis
excretion
extension
extrovert
eyestrain
fatty acid
fertility
fetishism
fever sore
focussing
folic acid
frigidity
frost bite
fulminant
gallstone
gastritis
germicide
gestation
gigantism
glossitis
haematoma
halitosis
hammertoe
heartbeat
heartburn
heart rate
hepatitis
herbalism
hirsutism
histamine

histology	occipital	roundworm	antisepsis
hunchback	occlusion	sclerosis	Apgar score
hydrocele	olfactory	scoliosis	apoplectic
hypnotism	open-heart	screening	apothecary
ileostomy	operation	serotonin	arrhythmia
impotence	osteology	sex change	asbestosis
incidence	osteopath	shivering	ascariasis
incubator	ovulation	silicosis	aspiration
induction	pacemaker	sinusitis	astringent
infection	palpation	skin graft	automatism
infirmary	papilloma	smear test	barium meal
influenza	paralysis	sterility	barotrauma
injection	paramedic	stimulant	BCG vaccine
inoculate	parotitis	stretcher	bed wetting
intellect	patch test	stricture	Bell's palsy
introvert	pathology	sunstroke	bionic limb
ischaemia	pemphigus	surrogate	Black Death
isolation	perfusion	symbiosis	blood cells
keratitis	perinatal	synergism	blood count
knock knee	pertussis	synovitis	blood donor
lactation	phenotype	teratogen	blood group
lassitude	phlebitis	toothache	brain death
leukaemia	physician	treatment	brainwaves
lithotomy	pneumonia	umbilicus	bronchiole
magnesium	poisoning	urine test	bronchitis
malignant	polygraph	urticaria	canker sore
masochism	pompholyx	vaginitis	carcinogen
medicinal	porphyria	varicella	cardiogram
menopause	precocity	vasectomy	cardiology
mesomorph	pregnancy	wrist drop	castration
metophase	prodromal	xeroderma	catabolism
methadone	prognosis		cellulitis
microtome	protazoan	**10**	chickenpox
mongolism	psoriasis		childbirth
myxoedema	psychosis	abreaction	chloroform
myxovirus	psychotic	acromegaly	colposcopy
nephritis	pulmonary	adenovirus	common cold
nephrosis	purgative	afterbirth	compulsion
neuralgia	pyelogram	alcoholism	conception
neurology	radiology	alkalaemia	concretion
nosebleed	reduction	amoebiasis	concussion
novocaine	rejection	amputation	congenital
nutrition	remission	antibiotic	congestion
nystagmus	retractor	antiseptic	consultant
obsession	rheumatic	antiemetic	contrecoup

conversion
convulsion
coprolalia
cystic duct
dependence
depilatory
depressant
depression
dermatitis
diphtheria
dipsomania
dispensary
dissection
DPT vaccine
ecchymosis
emaciation
embryology
episiotomy
euthanasia
exhaustion
extradural
eyeglasses
fallen arch
false teeth
fibrositis
filariasis
filtration
flatulence
geriatrics
gingivitis
glomerulus
gonorrhoea
grey matter
haematuria
haemolysis
hearing aid
heart block
heatstroke
hemiplegia
hypodermic
hypophysis
idiopathic
imbecility
immunology
inbreeding

infarction
inhalation
inhibition
insanitary
insanity
interferon
irrigation
kiss of life
lactic acid
laparotomy
laryngitis
Lassa fever
leucopenia
lightening
lung cancer
masectomy
meditation
meningitis
metabolism
microscope
moniliasis
mouth ulcer
narcissism
narcolepsy
nephrology
nerve block
nerve fibre
nettle rash
nucleotide
nyctalopia
obstetrics
ophthalmia
ornithosis
osteopathy
palliative
paraplegia
penicillin
perception
percussion
pharmacist
phrenology
physiology
post mortem
presbyopia
proctology
prokaryote

prostheses
prosthesis
psychiatry
psychology
peurperium
quarantine
quickening
relaxation
renal colic
repression
respirator
rheumatism
safe period
Salmonella
sanatorium
sanitation
scar tissue
seborrhoea
shell shock
sonography
spectacles
staff nurse
stomatitis
strabismus
subliminal
suggestion
swallowing
threadworm
thrombosis
tissue bank
tomography
tooth decay
tourniquet
toxicology
tracheitis
transplant
trench foot
trepanning
tryptophan
ulceration
ultrasound
urethritis
varicocele
withdrawal
xenophobia

11

acupuncture
adolescence
agoraphobia
air embolism
air sickness
albuminuria
amenorrhoea
amphetamine
anaesthesia
anaesthetic
anaphylaxis
anastomosis
anencephaly
anthracosis
antipyretic
antitussive
arteriogram
arthrodesis
astigmatism
ausculation
bacteraemia
barbiturate
barium enema
beta-blocker
biofeedback
bisexuality
blepharitis
borborygmus
bradycardia
breech birth
brucellosis
candidiasis
car sickness
carminative
cauterizing
charge nurse
cholesterol
choroiditis
chylomicron
circulation
cleft palate
climacteric
coagulation

coarctation
cold abscess
consumption
contact lens
contracture
corn plaster
crepitation
cryosurgery
cryotherapy
day hospital
dehydration
denervation
dental brace
dermatology
dislocation
drunkenness
dysfunction
ejaculation
electrolyte
embrocation
equilibrium
expectorant
farmer's lung
fibre-optics
fluoroscope
fomentation
food allergy
fulguration
gall bladder
genetic code
gerontology
gynaecology
habituation
haemophilia
haemorrhage
heart attack
heart murmur
homeostasis
homoeopathy
hydatid cyst
hydrophobia
hyperemesis
hyperplasia
hypertrophy
hypotension

hypothermia
indigestion
infantilism
infestation
infertility
inheritance
inkblot test
inoculation
intravenous
irradiation
kidney stone
kleptomania
kwashiorkor
lacrimation
laparoscopy
laughing gas
litholapaxy
locum tenens
malingering
malpractice
mammography
mammoplasty
mastication
melancholia
meningocele
menorrhagia
micturition
miscarriage
mustard bath
myelography
naturopathy
ovarian cyst
oxygenation
palpitation
paracetamol
paratyphoid
parturition
pediculosis
peptic ulcer
perforation
peristalsis
peritonitis
phantom limb
pharyngitis
photophobia

plantar wart
polypeptide
potentation
prickly heat
prosthetics
proteinuria
psittacosis
psychopathy
radiography
respiration
retardation
rhinoplasty
salpingitis
sea sickness
septicaemia
side-effects
slipped disc
spina bifida
spirochaete
spondylitis
spondylosis
stethoscope
stomach pump
sublimation
suffocation
sulpha drugs
suppository
suppression
suppuration
tachycardia
temperature
tennis elbow
thermometer
tonsillitis
torticollis
tracheotomy
transfusion
trans-sexual
trench fever
trichinosis
unconscious
vaccination
vasodilator
venereology
ventilation

visual field
X-chromosome
Y-chromosome
yellow fever

12

abortus fever
accouchement
acrocyanosis
anthelmintic
anthropology
antinauseant
antipruritic
aphrodisiacs
appendectomy
appendicitis
apperception
arthroplasty
articulation
athlete's foot
autoantibody
bacteriology
behaviourism
bilharziasis
biliary colic
biochemistry
biomechanics
birth control
blood alcohol
breast cancer
bromhidrosis
bronchoscopy
carbolic acid
cardiac cycle
chemotherapy
chiropractic
circumcision
claudication
colour vision
complication
conditioning
constipation
constitution
convalescent
corneal graft

decongestant
degeneration
dental caries
dental clinic
desalination
disinfectant
dissociation
diverticulum
double vision
electrolysis
emasculation
encephalitis
endocarditis
enteric fever
epidemiology
excitability
exophthalmos
extrasystole
faith healing
family doctor
feminization
fibrillation
folk medicine
friar's balsam
gamma gobulin
gastric juice
gastric ulcer
generic drugs
group therapy
haematemesis
haemorrhoids
hallucinogen
hallux valgus
heart disease
heart failure
heliotherapy
hiatus hernia
hydrotherapy
hyperkinesia
hypertension
hypnotic drug
hypochondria
hysterectomy
idiosyncrasy
immune system

immunization
implantation
incompetence
incontinence
inflammation
insemination
intelligence
intoxication
irritability
laryngectomy
malformation
malnutrition
manipulation
MAO inhibitor
menstruation
microbiology
microsurgery
neurosurgery
nematode worm
night terrors
nitrous oxide
oophorectomy
opisthotonos
orthopaedics
ossification
osteoporosis
otosclerosis
pancreatitis
paraesthesia
Parkinsonism
pericarditis
perspiration
pharmacology
pigmentation
pneumothorax
prescription
presentation
pressure sore
primigravida
progesterone
prophylactic
pulled muscle
quadriplegic
quartan fever
radiotherapy

referred pain
Rhesus factor
rheumatology
scarlet fever
sense of smell
Siamese twins
sleeping pill
sleepwalking
solvent abuse
somnambulism
somnambulist
St Vitus dance
steatorrhoea
subarachnoid
subconscious
subcutaneous
surgical boot
tertian fever
test-tube baby
thalassaemia
thermography
thoracic duct
tranquillizer
sense of touch
stroke volume
surgeon's knot
trephination
trichuriasis
tuberculosis
tunnel vision
typhoid fever
vasodilation
writer's cramp

13

accommodation
acetylcholine
agglutination
amniocentesis
anthropometry
anticoagulant
antihistamine
antirheumatic
antispasmodic

aphthous ulcer
atrial flutter
bacteriophage
battle fatigue
blastomycosis
blood pressure
bottle feeding
breast feeding
bubonic plague
calcification
callisthenics
carbon dioxide
cardiac arrest
cardiac output
cerebral palsy
certification
cholangiogram
cholecystitis
choriod plexus
clinical trial
compatability
consanguinity
consciousness
contraception
contraceptive
convalescence
Crohn's disease
defibrillator
dental surgery
district nurse
Down's syndrome
drug addiction
duodenal ulcer
elephantiasis
endocrinology
erogenous zone
exhibitionism
fertility drug
fertilization
food poisoning
genetic traits
German measles
Graves' disease
gynaecomastia
haemodialysis

hallucination
health visitor
helminthiasis
hermaphrodite
hydrocephalus
hypermetropia
hypoglycaemia
hyperactivity
intensive care
intramuscular
Ishihara tests
lead poisoning
leishmaniasis
materia medica
medical record
mental illness
metabolic rate
micro-organism
mononucleosis
neuromuscular
noradrenaline
ophthalmology
osteomyelitis
oxygen therapy
paternity test
periodontitis
pharmacopoeia
physiotherapy
plantar reflex
poliomyelitis
polyarteritis
portwine stain
Pott's fracture
pregnancy test
premedication
prostate gland
prostatectomy
psychosomatic
psychosurgery
psychotherapy
regurgitation
reinforcement
renal dialysis
resuscitation
Rorschach test

schizophrenia
sebaceous cyst
sensitization
serum sickness
smelling salts
speech therapy
sterilization
Streptococcus
tenosynovitis
tissue culture
toxoplasmosis
trace elements
tranquillizer
varicose ulcer
varicose veins
vital capacity
whooping cough
xerophthalmia
zygomatic arch

14

achondroplasia
adrenocortical
angina pectoris
anticonvulsant
antidepressant
aortic stenosis
appendicectomy
autosuggestion
Babinski reflex
barefoot doctor
benzodiazepine
blood poisoning
breathlessness
Bright's disease
bronchodilator
carbon monoxide
cardiac massage
cardiomyopathy
cardiovascular
cathode-ray tube
cervical collar
chelating agent
cholelithiasis

chromatography
claustrophobia
coeliac disease
Colles' fracture
community nurse
conjunctivitis
coronary by-pass
cross-infection
cryptorchidism
cystic fibrosis
cytotoxic drugs
dacryocystitis
defibrillation
detached retina
detoxification
disorientation
diverticulitis
electrotherapy
family planning
fringe medicine
frozen shoulder
fraternal twins
glandular fever
Hansen's disease
heat exhaustion
hip replacement
histoplasmosis
housemaid's knee
house physician
hydrocortisone
hyperglycaemia
hypothyroidism
identical twins
immune response
inguinal hernia
menstrual cycle
mental disorder
motion sickness
muscle relaxant
night blindness
nitroglycerine
nodes of Ranvier
Oedipus complex
ophthalmoscope
osteoarthritis

parapsychology
pasteurization
patent medicine
pharmaceutical
plasmapheresis
plaster of Paris
plastic surgery
pneumoconiosis
premature birth
psychoanalysis
puerperal fever
pyelonephritis
rehabilitation
relapsing fever
rheumatic fever
sexual medicine
speech disorder
spinal puncture
Staphylococcus
surgical spirit
tolerance level
tranquillizers
travel sickness
trichomoniasis
tuberculin test
whiplash injury

15

Addison's disease
adhesive plaster
adverse reaction
anabolic steriod
anorexia nervosa
aplastic anaemia
artificial heart
blackwater fever
body temperature
Bornholm disease
cat-scratch fever
circadian rhythm
colour blindness
cosmetic surgery
cottage hospital
delirium tremens

dental hygienist
general medicine
heart transplant
heterosexuality
Hodgkin's disease
intussusception
locomotor ataxia
manic depressive
Ménière's disease
Minimata disease
morning sickness
nuclear medicine
organ transplant
pyloric stenosis
sticking plaster
Sydenham's chorea
trypanosomiasis
venereal disease
X-linked disorder

16 +

alternative medicine
altitude sickness
aluminium hydroxide
Alzheimer's disease
ankylosing spondylitis
anti-inflammatory
aortic incompetence
artificial
    insemination
artificial kidney
artificial respiration
atrial fibrillation
autonomic nervous system
basal metabolic rate
behaviour therapy
biomedical engineering
blood transfusion
Caesarean section
cardiac pacemaker
carpal tunnel syndrome
cerebral haemorrhage
cerebral thrombosis
cervical vertebrae

Cheyne-Stokes breathing
chromatic aberration
coitus interruptus
colonic irrigation
comminuted fracture
communicable disease
community medicine
compound fracture
compressed air sickness
conditioned reflex
congenital disorder
contraceptive drug
coronary heart disease
coronary thrombosis
Coxsackie viruses
decompression sickness
deficiency disorders
dental technician
dilatation and curettage
Dupuytren's contracture
ectopic pregnancy
electron microscope
Epstein-Barr virus
extrasensory perception
Fallot's tetralogy
feedback mechanism
follicle-stimulating hormone
forensic medicine
functional disorder
general practioner
genetic counselling
genetic engineering
genetic fingerprints
glucose tolerance test
glyceryl trinitrate
granulation tissue
greenstick fracture
Hashimoto's disease
heart-lung machine
high blood pressure
holistic medicine
hormone replacement therapy
Huntingdon's chorea
incubation period
infectious disease

inferiority complex
ingrowing toenail
intelligence quotient
intelligence test
intermittent claudication
intrauterine device
intravenous pyelogram
in vitro fertilization
Jacksonian epilepsy
kidney transplant
Legionaire's disease
life-support machine
maintenance therapy
maternal deprivation
mental deficiency
mental retardation
mercury poisoning
monoclonal antibody
motor neurone disease
mountain sickness
multiple sclerosis
muscular dystrophy
myocardial infarction
natural childbirth
nephrotic syndrome
nervous breakdown
neuromuscular disorder
non-specific urethritis
obstructive lung disease
occupational therapy
open-heart surgery
opportunistic infection
painkilling drugs
paramedical services
Parkinson's disease
peritoneal dialysis
pernicious anaemia
premenstrual syndrome
prepatellar bursitis
presenile dementia
preventative medicine
psychosexual development
psychotropic drugs
radiation sickness
rapid eye movement

replacement surgery	spinal anaesthesia
respiratory arrest	Stokes-Adams syndrome
respiratory disorders	strawberry birthmark
respiratory failure	toxaemia of pregnancy
rheumatoid arthritis	transplant surgery
sex-linked disorders	tropical medicine
sexually transmitted disease	ventricular fibrillation
sickle-cell anaemia	ventricular flutter
sleeping sickness	vitamin deficiency
spare-parts surgery	withdrawal method

(Note: **haemo-** *compounds may appear* **hemo-**, *especially in American spelling.)*

Military ranks, titles, etc.

2 & 3	ulan	bomber	yeoman	redcoat	deserter
	WAAF	bowman	Zouave	regular	doughboy
AB	Wren	bow oar		reserve	engineer
AC1	WRNS	bugler	**7**	shipman	fencible
AC2		cooper		soldier	flag
ADC	**5**	cornet	admiral	skipper	rank
AOC		driver	ancient	steward	fugelman
CO	bosun	ensign	armorer	subadar	fusilier
Col.	cadet	fitter	aviator	surgeon	guerilla
CSM	diver	Ghurka	captain	Terrier	havildar
FO	fifer	gunner	cavalry	trooper	helmsman
GI	Lieut.	hetman	colonel	vedette	infantry
LAC	major	hussar	Cossack	veteran	leadsman
Lt.	middy	lancer	dragoon	warrior	janizary
MP	pilot	lascar	drummer		Landwehr
NCO	piper	marine	general	**8**	marksman
OC	scout	master	hoplite		messmate
OS	sepoy	purser	jemadar	adjutant	mutineer
PO	spahi	ranger	marshal	armourer	mechanic
RSM	subah	rating	matelot	bandsman	observer
RTO	Tommy	reefer	militia	cabin boy	partisan
	uhlan	rigger	officer	cavalier	rifleman
4		sapper	orderly	chaplain	sentinel
	6	seaman	pikeman	chasseur	sergeant
Capt.		sentry	pioneer	commando	ship's
C in C	airman	snotty	private	corporal	boy
cook	ataman	spahee	provost	coxswain	spearman
mate	batman	stoker	recruit	decurion	subahdar
peon					

205

turncoat
winchman

9

air gunner
artificer
artillary
beefeater
berserker
boatswain
brigadier
cannoneer
carbineer
centurion
combatant
commander
commodore
conscript
cook's mate
field army
field rank
drum-major
fife-major
grenadier
guardsman
guerrilla
Home Guard
irregular
janissary
mercenary
musketeer
navigator
paymaster
pipe-major
press gang
sailmaker
ship's cook
signaller
signalman
subaltern
tugmaster
volunteer

10

able seaman
aide-de-camp
air marshal
apprentice
bandmaster
bombardier
campaigner
carabineer
carabinier
cavalryman
coastguard
commandant
cuirassier
drummer-boy
halbardier
Life Guards
lansquenet
lieutenant
militiaman
midshipman
paratroops
rear gunner
shipmaster
shipwright

11

aircraftman
air mechanic
bashibazook
bersaglieri
chief stoker
condottière
crack troops
crossbowman
field cornet
flag captain
flag officer
foot soldier
gunner's mate
Horse Guards
horse marine
infantryman

landsknecht
master pilot
naval rating
paratrooper
rear-admiral
second pilot
Tommy Atkins
vice-admiral

12

air commodore
armour-bearer
artillaryman
cabin steward
camp-follower
chief officer
chief steward
ensign-bearer
field marshal
field officer
first officer
group captain
horse soldier
junior seaman
major-general
master-at-arms
master gunner
officer cadet
petty officer
pilot officer
powder monkey
second master
senior purser
ship's surgeon
staff officer
storm-trooper
telegraphist
third officer

13

armourer's mate
army commander
barrack master

captain's clerk
chief armourer
chief engineer
dispatch rider
drill sergeant
flying officer
fourth officer
generalissimo
harbourmaster
lance corporal
leading seaman
leading stoker
light infantry
machine-gunner
master aircrew
prisoner of war
quartermaster
radio operator
sergeant major
second officer
signal officer
staff sergeant
sub-lieutenant
third engineer
torpedo-gunner
wing commander

14

air vice-marshal
colonel-in-chief
colour sergeant
flag lieutenant
flight engineer
flight mechanic
flight sergeant
leading steward
liaison officer
master corporal
master engineer
master sergeant
medical officer
ordinary seaman

provost marshal
second corporal
second engineer
ship's carpenter
signals officer
squadron leader
standard bearer
warrant officer

15 +

adjutant-general
air chief marshal
Chelsea Pensioner
chief technician
corporal of horse
first lieutenant
gentleman-at-arms
household troops
master navigator
master signaller
officer's steward
ordnance officer
second lieutenant
soldier of fortune

16 +

admiral of the fleet
chief petty officer
flight lieutenant
junior technician
lieutenant colonel
lieutenant commander
lieutenant general
marshal of the Royal Air Force
master air electronic operator
master air loadmaster
military policeman
officer of the day
officer of the guard
second-leutenant
senior aircraftman
quartermaster-sergeant

Monday's child rhyme

Monday's child is fair of face
Tuesday's child is full of grace
Wednesday's child is full of woe
Thursday's child has far to go
Friday's child is loving and giving
Saturday's child works hard for a living
But a child that's born on the Sabbath day
Is bonny and blythe and good and gay.

Money

1

c (cent)
d (penny, pence)
f (farthing)
l (lira, pound, £)
p (penny, pence)
q (quadrans = farthing)
R (rand)
s (shilling)
$ (dollar)
Y (Yen, ¥)

2

as
at
DM (Deutschmark)
fl (florin/guilder)
xu

3

ban
bit
bob
écu
fen
fil

fin
hào
IOU
jon
kip
lek
lei
leu
lev
lsd
mil
öre
ore
pay
pie
pul
pya
sen
sol
sou
tin
won
yen

4

anna
ante
avos
baht
bani
bean
bill
birr
bits
buck
cash
cedi
cent
chon
coin
dime
doit
dong
fare
fils
gelt
gold
inti
jiao
jeon
kina
kobo
kyat
lira
lire
loot
loti
lwei
mark
mill
mint
mite
note
obol
para
pelf
peso
pice
pony
pula
puli
pund
punt
quid
rand
real
reis
rial
riel
ryal
sene
slug
syli
taka
tala
toea
vatu
yuan

5

agora
angel
asper
aurar
baiza
belga
booty
brass
bread
butut
colón
conto
crown
daric
dinar
dobra
dough
ducat
eagle
fiver
franc
funds
grand
groat

ingot	zaïre	monkey	bullion	**8**
khoum	zloty	moolah	capital	
kitty		nickel	carfare	banknote
kopek		obolus	centavo	bankroll
krona	**6**	pa'anga	centime	cruzeiro
krone		pataca	céntimo	currency
kurus	agorot	payout	chetrum	denarius
leone	assets	pennia	córdoba	doubloon
lepta	aureus	peseta	crusado	farthing
livre	balboa	pesewa	cruzado	finances
lolly	bawbee	poisha	denarii	finnmark
louis	boodle	qindar	drachma	groschen
lucre	cauris	qintar	ekpwele	hard cash
manna	change	ransom	guarani	louis d'or
means	cheque	Rappen	guilder	millième
mohur	copeck	riches	halalah	napoleon
möngö	copper	rouble	ha'penny	new pence
naira	credit	rupiah	hellers	new penny
ngwee	dalasi	salary	lempira	ngultrum
noble	denier	satang	lisente	picayune
oncer	dirham	seniti	lump sum	pin money
paisa	doblón	sequin	metical	round sum
paise	dollar	shekel	milreis	sesterce
paper	drachm	siglos	moidore	shilling
pence	ekuele	silver	nest egg	sixpence
penni	escudo	solidi	östmark	smackers
penny	filler	specie	ouguiya	sterling
perks	florin	spoils	peanuts	stotinki
piece	forint	stater	pfennig	tikchung
pound	gourde	stiver	piastre	tuppence
prize	groszy	tanner	quarter	two pence
purse	guinea	tariff	quetzal	windfall
qursh	gulden	tenner	readies	winnings
riyal	haléru	tester	red cent	zecchino
rupee	kopeck	teston	ringgit	
scudi	koruna	thaler	rufiyaa	
scudo	kwacha	tugrik	savings	**9**
senik	kwanza	wampum	sawbuck	
soldo	leptae	wealth	smacker	boliviano
sucre	lepton		solidus	centesimi
taler	likuta		stipend	centesimo
thebe	living	**7**	tambala	dupondius
tical	makata		testoon	easy money
toman	makuta	Afghani	two bits	emolument
wages	markka	Austral		fourpence
	mazuma	bolívar		fourpenny

gold piece
half-crown
half-eagle
half-noble
halfpenny
hush money
greenback
lilangeni
petty cash
pistareen
schilling
sovereign
spondulix

10

angel-noble
blood money
credit card
half-a-
  crown
money order
paper money
ready money
reichsmark
sestertium
threepence

11

bank account
bank balance
chickenfeed
danger money
decimal coin
deutschmark
double eagle
legal tender
Maundy Money
money for jam
pocket money
postal order
premium bond
sixpenny bit
small change
spondulicks
wherewithal

12

banker's draft
banker's order
hard currency
liquid assets
piece of eight
quarter-noble
remuneration

silver dollars
soft currency

13

brass farthing
caboverdianos
half-sovereign
pieces of eight
spending money
threepenny bit

14

certified check
coin of the realm
current account
letter of credit
peseta Guineana
promissory note

15+

checking account
conscience money
East Caribbean dollar
escudo caboverdianos
money for old rope
traveller's cheque

Mountain ranges, mountains, hills and volcanoes

2 & 3

Abu
Aso
Ida
K2
Kea (v.)

4

Alps
Blue
Caha
Cook
Ebal

Etna
  (v.)
Fuji
  (v.)
Harz
Iron
Jaya
Jura

Kibo
Meru
Ossa
Rosa
Rigi
Ural

5

Adams
Altai
Andes
Asama (v.)
Athos

Atlas
Baker (v.)
Black
Cenis
Coast
Cuzco
Eiger
Elgon
Galty
Ghats
Hecla (v.)
Huica
Kamet
Kenya
Hekla
Lenin (Peak)
Logan
Naipo
Misti
Ozark
Pelée
Rocky
Sayan
Sinai
Snowy
Table
Tatra
Weald (hills)
White

Hermon
Hoggar
Katmai
Kazbek
Koryak
Kunlun
Ladakh (range)
Lenina
Levick
Lhotse
Makula
Matopo (hills)
Mourne
Muztag
Nephin
Ochils (hills)
Olives (Mt of)
Pamirs
Pindus
Pissis
Pobedy
Purace (v.)
Sajama
Sangay (v.)
Scafel
Shasta
Sidlaw (hills)
Slioch
Taurus
Terror
Tunari
Vosges
Zagros

Errigal
Everest
Helicon
Illampu
Jorullo (v.)
Kilauea (v.)
Lliamna (v.)
Malvern (hills)
Mam Soul
Markham
Mendips (hills)
Muckish
Nan Ling
Nan Shan
Ollague
Olympus
Palomar
Peteroa
Rainier
Rockies
Roraima
Ruapehu (v.)
St. Elias
Samford
Scafell
Skiddaw
Snowdon
Socompa
The Peak
Tibesti
Tolimar
Triglav
Vulcano (v.)
Whitney

6

Ararat
Azufre
Balkan
Bonete
Brooks
Carmel
Darwin
Dumuyo
Egmont
Elbert
Elbrus
Elburz
Erebus (v.)

7

Ahaggar
Ben More
Bernina
Brocken
Cascade (range)
Cayambe
Chianti
Chillan (v.)
Copiapu

8

Anapurna
Ansuhuma
Antisana
Ardennes
Auvergne
Ben Attow
Ben Dearg
Ben Nevis

Ben Wyvis
Cambrian
Cameroon (v.)
Caucasus
Cevennes
Chachani
Cheviots
Chirripo
Coropuna
Cotopaxi (v.)
Cuillins
Demavend
Flinders (range)
Fujiyama
Goat Fell
Humphrey
Hymettus
Jungfrau
Hualalai (v.)
Kaikoura (ranges)
Kinabalu
Krakatoa (v.)
Knockboy
Mauna Loa (v.)
McKinley
Mitchell
Musgrave (ranges)
Palumani
Pennines
Pentland (hills)
Pyrenees
Quantock (hills)
St. Helens (v.)
Sgurr Nor
Stanovoi (range)
Sulaiman (range)
Tian Shan
Tien Shan
Vesuvius (v.)
Wrangell (v.)
Yerupaja
Yucamani

9

Aconcagua

Allegheny
Annapurna
Antofalla
Appenines
Beenoskee
Ben Lawers
Ben Lomond
Ben Macdui
Braeriach
Cairn Toul
Chilterns
Cotswolds
Cross Fell
Co del Toro
Dolomites
Dunsinane
Galtymore
Grampians
Hamersley (range)
Helvellyn (range)
Himalayas
Hindu Kush
Huascaran
Karakoram (range)
Kosciusko
Lochnager
Mangerton
Mont Blanc
Muztagata
Nanda Devi
Ngauruhoe (v.)
Pacaraima
Parnassus
Pikes Peak
Puy de Dome
Ras Dashan
Ruwenzori
Pen-y-Ghent
Pichincha
Rakaposhi
Sillajhua
Slieve Car
Sonequera
Stromboli (v.)
Tirich Mir

Tocorpuri
Tongariro (v.)
Villarica (v.)
Weisshorn
Whernside
Zugspitze

10

Adirondack
An Teallach
Arakam Yoma
Cader Idris
Cairngorms
Cantabrian
Carpathian
Chimborazo
Chomolhati
Col del Putro
Companario
Dent du Midi
Dhaulagiri
Erzgebirge
Gasherbrum
Kebnekaise
King George
Kommunisma
Konger Shan
Lammermuir
Lassen Peak
Macdonnell (ranges)
Majuba Hill
Matterhorn
Middleback (range)
Montserrat
Mount Lofty (ranges)
North Downs (hills)
Nyiragongo (v.)
St. Gotthard
South Downs (hills)
Torcurpure
Twelve Pins
Wetterhorn

11

Anti-Lebanon
Appalachian
Ben Cruachan
Drakensburg
Fairweather
Jotunheimen
Kangrinboqe
Kilimanjaro
Mendip Hills
Monadhliath
Namcha Barwa
Nanga Parbat
Nyamoragira (v.)
Scafell Pike
Sierra Madre

12

Appalachians

Cheviot Hills
Citlaltepetl
Godwin Austen
Golan Heights
Gran Paradiso
Ingleborough
Kanchenjunga
Kluchevskaya
Peak District
Popocatepetl
Schiehallion
Siding Spring
Sierra Morena
Sierra Nevada
Tinguiririca
Warrumbungle

13

Carrantuohill
Chiltern Hills

Co del Olivares
Communism Peak
Cotswold Hills
Grossglockner
Gurla Mandhata
Kangchenjunga
Kommunizma Pik
Ojas del Salado
Riesengebirge
Sierra Maestra

14 +

Bernese Oberland
Cleveland Hills
Fichtelgebirge
Finsteraahorn
Nevsojos del Salado
MacGillicuddy's
 Reeks
Shire Highlands
Xixabangma Feng

Muses

4

Clio - history

5

Erato - love songs

6

Thalia - comedy and
 pastoral poetry
Urania - astronomy

7

Euterpe - lyric poetry

8

Calliope - epic poetry
Polymnia - sacred song

9

Melpomene - tragedy

10

Polyhymnia - sacred song

11

Terpsichore - choral song
 and dance

Musical instruments

3

kit
lur
oud
oat
sax
saz
tar
uti

4

band
bass
bata
bell
biwa
drum
fife
gong
harp
horn
kena
khen
koto
lira
lute
lyra
lyre
mu yu
oboe
outi
pean
pipe
rote
ruan
sona
tuba
urua
vina

viol
whip

5

anvil
aulos
banjo
bells
block
bones
brass
bugle
bumpa
buzuq
cello
chang
cheng
ching
chime
cobza
corno
cornu
crwth
dauli
dhola
dobro
drone
fidla
flute
gaita
gajdy
gamba
hi-hat
huruk
kakko
kazoo
kerar
mbila
naker
nebel

okedo
organ
piano
rebab
rebec
reeds
regal
saron
shalm
shawm
shell
sheng
sitar
snare
strad
tabla
tabor
taiko
tibia
tudum
tupan
vibes
viola
zinke
zurla
zurna

6

alboka
arghul
atabal
bagana
bonang
bongos
buglet
carynx
chimes
citole
claves
corona

cornet
cymbal
darbuk
dehors
dulcet
fandur
fiddle
flugel
guitar
kettle
kissar
koboro
lirica
lirone
nakers
racket
rattle
rebeck
sacbut
sancho
santir
shaker
shofar
sopile
spinet
spoons
syrinx
tabour
tabret
tam-tam
timbal
tom-tom
trigon
tromba
tucket
tymbal
ventil
vielle
violin
yangum
zambra

zither

7

alp-horn
althorn
alto sax
atumpan
bagpipe
bandora
bandore
baryton
bassoon
bazooka
big band
bodhran
bow harp
box lyre
celesta
celeste
cembalo
chanter
chikara
cithara
cithern
cittern
clapper
clarion
clavier
cornett
cowbell
crotalo
cymbalo
cymbals
dichord
fagotto
fistula
fithele
flutina
gadulka
gamelan

gittern
harpist
hautboy
hornlet
kalungu
kithara
mandola
mandora
maracas
marimba
murumbu
musette
ocarina
octavin
orphica
pandora
pandura
pan-pipe
phonica
pianino
pianola
piccolo
posaune
sackbut
salpinx
sambuca
sambuke
samisen
santoor
sarangi
sarinda
saxhorn
saxtuba
serpent
sistrum
sithara
spinnet
taboret
tam am la
tambour
tambura
terbang
testudo
theorbo
tibicen

tiktiri
timbrel
timpani
timpano
trumpet
tubicen
ukulele
upright
vihuela
violone
warbler
whistle
zithern
zummara

8

alto-horn
arch-lute
autoharp
bagpipes
bandoura
bass drum
bass-horn
bass tuba
bass viol
bell harp
bombarde
bouzouki
calliope
carillon
castanet
chime bar
cimbalon
clappers
clarinet
clavecin
clavicor
continuo
cornpipe
crumhorn
ding-dong
dulcimer
gemshorn
handbell

harp lute
hornpipe
Jew's harp
keyboard
key-bugle
knackers
langspel
mandolin
melodeon
melodica
mirliton
pan pipes
pianette
pochette
polyphon
post horn
psaltery
recorder
reed pipe
side drum
slit drum
spinette
sringara
sticcado
surbahar
talambas
tamboura
tarabuka
tenor sax
timbales
triangle
trombone
tympanon
tympanum
violetta
virginal
vocalion
waldhorn
woodwind
zambomba

9

accordion
alpenhorn

alto-viola
angle harp
archilute
baby grand
balalaika
bandurria
banjolele
banjoline
bass-flute
bombardon
bongo drum
brass band
bugle-horn
castanets
celestina
chalumeau
chime bars
clarionet
claviharp
coach horn
cog rattle
componium
cornemuse
cornopean
crook horn
darabukke
decachord
drone-pipe
dulcitone
elbow-pipe
euphonium
flageolet
flexatone
flute-a-bec
gong ageng
hackbrett
hand organ
harmonica
harmonium
hydraulis
kelontong
könighorn
krummhorn
langspiel
mandoline

mandolone
mandolute
monochord
mouth harp
nose-flute
octachord
orchestra
orpharion
pantaleon
picco pipe
pipe organ
pitch-pipe
portative
reed organ
saxophone
semi-grand
seraphine
snare-drum
steel band
tabourine
tallharpa
tambourin
tenor horn
tenor tuba
tenor viol
tubophone
vibraharp
viola alto
washboard
wood block
Wurlitzer
xylophone
xylorimba

10

barrel drum
basset horn
bass fiddle
bass guitar
bird scarer
bongo drums
bull fiddle
bull-roarer
chittarone

choir-organ
clavichord
claviorgan
concertina
contrabass
cor anglais
didgeridoo
double bass
Eolian harp
Eolian lyre
euphonicon
flugelhorn
fortepiano
French harp
French horn
gong chimes
gramophone
grand piano
harmonicon
heptachord
hurdy-gurdy
instrument
kettle drum
lithophone
mandocello
mellophone
mouth-organ
oboe d'amore
ophicleide
pentachord
percussion
phonograph
pianoforte
piano-organ
saxotromba
sleighbell
soprano sax
sousaphone
spitzharpe
squeeze-box
Stradivari
string band
symphonion
symphonium
tamboureen

tambourine
thumb piano
tin whistle
tuning fork
vibraphone

11

Aeolian harp
Aeolian lyre
angel chimes
baritone sax
barrel organ
bell cittern
bladder pipe
cinema organ
fipple flute
German flute
graphophone
guitar-banjo
harmoniphon
harpsichord
heckelphone
hunting horn
hydraulicon
nickelodeon
orchestrina
orchestrion
piano-violin
player-piano
sleighbells
steel guitar
talking drum
viola d'amore
viol da gamba
violoncello
wobble-board

12

alto clarinet
alto trombone
bass recorder
cembal d'ambre
chamber organ

Chinese block
clavicembalo
concert grand
gansa gambang
gansa jongkok
glockenspiel
Hammond organ
hi-hat cymbals
kanteleharpe
mandolinetto
metallophone
military band
pandean pipes
penny whistle
rhythm guitar
sarrusophone
shoulder harp
Stradivarius
theatre organ
tromba marina
tubular bells
ukulele-banjo
upright piano
viola da gamba
whistle flute

13

alto saxophone
American organ
banjo-mandolin
contrabassoon
contrafagotto
cornet--piston
double bassoon
electric organ
hammerklavier
heckelclarina
marine trumpet
panharmonicon
positive organ
slide trombone
Swanee whistle
tenor recorder
tintinnabulum
valve trombone
viola bastarda

14

banjo-mandoline

brass instrument
clarinet d'amore
clavicytherium
electric guitar
flute-flageolet
piano accordion
regimental band
tenor saxophone
treble recorder
wind instrument

15 +

baritone saxophone
classical guitar
descant recorder
instrumentalist
Moog synthesizer
percussion instrument
soprano recorder
soprano saxophone
string instrument
string quartette
woodwind instrument

Musical terms

1	2					
		mf	air	key	run	aria
		mi	alt	lah	sfz	arja
A	al	mp	bar	lay	ska	ayre
B	CD	pp	bis	nut	soh	band
C	DC	re	bop	ped	sol	base
D	do	sf	bow	peg	ten	bass
E	fa	si	cue	pin	tie	beat
F	EP	te	dim	piu	vox	book
f	ff	ud	doh	piz		brio
G	fz	ut	duo	pop		buka
p	Hz		fah	rag	**4**	capo
	la		gig	ray		clef
	LP	**3**	hum	rib	alla	coda
	me		jig	rit	alto	desk
		aak			arco	

217

disc	riff	belly	kyrie	segno	valve
disk	ring	blare	largo	segue	vocal
duet	rock	blues	lento	senza	voice
echo	roll	break	lyric	shake	volta
fine	root	breve	major	sharp	volti
flat	rote	buffa	march	shift	waist
flue	scat	buffo	meter	sixth	waltz
form	sign	canon	mezzo	slide	wrest
fret	sing	canto	minim	soave	yodel
frog	sino	carol	minor	sol-fa	zoppa
glee	slur	catch	molto	sound	
heel	solo	cento	mosso	staff	**6**
hi-fi	song	chant	motet	stave	
high	soul	chime	motif	stick	accent
hold	stop	choir	music	stomp	accord
hymn	tail	chord	Muzak	strum	action
jack	tape	clang	ninth	suite	adagio
jazz	time	clank	nodal	swell	al fine
jive	toll	comma	nonet	swing	answer
lead	tone	conga	octet	table	anthem
Lied	trad	Credo	opera	tacet	arioso
lilt	trio	croma	paean	tango	atonal
mass	tune	crook	pause	tanto	attack
mese	turn	croon	pavan	tardo	attune
mode	vamp	dance	pedal	tempo	aubade
mono	vivo	dirge	piano	tenor	ballad
mood	voce	ditty	piece	tenth	ballet
mort	voix	dolce	pieno	theme	beebop
moto	wind	drone	piper	third	beemol
mute	wood	dumka	pitch	thrum	bolero
neck	work	duple	polka	tiple	boogie
node		elegy	primo	title	bourée
note	**5**	etude	psalm	tonic	bridge
opus		f-hole	quasi	tonus	bugler
part	acuta	fifth	quill	touch	burden
peal	ad lib	forte	quint	triad	cadent
play	album	fugal	reply	trill	can-can
poco	arsis	fugue	resin	trite	cantor
port	assai	galop	rondo	trope	cantus
punk	atone	gamut	round	tuner	catgut
raga	barré	gigue	samba	tutti	chaunt
rall	basso	grace	sansa	twang	chiuso
reed	basta	grave	scale	up-bow	choral
reel	baton	hertz	scena	valse	choric
rest	bebop	knell	score	value	chorus

contra	minuet	tenuto	big nabd	down-bow
crooks	monody	tercet	bitonal	drummer
da capo	morris	tierce	bravura	epicede
damper	motive	timbre	buccina	episode
design	niente	treble	cadence	estinto
diesis	nobile	tongue	cadency	euphony
ditone	oboist	treble	cadenza	eutonia
divisi	octave	triple	calando	fanfare
divoto	off-key	tune up	calypso	fermata
Dorian	ottava	tuning	cantata	fiddler
duetto	pavane	unison	canzona	flatten
eighth	peg-box	up-beat	canzone	flutist
encore	phrase	vamper	caprice	fuguist
entrée	piston	veloce	carioca	furioso
euphon	plagal	vivace	casette	gavotte
facile	plaint	volata	celeste	giocoso
fading	player	volume	cellist	gravita
figure	presto	warble	chamade	gravity
finale	quaver		chanson	G-string
fipple	record	**7**	chorale	harmony
follia	reggae		clapper	harpist
fourth	repeat	Aeolian	codetta	juke-box
fugato	revert	aeolist	comique	keynote
fujara	retenu	agitato	compass	lullaby
gallop	rhythm	allegro	con brio	machine
giusto	rubato	al segno	concert	maestro
ground	scales	amoroso	conduct	marcato
hammer	second	andante	console	mazurka
hummel	sempre	angelot	coranto	measure
intone	sennet	animato	counter	mediant
Ionian	septet	apotome	coupler	melisma
jingle	serial	apotomy	courant	melodic
lament	sestet	arietta	cremona	middle C
leader	sextet	ariette	crooner	mistune
legato	shanty	ars nova	csardas	morbido
Lieder	singer	art-song	czardas	mordent
litany	sketch	attacca	descant	morendo
lutist	snatch	attuned	descend	musette
Lydian	sonata	backing	descent	musical
lyrics	stanza	balance	diagram	natural
lyrist	stereo	ballade	dichord	nonette
manual	strain	Baroque	diplice	octette
marcia	string	bassist	discord	offbeat
medley	subito	battery	distune	organum
melody	tattoo	bellows	dolente	partita

219

pesante	sospiro	canticle	fandango	musicale
pianist	spagane	canzonet	fantasia	musician
pibcorn	stopped	castrato	fantasie	nocturne
pibroch	stretto	cavatina	festival	nonuplet
piffaro	strings	chaconne	flamenco	notation
piffero	strophe	chevalet	flautist	notturno
playing	sub-bass	cheville	flourish	obligato
plectre	subject	col canto	folk song	octuplet
pomposo	syncope	composer	folk tune	open note
pop song	taborer	composto	forzando	operatic
posaune	taboret	con amore	fughetta	operetta
prelude	tambura	con anima	galement	oratorio
quartet	tipping	concerto	galliard	organist
quintet	toccata	con fuoco	grazioso	ostinato
quinton	tone-row	conjusto	half-note	overtone
ragtime	tremolo	con mosso	harmonic	overture
rastrum	triplet	continuo	high note	part-song
recital	tuneful	courante	hornpipe	pastiche
refrain	twelfth	cromorna	infinito	pastoral
reprise	vamping	crotchet	interval	phantasy
requiem	vespers	dal segno	intonate	phrasing
ripieno	vibrato	demi-tone	isotonic	Phrygian
romance	violist	diapason	jongleur	plectrum
rondeau	voicing	diatonic	keyboard	pop music
rondino		diminish	langspil	portando
rosalia		doloroso	lentando	position
roulade	**8**	dominant	libretto	practice
Sanctus		down beat	ligature	practise
scherzo	a battuta	doxology	love-song	preludio
schisma	absonant	drumbeat	lutanist	putorino
sciolto	Agnus Dei	drum-head	lutenist	register
scoring	alto clef	duettino	madrigal	resonant
secondo	animando	duettist	maestoso	response
septole	antiphon	dulciana	major key	rhapsody
setting	arpeggio	eleventh	melodics	rigadoon
settino	backbeat	energico	melodist	rigaudon
seventh	baritone	ensemble	melodize	ritenuto
singing	barytone	entr'acte	minor key	saraband
skiffle	bassetto	euphonic	minstrel	semitone
slurred	bass note	euphonon	miserere	septette
soloist	bel canto	evensong	moderato	sequence
song hit	berceuse	exercise	modulate	serenade
soprano	blue note	faburden	monotone	serenata
sordino	boat song	falderal	monotony	sestetto
sordone	brillant	falsetto	movement	sextette
	cake-walk			

sforzato	allemande	flute-stop	monochord
sinfonia	andamento	folk music	monophony
sing-song	andantino	full organ	monotonic
smorzato	antiphony	full score	music book
sonajero	arabesque	frequency	obbligato
sonatina	arpanetta	furibondo	octachord
song form	atonality	gallopade	orchestra
songster	augmented	generator	organ-pipe
sound-bar	bacchanal	glissando	part music
sound-box	bagatelle	grace-note	paso doble
sourdine	bandstand	gradation	pastorale
spiccato	barcarole	grandioso	pianolist
staccato	barn dance	Gregorian	pizzicato
sticcado	bassonore	guitarist	plainsong
stopping	bow-string	half-close	polonaise
subtonic	brass band	half-shift	polyphony
symmetry	brillante	harmonics	polytonal
symphony	bugle call	harmonize	pressando
syntonic	cacophony	hexachord	principal
tabourer	cantabile	high pitch	quadrille
tabouret	cantilena	high-toned	quartette
tarogato	capriccio	homophony	quintette
terzetto	cassation	honky-tonk	quodlibet
threnody	charivari	imbroglio	recording
timoroso	chromatic	imitation	rehearsal
tonalist	conductor	impromptu	rendering
tonality	consonate	improvise	rendition
tone down	contralto	in harmony	resonance
tone poem	crescendo	inner part	resonator
trad jazz	dance tune	interlude	rhythmics
tremando	dead march	intonation	ricercare
trichord	death-bell	invention	rock'n'roll
vigoroso	decachord	inversion	roundelay
virtuoso	deep-toned	irregular	selection
vocalism	dissonant	lagrimoso	semibreve
vocalist	dithyramb	languente	semitonic
voce colo	Dixieland	larghetto	septimole
warbling	double bar	leger-line	seraphine
woodwind	drumstick	leitmotif	septuplet
	elevation	leitmotiv	sextuplet
	euphonism	melodious	sforzando
9	euphonize	meno mosso	siciliana
	extempore	metronome	siciliano
accompany	farandole	mezzo voce	signature
acoustics	fingering	modulator	slow march
adagietto			

10

soft pedal		dotted note	musica viva
solfeggio		double-flat	music-drama
sollecito	accidental	double time	musicology
song cycle	adaptation	eisteddfod	music-stand
sopranist	added sixth	embouchure	music-stool
sostenuto	affettuoso	enharmonic	nobilmente
sotto voce	allargando	escapement	opera buffa
sound-hole	allegretto	euphonious	opera music
sound-post	appoggiato	exposition	opera seria
spiritosa	background	expression	orchestral
spiritual	bandmaster	finger-hole	organ-point
steel band	barcarolle	folk singer	patter-song
strascino	bassanello	fortissimo	pedal-board
strumming	bassoonist	gramophone	pedal organ
succentor	binary form	grand opera	pedal point
symphonic	binotonous	ground bass	pentachord
syncopate	bitonality	heavy metal	percussion
tablature	cantatrice	homophonic	phonograph
tail-piece	cantillate	humoresque	pianissimo
tenor bass	canto fermo	incidental	piano stool
tenor clef	canzonetta	instrument	piped music
tessitura	chiroplast	intermezzo	plainchant
theme song	colascione	intonation	polyphonic
theorbist	coloratura	jam session	portamento
timpanist	comic opera	lentamente	prima donna
toccatina	common time	light music	quadruplet
torch-song	complement	light opera	quintuplet
trillando	concertino	Lydian mode	recitative
troubador	consonance	mainstream	recitativo
trumpeter	consonancy	major chord	rehearsing
tuning-key	con spirito	major scale	repertoire
tuning-peg	continuato	major third	repetition
twelve-row	cornettist	meditation	resolution
tympanist	corroboree	mezzoforte	ritardando
unmusical	dance music	minor chord	ritornello
untunable	demi-ditone	minor scale	rockabilly
variation	diastaltic	minor third	scherzando
violinist	diminished	minstrelsy	semiquaver
voluntary	diminuendo	Mixolydian	sonata form
vox humana	discordant	modern jazz	sound-board
whistling	disharmony	modulation	sourdeline
wind chest	dissonance	monotonous	staphyline
	dissonancy	mouth music	strathspey
	dolcemente	mouthpiece	strepitoso
	Dorian mode	musicality	string band

stringendo
submediant
supertonic
suspension
symphonist
syncopated
syncopator
swing music
tarantella
tetrachord
theme music
tonic chord
tonic major
tonic minor
tonic sol-fa
triple time
transition
treble clef
triple time
trombonist
tuning fork
twelve-note
twelve-tone
undulation
variamento
virtuosity
vistomente
vocal music
water music

11

accelerando
Aeolian mode
affrettando
alla capella
alto-ripieno
arrangement
ballad opera
bene-placito
bothy ballad
broken chord
canned music
capriccioso
chansonette

church music
clairschach
clarion note
common chord
composition
concertante
contra-basso
contrapunto
contra-tenor
counterpart
decrescendo
demi-cadence
development
diatessaron
discordance
discordancy
double-sharp
equisonance
extemporize
fiddlestick
figured bass
fingerboard
first violin
fundamental
gospel music
harmonizing
high-pitched
hunting song
incantation
leading note
madrigalist
mandolinist
minnesinger
music master
natural note
nickelodeon
open cadence
open harmony
opera bouffe
orchestrate
partial note
passacaglia
passing note
performance
polyphonism

prestissimo
progression
quarter-note
quarter-tone
rallentando
rock and roll
recessional
sacred music
saxophonist
schottische
senza rigore
square dance
stereophony
string music
subdominant
subsemitone
symphonious
syncopation
temperament
torch singer
transposing
transposing
tridiapason
unaccordant
vivacissimo
voce-di-petto
voce-di-testa
volti-subito

12

acciaccatura
accordionist
acoustic bass
alla cappella
allegrissimo
anticipation
appassionata
appoggiatura
assai allegro
audio casette
augmentation
backing group
bass baritone
boogie-woogie

cantus firmus
chamber music
chromaticism
clarinettist
close harmony
comedy ballet
compound time
concert pitch
concert waltz
contrapuntal
counterpoint
counter-tenor
divertimento
double-octave
extravaganza
false cadence
funeral march
high fidelity
inharmonious
instrumental
introduction
key signature
leggeramente
melodic minoe
mezzo-relievo
mezzo-soprano
military band
moto perpetuo
musical drama
musicologist
natural scale
opera comique
orchestrator
organ grinder
organ recital
passion music
perfect fifth
perfect pitch
philharmonic
philomusical
Phrygian mode
polytonality
quadraphonic
quadraphonic
registration

repercussion
sight-reading
sounding post
spheremelody
stereophonic
thorough-bass
vocalization
wedding march

13

absolute pitch
accompaniment
basso profondo
choral singing
closed cadence
common measure
concrete music
concertmaster
conservatoire
disharmonious
false relation
gospel singing
Gregorian mode
harmonic chord
harmonic minor
improvisation
musical comedy
music festival
operatic music

orchestration
plagal cadence
ranz-des-vaches
serialization
signature tune
sol-fa notation
staff notation
string octette
string quartet
superdominant
tetradiapason
time signature
transcription
transposition
violoncellist

14

Ambrosian chant
chromatic scale
contrary motion
demi-semi-quaver
direct interval
double-stopping
Gregorian chant
interpretation
mainstream jazz
Mixolydian mode
national anthem
perfect cadence

programme music
recapitulation
reed instrument
regimental band
wind instrument

15 +

augmented seventh
barber-shop quartet
barber-shop singing
brass instrument
diminished seventh
double-tongueing
electronic music
incidental music
instrumentalist
instrumentation
musical director
musique concrete
percussion instrument
perfect interval
serial technique
string instrument
string quartette
symphony concert
traditional jazz
triple-tongueing
woodwind instrument

Mythology

2 & 3	Ops	Argo	Iris	Styx	Arcas
	Orc	Dido	Isis	Troy	Arges
Ate	Roc	Echo	Juno	Tyro	Argus
Eos	Tiu	Eden	Leda		Arion
Ge	Tyr	Eris	Leto	**5**	Asura
Hel		faun	Loki		Atlas
Io		Gaea	Maia	Aegle	Balor
Ino	**4**	Garm	Mara	Aegus	Belus
Nox		Hebe	Ogam	Aello	Cernu
Nyx	Ajax	Hera	Rhea	Aeson	Chaos
	Ares				

Chloë	Wotan	Neleus	Coronis	Zagreus
Circe		nymphs	Cyanean	
Creon	**6**	Osiris	Cyclops	**8**
Ceryx		Orthos	Cyzicus	
Danae	Adonis	Pelion	Daphnis	Absyrtus
Delos	Aeacus	Pelias	Demeter	Achilles
dryad	Aeetes	Phoebe	Diomede	Aglaucus
Fates	Aegeus	Pollux	Echidna	Alcestis
Hades	Aegina	Psyche	Eleusis	Alcimede
Harpy	Agenor	Scylla	Elysium	ambrosia
Helen	Alecto	Semele	Erinyes	Anacreon
Helle	Amazon	Selene	Euryale	Antigone
Herse	Amycus	Sirens	Gorgons	Apollyon
Hydra	Apollo	Sphinx	Glaucus	Atalanta
ichor	Areion	Stheno	Goeteia	Arethusa
Ilium	Athene	Teucer	griffin	basilisk
Irene	Athens	Tiphys	griffon	Bebryces
Ixion	Boreas	Titans	gryphon	Bithynia
Jason	Cadmus	Triton	Harpies	Brunhild
Kakon	Castor	Typhon	Jocasta	Brynhild
Ladon	Chione	Uranus	Megaera	Caduceus
Laius	Chiron	Zethus	Minoans	Callisto
Lethe	Charon		Nemesis	Caucasus
Medea	Clotho		Nephele	Cephalus
Medus	Cybele	**7**	Ocypete	Cerberus
Metis	Europa		Oedipus	Chimaera
Midas	Fenrir	Achates	Olympus	Daedalus
Minos	Furies	Actaeon	Orestes	Damocles
Muses	fylgja	Alcides	Orpheus	Dardanus
naiad	Geryon	Alcmene	Orthrus	Dionysus
Niobe	Gorgon	Amphion	Pandora	Doliones
Nisus	Hector	Ancaeus	Pegasus	Endymion
Orion	Helios	Antaeus	Perseus	Erytheia
Paris	Hermes	Antenor	Phineus	Eumolpus
Perse	Hyades	Antiope	Phoenix	Euphemus
Phebe	Hygeia	Artemis	Phrixus	Eurydice
Priam	Icarus	Astarte	Pyrrhus	Eurynome
Remus	Ithaca	Athamas	Pyramus	Ganymede
Runes	Kronos	Atropos	Podarge	Hamingja
satyr	Mageia	Brontes	Romulus	Heracles
Sibyl	Matres	Busiris	Stentor	Hercules
Siren	Medusa	Celaeno	Telamon	Hesperus
Talos	Megara	centaur	Theseus	Hyperion
Tegea	Mopsus	Chimera	Ulysses	Lachesis
Woden	nectar	Chloris	Xanthus	Lapithae
		Colchis		

Menelaus	**9**	Valkyries	Proserpina
Minotaur		Yggdrasil	Proserpine
Nauplius	Agememnon		Telemachus
Nausicaa	Archelous	**10**	
Odysseus	Argonauts		**11**
Olympian	Asclepius	Amphimarus	
Pleiades	Autolycus	Amphitrite	Aesculapios
Poseidon	Bosphorus	Amphitryon	Amphilocous
Ragnorak	Charybdis	Brünnhilde	Bellerophon
Sarpedon	Deianoira	Bucephalus	Euphrostyne
Sleipnir	Eumenides	Dii majores	Helen of Troy
Steropes	Gilgamesh	Dii minores	Lyssianassa
Tantalus	Iphigenia	Fenriswolf	Philoctetes
Tartarus	Narcissus	Hephaestus	
Thessaly	Parnassus	Hesperides	**12 +**
Thyestes	Parthenon	Hippodamia	
Tiresias	Philomela	Orchomenus	Castor and Pollux
Typhoeus	Polynices	Persephone	Cyanean Rocks
Valhalla	Pygmalion	Polyphemus	Golden Fleece
Windingo	Scamander	Polydeuces	Golden Apples
	Thersites	Procrustes	Hecatoncheires
	Tisiphone	Prometheus	Hesperethusa
			Rhadamanthus
			Romulus and Remus

Numbers 1 to 10 in various languages

English	French	German	Greek	Italian
one	un	ein	heis	uno
two	deux	zwei	duo	due
three	trois	drei	treis	tre
four	quatre	vier	tessares	quattro
five	cinq	funf	pente	cinque
six	six	sechs	hex	sei
seven	sept	sieben	hepta	sette
eight	huit	acht	okto	otto
nine	neuf	neun	ennea	nove
ten	dix	zehn	deka	dieci

	Latin	Portugese	Spanish
(one)	unus/unum	um/uma	uno
(two)	duus/duum	dois	dos
(three)	tres/tria	tres	tres
(four)	quatuor	quatro	cuatro
(five)	quinque	cinco	cinco
(six)	sex	seis	seis
(seven)	septem	sete	siete
(eight)	octo	oito	ocho
(nine)	novem	nove	nueve
(ten)	decem	dez	diez

Operas and their characters

Operas

4 & 5

Aida
Aleko
Calaf
Faen
Faust
Halka
Iris
Lakme
Manon
Manru
Mavra
Medée
Mlada
Norma
Sapho
Sarka
Teseo
Thais
Tosca
Uthal
Zaide
Zaza

6

Alcina
Almira
Alzira
Amadis
Aniara
Attila
Carmen
Hamlet
Joseph
Julian
Mignon
Nerone
Oberon
Otello
Salomé
Sigurd
Tarare
Ulisse

7

Aladdin
Alceste
Arianna

Arminio
Bank Ban
Dalibor
Guntraw
Irmelin
Isabeau
Ivanhoe
L'Aiglon
La Juive
La Wally
Lowland
Macbeth
Mazeppa
Nabucco
Nose, The
Olympia
Orlando
Ormindo
Rusalka
Savitri
Wozzeck
Yolande

8

Ariodant

Berenice
Deidamia
Ebn-Hakia
Fevernot
Giustino
Gloriana
Goyescas
Guiditta
Ice Break
Jessonda
John Hary
La Boheme
Le Roi d'Ys
Loddiska
Maritana
Masks, The
May Night
Mona Lisa
Parisina
Polituto
Scipione
Tiefland
Turandot

9

Abu Hassan
Africaine
Agrippina
Angelique
Belisario
Billy Budd
Campiello
Capriccio
Cardillac
Consul, The
Der Vampyr
Dybbuk, The
Hary Janos
Herodiade
Il Tabarro
I Puritani
Joan of Arc
King Priam
King Roger
La Calisto
La Rondine
L'Erismena
Lodoletta
Löhengrin
Maskarade
Mother, The
Pagliacci
Perichole
Rigoletto
Rodelinda
Secret, The
Stiffelio

10

Alessandro
Anna Bolena
Archers, The
Artaxerxes
Danton's Tod
Der Revisor
Devil's Walk
Die Abreise

Donna Diana
Don Rodrigo
Fra Diavolo
Fra Gherado
Griselidis
Gwendoline
Intermezzo
Jacobin, The
Kazakhstan
L'Arlesiana
L'Atlantide
La Traviata
Le Comte Ory
Le Maschere
Le Prophete
Les Martyrs
Les Troyens
Masnadieri
Monna Vanna
Semiramide
Swallow, The
Tannhauser
Trojans, The
Uzbekistan

11

Dead City, The
Die Soldaten
Doktor Faust
Don Giovanni
Don Pasquale
I Due Foscari
Il Duca D'Alba
Il Trovatore
Jean de Paris
John of Paris
King of Ys, The
L'Amico Fritz
La Nazaraise
La Straniera
La Vida Breve
Mefistofele
Night Flight
Noyes Fludde

Peter Grimes
Prisoner, The
Si j'etais Roi
Volo di Notte
War and Peace
William Tell

12

Ban of Love, The
Bassarids, The
Boris Godunov
Cosi Fan Tutte
Danton's Death
Debora Jaele
Die Tote Stadt
Foreigner, The
Giulio Cesare
Kath Kabanova
Konigskinder
La Somnabula
Le Domino Noir
Les Huguenots
L'Oca del Cairo
Manon Lescaut
Maria di Rohan
Maria Stuarda
Moses und Aron
Olympians, The
Owen Wingrave
Porgy and Bess

13

Albert Herring
Andrea Chenier
Death in Venice
Der Corregidor
Der Freischutz
Die Drei Pintos
Fairy Queen, The
Giovanna d' Arco
Guillaume Tell
Hugh the Drover
Hunyadi Laszlo

Il Prigioniero
Khovanshchina
King's Henchmen
Knot Garden, The
La Cenerentola
La Reine de Saba
La Scala di Seta
L'Elisir d'amor
Marino Fallero
Merrie England
Mother of Us All
Peter Ibbetson
Poor Sailor, The
Sir John in Love
Snow Maiden, The
Tenderland, The
Torquato Tasso
Tsar's Bride, The

14

A Night in Venice
Castor et Pollux
Decembrists, The
Der Dorfbarbier
Devils of London
Die Berglnappen
Henry the Eighth
Il Piccolo Marat
Irische Legende
Jonny Soielt Auf
La Donna del Lago
L'Amore del Tre Re
Le Pré aux Clercs
Lucrezia Borgia
Madame Sans Gene
Perfect Fool, The
Riders to the Sea
Robert le Diable
Robert the Devil
Samson et Dalila
Silent Woman, The
Sleepwalker, The
Spanish Hour, The

15

A Life for the Tsar
Beatrice di Tenda
Beggars Opera, The
Bohemian Girl, The
Das Liebesverbot
Devil and Kate, The
Down in the Valley
Fair Maid of Perth
Goose of Cairo, The
Hansel and Gretel
Immortal Hour, The
Le Nozze di Figaro
Le Pauvre Matelôt
L'Heure Espagnole
Madame Butterfly
Orphée aux Enfers
Pearl Fishers, The
Poisoned Kiss, The
Queen of Sheba, The
Riders to the Sea
Romeo et Juliette
Simon Boccanegra
Tale of Two Cities

16

Benvenuto Cellini
La Buona Figliuola
L'Attaque de Moulin
Linda di Chamounix
Queen of Spades, The
Rakes Progress, The
Royal Children, The
Samson and Delilah
Tristan und Isolda

17

Adriana Lecouvreur
Barber of Bagdad, The
Boatswain's Mate, The
Boulevard Solitude
Die Königin von Saba

Flying Dutchman, The
Force of Destiny, The
Francesca da Rimini
Gentle Shepherd, The
Guglielmo Ratcliff
Iphigenie en Aulide
I Puritan di Scozia
La Campana Sommersa
La Forza del Destino
La Muette de Portici
L'Italiana in Algeri
Lucia di Lammermoor
Madonna's Jewels, The
Makropoulos Affair
Midsummer Marriage
Mozart and Salliers
Rape of Lucretia, The
Re di Creta Idomenso
Ruslan and Lyudmila
Turn of the Screw, The

18

Beatrice et Benedict
Die Schweigsame Frau
Eine Nacht in Venedig
Il Filosolo di Campagna
Il Crociato in Egitto
Iphigenie en Tauride
La Finta Giardiniera
Le Austuzie Femminili
Le Maître de Chapelle
Les Contes d'Hoffmann
Les Malheurs d'Orphée
Richard Coeur de Lion
Story of a Real Man, The

19

Admento re di Tessaglia
Allesa ndro Stradella
Cavelleria Rusticana
Der Barbier von Bagdad
Die Agyptische Helena
Die Frau Öhne Schatten
Elegy for Young Lovers
Il Campanello di Notte
Il Matrimonio Segreto
La Jolie fille de Perth
Les Pêcheurs de Perles
Marriage of Figaro, The
Much Ado About Nothing
Pilgrim's Progress, The
Secret of Marriage, The
Sorrows of Orpheus, The

20 +

Besuch der Alten Dame Der
Coronation of Poppea, The
Cunning Little Vixen, The
Der Fliegende Hollander
Dialogues des Carmelites
Duke Bluebeard's Castle
Dumb Girl of Portici, The
Gioielli della Madonna
Girl of the Golden West, The
I Capuleti e I Montecchi
Italian Girl in Algiers
La Cambiale di Matrimonio
Les Cloches de Cornville
L'Incoronazione di Poppea
Merry Wives of Windsor, The
Midsummer Night's Dream, A
Orpheus in the Underworld
Travelling Companion, The

Operatic characters

3						4
	Asa	Eva	Liu	Meg	Ugo	
	Cas	Lel	Mab	Mel		
Ada	Dov	Lev	Max	Pan		Aron

Bess	Tita	Flute	Osaka	Amazil	Hannah
Cuno	Toni	Folco	Osmin	Andres	Hecuba
Duke	Ursa	Frank	Paolo	Andrea	Hector
Elsa	Wurm	Fritz	Paris	Andrey	Hermes
Emmy	Yuri	Gayle	Pasha	Annina	Hermio
Ezio	Zaza	Gilda	Pedro	Armida	Janthe
Finn		Gomez	Pimen	Arnold	Janusz
Hero	**5**	Grant	Polly	Arsace	Judith
Hugh		Groma	Porgy	Arturo	Julien
Iago	Adele	Guido	Priam	Astron	Kaspar
Ilia	Adina	Hanna	Rajah	Balkis	Kunrad
Iris	Agnes	Helen	Ralph	Becket	Kupava
Inez	Alain	Henry	Ramon	Bertha	Lensky
Jack	Aleen	Herod	Reiza	Blonde	Libuse
Joan	Aleko	Jacob	Romeo	Bottom	Lionel
Jove	Alfio	Julia	Salvo	Castor	Lockit
Juno	Alice	Kyoto	Sapho	Chanon	Louise
Kate	Amina	Lapak	Senta	Claire	Lubino
Kath	Anita	Laura	Silva	Cobweb	Luther
Leah	Armel	Levko	Simon	Ctirad	Lycoan
Lina	Assad	Leila	Snook	Cyrano	Mangus
Lola	Assur	Lilla	Snout	Daland	Martha
Lucy	Aubry	Linda	Suzel	Daphne	Maurya
Luke	Avito	Luigi	Tasso	Daudon	Mignon
Manz	Barak	Luisa	Thais	Denise	Milada
Mark	Bassi	Luise	Tisbe	Dmitry	Miller
Mary	Bella	Lykov	Tonio	Dorvil	Minnie
Mimi	Benda	Mamon	Tosca	Eadgar	Mizgir
Mino	Benes	Manru	Trott	Egmont	Mozart
Moth	Beppe	Maria	Ulana	Elvino	Nadori
Nero	Bobyl	Magda	Venus	Elvira	Nerone
Nils	Canio	Marti	Zaide	Enrico	Noriva
Nora	Carlo	Mauri		Ernani	Oberon
Olga	Chloe	Melot	**6**	Fabien	Ortrud
Omar	Crown	Midas		Fanuel	Otello
Owen	Dalva	Midir	Adolar	Farlaf	Ottone
Oros	Danae	Moses	Agatha	Fatima	Pollux
Paco	Diana	Mylio	Agnese	Fatime	Pompeo
Paul	Edgar	Nadir	Alaide	Fiesco	Poppea
Pisa	Etain	Naina	Alfred	Figaro	Phoebe
Puck	Faber	Nancy	Alexey	Gerald	Premys
Rose	Fanny	Nardo	Alvise	Gerard	Quince
Sali	Faust	Nedda	Amalia	Giulia	Ramiro
Snug	Fides	Norma	Amelia	Gomatz	Rachel
Thea	Flora	Orest	Aminta	Gilfen	Robert

Operas and their characters

Roxane
Rozenn
Ruslan
Salomé
Samiel
Samson
Selika
Seneca
Silvio
Shadow
Sophie
Spring
Stella
Suzuki
Taddeo
Thisbe
Tichon
Timida
Vasily
Zamord
Zdenek

7

Adriano
Aegisth
Aladino
Aleskey
Alidono
Alfonso
Allazim
Amneris
Antinea
Antonia
Araquil
Armanro
Arminda
Asteria
Atlanta
Baculus
Barbara
Barnaba
Bartley
Bartolo
Basilio

Bellina
Belmont
Berlioz
Bertram
Calisto
Cellini
Charles
Charlot
Chemier
Chrudos
Claudia
Corrado
Dandini
Delaqua
Delilah
Despina
Die Feen
Douglas
Edoardo
Eleazar
Elektra
Ernesto
Eugenia
Ferrano
Fidelia
Foresto
Gellner
Gennaro
Germont
Geronte
Giacomo
Grigory
Guntran
Harasta
Hermann
Hoffman
Irmelin
Isolier
Jacobin
Jenifer
Juliett
Jupiter
Koanger
Krasava
Kudrjas

La Cieca
Leander
Leonora
Lesbina
Lescaut
Licinio
Lindoro
Lorenzo
Lysiart
Macbeth
MacDuff
Malcolm
Mariola
Masetto
May King
Mazeppa
Mercury
Metifio
Micaela
Michele
Missail
Musetta
Nabucco
Natasha
Nelusko
Octavia
Olympia
Ottavio
Orpheus
Palmide
Palmyra
Paolino
Parasha
Pauline
Paquiro
Piquillo
Pope Leo
Poliuto
Radames
Rambaud
Rinaldo
Rivière
Rodolfo
Romanov
Rosario

Rossane
Ruggero
Rusalka
Salieri
Shuisky
Slender
Sobinin
Sperata
Stahlay
Stankar
Statire
Susanin
Tatyana
Telaira
Terynka
Tigrana
Titzkan
Tristan
Trouble
Turiddu
Tytania
Variaam
Varvara
Vincent
Vivette
Wolfram
Wozzeck
Zempira
Zerlina

8

Achilles
Adalgisa
Adrienne
Aennchem
Alphonso
Almansor
Amonasro
Ambrosio
Angelina
Antonida
Aristeau
Beatrice
Blondell

Boniface
Brangane
Carolina
Cathleen
Claggart
Clarrisa
Cleophas
Clorinda
Comte Ory
Die Kluge
Don Pinto
Drusilla
Dufresne
Elmireno
Elisetta
Eochaida
Eutripio
Euridice
Eurydice
Fernando
Filandro
Floreski
Freihild
Geronimo
Giampolo
Giocondo
Giovanni
Gonsalve
Gretchen
Gryaznoy
Heinrich
Huguette
I Damante
Isabella
Isoletae
Jezibaba
Juliette
King Mark
King René
Kochubey
Kutwenal
Lefebvre
Lodoiska
Lothario
Lucrezia

Lysander	Aphrodite	Justinian	Don Alfonso
Lyubasha	Bluebeard	Kabanicha	Don Lisargo
Lyudmila	Bobylikha	Katherine	Don Pttavio
MacHeath	Butterfly	King Priam	Dourlinski
Maliella	Caramello	King Roger	Duke of Alba
Manfredo	Cassandra	Loddletta	Duke Robert
Marcello	Christian	Löhengrin	Fieramosca
Margiana	Christine	Leicester	Fransquita
Margared	Cherubino	Leporello	Fra Daviolo
Marietta	Chevreuse	MacGregor	Gianciotto
Mathilde	Ciboletta	Maddalena	Gwendoline
Meleager	Colombine	Militrisa	Henry Smith
Mercedes	Constanze	Nerodiade	Khlestakov
Mercutto	Coppelius	Orombello	King Fisher
Mrs. Grose	Cio-Cio-San	Pannochka	King Harald
Mireille	Demetrius	Poppacoda	Lady Pamela
Nemorino	Desdemona	Patroclus	Lord Walton
Niclause	Des Grieux	Pinkerton	Lucy Ashton
Nourabad	Dominique	Povarikha	Marcellina
Nureddin	Donabella	Richelieu	Margherita
Odabella	Don Andres	Rigoletto	Marguerite
Olympian	Don Alvaro	Rosalinde	Mary Stuart
Pedrillo	Don Gaston	Schaunard	Miss Jessel
Pollione	Donna Anna	Sharpless	Nick Shadow
Raffaele	Dulcamara	Sherasmin	Nilakantha
Raimbaud	Eglantine	Skradella	Peter Quint
Sandrina	Elisabeth	Simon Mago	Saxon Armel
Santuzza	Euryanthe	Sososstris	Sebastiano
Serafina	Escamillo	Stiffelio	Simon Perez
Serpetia	Faramondo	Sula Smith	Sir Morosus
Serverus	Françoise	Svyetozar	Spalanzini
Somarone	Francesco	Telramund	Starveling
Stolzius	Frau Fluth	Tkachikha	Tannhauser
Tio Lucas	Frau Reich	Tsar Peter	Torquemade
Titzikan	Frederica	Valentine	Tsar Sultan
Toreador	Friedhold	Venusberg	Valdeburgo
Turandot	Giorgetta		
	Guadalett		
	Gottfried	**10**	**11**
9	Guilielmo		
	Hagenbach	Aethewold	Anne Trulove
Abigaille	Harlequin	Ann Boleyn	Baba the Turk
Adonigram	Hilda Mack	Boccanegra	Captain Vere
Amaryllus	I Damanteo	Bourlinski	Chrysothems
Angelotti	Jack Rance	De Bretigny	Count of Moor
Angelique		Doctor Falke	Count Walter

Charlemagne
Dick Johnson
Doge of Genoa
Don Ruy Gomez
Duke Ferrara
Earl of Essex
Emir of Tunis
Fata Morgana
Friedenstag
George Brown
Jane Seymour
Jean Gaussin
King of Spain
King Solomon
Lady Billows
Lady Harriet
Lady Macbeth
La Perichole
Lord Ruthven
Malatestino
Massimician
Princivalle
Prince Calaf
Queen Roxane
Roderick Dhu
Snegurochka
Sparafucile
Tom Bakewell
Tormentilla
Vasca de Gama
Vasco de Saxe
William Tell

12

Baron de Mercy
Baron Douphol
Baron Soarpia
Count Douglas
Count Rodolfo
Don Magnifico
Don Triternio
Duke of Mantua
Duke of Norway
Duke of Venice

Duke of Urbino
Enzo Grimaldi
Fanny Legrand
Flora Bervoix
Hunyadi Lazlo
Madame Larina
Iola Gioconda
John of Leydon
Lord Cockburn
Miss Wingrave
Pease-blossom
Piccolo Marat
Prince Gremin
Prince Guidon
Prince Ramiro
Prince Ratmir
Quenn of Sheba
Rautendelein
Robert Storch
Spencer Coyle
Thomas Bouche
Tsar Berendey

13

Andrew Jackson
Byronic Onegin
Captain Zunica
Countess Adele
Count Robinson
Daniel Webster
Der Freischutz
Doctor Miracle
Don Inigo Gomez
Duke of Norfolk
Duke of Rothsay
Federico Manton
Friar Laurence
Il Mlle Blanche
Jacopo Foscari
Jennie Parsons
King of Castile
La Dame Blanche
L'Etoile du Nord
Major Kovalyon

Monsieur Emile
Peter Ibbetson
Prince Arindal
Queen of Spades
Sultan Aladino
Susan B. Anthony
Ulysses S. Grant

14

Alfredo Germont
Baron Desportes
Cardinal Brogni
Count Belifiore
Count of Chalais
Doctor Romaulda
Duke of Burgundy
John the Baptist
King Archibaldo
Prince Oriofsky
Queen Elizabeth
Queen Henrietta
Sir Tobias Mills
Tristan d'Acunha
William Meister

15

Catherine Glover
Colonel Ibbetson
Count of Eberbagh
Das Liebesverbot
Doctor Malatesta
Don Jose Martinez
Don Juan de Aragon
Duchess of Danzig
Duchess of Towers
Edgar Ravenswood
Der Evangelimann
Isabelle de Bearn
King Henry Eighth
Monsieur Triquet
Princess Irmelin
Princess Isabeau
Sergeant Belcore

Stella de Tolomel
William Ratcliff

16

Cardinal Salviati
Countess Cathleen
Councillor Kalina
Henry of Brunswick
Landgrave Hermann
Lord Arthur Talbot
Princess Bouillon
Princess Turandot
Princess of Navare
Sir Walter Raleigh

17

Alexander the Great

High Priest of Dagon
Katerina Izmaylova
Lord Arthur Bucklow
Marchese Attavanti
Marquis of San Marco
Parisina Malatesta

18 +

Bessie Throckmorton
Countess Violanta Onesti
Crown Prince of France
Eleandra di Scandiano
Filippo, Duke of Milan
Marguerite of Flanders
Marquis of Calatrava
Percy, Earl of
  Northumberland

Paper and board

2, 3 & 4

demy
ISO
leaf
MF
MG
post
pot
pott
ream
SG

5

atlas
brief
crown
folio
royal

6

bag cap
casing
metric
octavo
quarto
tissue

7

airmail
emperor
imperial
kent cap

8

artboard
art paper

elephant
foolscap
haven cap
imperial
quad demy

9

cartridge
cardboard
chipboard
colombier
large post
music demy
newsprint
onionskin
pulp board
quad crown
quad sheet

10

bible paper
double demy
double post
grand eagle
India paper
pasteboard
small royal
strawboard
super royal

11

antiquarian
crown quarto
double crown
imperial cap
pinched post
ticket board

board

12

drawing board
imitation art
quad foolscap

14

double elephant
double foolscap
double imperial
lined chipboard

15

double large post
double quad crown
double four pound

13

mounting

Parts of the body

2 & 3	foot	ankle	organ	**6**	genome
	gene	aorta	ovary		gullet
ADP	gums	atlas	penis	airway	humour
arm	hair	blood	pinna	areola	kidney
ATP	hand	bowel	pubis	armpit	lanugo
CNS	head	brain	pulse	artery	larynx
DNA	heel	bursa	pupil	atrium	lobule
ear	iris	chord	renin	axilla	lumbar
egg	knee	cilia	semen	biceps	marrow
eye	lens	colon	serum	breast	muscle
fat	lips	cones	sinus	caecum	myelin
gut	lobe	elbow	skull	canine	myosin
hip	lung	femur	sperm	carpal	neuron
jaw	nail	gland	spine	carpus	nipple
leg	node	gonad	talus	cervix	nodule
LH	nose	groin	tears	coccyx	palate
RNA	ovum	heart	teeth	corium	pelvis
rib	pore	hymen	thumb	cornea	pepsin
rod	ribs	ileum	tibia	cortex	plasma
toe	rods	ilium	tinea	dermis	pleura
	skin	incus	tooth	earwax	plexus
	ulna	joint	tract	embryo	radius
4	urea	labia	trunk	enzyme	rectum
	wart	liver	urine	eyelid	rennin
ACTH	womb	lymph	uvula	faeces	retina
anus	ulna	molar	valve	fascia	sacrum
axis	vein	mucus	vulva	fibula	saliva
axon		navel	wrist	flexor	sclera
bile		nerve		foetus	septum
bone	**5**	nares		fundus	smegma
disc		orbit		gamete	socket
cell	actin				

spleen
tarsal
tarsus
tendon
testis
thorax
thymus
tissue
tongue
ureter
uterus
vagina
venule
villus

7

abdomen
agonist
albumin
auricle
bladder
calcium
capsule
cardiac
carotid
choroid
cochlea
condyle
cranium
cuticle
eardrum
ethmoid
eyelash
femoral
fimbria
glottis
gristle
heparin
hormone
humerus
incisor
insulin
ischium
jejunum

malleus
mastoid
maxilla
medulla
melanin
neurone
nucleus
ossicle
papilla
patella
phallus
pharynx
prepuce
protein
pudenda
pylorus
scapula
scrotum
sternum
stomach
tonsils
trachea
urethra
vacuole
viscera

8

adenoids
alveolus
androgen
backbone
bile duct
bronchus
cerebrum
chlorine
clitoris
clavicle
collagen
cortisol
dendrite
duodenum
extensor
filament
follicle

foreskin
ganglion
globulin
glucagon
incisors
inner ear
ligament
mandible
masseter
mast cell
membrane
meninges
mesoderm
midbrain
monocyte
oxytocin
pancreas
pectoral
peduncle
perineum
pia mater
placenta
platelet
premolar
receptor
ribosome
secretin
shinbone
skeleton
steroids
thalamus
tympanum
tyrosine
uric acid
vena cava
vertebra
windpipe
xanthoma

9

arteriole
bilirubin
brainstem
calcaneus

capillary
cartilage
corpuscle
cortisone
diaphragm
dura mater
epidermis
forebrain
funny bone
genitalia
hamstring
hindbrain
hyoid bone
labyrinth
leukocyte
lymph node
mesentery
middle ear
milk teeth
nerve cell
oestrogen
olecranon
organelle
phagocyte
phalanges
prolactin
reflex arc
rhodopsin
serotonin
sphincter
thyroxine
ventricle
vestibule
vocal cord

10

acetabulum
Adam's apple
adrenaline
antagonist
birth canal
blood cells
blastocyst
blood sugar

bone marrow
breastbone
calcitonin
cerebellum
chromosome
collar bone
endorphins
epididymis
epiglottis
epithelium
fibrinogen
fontanelle
glomerulus
grey matter
heart valve
integument
intestines
lymphocyte
macrophage
metacarpal
metacarpus
metatarsal
metatarsus
myocardium
oesophagus
optic nerve
periosteum
peritoneum
pineal body
portal vein
protoplasm
spinal cord
vagus nerve

11

agglutinins
aldosterone
blood vessel
cauda equina
conjunctiva
endocardium
endometrium
erythrocyte
facial nerve

floating rib
granulocyte
haemoglobin
hippocampus
jugular vein
lipoprotein
loop of Henle
median nerve
mitral valve
motor cortex
nasal cavity
nasal septum
nasopharynx
nucleic acid
pericardium
sex hormones
solar plexus
vas deferens
vasopressin
white matter
wisdom teeth

12

adrenal gland
barorecepter
basal ganglia
dominant gene
eccrine gland
gonadotropin
hair follicle
hypothalamus
Langer's lines
limbic system
mammary gland
optic chiasma
organ of Corti
parathormone
phrenic nerve
red blood cell
sciatic nerve
smooth muscle
spermatozoon
spinal nerves
testosterone

thoracic duct
thyroid gland
urinary tract

13

deltoid muscle
ductless gland
exocrine gland
Fallopian tube
femoral artery
gamma globulin
gastric juices
gonadotropins
growth hormone
lacrimal gland
mitochondrion
nervous system
noradrenaline
parotid glands
recessive gene
salivary gland
shoulder blade
umbilical cord
zygomatic arch
zygomatic bone

14

Achilles tendon
Bowman's capsule
cerebral cortex
circle of Willis
coronary artery
corticosteroid
deciduous teeth
digestive tract
endocrine gland
Eustachian tube
exteroreceptor
Golgi apparatus
mucous membrane
olfactory nerve
oxyhaemaglobin
paranasal sinus

pituitary gland
proprioceptors
prostaglandins
sebaceous gland
semilunar valve
seminal vesicle
sinoatrial node
skeletal muscle
striated muscle
thoracic cavity
tricuspid valve
vitreous humour
white blood cell

15

alimentary canal
Haversian system
lumbar vertebrae
oculomotor nerve
ovarian follicle
ribonucleic acid
sacroiliac joint
trigeminal nerve
vertebral column

16 +

antidiuretic hormone

arachnoid membrane
basement membrane
cardiovascular system
cerebral hemispheres
cervical vertebrae
central nervous system
cerebrospinal fluid
connective tissue
extracellular fluid
glossopharyngeal nerve
glucocorticoid hormone
hepatic portal vein
hydrochloric acid
intervertebral disc
islets of Langerhans
luteinizing hormone
medulla oblongata
parathyroid glands
parathyroid hormone
peripheral nervous system
respiratory centre
reticular activating system
semicircular canals
seminiferous tubules
sympathetic nervous system
synovial membrane
thoracic vertebrae
thyroid-stimulating hormone
urogenital system

Patron saints

3 & 4

Anne - Canada; housewives
Elmo - sailors
Eloi - jewellers;
  metalworkers
Eric - Sweden
Ivo   - lawyers
Jude - afflicted;
  hopeless causes
Luke - artists; brewers;
  physicians; surgeons

Olaf - Norway
Zita - domestic servants

5

Amand - inkeepers; wine
  merchants
Asgar - Denmark
David - poets; Wales
Denys - France
Giles - beggers;
  blacksmiths; cripples

James – Spain
Menas – merchants
Vitus – epilepsy; nervous diseases

6

Adrian – soldiers
Agatha – bell founders; nurses
Albert – scientists
Andrew – Greece; Russia; Scotland
Antony – lost property; poor
Blaise – woolcombers
Canute – Denmark
Claude – sculptors
Dympna – insane
Dysmas – funeral directors
Fiacre – drivers; gardeners
George – England; farmers; scouts; soldiers
Hubert – huntsmen
Jerome – librarians
Joseph – Belgium; Canada; carpenters; workers
Julian – boatmen; inkeepers; travellers
Martha – cooks; housewives
Monica – Christian mothers
Teresa – foreign missions; Spain
Ursula – schools

7

Adelard – gardeners
Alexius – nurses
Barbara – architects; gunners; miners
Brendan – sailors
Bridget – Ireland; Sweden
Casimir – Poland
Cassian – secretaries
Cecilia – church music; musicians; poets

Crispin – shoemakers; leatherworkers
Dunstan – blacksmiths; goldsmiths; jewellers; locksmiths; musicians; singers
Eligius – metalworkers
Erasmus – sailors
Eulalia – sailors
Eustace – huntsmen
Florian – firemen
Gabriel – post; telecommunications
Isidore – farmers
Leonard – prisoners
Matthew – accountants; bankers; book-keepers; tax-collectors
Maurice – infantrymen
Michael – Germany; grocers; paratroopers; police officers
Patrick – Ireland
Raphael – nurses; physicians
Stephen – bricklayers; Hungary
Therese – florists

8

Boniface – Germany
Camillus – nurses
Cuthbert – sailors
Dorothea – florists; gardeners
Genesius – actors; lawyers; secretaries
Gertrude – West Indies
Ignatius – soldiers
Lawrence – cooks
Nicholas – apothecaries; bakers; children; Greece; merchants; pawnbrokers; perfumiers; Russia; sailors; unmarried girls

Venerius - lighthouse-
  keepers

9

Apollonia   - dentists
Catherine   - attorneys;
  scholars; teachers;
  wheelwrights
Joan of Arc - France;
  soldiers
John of God - booksellers;
  hospitals; nurses; printers
Pantaleon   - physicians
Procopius   - Czechoslovakia
Sebastian   - archers;
  athletes; soldiers
Valentine   - lovers
Wenceslas   - Bohemia;
  Czechoslovakia

10

Crispinian - leatherworkers
Frideswide - Oxford
Thomas More - lawyers
Willibrord - Holland

11

Christopher - motorists;
  sailors; wayfarers

12

Peter Nolasco - midwives

13

Frances of Rome   -
  motorists
Francis Xavier - foreign
  missions

John of Nepomuk   -
  Czechoslovakia
Thomas Aquinas - scholars
Vincent Ferrer - builders

14

Francis de Sales   -
  writers; journalists
Jerome Emiliani - orphans
  and abandoned children
Our Lady of Grace   -
  motorcyclists

15 +

Bernadine of Siena -
  advertising
Bernard of Mount Joux -
  mountaineers
Camillus of Lellis - nurses
Catherine of Siena - Italy
Elizabeth of Hungary -
  bakers
Francis of Assisi - animals;
  Italy
Francis of Cabrini -
  emigrants
Gregory the Great -
  musicians; singers;
  teachers
Joseph Cupertino - airmen
Joseph of Arimathea   -
  funeral directors
Katherine of Alexandria -
  scholars; philosophers;
  craftsmen
Our Lady Help of Christians
  - Australia; New Zealand
Our Lady of Loreto - airmen
Our Lady of the Assumption
  - India; South Africa
Therese of Lisieux - airmen;
  Russia

Phobias

9

apiphobia - bees
atephobia - being ruined
neophobia - change;
  anything new
zoophobia - animals

10

acrophobia - heights
aerophobia - air; aircraft
algophobia - pain
autophobia - being alone;
  oneself
cenophobia - empty spaces
cibophobia - food
cynophobia - dogs
demophobia - crowds
eosophobia - dawn
gynophobia - women
hemophobia - blood
hodophobia - travel
hylophobia - woods
kenophobia - empty spaces
monophobia - being alone
musophobia - mice
nosophobia - disease
panophobia - everything
polyphobia - many things
pyrophobia - fire
sitophobia - food
theophobia - God
xenophobia - strangers

11

acarophobia - insects
agoraphobia - open spaces
androphobia - men
anemophobia - wind

astraphobia - thunder and
  lightning
chionphobia - snow
dromophobia - crossing roads
gymnophobia - nakedness
haemophobia - blood
haphephobia - being touched
heliophobia - sunlight
hierophobia - sacred things
hippophobia - horses
hormephobia - shocks
hydrophobia - water
hygrophobia - moisture
hypnophobia - sleep
laliophobia - speaking
maniaphobia - insanity
microphobia - small objects
necrophobia - dead bodies
noctiphobia - night
nyctophobia - darkness; night
ochlophobia - crowds
ombrophobia - rain
pathophobia - disease
phobophobia - fear
phonophobia - speaking aloud
photophobia - light
scopophobia - being watched
scotophobia - darkness
stasiphobia - standing

12

ailurophobia - cats
anginophobia - choking,
  suffocation
brontophobia - thunder
chronophobia - time
entomophobia - insects
hedonophobia - pleasure
hyposophobia - heights
icthyophobia - fish

kinesophobia - motion
kleptophobia - stealing
megalophobia - large objects
odontophobia - dentistry
phasmophobia - ghosts
potamophobia - rivers
satanophobia - the Devil
stygiophobia - hell
thermophobia - heat
toxicophobia - poison
trichophobia - hair

13

arachnophobia - spiders
asthenophobia - weakness
erythrophobia - blushing;
red
climacophobia - stairs
harpaxophobia - thieves
melissophobia - bees
ophidiophobia - snakes

ornithophobia - birds
peccatiphobia - corruption
psychrophobia - cold
pteronophobia - feathers
scelerophobia - burglars
sidereophobia - stars
thanatophobia - death
tridekaphobia - the number 13

14

anthropophobia - people
ballistophobia - missiles
batrachophobia - frogs
chrematophobia - money
chromatophobia - colour
claustrophobia - being shut in
maieutiophobia - childbirth
parthenophobia - young women
pharmacophobia - medicine
thalassophobia - sea
traumatophobia - injury

Places in London

3	Euston	Clapton	The Oval	Highgate
Bow	Fulham	Croydon	Tooting	Highbury
	Harrow	Dulwich	Wapping	Holloway
4	Hendon	East End	Wembley	Hounslow
	Ilford	East Ham	West End	Hyde Park
Soho	Newham	Enfield	West Ham	Kingston
	Putney	Edgware		Lewisham
	Sutton	Hackney		Mill Hill
5		Holborn	**8**	Richmond
Acton		Kilburn		Southall
Brent	**7**	Lambeth	Barbican	Surbiton
	Aldgate	Mayfair	Chiswick	Victoria
	Barking	Mile End	Deptford	Vauxhall
6	Brixton	Mitcham	Edmonton	Wanstead
	Bromley	Peckham	Finchley	Waterloo
Barnet	Catford	Pimlico	Finsbury	Woodford
Camden	Chelsea	Stepney	Grays	Woolwich
Ealing	Clapham	The Mall	Inn	
			Haringey	

9

Battersea
Bayswater
Brentford
Docklands
Greenwich
Guildhall
Hampstead
Islington
Old Bailey
Redbridge
Rotten Row
Royal Mint
Southgate
Southwark
Stockwell
Stratford
Streatham
The Temple
Tottenham
Tower Hill
Tulse Hill
White City
Whitehall
Willesden
Wimbledon
Wood Green

10

Albert Hall
Bermondsey
Bloomsbury
Camberwell
Camden Town
County Hall
Earls Court
Hillingdon
Kennington
Kensington
Marble Arch
Marylebone
Paddington

Piccadilly
Serpentine
Shoreditch
Teddington
The Strand
Twickenham
Wandsworth

11

Bishopsgate
Blackfriars
Bond Street
Fleet Street
Hammersmith
Hither Green
Holland Park
Kentish Town
Notting Hill
Regents Park
Sloane Square
St. Johns Wood
Tate Gallery
Tower Bridge
Walthamstow
Westminster
Whitechapel

12

Bethnal Green
Billingsgate
Charing Cross
Covent Garden
Golders Green
Harley Street
Lavender Hill
London Bridge
Oxford Circus
Oxford Street
Primrose Hill
Regent Street
Royal Academy
Swiss Cottage

Tower Hamlets

13

Admiralty Arch
British Museum
Bank of England
Berkley Square
Crystal Palace
Downing Street
Knightsbridge
Lambeth Palace
Nelson's column
Shepherds Bush
Somerset House
Stock Exchange
Tower of London
Waltham Forest

14

Madame Tussaud's
Parliament Hill
St. James's Palace
Stoke Newington
The Planetarium
Wembley Stadium

15

Chelsea Hospital
Leicester Square
Liverpool Street
National Gallery
National Theatre
New Scotland Yard
Post Office Tower
Royal Opera House
Trafalgar Square

16 +

Buckingham Palace
Covent Garden Market

Elephant and Castle
Horse Guards Parade
Houses of Parliament
Imperial War Museum
Kensington Gardens
Kingston-upon-Thames
Lord's Cricket Ground
Natural History Museum

Royal College of Music
Royal Geographical Society
Royal Festival Hall
St. Paul's Cathedral
Threadneedle Street
Victoria and Albert Museum
Westminster Abbey
Westminster Cathedral

Planets and asteroids

4

Amor
Eros
Hebe
Iris
Juno
Mars

5

Earth
Ceres
Pluto
Vesta
Venus

6

Adonis
Apollo
Chiron
Hermes
Hygiea
Icarus
Pallas
Uranus
Saturn

7

Astreae
Eunomia
Hidalgo
Mercury
Jupiter

8

Achilles

10

Euphrosyne

Reptiles and amphibians

3 & 4

asp
boa
eft
frog
gila
newt
pipa
toad

5

adder

agama
cobra
draco
gecko
guana
krait
mamba
siren
skink
snake
swift
tokay
viper

6

caiman
cayman
garial
gavial
goanna
iguana
lizard
muggar
mugger
muggur
python
taipan

turtle

7

axolotl
gharial
ghavial
hognose
monitor
paddock
rattler
saurian
serpent
snapper

tadpole
tuatara
urodele

8

anaconda
basilisk
bullfrog
cerastes
colubrid
Congo eel
moccasin
mud puppy

ophidian
pit viper
polliwog
rat snake
rhingals
sea snake
slow worm
terrapin
tortoise
tree frog
stinkpot
rat snake
water boa

9

alligator
blindworm
blue racer
boomslang
bull snake
box turtle
caecilion
chameleon
chelonian
crocodile
frog spawn
galliwasp
hairy frog
hamadryad
hoop snake
iguanodon
jew lizard
king cobra
king snake
milk snake
mud turtle
puff adder
ring snake

rock snake
sea turtle
tiger snake
tree snake
whip snake

10

batrachian
black snake
bushmaster
chuckwalla
congo snake
copperhead
coral snake
fer-de-lance
flying frog
glass snake
grass snake
green snake
hellbender
horned toad
loggerhead
natterjack
rock python
salamander
sand lizard
sidewinder
tiger snake
wall lizard
water snake

11

amphisbaena
carpet snake
constrictor
cottonmouth
diamond back

draco lizard
fence lizard
flying snake
garter snake
gila monster
goliath frog
gopher snake
green turtle
horned viper
midwife toad
rattlesnake
smooth snake
Surinam toad

12

carpet python
dragon lizard
flying lizard
hognose snake
Komodo dragon
Komodo lizard
horned lizard

13

bearded lizard
frilled lizard
giant tortoise
monitor lizard
water moccasin

14 +

boa constrictor
leatherback turtle
marsh crocodile
painted terrapin
soft-shelled turtle

Rivers

1

E
Y

Hue
Ili
Ill
Inn
Jiu
Ket
Kur
Kwa
Lea
Lee
Lek
Lim
Lot
Lys
Moy
Nar
Nen
Obi
Oka
Ord
Pic
Pur
Red
Rib
Roe
Rur
Rye
Sid
Sir
Sow
Syr
Taw
Tay
Tom
Tye
Ure
Usa
Usk
Var
Ver
Wey

2

Aa
Ii
Ob
Po
Si

3

Aar
Ahi
Ain
Aln
Alt
Axe
Ayr
Bug
Cam
Can
Chu
Dal
Dee
Dja
Don
Dua
Ely
Ems
Esk
Exe
Fal
Fly
Han
Hay
Hex
Hsi

Wye
Yeo
Zab

4

Aare
Adda
Adur
Agra
Agri
Aire
Alma
Alph
Alta
Amoo
Amur
Anio
Arno
Arun
Aube
Aude
Avon
Back
Bann
Beas
Beni
Brue
Bure
Bush
Cart
Cary
Cher
Chew
Chir
Cole
Coln
Cree
Dart
Doon
Dora

Dove
Duna
Earn
Ebro
Eden
Elan
Elbe
Elwy
Enns
Erne
Eure
Fall
Finn
Geba
Gila
Glan
Glen
Gota
Grey
Ha Ha
Hase
Hull
Irin
Isar
Isis
Isla
Juba
Kama
Kura
Kusi
Lahn
Leaf
Lech
Lena
Lima
Loir
Lune
Lynd
Lyon
Maas
Main

Meon
Meta
Milk
Mole
Mooi
Moth
Naze
Nene
Neva
Nida
Nile
Nith
Nore
Oder
Ohio
Oise
Orne
Ouse
Oxus
Para
Peel
Pina
Plym
Prah
Prut
Qena
Ravi
Rede
Reno
Rock
Roer
Ruhr
Saar
Salt
Save
Seal
Spey
Styr
Suir
Swan
Taff

Tana
Tara
Tarn
Tawe
Tees
Teme
Test
Thur
Tons
Towy
Tyne
Tywi
Ugie
Umea
Ural
Vaal
Vire
Waag
Waal
Wear
Yaln
Yana
Yare
York
Yser
Zorn

5

Abana
Adige
Adour
Aeron
Agano
Agout
Aisne
Aldan
Alice
Allen
Aller
Annan

Apure	Gumti	Neuse	Tamar	Albert	Granta
Argun	Habra	Niger	Tapti	Allier	Hamble
Avoca	Havel	Oglio	Tarim	Almond	Hawash
Benue	Hondo	Onega	Teffe	Amazon	Hudson
Black	Huang	Osage	Teifi	Angara	Huelva
Blood	Hugli	Otter	Teign	Aragon	Humber
Bober	Hunza	Oykel	Teith	Arinos	Hwan-Ho
Bogie	Ikopa	Payne	Temes	Atbara	Iguacu
Boyne	Indre	Peace	Tiber	Bandon	Ijssel
Brent	Indus	Pearl	Tisza	Barcoo	Irtysh
Bride	Isère	Pecos	Torne	Barrow	Irwell
Brora	Ishim	Pei Ho	Traun	Barwon	Itchen
Cairn	Jelum	Pelly	Trent	Beauly	Japura
Camel	Jumna	Perak	Tweed	Bio-Bio	Javari
Cedar	Jurva	Piave	Usuri	Bolsas	Jhelum
Clare	Kabul	Plate	Vitim	Bourne	Jordan
Clwyd	Kafue	Pruth	Volga	Brazos	Kagera
Clyde	Karun	Purus	Volta	Buchan	Kaveri
Colne	Kasai	Rance	Wahgi	Buller	Kennet
Congo	Katun	Reuss	Warta	Bulloo	Kikori
Conwy	Kings	Rhine	Welle	Calder	Kolyma
Cothi	Koros	Rhone	Werra	Canton	Komati
Deben	Kowie	Roper	Weser	Caroni	Konkib
Derry	Kuram	Saale	Whale	Carron	Kwanza
Desna	Lagan	Saône	Whion	Chenab	Lehigh
Devon	Lenea	Sarre	White	Conway	Leitha
Douro	Lethe	Seine	Xingu	Coquet	Liddel
Dovey	Leven	Shari	Xiugo	Crouch	Liffey
Drina	Liard	Sheaf	Yanda	Cuanza	Loddon
Dvina	Lippe	Shiel	Yaqui	Cuiaba	Lomami
Eider	Loire	Shire	Yarty	Danube	Mamore
Ellen	Lotta	Siang	Yonne	Dihong	Medina
Etive	Marne	Siont	Yssel	Donets	Medway
Feale	Maroo	Slave	Ythan	Draava	Mekong
Fleet	Memel	Snake	Yukon	Elster	Mersey
Flint	Menam	Snowy	Zaïre	Escaut	Mincio
Forth	Meuse	Somme	Zenta	Farrar	Mobile
Fowey	Miami	Spree		Foyers	Modder
Foyle	Minho	Stolp	**6**	Fraser	Mohawk
Frome	Mosel	Stour		French	Moisie
Gabon	Moose	Swale	Abdiel	Gambia	Moldau
Garry	Nairn	Sugar	Agogno	Gandak	Monnow
Gogra	Neath	Sulir	Aguada	Ganges	Morava
Grand	Negro	Swale	Alagon	Glomma	Moskva
Green	Neman	Tagus	Albany	Grande	Murray

Neckar	Sutluj	Analong	Limpopo	Surinam
Neisse	Swakop	Annalee	Lualaba	Suwanee
Nelson	Swilly	Berbice	Luangwa	Tampico
Neutra	Tamega	Bermejo	Lugendi	Tapajos
Niemen	Tanana	Big Blue	Madeira	Thomson
Noatak	Tanaro	Big Horn	Marañón	Tobique
Ogowai	Teviot	Buffalo	Maritsa	Trinity
Oneida	Thames	Calabar	Maritza	Tsangpo
Orange	Theiss	Catawba	Mattawa	Ucayali
Orwell	Thurso	Cauvery	Mayenne	Uruguay
Ottawa	Ticino	Chambal	Meander	Vistula
Paraná	Tigris	Chelmer	Meklong	Waikato
Parima	Tormes	Chumbal	Meranon	Waitaki
Parret	Tornio	Cleddau	Moselle	Warrego
Platte	Tugela	Darling	Muluvar	Washita
Porali	Tummel	Derwent	Murghab	Waveney
Pripet	Turkey	Deveron	Narbuda	Welland
Pungwe	Ubangi	Dneiper	Niagara	Wichita
Quoile	Umpqua	Douglas	Olifant	Xanthus
Racket	Ussuri	Dubawnt	Orinoco	Yangtse
Ribble	Viatka	Dunajec	Orontes	Yarkand
Roding	Vienne	Durance	Owenboy	Yenesei
Rother	Vilyny	Ettrick	Parsnip	Ystwyth
Rovuma	Vilyui	Feather	Passaic	Yuruari
Rufiji	Vlatva	Fitzroy	Pechora	Zambezi
Rupert	Wabash	Gamtoos	Potomac	
Sabine	Waihou	Garonne	Red Deer	**8**
St. Paul	Wandle	Gauritz	Roanoke	
Salado	Warthe	Genesee	Rubicon	Amu Darya
Salmon	Weaver	Gilbert	Salween	Araguaia
Sambre	Wensum	Gironde	San Juan	Arkansas
Sarthe	Wharfe	Glenelg	Sankuru	Beaulieu
Salwin	Wipper	Glommen	St. Johns	Beresina
Sambre	Witham	Guapore	Salween	Big Black
Santee	Yamuna	Helmand	Schelde	Blue Nile
Scheld	Yarrow	Heri Rud	Scheldt	Brisbane
Scioto	Yavari	Huang He	Selenga	Campaspe
Seiont	Yellow	Hooghli	Semliki	Cape Fear
Seneca	Zarang	Hwangho	Senegal	Chambezi
Sereth	Zontag	Juniata	Shannon	Cherwell
Severn		Kanawha	Shibeli	Cheyenne
Slaney	**7**	Krishna	Si Kiang	Chindwin
Stroma		Kubango	Spokane	Clarence
Sunday	Abitibi	Lachlan	Sundays	Colorado
Sutlej	Alabama	La Plata	Sungari	Columbia

Delaware
Demerara
Dneister
Dordogne
Eastmain
Evenlode
Findhorn
Flinders
Gallinas
Gascoyne
Gatineau
Georgina
Godavari
Goulburn
Great Kei
Guadiana
Guiviari
Hamilton
Hankiang
Huallaga
Humboldt
Illinois
Irtysh Ob
Itimbiri
Kankakee
Kelantan
Kennebec
Klondyke
Kootenay
Mahanadi
Mazaruni
Merrimac
Missouri
Mitchell
Nebraska
Ob Irtish
Paraguay
Paracuta
Parnaíba
Putumayo
Red River
Richmond
Rimouski
Rio Negro
Rio Tinto

Saguenay
St. Claire
Santiago
Savannah
Stinchor
Suwannee
Syr Daria
Torridge
Tunguska
Umvolosi
Victoria
Wanganui
Wansbeck
Windrush
Winnipeg

9

Abbitibee
Athabaska
Churchill
Crocodile
East River
Esmeralda
Essequibo
Euphrates
Gala Water
Great Fish
Great Ouse
Guadelete
Helmsdale
Indigirka
Irrawaddy
Kalamazoo
Kizil Uzen
Mackenzie
Magdalena
Mallagami
Miramichi
Murchison
Nipisquit
Paranaíba
Penobscot
Pilcomayo
Porcupine

Qu' Appelle
Rede River
Richelieu
Rio Branco
Rio Grande
Roosevelt
Saint John
Saint Paul
Salt River
Tennessee
Tocantins
Toombudra
Trombetas
White Nile
Wisconsin
Zarafshan

10

Allenwater
Black River
Blackwater
Blood River
Great Slave
Green River
Hackensack
Hawkesbury
Kizil Irmak
Lackawanna
Manzanares
Paranahiba
Parramatta
Republican
Sacramento
San Joaquin
Saint John's
St. Lawrence
Shat-el-Arab
Shenandoah
Snake River
White River
Yarra Yarra

11

Bonaventure

Brahmaptura
Chiang Jiang
Desaguadero
Madre de Dois
Mississippi
Modder River
Monongahela
Restigouche
Rio del Norte
Saint Claire
Susquehanna
Upper Paraná

Yarrowwater
Yellow River
Yellowstone

12

Big Blue River
Big Horn River
Ettrickwater
Great Kanawka
Guadalquivir
Murrumbidgee

Rappahannock
Sao Franciso
Saskatchewan
Shubenacadia
Yangtse Kiang

13

Big Black River
Big Sandy River
Big Sioux River
Saint Lawrence

Roman emperors

3

Leo (I&II)

4

Geta
Nero
Otho

5

Carus
Galba
Nerva
Titus

6

Avitus
Decius
Gallus
Jovian
Julian
Julius
Philip
Probus

Trajan
Valens

7

Carinus
Gordian
 (I-III)
Gratian
Hadrian
Marcian
Maximin
Maximus
Severus
Tacitus

8

Arcadius
Augustus
Aurelian
Balbinus
Caligula
Claudius
 (I&II)
Commodus
Constans

Domitian
Eugenius
Galerius
Honorius
Lucinius
Macrinus
Majorian
Maximian
Olybrius
Pertinax
Tiberius
Valerian

9

Anthemius
Caracalla
Florianus
Gallienus
Glycerius
Maxentius
Vespasian
Vitellius

10

Aemilianus

Diocletian
Magnentius
Numerianus
Theodosius (I&II)

11

Constantine (I&II)
Constantius (I-III)
Hostilianus
Julius Nepos
Lucius Verus
Valentinian (I-III)

12

Heliogabalus

13

Antoninus Pius
Libius Severus

14

Didius Julianus
Marcus Aurelius

15

Pupienus
 Maximus

16 +

Alexander Severus
Julian the Apostate

Petronius Maximus
Philip the Arabian
Romulus Augustulus
Theodosius the Great

Roman numerals

1 = I	6 = VI	11 = XI	91 = XC	600 = DC
4 = IV	9 = IX	50 = L	100 = C	900 = CM
5 = V	10 = X	51 = LI	200 = CC	1000 = M
			500 = D	2000 = MM

*(This list only includes letters that might be useful in a
 crossword solution.)*

Rulers of Britain and Royal Houses

Royal Houses

4

York

5

Blois

Tudor

6

Stuart

7

Hanover
Windsor

8

Normandy

9

Lancaster

10

Saxe-
 Coburg

11

Plantagenet

Rulers of England and Britain

4

Anne
Edwy
John
Mary (I &
 II)

5

David (I & II)
Edgar
Edred
Henry (I-VIII)
James (I & II
 Eng; I-VI
 Scot)

6

Alfred
Canute
Dafydd
Duncan
Edmund
Edward (I-VIII)
Egbert

George (I-VI)
Harold (II)
Robert (I-III)

7

Charles (I & II)
Macbeth

Malcolm (III)
Richard (I-III)
Stephen
William (I-IV)

8

LLewelyn
Margaret
Victoria

9

Aethelred
Alexander (II & III)
Athelstan
Elizabeth (I & II)
Rhodn Mawr

10

Aethelbald

Aethelbert
Aethelwulf

11

John Balliol

12

Harthacanute
William Rufus

13

David the Saint
Owen Glendower

14

Alfred the Great
Council of State
Edmund Ironside

Edward the Elder
Harold Harefoot
Malcolm Canmore
Oliver Cromwell
Robert the Bruce
William the Lion

15 +

Aethelred the Unready
Edward the Confessor
Edward the Martyr
LLewelyn ap Gruffydd
LLewelyn the Great
Margaret of Norway
Richard Coeur de Lion
Richard Cromwell
Richard the Lionheart
William the Conqueror

Russian rulers

4

Anna
Ivan (III-VI)
Paul (I)

5

Peter (I-III)

6

Alexis
Dmitri
Feodor (I-III)

Vasily (III-IV)

7

Michael

8

Nicholas (I&II)

9

Alexander (I-III)

Elizabeth
Catherine (I&II)

12

Boris Godunov
Ivan the Great

13

Peter the Great

15 +

Catherine the Great
Ivan the Terrible

Scientific terms

2	NTP	fuse	watt	earth	molar
	OCR	gain	X-ray	emery	nacre
aa	ohm	gall	yoke	epoxy	nadir
a.c.	PVA	gate	zeta	ester	niche
AM	PVC	germ		ether	nitre
AU	rad	gill	**5**	facet	nymph
d.c.	RAM	gram		farad	ochre
FM	r.a.m.	gray	adder	fault	optic
pH	rem	haem	agate	field	orbit
	RNA	heat	ALGOL	flame	order
3	ROM	host	alloy	flint	organ
	sol	hypo	amber	fluid	oxide
air	STP	lava	amide	focus	ozone
AMU	SHM	lens	amine	force	petal
arc	VDU	mass	anion	Freon	phase
bar	VHF	mica	anode	gauss	polyp
bel		Moho	ascus	genus	power
bit	**4**	mole	atoll	gluon	prism
BTU		muon	auxin	gonad	quark
CCD	acid	node	basic	graph	radar
CFC	agar	onyx	beats	henry	radio
CRO	alum	opal	beryl	hertz	redox
day	atom	palp	biome	hypha	relay
DDT	barn	peat	borax	image	scion
dip	base	phon	boson	imago	serac
DNA	beam	pole	brine	index	shale
erg	bond	pome	carat	inert	shunt
gas	byte	pupa	chalk	joule	solum
gel	cell	ruby	chert	larva	sonar
GeV	clay	seif	choke	laser	spark
ion	coal	sere	clone	latex	spore
jet	coke	sial	COBOL	lever	steam
keV	core	sima	coral	light	stele
LCD	data	slag	curie	lipid	stoke
LED	deme	soda	cycle	litre	stoma
lux	disk	talc	daraf	lumen	style
lye	dyne	till	debug	lysis	taiga
MHD	echo	tone	decay	magma	taxis
mho	flex	torr	diazo	maser	tesla
mil	flux	tufa	dimer	meson	testa
NMR	foci	unit	diode	metre	tilth
TNT	fold	volt	donor	modem	titre

tonne	charge	ice age	phloem	tetrad
topaz	chitin	instar	photon	theory
toxin	cilium	in vivo	phylum	thorax
tribe	cirque	iodide	pileus	thrust
weber	convex	isomer	plasma	tincal
xeric	corona	kaolin	potash	tissue
xylem	couple	kelvin	proton	torque
zooid	cresol	ketone	pulsar	toxoid
	cupric	labile	pumice	trimer

6

	cyclic	labium	quanta	triode
	dalton	labrum	quartz	triton
achene	decant	lamina	quasar	tropic
action	defect	lepton	qwerty	tundra
adduct	dilute	ligand	radian	turgor
aerial	dipole	lignin	radome	vacuum
aerobe	domain	lipase	radula	vapour
agonic	dorsal	litmus	raster	venule
air sac	dry ice	maglev	ratite	vernal
albedo	dynamo	magnet	relict	volvox
albite	eluate	marble	retort	zenith
alkali	eluent	mascon	retrix	zygote
alkane	embryo	matrix	reflex	
alkene	energy	matter	reflux	

7

allele	enzyme	micron	saline	
ampere	factor	mirror	samara	abyssal
anther	farina	moment	scaler	acetate
antrum	ferric	mosaic	sensor	acetone
apical	filter	motile	silica	actinic
apogee	fossil	mutant	siphon	acyclic
atomic	fusion	nastic	slurry	adapter
aurora	gabbro	natron	solder	adaptor
azo dye	galena	nectar	solute	address
baleen	gamete	nekton	spinel	aerobic
baryon	garnet	newton	stator	aerosol
basalt	genera	nodule	sterol	agonist
binary	genome	on-line	stigma	airlock
bionic	gimbal	oocyte	stolon	airpump
bleach	glycol	oogamy	strain	alchemy
bolide	gneiss	opaque	strata	alcohol
botany	gramme	operon	stress	alumina
buffer	gypsum	optics	stroma	amalgam
carpel	hadron	parsec	syphon	ammeter
casein	halide	pascal	syrinx	ammonia
cation	halite	pectin	telson	aneroid
cermet	hybrid	phenol	tephra	aniline

annulus	crystal	gilbert	nitrite	somatic
antenna	cuprite	glacial	nucleon	species
antigen	cuprous	granite	nucleus	spectra
apatite	current	gravity	ocellus	spindle
aqueous	cuticle	habitat	oersted	stannic
aquifer	cyanide	halogen	ohmeter	statics
asexual	dash-pot	haploid	Ohm's	steroid
azimuth	decibel	hormone	law	stomata
back emf	degauss	hydrate	olivine	stratum
balance	dendron	hydride	oospore	strigil
bar code	density	hydrous	ootecha	styrene
battery	dibasic	hyperon	orbital	sucrose
bauxite	digital	igneous	osmosis	synapse
bearing	diluent	impulse	panicle	synergy
benthos	dioptre	inertia	phellem	tektite
benzene	diploid	in vitro	physics	tensile
beta ray	diurnal	isogamy	pipette	ternate
Big Bang	dry cell	isotone	plastid	thermal
bipolar	ductile	isotope	plumule	thallus
biology	ecdysis	kainite	polymer	titrant
biomass	ecology	keratin	polypus	tokamak
bitumen	elastic	kinesis	program	torsion
bromide	element	labiate	propane	transit
burette	elution	lamella	protein	tritium
calcite	emerald	lanolin	quantum	trophic
calomel	entropy	lattice	quinine	tropism
calorie	epigeal	lignite	radiant	turbine
camphor	equinox	linkage	radical	ungular
candela	ethanol	magneto	radicle	valence
carbide	exogamy	maxwell	rare gas	valency
cathode	fall-out	methane	reagent	variety
caustic	faraday	microbe	reactor	velamen
Celsius	fatigue	mimicry	reflect	ventral
ceramic	felspar	mitosis	refract	venturi
chelate	ferrite	monomer	rhizoid	vernier
chloral	ferrous	monitor	rhizome	vesicle
circuit	fissile	mordant	rontgen	vitriol
coal gas	fission	mutagen	rostrum	voltage
coal-tar	food web	naphtha	sagitta	wolfram
colloid	formula	neoteny	scanner	yardang
complex	FORTRAN	neritic	sessile	zeolite
concave	fuel rod	network	siemens	zincite
coolant	funicle	neutral	sievert	zoology
coulomb	geodesy	neutron	soluble	zymogen
counter	geology	nitrate	solvent	

8

	catalyst	emission	hydrated	nucellus
	centroid	emulsion	hypogeal	nucleate
ablation	ceramics	endoderm	ignition	nutation
acid rain	charcoal	enthalpy	impeller	oestrous
acrosome	chimaera	epiblast	inductor	oil shale
actinide	chlorate	epigamic	inert gas	omnivore
addition	chloride	epiphyte	infra-red	ontogeny
adhesion	chlorite	eutectic	iriscope	overload
aerostat	chromite	fascicle	isostasy	overtone
affinity	cinnabar	feedback	isotherm	paraffin
agronomy	cleavage	feldspar	isotonic	parallax
aldehyde	cohesion	filtrate	kerosene	parasite
alkaline	compiler	filament	kinetics	paradigm
alkaloid	compound	fireclay	klystron	particle
allogamy	computer	firedamp	laser gun	peak load
alluvial	constant	fixation	laterite	pendulum
alpha ray	corundum	flip-flop	latitude	peroxide
altitude	coupling	fluidics	leaching	phosphor
amethyst	covalent	fluidity	lecithin	plankton
ammonium	cracking	fluoride	lenticel	polarity
anaerobe	cryolite	fluorite	light pen	porosity
analysis	cytology	follicle	limonite	positive
anaphase	data bank	free fall	liposome	positron
anechoic	data base	friction	lysosome	predator
angstrom	delta ray	fuel cell	lysozome	pressure
anterior	dendrite	galvanic	magneton	print-out
antibody	deuteron	gamma ray	meniscus	promoter
antinode	dew point	gas laser	meridian	prophase
aperture	dialysis	genetics	mesoderm	radiance
aphelion	diapause	geodesic	mesoglea	radiator
apoplast	diastema	geotaxis	methanol	reactant
armature	diatomic	glove box	miscible	reaction
artesian	dilution	glycerol	molality	receiver
asbestos	diskette	gradient	molarity	receptor
atomizer	divalent	graphite	molecule	red shift
autogamy	dolomite	graviton	momentum	refining
autosome	dominant	half-life	momocyte	resistor
biconvex	dormancy	hard disk	mucilage	rheostat
bioassay	dynamics	hardware	mutation	rock salt
biometry	ecliptic	harmonic	mycelium	roentgen
bistable	ectoderm	heat sink	mycology	ruminant
bivalent	effectoe	heredity	narcotic	sapphire
buoyancy	efferent	hologram	neotenin	scissile
calamine	effusion	holozoic	neutrino	sediment
carboxyl	electron	humidity	noble gas	serology

silicate
silicone
sine wave
smelting
software
solenoid
solution
spectrum
spiracle
stannous
steatite
stimulus
sub-imago
subsonic
sulphate
sulphide
sulphite
symplast
syncline
tartrate
taxonomy
tetrapod
thrombin
tracheid
ungulate
ungulate
upthrust
vagility
vascular
velocity
venation
vesicant
volatile
water gas
watt-hour
waveform
xenolith
zoetrope

9

acellular
acetylene
acoustics
adiabatic

adsorbent
advection
afterglow
air pocket
alabaster
algorithm
alicyclic
aliphatic
allotrope
allotropy
altimeter
ambergris
amino acid
amorphous
amphibole
amplifier
amplitude
anabolism
anaerobic
analogous
anhydride
anhydrite
anhydrous
anisogamy
annealing
anodizing
anticline
aperiodic
aqua regia
aragonite
aspirator
astrolabe
atomicity
autoclave
autolysis
autotroph
azeotrope
bandwidth
barograph
barometer
baroscope
base metal
batholith
becquerel
bentonite

beta decay
biconcave
biorhythm
biosphere
black body
black hole
bolometer
Boyle's
  law
capacitor
capillary
carbonate
cataltsis
cellulose
character
chemistry
chirality
chromatid
chromatin
clathrate
clinostat
community
component
composite
condenser
conductor
converter
copolymer
corrosion
cosmic ray
cosmogony
cosmology
countdown
cyclotron
cytoplasm
Darwinism
deflector
deionizer
desiccant
detonator
deuterium
diaphragm
diatomite
dichroism
diffusion

dioecious
discharge
dosimeter
ductility
ecosphere
ecosystem
ectoplasm
elastomer
electrode
empirical
endoplasm
endosperm
endospore
ephemeral
eukaryote
eutrophic
evolution
exogenous
exosphere
explosion
factorial
field coil
filoplume
flagellum
flame test
flotation
fluorspar
fluxmeter
food chain
foot-pound
frequency
fungicide
galvanize
gamma rays
generator
gestation
glycerine
guard cell
gynaecium
gyroscope
haematite
halophyte
heliostat
herbicide
histogram

histology
homologue
hydration
hydraulic
hydrology
hydrostat
hydroxide
hygrostat
hypotonic
ilmentite
imbricate
impedance
implosion
indicator
induction
inelastic
inorganic
insoluble
insulator
intensity
interface
inversion
isomerism
isotropic
jet stream
koalinite
laser beam
Leyden jar
light wave
light year
limestone
lime water
limnology
lodestone
longitude
lubricant
luciferin
luminance
lyophilic
lyophobic
magnesite
magnetism
magnetite
magnetron
magnifier

magnitude
malleable
manometer
mechanics
megascope
metalloid
mesophyte
metaphase
micropyle
microtome
microtron
microwave
moderator
molecular
monatomic
multipole
mutualism
Newtonian
nitration
objective
occlusion
oogenesis
operculum
oviparity
oxidation
pachytene
passivity
pearl spar
periscope
permeable
petroleum
petrology
phenotype
pheromone
phosphate
photocell
phylogeny
pitot tube
pneumatic
pollution
polyester
posterior
potential
precursor
proboscis

proton gun
pyrolysis
pyrometer
pyrometry
quicklime
radiation
radiology
rare earth
reactance
recessive
rectifier
reduction
reflector
refractor
resonance
reticulum
rotoscope
saccharin
saltpetre
sandstone
saprolite
serotinal
shock wave
short-wave
silica gel
sintering
soapstone
soft water
solar cell
solvation
sonometer
sound wave
statocyst
steradian
stopclock
striation
strobilus
subatomic
sublimate
substrate
succulent
symbiosis
synthesis
synthetic
tachytely

tectonism
telemeter
telemetry
telephony
telescope
telophase
telotaxis
teratogen
thelytoky
thyratron
thyristor
time clock
titration
transient
triatomic
trilobite
trivalent
turquoise
unisexual
univalent
uraninite
variation
verdigris
vernation
vestigial
vibration
viscosity
voltmeter
wattmeter
waveguide
wire gauge
xerophyte

10

aberration
abscission
absorption
access time
acetic acid
achromatic
activation
active mass
adaptation
admittance

adsorption
air bladder
alternator
amphoteric
androecium
anemometer
angiosperm
antagonist
anthracite
antimatter
antiproton
aposematic
aqua fortis
aquamarine
arenaceous
atmosphere
atomic mass
auriferous
ballistics
bimetallic
binary code
biogenesis
biophysics
bituminous
bond energy
Böhr theory
carboxylic
carnallite
catabolism
cathode ray
centigrade
centrifuge
centromere
chalcedony
chemotaxis
chloroform
chromosome
citric acid
collimator
combustion
commutator
conduction
convection
cryogenics
degaussing

derivative	hydrolysis	nematocyst	seismograph
desiccator	hydrometer	nephridium	senescence
desorption	hydrophone	nitric acid	slaked lime
Dewar flask	hydrophyte	noble metal	solubility
diakinesis	hygrometer	nucleonics	solvolysis
dielectric	hygroscope	nucleotide	spallation
dimorphism	hypodermis	nyctinasty	spartalite
dispersion	hypothesis	ommatidium	sporangium
distillate	hysteresis	orgamology	sporophyll
distortion	imprinting	orogenesis	sporophyte
elasticity	incubation	oscillator	sputtering
embryology	inductance	ovipositor	stalactite
endodermis	infrasound	oxalic acid	stalagmite
endogenous	insulation	ozone layer	subspecies
etiolation	integument	parasitism	succession
eukaryotic	interferon	pentatomic	superfluid
excitation	interphase	photometer	supersonic
exothermic	ionization	photometry	surfactant
experiment	ionosphere	phototaxis	suspension
Fahrenheit	isonuclear	physiology	synchroton
filtration	isothermal	plasticity	tachograph
flash point	kieselguhr	polyploidy	tachometer
floppy disk	kinematics	precession	technology
fossil fuel	laboratory	primordium	telegraphy
free energy	lactic acid	propellant	television
geocentric	lanthanide	propulsion	tetratomic
geophysics	latent heat	prothallus	tetraploid
geothermal	luminosity	protoplasm	thanatosis
geotropism	Mach number	pseudocarp	theodolite
glaciation	macroprism	radiograph	thermionic
glycolysis	mass defect	radioscope	thermistor
goniometer	mass number	reactivity	thermopile
gravimeter	meerschaum	receptacle	thermostat
gymnosperm	mesomerism	reflection	thixotropy
halophilic	mesosphere	refraction	tourmaline
heat shield	metabolism	refractory	trajectory
heavy water	metallurgy	regelation	transducer
helioscope	micrometer	relativity	transistor
holography	micrometre	reluctance	trinoscope
holophytic	microphone	resilience	triple bond
homologous	microscope	resistance	trochotron
homozygous	modulation	saprophyte	turbulence
hornblende	monoclinic	saturation	ultrasonic
horsepower	morphology	schizogony	vacuum tube
hydraulics	multimeter	sciaphilic	vicariance

viscometer
viviparous
voltameter
water glass
wavelength
wave number
white light
white noise
winchester
wind tunnel
xerography
Zener diode
zwerschaum

11

abiogenesis
absorptance
accelerator
accumulator
achromatism
actinometer
aestivation
agamospermy
agglomerate
air pressure
anisotropic
antheridium
antherozoid
anticathode
antineutron
anticyclone
antioxidant
archegonium
aromaticity
atomic clock
attenuation
Auger effect
avoirdupois
Baily's beads
barycentric
bathyscaphe
bathysphere
boulder clay
bulk modulus

calcination
calibration
calorimeter
candle power
capacitance
capillarity
carbon black
carbon cycle
carborundum
Carnot cycle
carrier wave
cassiterite
caustic soda
chlorophyll
chloroplast
cholesterol
chronometer
colorimeter
conductance
conjugation
crystalline
crystalloid
cybernetics
Daniell cell
deamination
declination
degradation
dehydration
dicotyledon
diffraction
dislocation
dynamometer
eddy current
electricity
electrolyte
electron gun
electronics
endothermic
environment
epidiascope
equilibrium
evaporation
exoskeleton
expansivity
fibre optics

fissionable
fluorescein
fluorescent
fluoroscope
focal length
free radical
galvanizing
gametangium
gametophyte
gas exchange
Gegenschein
genetic code
germination
gibberellin
gravimetric
gravitation
ground state
habituation
heterolytic
hibernation
homeostasis
homogametic
homogeneous
hydrocarbon
hydrography
hydrophilic
hydrophobic
hydroponics
hydrosphere
hygroscopic
Iceland spar
ignus fatuus
impermeable
indehiscent
insecticide
interaction
ion exchange
iridescence
irradiation
isoelectric
isomorphism
lapis lazuli
linear motor
line printer
lithosphere

macroscopic
mensuration
metamorphic
meteorology
naphthalene
nucleophile
occultation
open circuit
outbreeding
periodicity
photosphere
pitchblende
plasticizer
polarimeter
polarimetry
polystyrene
precipitate
primary cell
producer gas
prussic acid
qualitative
quantum leap
radiant heat
radioactive
radio opaque
Raman effect
refrigerant
reluctivity
respiration
restitution
röntgen rays
sal volatile
sedimentary
seismograph
silicon chip
slickenside
Solar System
spherometer
spirochaete
stereophony
stereoscope
stratopause
stroboscope
sublimation
substituent

supercooled
supernatant
synchrotron
tau-particle
tautomerism
temperature
thermionics
thermograph
thermometer
thrombocyte
transformer
translation
translucent
transmitter
transparent
triple point
troposphere
tunnel diode
ultrasonics
ultraviolet
unicellular
unsaturated
vacuum flask
vermiculite
voltaic cell
xylophagous
zooplankton

12

absolute zero
absorptivity
acceleration
acetaldehyde
actinic glass
adventitious
aerodynamics
alphanumeric
angstrom unit
annihilation
anthropology
antineutrino
antiparticle
argillaceous
assimilation

astrophysics
atomic energy
atomic number
atomic theory
atomic weight
autotrophism
backing store
beta particle
biochemistry
biosynthesis
blast furnace
boiling point
borosilicate
Bourdon gauge
Bunsen burner
calcium oxide
carbohydrate
carbolic acid
centre of mass
chemotropism
chlorination
chromosphere
cloud chamber
commensalism
condensation
conductivity
conformation
conglomerate
critical mass
cytogenetics
daughter cell
deceleration
deionization
deliquescent
demodulation
desalination
diamagnetism
dipole moment
displacement
dissociation
distillation
echolocation
ectoparasite
elastic limit
electric cell

electrolysis
electrolytic
electrophile
electroscope
endoparasite
endoskeleton
experimental
extranuclear
fermentation
flocculation
fluidization
fluorescence
fluoridation
fluorination
fluorocarbon
fullers earth
galvanometer
Geissler tube
geochemistry
geomagnetism
halogenation
heat capacity
heliocentric
heterozygous
hydrostatics
hydrotropism
hyperphysics
implantation
inclinometer
iatrophysics
interference
intermediate
interstitial
irritability
Kelvin effect
liquefaction
low frequency
luminescence
macrophysics
magnetic flux
magnetometer
mean free path
microammeter
microbalance
microbiology

Moire pattern
neo-Darwinism
Newton's rings
nuclear power
nuclear waste
oceanography
oligotrophic
optical laser
orthotropism
oscilloscope
output device
paedogenesis
palaeolithic
permeability
permittivity
pharmacology
phototropism
polarization
polarography
polyethylene
polymorphism
polyurethane
pteridophyte
putrefaction
pyrotechnics
quantitative
racemization
radiobiology
radio compass
radio-isotope
regeneration
reproduction
short circuit
solar battery
solar physics
specific heat
spectrometer
spectrometry
spectroscope
spectroscopy
stasigenesis
stereoisomer
stereoscopic
stratigraphy
stratosphere

stridulation
substitution
sulphonation
supercooling
sup
tartaric acid
thermocouple
thermography
thermosphere
thiosulphate
trace element
translusence
transmission
visible light
Wankel engine
zone refining

13

accelerometer
aerogenerator
alpha particle
amplification
Appleton layer
argentiferous
asthenosphere
autocatalysis
beta radiation
binding energy
bioenergetics
biotechnology
bubble chamber
camera obscura
carbon dioxide
caustic potash
chain reaction
chemoreceptor
chromatograph
compressed air
concentration
configuration
decomposition
decompression
decrepitation
deliquescence

direct current
discharge tube
Doppler effect
effervescence
efflorescence
electromagnet
electrophilic
electrophorus
electrostatic
electrovalent
extracellular
ferromagnetic
fertilization
fractionation
freezing point
Geiger counter
geomorphology
geostationary
graticulation
heat exchanger
hermaphrodite
heterogeneous
high frequency
homoiothermic
hybridization
hydrodynamics
hydroelectric
hydrogenation
incandescence
induction coil
inflorescence
intercellular
intracellular
kinetic energy
kinetic theory
magnetic field
magnetization
magnetosphere
magnification
metamorphosis
microcomputer
micro-organism
monochromatic
monocotyledon
morphogenesis

multicellular
nitrification
nitrogen cycle
nuclear fusion
ovoviviparity
palaeontology
paramagnetism
Periodic Table
perissodactyl
petrochemical
photochromism
photoelectric
phytoplankton
piezoelectric
polypropylene
potentiometer
precipitation
pressure gauge
primary colour
quantum theory
radioactivity
recombination
rectification
reducing agent
scintillation
sedimentation
self-induction
semiconductor
spring balance
splanchnology
sterilization
stoichiometry
sulphuric acid
supercritical
thermonuclear
thermoplastic
thigmotropism
transcription
translocation
transmittance
transpiration
triploblastic
word processor
zodiacal light

14

alpha radiation
atomic mass unit
audio frequency
Aurora Borealis
binary notation
biodegradation
bioengineering
breeder reactor
carbon monoxide
cathode-ray tube
chromatography
circuit breaker
counter-current
depolarization
differentiator
electrostatics
eutrophication
ferromagnetism
gamma radiation
harmonic motion
harmonic series
Heaviside layer
heterotrophism
image converter
induction motor
interferometer
intermolecular
keratinization
magnetic moment
microprocessor
neutralization
nitrocellulose
nitroglycerine
nuclear fission
nuclear reactor
organometallic
osmoregulation
oxidizing agent
pasteurization
photochemistry
photogrammetry
photosynthesis
plate tectonics
poikilothermic
polarized light
polymerization
radio astronomy
radiochemistry
radio frequency
radio telescope
saponification
servomechanism
sodium chloride
sulphur dioxide
superconductor
supersaturated
surface tension
susceptibility
thermodynamics
transformation
transverse wave
trickle charger
vapour pressure
weightlessness

15

acclimatization
activated carbon
angular momentum
bioluminescence
bleaching powder
bomb calorimeter
centre of gravity
cosmic radiation
crystallization
crystallography
daughter element
demagnetization
denitrification
devitrification
electroanalysis
electrodialysis
electrodynamics
electrokinetics
electronegative
electrophoresis
electropositive
freezing mixture
horseshoe magnet
incompatability
Lissajou's figure
molecular weight
montmorillonite
nuclear reaction
palaeomagnetism
packing fraction
parthenogenesis
partial pressure
phosphorescence
photomicrograph
photomultiplier
Planck's constant
potential energy
refractive index
relative density
ribonucleic acid
rotary converter
sodium carbonate
sodium hydroxide
specific gravity
stereochemistry
sulphur trioxide
superheterodyne
thermobarograph
ultramicroscope

16

astronomical unit
calcium carbonate
calcium hydroxide
centrifugal force
centripetal force
continental drift
continental shelf
data transmission
central processor
greenhouse effect
mass spectrograph
mass spectrometer
molecular biology
natural selection

negative feedback
organic chemistry
polyvinyl acetate
positive feedback
relative humidity
Wheatstone bridge

17 +

absolute temperature
absorption spectrum
adaptive radiation
alternating current
background radiation
Bessemer converter
catalytic converter
celestial mechanics
centre of curvature
charge-coupled device
diffraction grating
electrometic force
electron microscope
elementary particle

frequency modulation
gas chromatography
genetic engineering
glyceryl trinitrate
information retrieval
integrated circuit
light-emitting diode
linear accelerator
liquid-crystal display
mechanical advantage
photoelectric cell
polyvinyl chloride
potential difference
simple harmonic motion
sodium bicarbonate
solid-state physics
solvent extraction
spontaneous combustion
spontaneous generation
statistical mechanics
transition element
vacuum distillation
vegetative propagation

*(Note: **metre** is preferred to **meter** in British English.)*

Scientists, engineers and inventors

3	Ader	Born	Gahn	Ives	Otis
	Airy	Bose	Gall	King	Otto
Dam	Babo	Cohn	Gold	Koch	Rabi
Ged	Baer	Coke	Gray	Kuhn	Reid
Kay	Ball	Colt	Hahn	Land	Rose
Lee	Bell	Cort	Hale	Lanz	Ryle
Ohm	Benz	Davy	Hero	Lenz	Salk
Ray	Berg	Dean	Hess	Laue	Swan
	Best	Dorn	Holt	Loeb	Todd
4	Biro	Eads	Hope	Mach	Tull
	Bode	Ford	Howe	Mayo	Urey
Abel	Bohr	Fust	Hunt	Mohs	Urie

Watt	Cooke	Lawes	Weber	Darwin	Isaacs
Webb	Creed	Libby	White	Dawson	Jansky
Wren	Crick	Lodge	Young	de Bary	Jenner
Yale	Cross	Loewi		de Duve	Jenson
Yang	Curie	Lowry		Diesel	Joliot
Zinn	Debye	Lyell	**6**	Dreyer	Judson
	Dewar	Magee		Duggar	Karrer
5	Diels	Marsh	Achard	du Mont	Kelvin
	Dirac	Maxim	Adrian	Dulong	Kepler
Adams	Elton	Mayer	Agnesi	Dunlop	Kinsey
Aiken	Euler	Monge	Aitkin	Eckert	Koller
Amici	Evans	Milne	Alfven	Edison	Kotter
Arago	Ewing	Monod	Ampère	Elster	Landau
Aston	Ewins	Morse	Appert	Enders	Lartet
Auger	Fabre	Nobel	Archer	Engler	Lawler
Avery	Fabry	Papin	Aselli	Euclid	Leakey
Bacon	Fermi	Pasch	Baeyer	Fermat	Lenoir
Baade	Frege	Pauli	Balmer	Finsen	Liebig
Baily	Freud	Petit	Beadle	Fizeau	Lister
Baird	Gabor	Petri	Berger	Fokker	Lorenz
Baker	Galen	Popov	Bodoni	Franck	Lovell
Banks	Galle	Prout	Bolyai	Frisch	Lowell
Bates	Gauss	Raman	Bottet	Frasch	Manson
Beebe	Geber	Raven	Bordet	Froude	Markov
Bethe	Gibbs	Reber	Boveri	Fulton	Martin
Bevan	Godel	Rhine	Bramah	Galois	Martin
Black	Haber	Ritty	Brandt	Galton	McAdam
Bloch	Hardy	Romer	Briggs	Geiger	Mendel
Bondi	Henry	Rosse	Brunel	Geitel	Morgan
Boole	Hertz	Sabin	Buffon	Gesner	Morley
Booth	Hills	Saint	Bunsen	Glaser	Morris
Bosch	Hirst	Salva	Calvin	Graham	Morton
Bothe	Hooke	Segré	Cantor	Gregor	Muller
Bovet	Hoyle	Smith	Carnot	Grosse	Napier
Bowen	Hyatt	Soddy	Carrel	Hadley	Nernst
Bower	Ivatt	Stahl	Carver	Halley	Newton
Boyle	Jacob	Tatum	Cauchy	Harvey	Niepce
Bragg	Jeans	Tesla	Caxton	Hevesy	Norman
Brahe	Jones	Tsvet	Cayley	Hewish	Olbers
Brand	Joule	Volta	Cayley	Holden	Parkes
Braun	Kilbe	Weber	Chappé	Hooker	Pascal
Brown	Kolff	Wells	Cierva	Hubble	Pavlov
Burge	Konig	Whale	Claude	Hughes	Penney
Carre	Krebs	White	Cugnot	Hutton	Perkin
Chain	Kühne	Young	Cuvier	Huxley	Perrin
			Dalton		

Planck	Audubon	Fresnel	Macleod	Siemens
Powell	Babbage	Gadolin	Malthus	Simpson
Proust	Banting	Gagarin	Marconi	Sobrero
Raoult	Bardeen	Galileo	Mauchly	Spenser
Ramsay	Barnard	Galvani	Maxwell	Stanley
Rennie	Bateson	Gatling	Medawar	Steptoe
Ritter	Battani	Gilbert	Meitner	Swinton
Roscoe	Beattie	Glidden	Messier	Szilard
Sanger	Bergius	Goddard	Michaux	Telford
Savery	Borlaug	Gossage	Midgley	Tennant
Schick	Bradley	Gregory	Moseley	Thenard
Sholes	Braille	Gresley	Nasmyth	Thomson
Singer	Brouwer	Haeckel	Neumann	Travers
Sloane	Burbank	Harteck	Nielson	Tupolev
Solvay	Candela	Hawking	Oersted	Tyndall
Sperry	Cardano	Haworth	Onsager	van Laue
Stokes	Carlson	Helmont	Ostwald	Vavilov
Struve	Cassini	Hermite	Parsons	Veksler
Sutton	Charles	Hilbert	Pasteur	Vernier
Talbot	Chladni	Hodgkin	Pauling	Virchow
Taylor	Collett	Holland	Peligot	Waksman
Teller	Compton	Hopkins	Philips	Wallace
Thales	Correns	Huggins	Piccard	Wegener
Tilden	Coulomb	Huygens	Poisson	Whitney
Townes	Crookes	Janssen	Pollitt	Whittle
Urbain	Curtiss	Johnson	Poulsen	Wilkins
Vauban	d'Abbans	Jussieu	Prandtl	Ziegler
Wallis	Daimler	Kapitza	Ptolemy	
Walter	Daniell	Kendall	Purcell	
Walton	Da Vinci	Kendrew	Reaumur	**8**
Watson	de Graaf	Khorana	Richter	
Wiener	de la Rue	Kidinnu	Riddles	Agricola
Wigner	Deville	Kozirev	Riemann	Amontons
Wilson	de Vries	Lalande	Röntgen	Anderson
Wohler	Doppler	Lamarck	Rumford	Angström
Wright	Driesch	Lambert	Russell	Appleton
Yukawa	Eastman	Langley	Ruzicka	Aspinall
Zeeman	Edwards	Laplace	Rydberg	Avogrado
	Eichler	Leavitt	Sandage	Bakewell
	Ekeberg	Leibniz	Scheele	Beaufort
7	Faraday	Lesseps	Scholes	Berliner
	Feynman	Lockyer	Schwann	Bessemer
Agassiz	Fischer	Lorentz	Seaborg	Birdseye
Allbutt	Fleming	Lumiere	Seyfert	Birkhoff
Alvarez	Fourier	Lysenko	Shepard	Bjerknes
Andrews				Blackett

Brattain	Klaproth	Sturgeon	de Elhuyar
Brewster	Kornberg	Sturrock	Descartes
Bridgman	Koroliov	Thompson	Dutrochet
Brindley	Lagrange	Tombaugh	Eddington
Bronsted	Langmuir	Van Allen	Einthoven
Browning	Lawrence	Van't Hoff	Endlicher
Bushnell	Legendre	Vesalius	Eustachio
Calmette	Lemaître	von Mayer	Fabricius
Caventou	Leuckart	Waterman	Fairbairn
Chadwick	Linnaeus	Weismann	Falloppio
Clausius	Lipscomb	Woodward	Fessenden
Cockroft	Lonsdale	Worsdell	Fibonacci
Coriolis	Malpighi	Zeppelin	Flamsteed
Courtois	Maudslay	Zernicke	Fox Talbot
Cousteau	Maunsell	Zworykin	Friedmann
Crampton	McMillan		Gascoigne
Crompton	Mercator		Gay-Lussac
Culpeper	Meyerhof	**9**	Goodricke
Daguerre	Millikan		Gutenberg
Dedekind	Milstein	Abu Al-Wafa	Heaviside
de Fermat	Mitchell	Aristotle	Helmholtz
De Forest	Mosander	Arkwright	Heyrovsky
De Morgan	Mulliken	Armstrong	Hopkinson
Drummond	Newcomen	Arrhenius	Johannsen
Edgerton	Oliphant	Baekeland	Josephson
Einstein	Ortelius	Bartholin	Kirchhoff
Ericsson	Oughtred	Becquerel	Kurchatov
Foucault	Poincare	Bernoulli	Lankester
Franklin	Rayleigh	Berthelot	Lavoisier
Gassendi	Rheticus	Berzelius	Lederberg
Gauthier	Robinson	Boltzmann	Lenormand
Gell-Mann	Roebling	Bronowski	Leverrier
Gillette	Roentgen	Butenandt	Liouville
Goldmark	Sabatier	Cailletet	McCormick
Goodyear	Sakharov	Carothers	Macintosh
Guericke	Saussure	Cavendish	Macmillan
Hamilton	Schaefer	Chebishev	Michelson
Harrison	Sefstrom	Cherenkov	Mottelson
Herschel	Servetus	Cockcroft	Nicholson
Hisinger	Shockley	Cockerell	Nirenberg
Humboldt	Shrapnel	Cornforth	Pelletier
Ilyushin	Sidgwick	Cronstedt	Pettigrew
Ipatieff	Sikorsky	d'Alembert	Priestley
Jacquard	Stenning	Daubenton	Remington
Kennelly	Stirling	Davenport	Schleiden
		de Broglie	

Schonbein
Serturner
Steinmetz
Stroudley
Tartaglia
Tinbergen
Vauquelin
Whitelegg
Wilkinson
Withering
Wollaston
Zsigmondy
Zuckerman

10

Archimedes
Arrowsmith
Barkhausen
Berthollet
Blenkinsop
Bowen-Cooke
Cannizzaro
Cartwright
Cassegrain
Chardonnet
Churchward
Copernicus
Dobereiner
Dobzhansky
du Vigneaud
Fahrenheit
Fitzgerald
Fourneyron
Fracastoro
Fraunhofer
Hargreaves
Hawksworth
Heisenberg
Hipparchus
Hofmiester
Hounsfield
Ingen-Hausz
Kolmogorov
Lilienthal

Lindenmann
Lippershey
Lord Kelvin
Maupertuis
Mendeleyev
Metchnikov
Paracelsus
Richardson
Rutherford
Sanctorius
Schweigger
Senefelder
Sommerfeld
Staudinger
Stephenson
Swammerdam
Torricelli
Tournefort
Trevithick
van de Graaf
van Drebbel
von Purbach
Wainwright
Watson-Watt
Wheatstone

11

Al-Khwarizmi
Baskerville
Chamberlain
Goldschmidt
Hertzsprung
Hinshelwood
Joliot-Curie
Landsteiner
Le Chatelier
Leeuwenhoek
Lobachevski
Montgolfier
Nostradamus
Oppenheimer
Pickersgill
Schrodinger
Sherrington

Spallanzani
Szent-Györgi
Tsiolkovski
van der Waals
von Guericke
von Welsbach

12

Ambartsumian
Boussingault
Lord Rayleigh
Mergenthaler
Szent-Györgyi

13

Arago Francois
Brandenberger
Chandrasekhar
von Sauerbronn

14

Galileo Galilei
Eudoxus of Cnidus

15 +

Apollonius of Perga
Aristarchus of Samos
Boyd-Orr of Brechin
  Mearns
Cagniard de la Tour
Diophantus of
  Alexandria
Dioscorides Pedanius
Eratosthenes of Cyrence
Geoffroy Saint-Hilaire
Hero of Alexandria
Kamerlingh-Onnes
Kekule von Stradonitz
Lecoq de Boisbaudran
Pappus of Alexandria
Sosigenes of Alexandria

Sea creatures

4

clam
crab
cray

5

conch
coral
gaper
hydra
monad
murex
ormer
polyp
prawn
razor
salpa
squid
whelk

6

cockle
cowrie
cultch
cuttle
limpet
medusa
mussel
oyster
partan
quahog
scampi
sea-ear
sea fan
sea fir
sea pen
shrimp

sponge
squill
urchin
winkle
wampum

7

abalone
acaleph
actinia
bivalve
copepod
cyclops
dog-crab
fiddler
hydroid
lobster
man-o'-war
medusan
mollusc
octopod
octopus
pandora
pea crab
rotifer
scallop
sea hare
sea lily
sea slug
sea wasp
sea worm
toheroa
trepang

8

argonaut
ark shell
barnacle
crawfish

crayfish
ear shell
escallop
king crab
land crab
man-of-war
medusoid
nauplius
nautilus
pteropod
sea jelly
sea mouse
sea onion
sea snake
starfish
top shell
univalve

9

acorn worm
comb jelly
cone shell
date shell
ear cockle
fish louse
gastropod
ghost crab
giant clam
harp shell
horsefoot
jellyfish
lamp shell
langouste
moon jelly
razor clam
round clam
sea flower
sea squirt
sea urchin
sea walnut

shellfish
shore crab
tusk shell
wing shell

10

acorn shell
auger shell
bêche-de-mer
coelacanth
crustacean
cuttlefish
heart shell
hermit crab
lion's mane
mitre shell
oyster crab
periwinkle
palolo worm
quahog clam
razor shell
robber crab
sand dollar
sea anemone
seed oyster
spider crab
swan mussel
tooth shell
tulip shell
velvet crab
venus shell
xyphosuran

11

brine shrimp
bubble shell
calling crab
fiddler crab
heart cockle

heart urchin
helmet shell
horse mussel
mussel shell
pearl mussel
pearl oyster
sea cucumber
soldier crab
spectre crab
trough shell
venus' girdle

mantis shrimp
pelican's foot
sea butterfly
sentinel crab
spectre shrimp
spindle shell
spiny lobster
trumpet shell
unicorn shell

pilgrim's shell
sea gooseberry
slipper limpet
soft-shell crab
soft-shell clam

14 +

chamber nautilus
lion's mane jellyfish
opossum shrimp
paper nautilus
pearly nautilus
Portugese man-of-war
skeleton shrimp
wheel animalcule

12

box jellyfish
coelanterate

13

acorn barnacle
goose barnacle
horseshoe crab
keyhole limpet

Seas and Oceans

3 & 4

Aral
Azov
Bali
Dead
Java
Kara
Red
Ross
Sawu
Sulu

5

Banda
Black
Ceram
China
Coral
Crete
Davis
Irish

Japan
North
Timor
White

6

Aegean
Arctic (O.)
Baltic
Bering
Celtic
Flores
Indian (O.)
Inland
Ionian
Laptev
Scotia
Tasman
Yellow

7

Andaman

Arabian
Arafura
Barents
Caspian
Celebes
Chukchi
Galilee
Lincoln
Marmara
Molucca
Okhotsk
Pacific (O.)
Wandels
Weddell

8

Adriatic
Amundsen
Atlantic (O.)
Beaufort
Labrador
Ligurian
Sargasso

9

Antarctic (O.)
Caribbean
East China
Greenland
Hudson Bay
Norwegian

10

Sea of Japan
South China
Tyrrhenian

12 +

Bellinghausen
Dumont d' Urville
East Siberian
Mediterranean
Sea of Galilee
Sea of Okhotsk
Sea of Marmora

Sevens

Seven Deadly Sins

4	**5**	**7**	**8**
envy	pride	avarice	gluttony
lust	sloth		
	wrath		

Seven Hills of Rome

7	**8**	**9**
Caelian	Aventine	Esquiline
Colline (or	Palatine	
Quirinal)	Quirinal (or Colline)	**10**
Viminal		Capitoline

Seven Sages (or Wise Men of Greece)

Bias of Priene – 'Most men are bad'
Chilo of Sparta – 'Consider the end'
Cleobulus of Lindos – 'Avoid extremes'
Periander of Corinth – 'Nothing is impossible to industry'
Pittacus of Mitylene – 'Seize time by the forelock'
Solon of Athens – 'Know thyself'
Thales of Miletus – 'Who hateth suretyship is sure'

Seven Seas

6	**11**	South Pacific
Arctic	Indian Ocean	Indian Ocean
9	**13**	**14**
Antarctic	North Pacific	North Atlantic
		South Atlantic

Seven Virtues

4

hope

5

faith

7

charity
justice

8

prudence

9

fortitude

10

temperance

Seven Wonders of the Ancient World

(The) Tomb of Mausolus
(The) Pyramids of Egypt
(The) Colossus of Rhodes
(The) Pharos of Alexandria
(The) Hanging Gardens of Babylon
(The) Temple of Diana at Ephesus
(The) Statue of Jupiter by Phidias

Shakespeare

Plays by Shakespeare

6

Hamlet (Prince of Denmark)
Henry V

7

Henry IV (Parts 1&2)
Henry VI (Parts 1-3)
Macbeth
Othello (The Moor of
  Venice)

8

King John

King Lear
Pericles (Prince of Tyre)

9

Cymbeline
Henry VIII
Richard II

10

Coriolanus
King Henry V
Richard III
Tempest, The

11

As You Like It
King Henry IV (Parts 1&2)
King Henry VI (Parts 1-3)

12

Julius Caesar
Twelfth Night
What You Will

13

King Henry VIII
King Richard II
Timon of Athens

14

King Richard III
Romeo and Juliet

Winter's Tale, The

15

Comedy of Errors, A
Titus Andronicus

Over 15

All's Well that Ends Well
Antony and Cleopatra
Hamlet, Prince of Denmark
Love's Labour's Lost
Measure for Measure
Merchant of Venice, The
Merry Wives of Windsor
Midsummer Night's Dream, A
Much Ado About Nothing
Othello, The Moor of Venice
Pericles, Prince of Tyre
Taming of the Shrew, The
Troilus and Cressida
Two Gentlemen of Verona

Shakespearean Characters

3 & 4

Adam
Ajax
Anne (Lady)
Bona
Cade
Cato
Davy
Dick
Dion
Dull
Eros
Fang
Ford
Ford (Mrs.)
Grey
Grey (Lady; Lord)

Hero
Hume
Iago
Iden
Iris
Jamy
John
John (Don; King;
  Prince)
Juno
Kent (Earl of)
Lear (King)
Lion
Luce
Lucy
Moth
Nym
Page

Page (Mrs.)
Peto
Puck
Ross
Ross (Lord)
Say (Lord)
Snug
Time
Vaux
Wall
Wart
York (Archbishop
  of; Duchess of;
  Duke of)

5

Aaron

Abram	Louis (Dauphin;	Angelo
Alice	King; Lord)	Antony
Angus	Lucio	Armado
Ariel	March (Earl of)	Arthur
Bagot	Maria	Audrey
Bates	Melun	Banquo
Belch	Menas	Basset
Bigot	Milan (Duke of)	Bianca
Biron	Mopsa	Blanch
Blunt	Osric	Blount
Boult	Paris	Bottom
Boyet	Pedro (Don)	Brutus
Bushy	Percy	Bullen
Butts	Percy (Lady)	Cadwal
Caius	Peter	Caesar
Casca	Phebe	Caphis
Celia	Philo	Cassio
Ceres	Pinch	Chiron
Cinna	Poins	Cicero
Cleon	Priam	Clitus
Clown	Regan	Cloten
Corin	Robin	Cobweb
Court	Romeo	Curtis
Curan	Rugby	Dennis
Curio	Sands (Lord)	Dorcas
Denny	Smith	Dorset (Marquis of)
Diana	Snare	Dromio
Edgar	Snout	Dumain
Egeus	Speed	Duncan (King)
Elbow	Timon	Edmund
Essex	Titus	Edward
Evans	Tubal	Edward (Earl; King;
Feste	Varro	Prince of Wales)
Flute	Viola	Elinor (Queen)
Froth	Wales (Prince of)	Emilia
Ghost		Exeter (Duke of)
Gobbo	**6**	Fabian
Gower		Feeble
Green	Adrian	Fenton
Helen	Aegeon	France (King of;
Henry	Aeneas	Princess of)
Henry (King; Prince)	Albany (Duke of)	Gallus
Julia	Alexas	George
Lafeu	Alonso	Gremio
Lewis (Dauphin)	Amiens	Grumio

Gurney
Hamlet
Hecate
Hector
Helena
Henry V (King)
Hermia
Horner
Imogen
Isobel (Queen)
Jaques
Juliet
Launce
Le Beau
Lennox
Lovell
Lucius
Marina
Morgan
Morton
Mouldy
Mr. Ford
Mr. Page
Mutius
Nestor
Oberon
Oliver
Olivia
Orsino
Oscric
Oswald
Oxford (Duke of; Earl of)
Pedant
Philip (King)
Pierce
Pistol
Pompey
Porter
Portia
Scarus
Quince
Rivers (Earl; Lord)
Rogero
Rumour

Scales (Lord)
Scroop
Scroop (Lord)
Seyton
Shadow
Silius
Silvia
Simple
Siward
Strato
Surrey (Duke of; Earl of)
Talbot
Talbot (Lord)
Tamora
Taurus
Thiasa
Thisbe
Thomas
Thurio
Tranio
Tybalt
Tyrrel
Ursula
Venice (Duke of)
Verges
Vernon
Wolsey (Lord)

7

Abraham
Adriana
Aemilia
Agrippa
Alarbus
Alencon (Duke of)
Antenor
Antonio
Arragon
Aumerle (Duke of)
Bedford (Duke of)
Berkley (Earl)
Berowne
Bertram

Bourbon (Duke of)
Brandon
Calchas
Caliban
Camillo
Capulet
Capulet (Lady)
Cassius
Catesby
Cerimon
Charles
Charles (Dauphin; King)
Claudio
Conrade
Costard
Cranmer (Archbishop)
Dauphin, The
Dionyza
Don John
Douglas (Earl of)
Dr. Butts
Eleanor
Escalus
Escanes
Flavius
Fleance
Francis
Gloster (Duchess of; Duke of; Earl of; Prince of)
Goneril
Gonzalo
Gregory
Helenus
Henry IV (King)
Henry VI (King)
Herbert
Horatio
Hostess
Hotspur
Iachimo
Jessica
Laertes

Lavache
Lavinia
Leonato
Leonine
Leontes
Lepidus
Lincoln (Bishop of)
Lord Say
Lorenzo
Lucetta
Luciana
Macbeth
Macbeth (Lady)
Macduff
Macduff (Lady)
Malcolm
Marcade
Marcius
Mardian
Mariana
Martext
Martius
Mercade
Messala
Michael
Michael (Sir)
Miranda
Montano
Morocco (Prince of)
Mowbray
Mowbray (Lord)
Mrs. Ford
Mrs. Page
Nerissa
Nicanor
Norfolk (Duke of)
Octavia
Ophelia
Orlando
Orleans (Duke of)
Othello
Paulina
Perdita
Phrynia
Pisanio

Proteus
Publius
Pucelle
Pyramus
Quickly (Mrs.)
Quintus
Richard
Richard (Duke;
    King)
Salanio
Salerio
Sampson
Setebos
Shallow
Shylock
Silence
Silvius
Simpcox
Slender
Solinus
Stanley
Stanley (Lord)
Steward
Suffolk (Duke;
    Earl)
Theseus
Thyreus
Titania
Travers
Tressel
Troilus
Ulysses
Urswick
Valeria
Varrius
Vaughan
Velutus
Warwick (Earl of)
William

8

Abhorson
Achilles
Aemilius

Aufidius
Auvergne (Countess
    of)
Baptista
Bardolph
Bardolph (Lord)
Bassanio
Beatrice
Beaufort
Beaufort (Cardinal)
Belarius
Benedick
Benvolio
Berkeley
Bernardo
Borachio
Bullcalf
Burgundy (Duke of)
Campeius (Cardinal)
Canidius
Capucius
Charmian
Clarence (Duke of)
Claudius
Claudius (King)
Clifford
Clifford (Lord)
Colville
Cominius
Cordelia
Cornwall (Duke of)
Cressida
Cromwell
Dercetas
Diomedes
Dogberry
Don Pedro
Edward VI (King)
Eglamour
Falstaff
Fastolfe
Florence
Florizel
Fluellen
Gadshill

Gardiner
Gargrave
Gertrude (Queen)
Grandpre
Gratiano
Griffith
Harcourt
Hastings (Lord)
Hermione
Humphrey
Isabella
Jack Cade
John Hume
Jourdain
King John
King Lear
Lady Anne
Lady Grey
Lawrence
Leonardo
Leonatus
Ligarius
Lodovico
Lord Grey
Lord Ross
Lucentio
Lucilius
Lucullus
Lysander
Malvolio
Margaret
Margaret (Queen)
Maecenas
Menelaus
Menteith
Mercutio
Montague
Montague (Lady)
Montague
  (Marquis of)
Mortimer
Mortimer (Lady)
Mountjoy
Old Gobbo
Overdone (Mrs.)

Pandarus
Pandulph (Cardinal)
Panthino
Parolles
Patience
Pembroke (Earl of)
Pericles
Philario
Philemon
Philotus
Pindarus
Polonius
Polydore
Prospero
Rambures
Ratcliff
Reignier
Reynaldo
Richmond (Earl of)
Roderigo
Rosalind
Rosaline
Rotheram
Salarino
Seleucus
Somerset (Duke of)
Stafford
Stafford (Lord)
Stephano
Thaliard
Timandra
Titinius
Trinculo
Vicentio
Violenta
Virgilia
Volumnia
Whitmore
Williams

9

Agamemnon
Aguecheek
Alexander

Antigonus
Antiochus
Apemantus
Archibald
Arviragus
Autolycus
Balthazar
Bassianus
Biondello
Bourchier (Cardinal)
Brabantio
Caithness
Cambridge (Earl of)
Cassandra
Chatillon
Cleomenes
Cleopatra
Constance
Cornelius
Cymbeline
Dardanius
Deiphobus
Demetrius
Desdemona
Dolabella
Donalbain
Elizabeth
Enobarbus
Erpingham
Ferdinand
Ferdinand (King)
Fitz-Peter
Fitzwater (Lord)
Flaminius
Francisca
Francisco
Frederick
Friar John
Glansdale
Glendower
Grandpree
Guiderius
Guildford
Helicanus
Henry VIII (King)

Hippolyta
Hortensio
Katharina
Katherine
Katharine
 (Princess)
King Henry (IV; V;
 VI & VIII)
King Louis
Lady Percy
Lancaster (Duke of)
Lancaster (Prince
 of)
Longsword
Lord Bigot
Lord Lewis
Lord Lovel
Lord Sands
Lychorida
Macmorris
Mamillius
Marcellus
Mareshall
Moonshine
Nathaniel
Patroclus
Petruchio
Polixenes
Richard II (King)
Rousillon (Count
 of)
Rousillon
 (Countess of)
Salisbury (Earl of)
Sebastian
Servilius
Simonides
Southwell
Tearsheet
Thersites
Trebonius
Valentine
Ventidius
Vincentio
Voltimand

Volumnius
Woodville
Worcester (Earl of)
Young Cato

10

Alcibiades
Andromache
Andronicus
Anne Bullen
Antipholus
Archidamus
Barnardine
Brakenbury
Buckingham (Duke
 of)
Calphurnia
Canterbury
 (Archbishop of)
Coriolanus
Duke of York
Earl of Kent
Earl Rivers
Euphronius
Fortinbras
Henry Percy
Holofernes
Hortensius
Jaquenetta
John Talbot
John Morton
King Duncan
King Edward
King Henry V
King Philip
Longaville
Lord Rivers
Lord Sandys
Lord Scales
Lord Scroop
Lord Talbot
Lord Wolsey
Lysimachus
Mark Antony

Margarelon
Menacrates
Montgomery
Mrs. Quickly
Prince John
Proculeius
Richard III (King)
Saturninus
Sempronius
Sir Michael
Somerville
Starveling
The Dauphin
Thomas Wart
Touchstone
Willoughby (Lord)
Winchester (Bishop
 of)

11

Abergavenny (Lord)
Artimidorus
Bishop of Ely
Bolingbroke
Caius Lucius
Dame Quickly
Doctor Butts
Doctor Caius
Duke of Anjou
Duke of Milan
Earl Berkely
Earl of Derby
Earl of Essex
Earl of March
Edward Poins
George Bevis
James Gurney
John Holland
John of Gaunt
King Charles
King Henry IV
King Henry VI
King Richard (II &
 III)

Lady Capulet
Lady Macbeth
Lady Macduff
Lord Mowbray
Lord Stanley
Mayor of York
Mrs. Anne Page
Mrs. Overdone
Mustardseed
Peasblossom
Philostrate
Plantagenet
Prince Henry
Queen Elinor
Queen Isobel
Ralph Mouldy
Robert Bigot
Rosencrantz
Simon Shadow
Thomas Percy
Westminster (Archbishop of)
William Page
Young Lucius
Young Siward

Lady Montague
Lady Mortimer
Lord Bardolph
Lord Clifford
Lord Hastings
Lord Stafford
Marcus Brutus
Matthew Goffe
Mistress Ford
Mistress Page
Peaseblossom
Popilius Lena
Sir Hugh Evans
Sir Nathaniel
Sir Toby Belch
Thomas Horner
Three Witches
Titus Lartius
Westmoreland (Earl of)
Young Marcius

13

Alexander Iden
Doll Tearsheet
Duchess of York
Duke of Alençon
Duke of Aumerle
Duke of Bedford
Duke of Bourbon
Duke of Gloster
Duke of Norfolk
Duke of Orleans
Duke of Suffolk
Earl Mortimer
Earl of Douglas
Earl of Gloster
Earl of Suffolk
Earl of Warwick
Faulconbridge
Faulconbridge (Lady)
Francis Feeble
Friar Lawrence
Henry Beaufort (Bishop)
Henry Gildford (Sir)

12

Caius Marcus
Decius Brutus
Duke of Albany
Duke of Exeter
Duke of Oxford
Duke of Surrey
Duke of Venice
Earl Berkeley
Earl of Oxford
Earl of Surrey
Friar Francis
Guildenstern
John Beaufort (Earl)
Julius Caesar
Junius Brutus
King Claudius
King Edward VI
King of France

Hubert de Burgh
Joan la Pucelle
John Southwell
King Ferdinand
King Henry VIII
King Richard II
Lord Fitzwater
Mayor of London
Owen Glendower
Peter Bullcalf
Pierce of Exton (Sir)
Prince of Wales
Richard Vernon (Sir)
Robert Shallow
Stephen Scroop (Sir)
Queen Gertrude
Queen Margaret
Sir Thomas Grey
Thomas Mowbray
Thomas Vaughan (Sir)
Walter Herbert (Sir)
William Brando (Sir)
Young Clifford

14

Baptista Minola
Cardinal Wolsey
Christopher Sly
Clerk of Chatham
Duke of Burgundy
Duke of Clarence
Duke of Cornwall
Duke of Florence
Duke of Somerset
Earl of Pembroke
Earl of Richmond
Edmund Mortimer (Earl)
Hostess Quickly
John Somerville (Sir)
Justice Shallow
King Richard III
Launcelot Gobbo
Lord Willoughby
Marcus Antonius

Metellus Cimber
Northumberland (Earl of)
Northumberland (Lady of)
Octavius Caesar
Peter of Pomfret
Pompeius Sextus
Prince Humphrey
Queen Elizabeth
Queen Katharine
Saunder Simpcox
Sextus Pompeius
Sir James Blount
Sir James Tyrrel
Sir John Stanley
Sir Walter Blunt
Sir William Lucy
Smith the Weaver
Thomas Beaufort (Duke)
Thomas Gargrave (Sir)
Tullus Aufidius
Walter Whilmore

15

Aemilius Lepidus
Bishop of Lincoln
Dromio of Ephesus
Duke of Lancaster
Earl of Cambridge
Earl of Salisbury
Earl of Worcester
Edmund of Langley
Governer of Paris
Lord Abergavenny
Margery Jourdain
Marquis of Dorset
Mayor of St. Albans
Menenius Agrippa
Mistress Quickly
Prince of Arragon
Prince of Morocco
Robin Goodfellow
Sicinius Volutus
Sir Anthony Denny
Sir Hugh Mortimer

Sir John Colville
Sir John Falstaff
Sir John Fastolfe
Sir John Mortimer
Sir Nicholas Vaux
Sir Thomas Lovell
Titus Andronicus
William Stafford

16 +

Abbot of Westminster
Archbishop of Canterbury
Archbishop Cranmer
Archbishop of York
Bastard of Orleans
Bishop of Carlisle
Cardinal Beaufort
Cardinal Bourchier
Cardinal Campeius
Cardinal Pandulph
Countess of Auvergne
Countess of Rousillon
Count of Rousillon
Domitius Enobarbus
Don Adriano de Armado
Dromio of Syracuse
Duchess of Gloster
Duke of Buckingham
Duke of Gloucester

Earl of Northumberland
Earl of Westmoreland
Governor of Harfleur
Henry Bolingbroke
Henry Percy Hotspur
King Philip of France
Lady Falconbridge
Lady of Northumberland
Margaret Plantagenet
Marquis of Montague
Mistress Anne Page
Mistress Overdone
Philip the Bastard
Posthumus Leonatus
Prince of Lancaster
Princess Katherine
Princess of France
Richard Plantagenet
Robert Falconbridge
Roger Bolingbroke
Sir Andrew Aguecheek
Sir Humphrey Stafford
Sir Pierce of Exton
Sir Richard Ratcliff
Sir Richard Vernon
Sir Robert Glansdale
Sir Stephen Scroop
Sir Thomas Vaughan
Sir Thomas Erpingham
Sir William Glansdale
Sheriff of Wiltshire

Shipping forecast areas and stations

4	5	Wight	Fisher	7
			Humber	
Sole	Dover	**6**	Jersey	Faeroes
Tyne	Forth		Thames	Fastnet
	Lundy	Bailey	Viking	Forties
	Malin	Biscay		Rockall
	Tiree	Dogger		Shannon

8

Cromarty
Fair Isle
Hebrides
Irish Sea
Land's End
Plymouth
Portland
Sumburgh
Valentia

9

Malin Head

10

Finisterre
Ronaldsway
St Abb's Head

11

Butt of Lewis

German Bight
North Utsire
Smith's Knoll
South Utsire

14

Royal Sovereign

Over 15

Channel Light-Vessel
South-East Iceland

Signs of the Zodiac

3

Leo - Lion

5

Aries - Ram
Libra - Scales
Virgo - Virgin

6

Cancer - Crab
Gemini - Twins
Pisces - Fishes
Taurus - Bull

7

Scorpio - Scorpion

8

Aquarius - Watercarrier

9

Capricorn - Goat

11

Sagittarius - Archer
Capricornus - Goat

Solomon Grundy

Born on Monday
Christened on Tuesday
Married on Wednesday
Took ill on Thursday
Got worse on Friday
Died on Saturday
Buried on Sunday ...
and that was the end of Solomon Grundy.

Sports and games

2 & 3	**4**			**5**	
	tie	game	pool	yoga	extra
	TT	goal	port		fault
ace	try	golf	post		feint
bat	win	grid	puck	**5**	field
bar		grip	punt		final
bat		hank	putt	alley	fives
bet	**4**	hare	race	arena	float
bob		heat	reel	arrow	fluke
bow	bail	hold	rest	bails	frame
box	ball	hole	ride	baton	green
bye	bars	home	ring	blade	guard
cox	barb	hook	rink	board	gully
cue	base	hoop	rope	bogey	horse
cup	beam	hunt	sail	bowls	inner
dan	bias	iron	seed	boxer	jetty
fly	bike	jack	shot	break	joust
gun	boat	jess	show	bully	kayak
gym	bout	judo	side	caber	kendo
jab	bowl	jump	skip	caddy	lasso
lap	buck	lane	slam	carom	links
lbw	buoy	lido	sled	chalk	loose
let	card	lift	slip	chase	loser
lie	cast	line	solo	check	lunge
lob	chip	lock	spar	chute	match
mat	chop	love	spin	coach	medal
nap	club	luge	spot	coupé	mid on
net	coup	lure	sumo	court	miler
oar	crew	meet	swim	crawl	mount
out	dart	mile	tack	cycle	pacer
par	dash	miss	team	darts	pairs
PE	dive	nock	toss	decoy	parry
pot	drag	Oaks	tote	Derby	pilot
PT	duck	oche	trap	deuce	pitch
put	duel	odds	trot	diver	piton
rod	épée	Oval	turf	divot	point
run	eyas	over	walk	dormy	pro-am
set	fall	pace	whip	drive	prize
ski	flag	pack	wide	dummy	racer
sod	foil	play	wing	eagle	rally
tag	fore	pole	wood	evens	range
tee	foul	polo	xyst	event	reins
	gaff				

284

relay	borrow	header	riding	TT race
rider	boules	hiking	ringer	umpire
rifle	bowler	hockey	roll in	victor
rings	bowman	hooker	roquet	volley
rodeo	boxing	hunter	rowing	wicket
rough	bullet	hurdle	rugger	willow
round	bunker	ice axe	runner	winger
rugby	caddie	jesses	saddle	xystos
sabre	cannon	jockey	savate	xystus
scent	canter	jumper	scorer	yorker
score	caving	karate	sculls	
scuba	chukka	kicker	second	
scull	clinch	kung fu	shinny	**7**
silks	corner	lariat	shinty	
skate	course	leg bye	single	acrobat
skeet	crease	loader	skater	address
skier	crosse	mallet	skibob	also ran
slice	cup tie	manege	skiing	amateur
smash	curler	marker	slalom	angling
stalk	dedans	mashie	sledge	archery
stall	defeat	nelson	sleigh	arm lock
stick	discus	no-ball	snatch	assault
stump	diving	not out	soccer	athlete
sweep	dog leg	opener	spider	axe kick
swing	driver	outrun	spiral	barbell
sword	dry fly	paddle	sprint	batsman
thole	eleven	pelota	squash	batsmen
throw	etrier	pistol	stable	batting
touch	falcon	player	stakes	beagles
track	fencer	pocket	stalls	bicycle
train	finish	pommel	stance	bowling
vault	flight	punter	stands	brassie
wager	flying	putter	sticks	captain
wedge	fly rod	quarry	strike	catcher
yacht	gallop	quarte	string	century
	gambit	quiver	stroke	chicane
6	gillie	quoits	stumps	chipper
	glider	rabbit	stymie	chukker
aikido	go-cart	racket	tackle	circuit
anchor	go-kart	rapids	target	classic
archer	googly	rapier	tennis	compass
birdie	gulley	record	torero	contest
bisque	gutter	remise	toss-up	couloir
blocks	hammer	replay	touché	crampon
bookie	hazard	result	trophy	cricket
				croquet

cue ball	kick-off	scratch	aqualung	fast ball
curb bit	knock-up	sculler	aquatics	fielding
curling	last lap	service	armguard	finalist
cushion	line out	shin pad	away game	fish-hook
cutlass	long bow	shot put	backhand	flat race
cycling	love all	shuttle	backspin	flippers
cyclist	love set	singles	baseball	foilsman
decider	lugeing	skating	baseline	football
declare	matador	skid lid	biathlon	foothold
defence	midiron	ski jump	boat race	footwork
descent	netball	ski lift	body blow	forehand
diamond	net cord	ski pole	bonspiel	foul play
doubles	niblick	snaffle	boundary	foul shot
dribble	ninepin	snooker	bullring	foxhound
fairway	oarsman	snorkle	bull's eye	free kick
fencing	oarsmen	stadium	bully off	free shot
fielder	oassade	starter	canoeing	full back
fifteen	offside	stirrup	car rally	full time
fishing	on guard	St. Leger	champion	full toss
fixture	overarm	striker	chip shot	gauntlet
flipper	over par	stumped	climbing	glass jaw
fly half	own goal	sub-aqua	coursing	goal area
fly kick	paddock	surfing	coxswain	goal kick
fly line	penalty	tacking	crossbar	goal line
forward	picador	take-off	cup final	goal post
fox hunt	pinfall	tally-ho	dark blue	golf ball
frogman	pitcher	The Oaks	dead ball	golf club
gliding	pit stop	The Oval	dead heat	gridiron
goggles	play off	throw in	deadlock	gymkhana
golf-bag	press up	tilting	dead shot	half back
gymnast	putting	toe-hold	deck game	half-ball
hairpin	quarter	top spin	delivery	half-blue
harmony	rackets	tourney	drag hunt	half-mile
harness	racquet	trained	dragster	handball
harpoon	rebound	trainer	dressage	handicap
harrier	referee	trapeze	drop goal	hat trick
hunting	regatta	vaulter	drop kick	haymaker
hurling	reserve	walking	drop shot	head-lock
ice pick	ripcord	weights	duelling	helmsman
in field	riposte	whistle	dumb bell	high dive
innings	rosette	workout	even keel	high jump
javelin	rowlock	wrestle	eventing	holed out
jogging	running	**8**	exercise	home base
jujitsu	sailing		falconer	home game
karting	scoring	après ski	falconry	horseman

how's that
huntsman
hurdling
iron shot
jousting
joystick
knockout
korfball
lacrosse
left back
left half
left hook
left wing
leg break
leg guard
leg sweep
lifeline
linesman
long jump
long odds
long shot
long slip
long stop
lost ball
love game
marathon
marksman
natation
ninepins
nosedive
olympiad
olympics
opponent
outfield
outsider
oval ball
pall mall
pavilion
pétanque
pike dive
ping-pong
pole jump
polo pony
pony race
port tack

pugilism
pugilist
pushball
pyramids
quintain
racegoer
rambling
recovery
ricochet
ringside
rink polo
rounders
runner-up
sand iron
sand trap
scramble
sculling
set point
shooting
short leg
shot putt
side blow
sideline
side slip
skipping
ski slope
ski stick
skittles
sledding
slow ball
snow line
softball
southpaw
sparring
speedway
stand off
stock-car
stop shot
straddle
stumping
stun shot
swimming
teamwork
The Ashes
third man

tholepin
tie-break
toboggan
toreador
tracking
trailing
training
transfer
trial run
trotting
tug of war
tumbling
turf club
underarm
undercut
under par
upper cut
vaulting
walkover
wall bars
wall game
water ski
wing area
wood shot
yachting

9

abseiling
advantage
aiki-jutsu
all square
anchorman
apparatus
aquaboard
aquaplane
athletics
aunt sally
backswing
badminton
belly-flop
bicycling
billiards
black belt
black flag

black pawn
bladework
bobsleigh
bodycheck
body punch
bowstring
brown belt
bull fight
butterfly
caddie car
cannonball
camelspin
chair lift
challenge
clubhouse
cock fight
combatant
conqueror
crackshot
cricketer
crossjack
cup winner
cycle race
cycle tour
dartboard
decathlon
decoy duck
deep field
dirt track
disengage
dog racing
dolly drop
double top
drawn game
dumbbells
enclosure
en passant
equalizer
Eton fives
extra time
faceguard
favourite
field game
fieldsman
first base

first half
first seed
first slip
fisherman
fixed odds
fletching
flight bow
foot fault
forty love
free reach
freestyle
freewheel
game point
gate money
goal posts
golf clubs
golf links
golf range
golf widow
good sport
grand prix
grand slam
greyhound
gum shield
gymnasium
handstand
hard court
hill climb
infielder
ice hockey
in-fielder
jackknife
judo throw
kennelman
king's rock
lawn bowls
light blue
lob bowler
long field
loose ball
loose rein
love match
low volley
match play
mid mashie

midwicket
moto-cross
motorboat
Newmarket
pacemaker
palaestra
pole vault
pot holing
pot hunter
programme
puissance
punchball
racehorse
race track
racing cap
relay race
relay team
right back
right half
right hook
right wing
safety net
sand wedge
sand yacht
sauna bath
schnorkel
score card
screw dive
screw shot
scrimmage
scrum half
scrummage
semi-final
shin guard
short stop
short slip
signal gun
skindiver
ski runner
skydiving
sleighing
small bore
small slam
spectator
speedboat

spin parry
split shot
square-leg
stable boy
stable lad
stalemate
starboard
steersman
stopwatch
stroke oar
surf board
sweat-band
swordplay
swordsman
tennis net
test match
third base
third slip
the sticks
tight rein
touch-down
touch goal
touchline
tracksuit
tramlines
twist dive
water jump
water polo
whipper-in
wrestling
wrist lock
yacht race

10

acrobatics
aerobatics
agility mat
back marker
backstroke
ballooning
banderilla
basketball
battledore
binoculars

Boston crab
boxing ring
catch a crab
centre half
centre spot
challenger
checkpoint
clay pigeon
competitor
contestant
corner flag
counted out
cover point
cricket bat
crown green
cyclo-cross
deck quoits
deck tennis
diving bell
dolly catch
double axle
drag racing
draw stumps
drop cannon
drop volley
eel fishing
eliminator
equitation
Eskimo roll
fast bowler
field event
field games
field sport
first blood
fishing net
fishing rod
fisticuffs
fives court
flat racing
fly-fishing
flying mare
footballer
forced move
Formula One
Formula Two

full nelson
foxhunting
goal circle
goal crease
goalkeeper
goal kicker
golf course
grandstand
gymnastics
half-nelson
half-volley
halved hole
handspring
hard tackle
hazard side
headhunter
heel and toe
horsewoman
hunting bow
hurdle race
ice dancing
ice sailing
ice skating
Indian club
indoor golf
injury time
inside lane
inside left
inside lock
in the rough
in training
isometrics
Jockey club
jump the gun
karate chop
landing net
lawn tennis
league game
little slam
lob bowling
love thirty
maiden over
marker buoy
mashie iron
match point

Monte Carlo
non-starter
opening bat
open season
open target
outfielder
paper-chase
par contest
pari-mutuel
passed pawn
penalty try
point of aim
polo ground
pony racing
pot hunting
prize fight
prize money
punch-drunk
push stroke
racecourse
real tennis
relegation
riding whip
rifle range
right bower
right innner
right swing
rowing boat
rugby fives
rugby match
rugby pitch
rugby union
run through
rush stroke
safety play
safety shot
scoreboard
second base
second half
second slip
seconds out
second wind
seven-a-side
short tacks
show-jumper

sidesaddle
side stroke
silly mid on
silly point
ski-jumping
ski-running
slow bowler
somersault
speed trial
spin bowler
sportswear
stable-mate
stake money
stop thrust
strokeplay
strokesman
submission
substitute
surf riding
suspension
sweepstake
swerve shot
switchback
team spirit
tennis ball
thrown goal
timekeeper
title fight
tournament
track event
trampoline
tricycling
triple jump
tumble turn
twelfth man
Vardon grip
volleyball
weighing-in
white water
win by a head
win by a nose

11

accumulator

athleticism
bear baiting
biased bowls
blood sports
bobsledding
boxing glove
bull baiting
canoe slalom
casual water
Channel swim
cheerleader
cinder track
class racing
close season
competition
county match
coup de grâce
crawl stroke
cricket pads
croquet arch
croquet ball
croquet hoop
curling rink
cycle racing
daisy cutter
deep fine leg
declaration
discus throw
diving board
double fault
downhill run
driving iron
fast bowling
fell walking
fencing mask
fifteen-love
field hockey
first eleven
fishing line
flick stroke
flying start
forced error
forward line
forward pass
Fosbury flop

free skating
game fishing
grass skiing
hairpin bend
hammer throw
hang-gliding
hockey pitch
hockey stick
home stretch
horse racing
horse riding
horse trials
hunting crop
hunting horn
ice yachting
inside right
inter-county
lap of honour
league table
loop the loop
martial arts
medlay relay
motor racing
neck and neck
Olympic team
out of bounds
outside lane
outside left
pairs skating
parachuting
penalty area
penalty goal
penalty kick
penalty line
penalty spot
pentathalon
photo finish
pools coupon
prizewinner
prop-forward
protagonist
public stand
quarterback
rabbit punch
race meeting

regatta card
return match
rising block
rising punch
round of golf
royal tennis
rugby league
sand sailing
scuba diving
seam bowling
self-defence
service line
service side
show jumping
shuttlecock
silly mid-off
simple parry
skating rink
slow bowling
snowshoeing
soft landing
spade mashie
springboard
squash court
starting gun
striker ball
sudden death
swallow dive
sweep rowing
table tennis
target arrow
test cricket
tennis court
third player
tobogganing
track record
transfer fee
uncontested
walking race
water hazard
Western roll
water skiing
windsurfing
wing forward
winning post

winning side
winning team
win on points
wooden horse
world record
yacht racing

12

anchor cannon
approach shot
back straight
banger racing
batting order
billiard ball
boardsailing
bobsleighing
bowling alley
bowling green
breast stroke
bullfighting
caber tossing
century break
championship
change bowler
change of ends
climbing rope
cockfighting
crash barrier
cricket match
cricket pitch
croquet court
curling stone
cut and thrust
dead ball line
deer stalking
direct cannon
double sculls
doubles match
dressing room
electric hare
field glasses
figure skater
first defence
first innings

first reserve
first service
flying tackle
Eton wall game
gamesmanship
googly bowler
ground-stroke
handicap race
hare coursing
head scissors
home straight
hundred yards
in the running
long distance
loose forward
losing hazard
javelin throw
maiden stakes
marathon race
medicine ball
mixed doubles
National Hunt
netball match
nursery slope
Olympic games
Olympic torch
opposing side
orienteering
outside right
parellel bars
penalty bully
penalty throw
pigeon racing
pitch and toss
playing field
point-to-point
pole position
pole vaulting
pony trekking
postponement
prize fighter
professional
putting green
quarter-final
racing stable

receiving end
record holder
return crease
ride to hounds
ringside seat
rock climbing
rope climbing
rope spinning
rope throwing
running strip
running track
scissors jump
second eleven
service court
shadow boxing
sharpshooter
single combat
single sculls
singles match
skipping rope
slice service
speed skating
sport of kings
squash racket
stabbing blow
stand-off half
starting gate
starting grid
starting post
staying power
steeplechase
sticky wicket
straddle jump
strong finish
swimming gala
swimming pool
sword fencing
tennis racket
thoroughbred
trampolining
trap shooting
treble chance
wicket keeper
winter sports

13

aquatic sports
billiard table
bowling crease
centre forward
checkered flag
chequered flag
coarse fishing
counter attack
county cricket
cricket ground
cricket stumps
croquet mallet
figure of eight
figure skating
finishing line
finishing post
fishing tackle
follow-through
football pitch
Grand National
half-time score
harness racing
horizontal bar
hundred metres
isometric bars
mashie niblick
mixed foursome
mountaineering
nightwatchman
one-day cricket
pitch invasion
popping-crease
qualification
record breaker
return service
rifle shooting
roller-skating
scratch player
second innings
shooting range
skateboarding
sportsmanship
sports stadium

starting price
starting stall
swordsmanship
track and field
vaulting horse
victor ludorum
weight lifting
wicketkeeping

14

all-in wrestling
American karate
approach stroke
asymmetric bars
billiard marker
cauliflower ear
discus throwing
downhill skiing
football league
Gaelic football
glorius twelfth
greyhound Derby
grouse shooting
hammer throwing
league football
master of hounds
mountaineering
nineteenth hole
opening batsman
sheepdog trials
sporting chance
starting blocks
starting stalls
pistol shooting
starting pistol
stock-car racing
thousand metres
weight training

wrestling match

15

appearance money
badminton racket
bodyline bowling
bowl a maiden over
butterfly stroke
cannonball serve
football stadium
greyhound racing
nursery handicap
public enclosure
shooting gallery
sparring partner
stable companion

16 +

aggressive offence
American football
association football
Australian Rules football
freestyle wrestling
game, set and match
hit below the belt
hot-air ballooning
leg before wicket
modern pentathalon
motorcycle racing
odds-on favourite
parachute jumping
pipped at the post
Royal and Ancient
rugby league football
synchronized swimming
throw in the towel
volunteer snooker

Threes

Three Graces

Aglaia
Thalia
Euphrosyne

Three Musketeers

Athos
Aramis
Porthos

Three Wise Men

Gaspar or Casper
Melchior
Balthazar
who gave:
gold
myrrh
frankincense

Titles, officials and forms of address

1 & 2	4		5		6
HE	agha	inca	ameer	imaum	rajah
M	aide	kadi	baboo	junta	ranee
Mr	amir	khan	baron	junto	reeve
S	amma	king	bedel	jurat	ruler
	babu	lady	begum	kalif	sagan
3	cadi	lama	boyar	laird	saheb
	cham	Lord	brenn	liege	sahib
aga	czar	Ma'am	calif	macer	Señor
beg	dame	Miss	chief	Madam	sheik
bey	dato	M'Lud	comte	mayor	subah
cid	dean	naib	conte	mirza	thane
dey	doge	naik	count	mogul	wazir
Dom	Doña	peer	dewan	mpret	
Don	ducé	raja	diwan	mufti	**6**
HRH	duke	rana	Donna	nabob	
Mme	earl	rani	doyen	nawab	archon
Mrs	emir	shah	elder	negus	ataman
mir	foud	Sire	emeer	nizam	bailie
ras	graf	tsar	envoy	noble	bashaw
rex	heir	tzar	ephor	omrah	beadle
Sir	imam	vali	hakam	pacha	bigwig
		wali		pasha	bursar
		zaim		queen	caesar

caliph	sherif	headman	subadar	heptarch
censor	shogun	hidalga	sultana	hierarch
chagan	sirdar	hidalgo	supremo	Highness
cherif	soldan	infanta	toparch	His Grace
consul	squire	infante	tribune	hospodar
daimio	sultan	jemadar	tsarina	interrex
daimyo	tycoon	justice	tzarina	kingling
deputy	vidame	karling	vavasor	Ladyship
despot	vizier	khedive	viceroy	Landgraf
doctor	yeoman	kinglet	vaivode	laureate
duenna		Law Lord	voivode	lawgiver
dynast	**7**	maestro		lawmaker
exarch		magnate		life peer
Führer	akhoond	maharao	**8**	lordling
Gräfin	alcalde	mahatma		Lordship
herald	armiger	Majesty	alderman	maharaja
hetman	attaché	marquis	archduke	maharani
holkar	bailiff	marshal	atheline	manciple
Junker	baronet	matgraf	autocrat	mandarin
kabaka	brenhin	monarch	banneret	marchesa
kaiser	burgess	Mr Mayor	baroness	marchese
knight	cacique	notable	Black Rod	margrave
legate	cazique	officer	burgrave	marquess
lictor	candace	padisha	cardinal	marquise
lucumo	comtess	paladin	caudillo	martinet
Master	consort	peeress	chairman	mayoress
mikado	coroner	pharoah	cicerone	memsahib
Mister	curator	podesta	contessa	minister
mullah	czarina	praetor	co-regent	Mistress
My Lady	dauphin	prefect	countess	monocrat
My Lord	dowager	premier	czarevna	Monsieur
notary	duchess	proctor	dauphine	nobility
peshwa	duumvir	questor	deemster	nobleman
pretor	effendi	royalty	delegate	official
prince	elector	sea-king	dictator	oligarch
puisne	emperor	sea-lord	diplomat	overlord
rajput	empress	senator	director	overseer
rector	equerry	shereef	dukeling	padishah
regent	esquire	sheriff	emeritus	palatine
regina	Fuehrer	Signior	emissary	placeman
sachem	gaekwar	Signora	Eminence	pontifex
satrap	gaikwar	Signore	ethnarch	princess
Senora	grafine	skipper	eupatrid	quaestor
shaikh	grandee	Speaker	guardian	queenlet
sheikh	Head Boy	steward	Head Girl	recorder
			headsman	

sagamore
Seigneur
Seignior
Señorita
squireen
subahdar
suzerain
talukdar
tetrarch
tipstaff
triumvir
tsarevna
tzarevna
vavasour
vavassor
verderer
viscomte
viscount
zamindar
zemindar

9

abimelech
authority
bodyguard
bretwalda
burggrave
castellan
catchpole
centurion
chevalier
chieftan
Chief Whip
commander
commadore
constable
custodian
dictatrix
dignitary
diplomate
electress
escheator
exciseman
executive

Gauleiter
Gold Stick
grand duke
His Honour
imperator
inspector
justiciar
Landgrave
liege-lord
liveryman
lord mayor
magnifico
maharajah
maharanee
maharawal
majordomo
matriarch
monsignor
ombudsman
palsgrave
patrician
pendragon
policeman
portreeve
president
pretender
princekin
princelet
principal
proconsul
registrar
secretary
Seigniore
seneschal
Signorina
sovereign
statesman
sub-beadle
sultaness
town clerk
town crier
treasurer
venerable
waldgrave
whipper-in

Your Grace

10

adelantado
aide-de-camp
ambassador
areopagite
aristocrat
baronetess
burgomaster
bumbailiff
chancellor
commandant
commissary
controller
councillor
crown agent
dauphiness
door-keeper
Excellency
headmaster
Honourable
inquisitor
King-at-Arms
legislator
lieutenant
mace-bearer
Madam Mayor
magistrate
margravine
mayor-elect
noblewoman
palsgravine
priest-king
princeling
procurator
ringmaster
tsarevitch
vice-consul
vice-regent
viscomtess
Your Honour

11

archduchess
aristocracy
burgomaster
cesarevitch
chamberlain
comptroller
crowned head
crown lawyer
crown prince
diplomatist
earl-marshal
functionary
grand master
grand vizier
His Eminence
Her Highness
His Highness
His Holiness
landgravine
life peeress
marchioness
Mister Mayor
Monseigneur
Mr President
My Lord Abbot
My Lord Mayor
palsgravine
policewoman
prince royal
Queen Mother
queen-regent
stadtholder
subordinate
sword-bearer
viscountess
waldgravine

12

agent-general
ambassadress
armour-bearer
chief justice

chief of staff
civil servant
commissioner
crown equerry
earl palatine
grand duchess
headmistress
heir-apparent
jack-in-office
knight errant
lady mayoress
lord temporal
maid of honour
Madamoiselle
Most Reverend
notary public
peace officer
price-bishop
prince regent
queen consort
queen dowager
queen-regnant
staff officer
temporal peer
Very Reverend
water bailiff
Your Eminence
Your Highness
Your Holiness

13

administrator
consul-general
count palatine
district judge
generalissimo
Grand-Seigneur
high constable
judge-advocate
lord spiritual
prime minister
prince consort
Prince of Wales
princess royal
public trustee
spittual peer
vice-president

14

archchancellor
auditor-General
chief constable
crown solicitor
dowager duchess
lord of the manor
hereditary peer
high court judge
king's messenger
knight-bachelor

knight-banneret
lord chancellor
lord lieutenant
My Lady Mayoress
prince imperial
provost-marshal
superintendent
town councillor
vice-chancellor
Your Excellency

15 +

advocate-general
attorney-general
cabinet minister
chargé d'affaires
district officer
governor general
heir-presumptive
hereditary peeress
Her Royal Highness
His Royal Highness
Mister President
plenipotentiary
privy councillor
queen's messenger
Right Honourable
Right Worshipful
vice-chamberlain
vice-chancellor
Your Royal Highness

Tools and implements

3	fan	zax	burr	hink	mole	rasp
	gad		cart	hook	mule	rule
adz	gin	**4**	celt	hose	nail	sock
awl	hod		crab	jack	pick	spud
axe	hoe	adze	file	last	pike	tool
bit	jig	bill	fork	loom	plow	trug
die	loy	bore	frow	mall	pump	vice
dog	saw	brog	gage	maul	rake	whim

5

anvil
auger
beele
bench
besom
betty
bevel
blade
borer
brace
burin
chuck
churn
clamp
clams
clasp
cleat
cramp
crane
croom
croze
cupel
dolly
drill
flail
flang
forge
gauge
gavel
gouge
hoist
incus
jacks
jemmy
jimmy
knife
lathe
level
lever
mower
parer
plane
plumb

preen
prise
prong
punch
quern
quoin
ratch
razor
sarse
scoop
screw
spade
spike
spile
spill
swage
temse
tommy
tongs
tromp
trone
wedge
winch

6

barrow
beetle
bender
blower
bodkin
borcer
bow-saw
brayer
broach
burton
chaser
chisel
colter
crevet
cruset
dibber
dibble
digger
doffer

dredge
driver
eolith
fanner
faucet
ferret
folder
gadget
gimlet
grater
graver
hackle
heckle
hammer
harrow
jagger
jigger
jig saw
ladder
mallet
mortar
muller
oil gun
oliver
pallet
pencil
pestle
pitsaw
planer
pliers
plough
pontee
pooler
rammer
ramrod
rasper
reaper
riddle
ripsaw
roller
rubber
sander
saw-set
scales
screen

scythe
segger
shaver
shears
shovel
sickle
sifter
skewer
sledge
slicer
spigot
square
stiddy
stithy
strike
stylus
tackle
tedder
tenter
trepan
trowel
tubber
turrel
wimble
wrench

7

band saw
boaster
bradawl
buzz saw
capstan
catling
cautery
chamfer
chip-axe
chopper
cleaver
couloir
coulter
crampon
crisper
crowbar
cuvette

derrick
diamond
dog-belt
drudger
fistuca
forceps
fretsaw
fruggin
gradine
grainer
grapnel
gripper
grub axe
hacksaw
handsaw
hatchel
hatchet
hayfork
hayrake
jointer
mandrel
mattock
nippers
nut hook
pickaxe
piercer
pincers
plummet
pole axe
pounder
pricker
riffler
rotator
salt-pan
scalpel
scauper
scraper
screwer
scriber
seed lop
shuttle
spaddle
spanner
spatula
sprayer

stapler
strocal
tenoner
thimble
trestle
triblet
T-square
twibill
twister
whip-saw
whittle
wood saw
woolder

8

airbrush
andirons
bark mill
bar shear
beakiron
bench peg
billhook
bistoury
bloomary
blowlamp
blowpipe
boathook
bowdrill
bull nose
butteris
calender
calipers
canthook
chainsaw
chopness
cross bit
crow mill
crucible
die stock
dividers
dowel bit
drill bow
Dutch hoe
edge tool

filatory
fire kiln
flame gun
flat iron
flax comb
gavelock
gee cramp
handloom
handmill
handtool
hand vice
hay knife
haymaker
hoof pick
horse hoe
lapstone
lead mill
nitre box
molegrip
muck rake
nut screw
oilstone
paint pad
panel saw
penknife
picklock
pinchers
plumb bob
polisher
power saw
prong-hoe
puncheon
reap hook
saw knife
saw wrest
scissors
scuffler
shoehorn
slate axe
spray gun
stiletto
strickle
strimmer
tenon saw
throstle

tommy bar
tooth key
tweezers
twist bit
weed hook
windlass
windmill

9

air hammer
arc welder
belt punch
bench hook
blowtorch
bolt auger
boot crimp
calllipers
can opener
cement gun
centre bit
compasses
corkscrew
cotter pin
cramp iron
curry comb
cutter bar
dog clutch
draw knife
draw-plate
drop forge
excavator
eyeleteer
fillister
fining pot
fork chuck
gas pliers
grease gun
hair dryer
hammer axe
hand brace
hand drill
handspike
holing axe
hummeller

implement
jackknife
jackplane
jackscrew
lace frame
lawnmower
mousetrap
nail punch
nut wrench
pitch fork
plane iron
planisher
plumbline
plumb-rule
road drill
screwjack
scribe awl
secateurs
shearlegs
sheep hook
staple gun
steam iron
steelyard
sugar mill
telescope
tin opener
try square
turf spade
turn bench
turnscrew
tyre lever
watermill

10

bowie knife
box spanner
bread knife
bush harrow
claspknife
clawhammer
coal shovel
cold chisel
crane's bill
cultivator

dray plough
drift bolts
drill press
drillstock
drop hammer
edging tool
emery wheel
fire engine
firing iron
fly swatter
garden fork
grindstone
instrument
keyhole saw
masonry bit
masticator
mitre block
motor mower
mould board
nail drawer
paintbrush
paper knife
perforator
pipe wrench
pointed awl
power drill
safety lamp
screw press
sleek stone
snowplough
spokeshave
steam press
stepladder
tenterhook
thumbscrew
thumbstall
tilt hammer
trip hammer
turf cutter
turnbuckle
twist drill
watercrane
watergauge
waterlevel
wheel brace

11

brace and bit
breast drill
butcher's saw
chaff cutter
chain blocks
chain wrench
cheese press
cigar cutter
circular saw
countersink
crisping pin
crosscut saw
dovetail saw
drill harrow
electric saw
fanning mill
garden spade
glass cutter
grubbing hoe
helvehammer
jagging iron
machine tool
monkey block
paring knife
paint roller
ploughshare
pocketknife
power shovel
pruning hook
rabbet plane
reaping-hook
ring spanner
rotary drill
safety razor
sanding disc
sawing stool
screwdriver
side-cutters
skim coulter
snatch block
spirit level
squaring rod
steam hammer

steam shovel
stone hammer
straw cutter
strike block
stubble rake
sward cutter
swingplough
tamping iron
tape measure
turfing iron
two-foot rule
warping hook
warping post
watering can
weeding fork
weeding hook
weeding rhim
wheelbarrow

12

barking irons
belt adjuster
branding iron
breastplough
carving knife
caulking tool
counter gauge
cradle scythe
cramping iron
crimping iron
crisping iron
curling tongs
drill grubber
driving shaft
driving wheel
electric iron
emery grinder
flour dresser
garden roller
garden shears
garden trowel
glass furnace
hedge trimmer
hydraulic ram

mandrel lathe
marline spike
masonry drill
monkey wrench
palette knife
pruning knife
pulley blocks
ratchet drill
running block
scribing iron
sledgehammer
sliding bevel
socket chisel
stone breaker
straightedge
swingle knife
touch needles
trench plough
turfing spade
turning lathe
two-handed saw
water bellows
weeding tongs

13

butcher's broom
chopping block
chopping knife
cylinder press
electric drill
grappling-iron
hydraulic jack
packing needle
pinking shears
scribing block
sewing machine
single-cut file
soldering bolt
soldering iron
sowing machine
spinning jenny
spinning wheel
stocking frame
subsoil plough
three-foot rule
two-hole pliers
weeding chisel

14

blowing machine
carding machine
draining engine
draining plough
pneumatic drill
reaping machine
shepherd's crook
smoothing plane
swingling knife
thrusting screw
weeding forceps

15

carpenter's
 bench
crimping machine
dredging machine
drilling machine
entrenching tool
pestle and mortar
pump screwdriver
weighing machine

Trades, professions and occupations

2	dip	**4**	chef	help	seer	**5**
GP	doc		cook	herd	serf	actor
MD	don	alto	dame	hind	sice	ad-man
MO	gyp	amah	dean	hoer	snip	agent
MP	ham	ayah	dick	hood	snob	baker
PA	lad	baas	diva	lead	star	baler
PM	lag	bard	doge	maid	syce	bobby
	pro	bass	dyer	mate	temp	bonze
	rep	beak	G-man	mime	thug	boots
3	spy	boss	grip	mute	tout	bosun
	sub	bull	hack	page	ward	boxer
boy	tec	cadi	hand	peon	whip	bride
cop	vet	char	head	poet		

buyer	mason	usher	bursar	drover	hawker
cabby	mayor	valet	busker	drudge	header
caddy	medic	viner	busman	duenna	healer
chips	mimer	walla	butler	duffer	heaver
clerk	mimic	watch	cabbie	earner	hedger
clown	miner	waxer	cabman	editor	helper
coach	model	wench	calker	escort	herald
comic	navvy	wirer	canner	etcher	hit-man
crier	nazir		carter	fabler	hodman
crimp	nurse	**6**	carver	factor	hooper
crook	oiler		casual	farmer	horner
curer	pasha	airman	censor	feller	hosier
daily	paver	archer	cleric	fisher	hunter
dhobi	pilot	artist	codist	fitter	husker
diver	piper	au pair	coiner	flayer	iceman
druid	poser	aurist	comber	fly-man	intern
envoy	pupil	author	commis	forger	ironer
extra	quack	bagman	conder	flower	issuer
fakir	raker	bailee	conman	fluter	jagger
fence	reeve	bailer	consul	framer	jailer
fifer	rimer	bailie	coolie	fuller	jailor
filer	roper	bailor	cooper	gaffer	jester
finer	rover	balker	copper	ganger	jobber
flier	saice	bandit	corker	gaoler	jockey
fraud	sawer	banker	co-star	garçon	joiner
gipsy	scout	barber	coster	gaucho	jurist
gluer	screw	bargee	cowboy	gauger	keeler
groom	sewer	barker	cowman	gelder	keeper
guard	sepoy	barman	critic	geisha	killer
guide	shoer	batman	culler	gigolo	lackey
hakim	slave	beadle	cupper	gilder	lagger
heavy	smith	beagle	cutler	gillie	lapper
helot	sower	bearer	cutter	glazer	lascar
hewer	staff	bigwig	dacoit	glover	lawman
hirer	super	binder	dancer	graver	lawyer
inker	sweep	boffin	dealer	grocer	leader
judge	tamer	bookie	deputy	grower	lector
knave	tawer	bowman	digger	guider	legate
layer	taxer	bowyer	dipper	guidon	leg-man
leech	tenor	brewer	docker	gunman	lender
liner	thief	broker	doctor	gunner	lictor
locum	tiler	buffer	dowser	guv'nor	loader
luter	tuner	bugler	draper	harlot	logger
madam	tutor	bumble	drawer	harper	logman
mammy	tyler	burler	driver	hatter	looter

lopper	pinder	sawyer	tiller	**7**
lumper	pin-man	scaler	tinker	
lutist	pirate	scribe	tinman	abettor
lyrist	pitman	sea-dog	tinner	abigail
mahout	planer	sealer	toiler	acolyte
marker	plater	seaman	toller	acolyth
master	player	seamer	tonsor	acrobat
matron	porter	seiner	tapman	actress
medico	pot-boy	seller	totter	acutary
mender	pot-man	server	touter	adviser
menial	potter	setter	tracer	advisor
mercer	priest	sexton	trader	alewife
milker	prover	shaman	trusty	almoner
miller	pruner	shaver	tubber	alnager
minter	purser	shroff	tubman	analyst
monger	pusher	singer	turner	arabist
mooter	querry	sister	tweeny	arbiter
mopper	racker	sitter	tycoon	artisan
mugger	ragman	skivvy	typist	artiste
muller	raider	slater	usurer	assayer
mummer	ranger	slaver	valuer	assizer
mystic	rapist	slavey	vamper	assurer
nailer	ratter	slayer	vandal	attaché
nailor	reader	sleuth	vassal	auditor
nautch	reaper	snarer	vender	aviator
notary	reever	socman	vendor	bailiff
nuncio	rector	sorter	verger	bandman
oboist	regent	soutar	verser	barmaid
oilman	relief	spicer	vibist	baulker
old lag	renter	squire	viewer	bell-boy
orator	rhymer	stager	vizier	bell-hop
ostler	rigger	stoker	waiter	bellman
outlaw	ringer	stooge	wallah	bencher
packer	robber	stoner	waller	best boy
parson	roofer	storer	warden	best man
pastor	rooter	sutler	warder	big-shot
patron	rozzer	tailor	warper	birdman
pavior	runner	tamper	washer	blaster
pedant	sacker	tanner	weaver	blender
pedlar	sailor	tapper	weeder	boatman
peeler	salter	tasker	welder	bondman
penman	salvor	taster	whaler	bookman
picker	sapper	taxman	worker	botcher
piecer	sartor	teller	wright	bottler
pieman	satrap	tester	writer	bouncer

breeder	crooner	fuguist	knitter	patcher
brigand	cropper	furrier	lace-man	paviour
buffoon	curator	gateman	lineman	peatman
builder	currier	girdler	linkboy	peddler
burgess	danseur	glazier	linkman	pianist
burgher	daysman	gleaner	lockman	picador
burglar	dentist	gleeman	lorimer	pickler
butcher	dialist	glosser	maestro	pierrot
buttons	diarist	grafter	mailman	pig-herd
call-boy	dietist	grainer	maltman	pikeman
cambist	ditcher	granger	manager	pioneer
carrier	dobhash	grantor	mangler	planner
caseman	dominie	grazier	marbler	planter
cashier	doorman	greaser	mariner	pleader
caterer	dragman	grinder	marshal	plumber
caulker	drapier	gumshoe	masseur	poacher
cellist	drawboy	gymnast	matador	poetess
changer	drayman	hackler	matcher	pop star
chanter	dredger	haggler	matelot	postboy
chapman	dresser	handler	mealman	postman
checker	drifter	hangman	meatman	praetor
chemist	drummer	harpist	midwife	prefect
cleaner	dustman	haulier	mildman	premier
clicker	duumvir	heckler	milkman	presser
clippie	elegist	herbist	mobster	printer
clogger	equerry	herdman	modiste	proctor
coalman	famulus	heritor	moneyer	provost
cobbler	fancier	hobbler	monitor	puddler
cockler	farrier	hogherd	moulder	puncher
collier	fiddler	hoodlum	mountie	quilter
comique	firebug	hostler	mourner	rancher
commere	fireman	hurdler	needler	realtor
compère	flesher	indexer	newsboy	referee
convict	florist	inlayer	newsman	refiner
co-pilot	flunkey	insurer	oculist	reviser
copyist	flusher	janitor	officer	revisor
coroner	flutist	juggler	operant	riddler
corsair	footboy	junkman	orderer	riveter
counsel	footman	juryman	orderly	roadman
courier	footpad	justice	ostiary	roaster
cowgirl	foreman	keelman	packman	roper-in
cowhand	founder	khedive	pageboy	rouster
cowherd	friseur	knacker	painter	rustler
cowpoke	frogman	knapper	palmist	sacrist
crofter	fueller	kneader	partner	saddler

sampler	stylist	**8**	cabin boy	emissary
samurai	surgeon		call girl	employee
scanner	swabber	abductor	caroller	employer
scourer	sweeper	advocate	castrato	engineer
scraper	taborer	aeronaut	cellarer	engraver
sea-cook	tallier	alderman	chairman	enroller
securer	tapster	alienist	chandler	epic poet
senator	taxi-man	analyser	charlady	essayist
servant	teacher	animator	charwoman	examiner
settler	tipster	annalist	choirboy	executor
sharper	tracker	annealer	claqueur	exorcist
shearer	trainee	aphorist	clothier	explorer
sheller	trainer	apiarist	coachman	exponent
sheriff	traitor	aquarist	co-author	exporter
shifter	trapper	arborist	codifier	fabulist
shipper	trawler	armorist	collator	factotum
shopboy	tribune	armourer	comedian	falconer
shopman	trimmer	arsonist	compiler	farcense
showman	trouper	arrestor	composer	farmhand
shunter	trucker	assassin	conjurer	ferreter
simpler	trusser	assessor	convener	ferryman
skimmer	trustee	attorney	conveyor	figurant
skinner	tumbler	bagmaker	courtier	film star
skipper	turnkey	bagpiper	coxswain	finisher
slipper	viceroy	bandsman	cremator	fishwife
smelter	villain	banjoist	criminal	flatfoot
snuffer	vintner	bargeman	croupier	flautist
socager	violist	baritone	cutpurse	fletcher
soldier	voyager	beadsman	dairyman	fodderer
soloist	wagoner	bedesman	danseuse	forester
soprano	warbler	bedmaker	deckhand	forgeman
sounder	warrior	bigamist	deemster	front man
speaker	webster	bit-maker	defender	fugitive
special	weigher	Black Rod	delegate	gangsman
spencer	whetter	blazoner	diplomat	pugleman
spinner	wireman	bleacher	designer	gangster
spotter	woodman	boatsman	director	gaol-bird
stainer	woolman	bondmaid	domestic	gardener
stamper	workman	bondsman	doughboy	gavelman
stapler	wrapper	botanist	dragoman	gendarme
starlet	wrecker	bothyman	druggist	geometer
statist	yardman	bowmaker	druidess	glassman
steerer		boxmaker	duettist	goatherd
steward		brewster	educator	godsmith
sticker		broacher	embalmer	governor
			embosser	

guardian	lecturer	observer	provisor	servitor
gunmaker	libeller	offender	psalmist	shearman
gunsmith	licensee	official	publican	shepherd
hammerer	linesman	onion-man	pugilist	shipmate
handmaid	linguist	oologist	purveyor	ship's boy
handyman	logician	operator	quaestor	shopgirls
hatmaker	lumberer	optician	quarrier	showgirl
haymaker	lutanist	ordainer	rabbiter	sidesman
head chef	lyricist	ordinand	raftsman	sitter-in
head cook	magician	organist	ragtimer	sketcher
headsman	magister	outrider	ragwoman	smuggler
helmsman	maltster	overseer	ranchero	solderer
henchman	mameluke	palatine	rapperee	soldiery
herdsman	mandarin	paper-boy	receiver	songster
hijacker	man of law	pargeter	recorder	spaceman
hireling	map-maker	parodist	regrater	spearman
home help	marauder	penmaker	releaser	speed-cop
hotelier	marketer	penwoman	repairer	spurrier
houseboy	masseuse	perfumer	reporter	starcher
houseman	mayoress	perjurer	resetter	star turn
huckster	measurer	peterman	resident	stitcher
humorist	mechanic	pewterer	restorer	stockman
huntsman	medalist	picaroon	retailer	storeman
importer	mediator	pig-woman	retainer	streamer
improver	melodist	pilferer	reveiwer	stripper
inkmaker	merchant	pillager	rewriter	strummer
indentor	merryman	plateman	riverman	stuntman
inventor	metal-man	plougher	rivetter	supplier
jail-bird	milkmaid	poisoner	roadsman	surfacer
jet pilot	millhand	polisher	romancer	surveyor
jeweller	milliner	politico	rugmaker	swindler
jig-borer	mimester	portress	saboteur	tabourer
jongleur	mimicker	postiler	salesman	tallyman
kipperer	minister	potmaker	satirist	taverner
knife-boy	minstrel	preacher	sawbones	teamster
labourer	mistress	prefacer	scrubber	thatcher
landgirl	modeller	preluder	scullion	theorist
landlady	motorman	pressman	sculptor	.thespian
landlord	muleteer	prisoner	seamster	thrasher
lapidary	muralist	procurer	searcher	thresher
larcener	murderer	producer	sea-rover	tin miner
larderer	musician	promoter	seasoner	tinsmith
law-giver	narrator	prompter	seedsman	tipstaff
law-maker	newshawk	prosaist	sempster	top-liner
leadsman	novelist	provider	sergeant	torturer

toymaker	anatomist	cameraman	cupbearer	film extra
trackman	anchorman	canvasser	custodian	film-maker
trencher	annotator	car driver	cut-throat	financier
triumvir	announcer	caretaker	cymbalist	fire-eater
truckman	antiquary	carpenter	daily help	fish-curer
turncock	appraiser	carvanner	dairymaid	fisherman
turnspit	arborator	casemaker	decorator	fish-woman
unionist	architect	catchpole	desk clerk	flag-maker
usheress	archivist	catechist	detective	flyfisher
valuator	art critic	celebrity	dice-maker	forewoman
veneerer	art dealer	cellarman	die-sinker	fraudster
verderer	art editor	cembalist	dietetist	freelance
vintager	artificer	charwoman	dietician	freighter
virtuoso	art master	chanteuse	dietitian	fripperer
vocalist	assembler	chauffeur	dignitary	fruiterer
volumist	assistant	cheapjack	dispenser	full-timer
waggoner	astronaut	Chief Whip	dissector	furbisher
waitress	attendant	chorister	distiller	furnisher
walker-on	authoress	citharist	draftsman	galvanist
wardress	auxiliary	clergyman	dramatist	gasfitter
warrener	balladeer	clinician	drum-maker	gazetteer
watchman	balladist	clogmaker	drysalter	gem-cutter
waterman	ballerina	coalminer	ecdysiast	geologist
water-rat	bar-keeper	collector	ecologist	gladiator
wet nurse	barrister	colourist	economist	gluemaker
whaleman	barrowboy	colourman	embezzler	goldminer
whiffler	bartender	columnist	enameller	goldsmith
whistler	beefeater	commissar	engineman	gondolier
whitener	beekeeper	companion	engrainer	gooseherd
wigmaker	biologist	concierge	engrosser	gospeller
winchman	boatswain	conductor	errand-boy	governess
winnower	bodyguard	conserver	estimator	guardsman
woodsman	boilerman	constable	excavator	guerrilla
wool-dyer	bondslave	contralto	excerptor	guitarist
wrestler	bondwoman	co-partner	exchanger	gun-runner
yodeller	bookmaker	corrector	exciseman	half-timer
	bootblack	cosmonaut	executive	harlequin
	bootmaker	cost clerk	exorciser	harmonist
9	brakes-man	costumier	eye doctor	harpooner
	buccaneer	courtisan	fabricant	harvester
absconder	burnisher	couturier	fagottist	herbalist
accessory	bus driver	cowfeeder	fan dancer	herbarian
adulterer	bush pilot	cowkeeper	fashioner	herborist
alchemist	cab driver	cracksman	felt-maker	herb-woman
analogist	café owner	craftsman	film actor	hired hand
anarchist				

hired help	lumberman	pantaloon	protector
historian	machinist	paramedic	psaltress
homeopath	major-domo	part-timer	publicist
hop-picker	make-up man	patrolman	publisher
horologer	male model	paymaster	pulpiteer
hosteller	male nurse	pedagogue	punctator
housemaid	man-at-arms	pen-pusher	puppeteer
housewife	Man Friday	performer	qualifier
hygienist	mannequin	physician	quarryman
hypnotist	mechanist	physicist	racketeer
incumbent	medallist	pierrette	railmaker
ingrafter	memoirist	pinkmaker	ransacker
innkeeper	mercenary	pin-up girl	recruiter
inscriber	mesmerist	pipe-layer	reformist
inspector	messenger	pit-sawyer	registrar
intendant	metallist	planisher	regulator
ironsmith	metrician	plasterer	rehearser
job-master	middleman	play-actor	repairman
joculator	mill-owner	ploughboy	retoucher
justiciar	mine owner	ploughman	ribbonman
kennel-man	model girl	plunderer	roadmaker
kidnapper	moderator	pluralist	rocketeer
kitchener	mortician	poetaster	ropemaker
knocker-up	muffin-man	pointsman	roundsman
lacemaker	murderess	policeman	rum-runner
lacquerer	musketeer	pop artist	sacristan
lady's maid	musketoon	pop singer	safemaker
lampooner	myologist	portrayer	sailmaker
land agent	navigator	portreeve	scarifier
landreeve	negotiant	postilion	scavenger
larcenist	neologian	postwoman	scenarist
launderer	neologist	poulterer	scholiast
laundress	newsagent	practiser	schoolman
legionary	newshound	precentor	scientist
librarian	nursemaid	preceptor	scribbler
lifeguard	odd-jobber	predicant	scrivener
life-saver	odd-job man	prelector	scytheman
linotyper	office boy	presenter	sea-robber
lion-tamer	ombudsman	president	second man
liveryman	operative	priestess	secretary
loan agent	ordinator	principal	seneschal
lockmaker	organiser	privateer	serenader
locksmith	osteopath	processer	shampooer
log-roller	otologist	proconsul	shantyman
Lord Mayor	outfitter	professor	shipowner

ship's mate
shoeblack
shoemaker
shopwoman
sightsman
signalman
slanderer
soapmaker
solicitor
songsmith
sonneteer
sorceress
soubrette
spiderman
spokesman
stableboy
stableman
stagehand
statesman
stationer
stay-maker
steersman
stevedore
strangler
stud groom
sub-editor
subwarden
succentor
sur-master
swan-upper
swineherd
switchman
swordsman
tablemaid
tactician
tailoress
tap-dancer
tattooist
tea-taster
tentmaker
test pilot
theorbist
therapist
theurgist
throwster

tic-tac man
timberman
timpanist
tool-maker
toolsmith
town clerk
town crier
tradesman
tragedian
traveller
treasurer
trepanner
tributary
trumpeter
tympanist
undercook
usherette
van driver
varnisher
versifier
vigilante
violinist
volcalist
wadsetter
waldgrave
warrantee
warranter
washerman
waxworker
wherryman
whitester
winemaker
wood-reeve
workwoman
wrong-doer
zookeeper
zoologist

10

able seaman
abstractor
accomplice
accomptant
accoucheur

accountant
adulteress
advertiser
aerologist
agrologist
agronomist
air hostess
air steward
algebraist
amanuensis
ambassador
apothecary
apprentice
arbalister
arbitrator
astrologer
astronomer
atmologist
auctioneer
audit clerk
baby-farmer
baby-sitter
balloonist
ballplayer
bandleader
bandmaster
baseballer
bassoonist
beadswoman
beautician
bell-hanger
bell-ringer
billposter
biochemist
biographer
blacksmith
bladesmith
blockmaker
blue jacket
bombardier
bondswoman
bone-setter
bookbinder
bookholder
bookkeeper

bookseller
bootlegger
boot-mender
bricklayer
brickmaker
brushmaker
bryologist
bumbailiff
bureaucrat
bushranger
butterwife
career girl
cartoonist
cartwright
cash-keeper
cataloguer
cat breeder
cat burglar
ceramicist
chair-maker
chairwoman
chancellor
chargehand
charioteer
chauffeuse
chirurgion
chorus girl
chronicler
chucker-out
circuiteer
city editor
claim agent
clapper-boy
clockmaker
clog-dancer
cloth maker
clubmaster
coachmaker
coal-backer
coal-fitter
coalheaver
coal-master
co-assessor
coastguard
collocutor

colloquist	drummer-boy	governante	law-breaker
colporteur	dry cleaner	grammarian	law officer
comedienne	emblazoner	groundsman	leading man
commissary	enamellist	gunslinger	legislator
compilator	ephemerist	hackney-man	librettist
compositor	epitaphist	hall porter	lighterman
compounder	epitomizer	handmaiden	lime-burner
concordist	ergonomist	harmonizer	linotypist
consultant	errand-girl	harvestman	liquidator
contractor	ethologist	hatcheller	lobsterman
controller	evangelist	hatchet man	lock-keeper
copyholder	eye-servant	headmaster	lumberjack
copywriter	fell-monger	head porter	mace-bearer
cordwainer	file-cutter	head waiter	machineman
cork-cutter	filibuster	hedge layer	magistrate
corn-cutter	film editor	hierophant	manageress
cornettist	firemaster	highwayman	manicurist
councillor	fire-raiser	homoeopath	manservant
counsellor	fire-walker	horn player	master-hand
couturiere	fire-worker	horologist	matchmaker
cowpuncher	fishmonger	horse-thief	meat-hawker
crop-duster	flight crew	house agent	medical man
Crown Agent	flowergirl	husbandman	merceriser
cultivator	folk-dancer	impressario	militiaman
customs man	folk-singer	incendiary	millwright
cytologist	folklorist	inoculator	mineralist
delineator	forecaster	inquisitor	mine worker
delinquent	frame-maker	institutor	missionary
deputy head	freebooter	instructor	moonshiner
dinner lady	fund raiser	interagent	mouthpiece
disc jockey	gamekeeper	ironmaster	naturalist
discounter	game warden	ironmonger	naturopath
discoverer	gatekeeper	ironworker	nautch girl
dishwasher	gear-cutter	journalist	negotiator
dispatcher	geisha girl	journeyman	newscaster
distrainer	gemologist	junk dealer	news editor
distrainor	geneticist	justiciary	newsmonger
dockmaster	geographer	kennelmaid	newsreader
dog breeder	glee-singer	keyboarder	newsvendor
dog-fancier	glossarist	knockabout	newswriter
doorkeeper	glue-boiler	lady doctor	night nurse
dope-pedlar	go-go dancer	lampoonist	nosologist
drag artist	gold-beater	land-worker	nurseryman
dramaturge	gold-digger	lapidarist	obituarist
dressmaker	gold-panner	laundryman	office girl

oil painter	quiz-master	soap-boiler	typesetter
one-man band	railwayman	songstress	understudy
osteologer	rat-catcher	sound-mixer	undertaker
overlooker	recidivist	specialist	unicyclist
panegyrist	recitalist	staff nurse	veterinary
pantrymaid	researcher	steersmate	vice consul
paper-maker	rheologist	stenciller	victualler
park-keeper	ringmaster	step-dancer	virologist
park-ranger	roadmender	stewardess	vivandière
pasquilant	rope-dancer	stipulator	vocabulist
pastry-cook	rope-walker	stocktaker	wage-earner
pathfinder	roughrider	stone-borer	wainwright
pawnbroker	roustabout	stonemason	ward sister
pearl-diver	safeblower	street-ward	watchmaker
pediatrist	saleswoman	sub-prefect	waterguard
pedicurist	scaffolder	supervisor	weather man
peltmonger	scat singer	surface-man	wharfinger
penologist	schoolmarm	swan-keeper	whipper-in
perruquier	scrutineer	symphonist	whitesmith
personator	sculptress	tally clerk	wholesaler
pharmacist	sea-captain	taskmaster	winegrower
philologer	seal-fisher	taxi-driver	wine taster
piano tuner	seamstress	taxonomist	wine-waiter
pickpocket	second mate	tea-blender	wire-dancer
platelayer	seminarist	tea planter	wire-drawer
playwright	sempstress	technician	wire-walker
polemicist	serologist	technocrat	wireworker
politician	serving-man	theogonist	woodcarver
postillion	sexologist	theologian	woodcutter
postmaster	ship-broker	theologist	wood-monger
practician	ship-holder	threnodist	woodworker
prescriber	shipmaster	timekeeper	wool-carder
press agent	shipwright	tractarian	wool-comber
prima donna	shire-reeve	traffic cop	wool-driver
print buyer	shopfitter	trafficker	wool-grower
private eye	shopkeeper	tram-driver	wool-sorter
procurator	shoplifter	transactor	wool-trader
programmer	shopwalker	translator	wool-winder
pronouncer	signwriter	trawlerman	working man
proprietor	silk-mercer	treasuress	yardmaster
prosecutor	silk-weaver	trespasser	zoographer
prospector	sinologist	trolley-man	zymologist
prostitute	skirmisher	trombonist	
protractor	slop seller	troubadour	
puncturist	sneak thief	type-cutter	

11

accompanist
accoucheuse
adjudicator
allopathist
annunciator
antiquarian
apple-grower
arch-villian
army officer
arquebusier
art mistress
assemblyman
audiologist
audio typist
backbcomber
bank cashier
bank manager
bargemaster
barnstormer
basketmaker
batti-wallah
beachcomber
bell-founder
belly-dancer
bill-sticker
bird-catcher
bird-fancier
bird-watcher
blackmailer
boatbuilder
body servant
boilermaker
boilersmith
bondservant
boot-catcher
breadwinner
broadcaster
bullfighter
burgomaster
businessman
candlemaker
carol singer
car salesman

cattle thief
cat's-meat-
   man
chair-minder
chalk-cutter
chamberlain
chambermaid
charge nurse
chiffonnier
child minder
chirologist
chiromancer
chiropodist
choirmaster
chronologer
clairvoyant
clock-setter
cloth-worker
coffin-maker
cognoscente
collar-maker
commentator
comptroller
conciliator
condisciple
condottière
conductress
confederate
congressman
consecrator
conservator
conspirator
constituent
contributor
conveyancer
coppersmith
cosmologist
court jester
crane driver
crime writer
crown lawyer
cub reporter
cypher clerk
dancing girl
day labourer

delivery man
demographer
diplomatist
dispensator
distributor
double agent
draughtsman
duty officer
electrician
emblematist
embroiderer
entertainer
equilibrist
estate agent
ethnologist
etymologist
executioner
extortioner
factory hand
faith healer
field worker
figure-maker
filing clerk
finestiller
fire-fighter
fire insurer
fire-watcher
flax-dresser
flesh-monger
floorwalker
fourbisseur
fringe-maker
fruit picker
funambulist
funtionary
galley-slave
games master
gemmologist
genealogist
ghost writer
glass-bender
glass-blower
glass-cutter
glass-worker
grave-digger

greengrocer
green keeper
haberdasher
hagiologist
hairdresser
hair stylist
handicapper
hardwareman
heirologist
High Sheriff
histologist
homesteader
horse doctor
horse trader
hospitaller
hotel-keeper
housefather
housekeeper
housemaster
housemother
hydrologist
hymnologist
illuminator
illusionist
illustrator
infantryman
internuncio
interpreter
interviewer
invigilator
iron-founder
ivory-carver
ivory-turner
ivory-worker
kerb-crawler
kitchenmaid
lamplighter
land steward
laundrymaid
leading lady
ledger clerk
lifeboatman
lightkeeper
limbo dancer
linen draper

lithologist
lithotomist
lollipop man
Lord Provost
lorry driver
madrigalist
maidservant
mammalogist
master baker
matinée idol
mechanician
medicine man
memorialist
merchantman
metal worker
miniaturist
minnesinger
mole-catcher
money-broker
money-lender
monographer
monologuist
moonlighter
mule-spinner
music critic
music master
mythologist
necrologist
necromancer
needlewoman
neurologist
neurotomist
night porter
night sister
nightworker
nomenclator
numismatist
office staff
onion-seller
opera singer
ophiologist
orientalist
osteologist
pamphleteer
panel-beater

paperhanger
parlourmaid
pathologist
pearlfisher
petrologist
pettifogger
philatelist
philologist
phonologist
phthologist
piano player
piece-worker
play-actress
policewoman
polyphonist
pork butcher
print-seller
probationer
promulgator
proofreader
property man
questionary
radiologist
rag merchant
representer
republisher
rhetorician
rhinologist
roadsweeper
safebreaker
safe-cracker
salesperson
sandwich man
saxophonist
scoutmaster
scrap dealer
scripholder
secret agent
seditionary
secret agent
seditionary
semanticist
servant girl
serving maid
share-broker

sheep-farmer
shepherdess
shipbreaker
shipbuilder
ship's master
shopbreaker
shop steward
silversmith
slaughterer
slave-driver
slave-holder
smallholder
sociologist
stage-driver
steel-worker
steeplejack
stilt-walker
stockbroker
stockjobber
stonecutter
storekeeper
storyteller
straight man
strip-teaser
sundriesman
system-maker
talent scout
tax gatherer
taxidermist
telegrapher
telephonist
ticket agent
toastmaster
tobacconist
tooth-drawer
topographer
torch-bearer
torch-singer
touch-typist
town planner
tragedienne
train driver
transcriber
transporter
transhipper

travel agent
type founder
typographer
underbearer
underwriter
upholsterer
versemonger
vine-dresser
washerwoman
watchkeeper
watch-mender
wax-chandler
wheel-cutter
wheelwright
whitewasher
witch-doctor
witch-finder
wool-stapler
xylophonist

12

accordionist
actor-manager
ambulanceman
anaesthetist
animalculist
archeologist
artilleryman
artist's model
baby-snatcher
ballet dancer
ballet master
bellows-maker
bibliologist
body-snatcher
booking clerk
bottle-washer
bus conductor
cabinet-maker
calligrapher
cardiologist
caricaturist
carpet-fitter
cartographer

cerographist
cheesemonger
chief cashier
chimney-sweep
chiropractor
chronologist
churchwarden
circuit judge
civil servant
clarinettist
clerk of works
cloth-shearer
coach-builder
coleopterist
commissioner
conchologist
confectioner
corn chandler
corn merchant
cosmographer
costermonger
counter-tenor
crafts-master
craniologist
cryptogamist
cryptologist
crystal gazer
dance hostess
deep-sea diver
demonologist
demonstrator
dendrologist
dock labourer
drama teacher
drug smuggler
ecclesiastic
educationist
egyptologist
electrotyper
elocutionist
embryologist
engine-driver
entomologist
entrepreneur
enzymologist

escapologist
ethnographer
experimenter
exterminator
family doctor
farm labourer
film director
film producer
first officer
flint-knapper
flying doctor
footplateman
front-bencher
funambulator
geometrician
glass-grinder
glossologist
grease monkey
guild brother
hagiographer
harness-maker
head gardener
head mistress
horse-breaker
horse-courser
horse-knacker
hotel manager
house-breaker
house husband
housepainter
house steward
house surgeon
hydrographer
immunologist
impersonator
instructress
investigator
invoice clerk
jerry-builder
joint-trustee
juvenile lead
King's Counsel
kitchen-wench
knife-grinder
knife-thrower

labouring man
land surveyor
lath-splitter
leader writer
lexicologist
lithographer
lollipop lady
longshoreman
loss adjuster
lumber-dealer
maid of honour
maître d'hotel
make-up artist
manual worker
manufacturer
mass producer
meat-salesman
messenger-boy
metallurgist
mezzo soprano
microscopist
mineralogist
miscellanist
money-changer
Morris-dancer
mosaic-artist
mosaic-worker
musicologist
mythographer
neurosurgeon
newspaperman
notary public
nutritionist
obstetrician
office junior
orchestrator
organ-builder
organ-grinder
orthodontist
orthographer
paper-stainer
pattern-maker
photographer
phrenologist
physiologist

plant manager
ploughwright
plumber's mate
plyer-for-hire
postmistress
practitioner
press officer
prestigiator
principal boy
prison warder
prize-fighter
professional
propagandist
proprietress
psephologist
psychiatrist
psychologist
publicity man
pupil-teacher
puppet-player
quarry master
racing driver
radiographer
receptionist
restaurateur
riding-master
right-hand man
rubber-grader
sales manager
scene-painter
scene-shifter
school doctor
schoolmaster
screenwriter
scriptwriter
scullery-maid
seed-merchant
seismologist
selenologist
senior master
serving-wench
sharecropper
sharpshooter
sheep-shearer
sheep-stealer

ship chandler
ship's husband
shoe-repairer
silver-beater
slaughterman
snake-charmer
social worker
soil mechanic
special agent
speechwriter
spice-blender
spokesperson
sportscaster
sports master
sportswriter
stage manager
stand-up comic
statistician
steel erector
stenographer
stonebreaker
stonedresser
street trader
street-walker
sugar-refiner
tax collector
technologist
telegraph boy
telegraphist
tenant farmer
test engineer
therapeutist
timber trader
toll-gatherer
tourist agent
toxicologist
tradespeople
transplanter
trichologist
trick cyclist
undermanager
underservant
veterinarian
vibraphonist
vice-chairman

waiting-woman
warehouseman
water diviner
wine merchant
wood-engraver
works manager
zincographer

13

administrator
agriculturist
antique dealer
arachnologist
archaeologist
arithmetician
articled clerk
barber-surgeon
basso-profundo
bibliographer
biology master
businesswoman
calico-printer
calypso singer
campanologist
chartographer
chicken-farmer
chirographist
choreographer
civil engineer
contortionist
contrabandist
contrapuntist
correspondent
cotton-spinner
counter-caster
counterfeiter
craniometrist
criminologist
cryptographer
dancing master
debt collector
dental surgeon
deipnosophist
dermatologist

diagnostician
diamond-cutter
district nurse
draughtswoman
drawing-master
dress designer
drill sergeant
dubbing editor
electroplater
electrotypist
encyclopedist
entozoologist
epigrammatist
estate manager
exhibitionist
fencing-master
fortune-teller
freight-broker
galvanologist
games mistress
glossographer
glyphographer
ground-bailiff
gynaecologist
haematologist
harbour master
heieroglyphist
High Constable
horse-milliner
hospital nurse
housemistress
ichthyologist
impressionist
industrialist
intelligencer
kettledrummer
lady-in-waiting
laryngologist
lepidopterist
letter-carrier
letter-founder
lexicographer
lighthouseman
literary agent
lollipop woman

machine-minder
maid-of-all-work
master builder
master mariner
mathematician
maths mistress
meistersinger
melodramatist
metaphysician
meteorologist
music mistress
night-watchman
oceanographer
old-clothes-man
ornithologist
orthographist
paediatrician
park attendant
peasant-farmer
periodicalist
pharmaceutist
physiognomist
physiographer
police officer
posture-master
poultry farmer
prime minister
printer's devil
prison officer
privateersman
process-server
projectionist
psalmographer
psychoanalyst
pteridologist
public speaker
Queen's Counsel
racing-tipster
rag-and-bone-man
rent collector
revolutionary
revolutionist
rubber-planter
sailing master
schoolteacher

science master
shop assistant
seismographer
selenographer
singing-master
sports teacher
stage-coachman
stationmaster
sterioscopist
straight actor
street-sweeper
sub-contractor
superintender
supernumerary
supply teacher
toll collector
trade unionist
traffic warden
tramcar-driver
tram conductor
trapeze artist
ventriloquist
vice-president
vice-principal
vulcanologist
welfare worker
violoncellist
window-cleaner
window-dresser
woollen-draper
writing-master
zoogeographer

14

anthropologist
astrophysicist
autobiographer
bacteriologist
ballet mistress
billiard-marker
billiard-player
black marketeer
bus conductress
casual labourer

chamber counsel
character actor
chief executive
chimney-sweeper
citizen-soldier
classics master
colour sergeant
commissionaire
cost accountant
customs officer
dancing partner
design engineer
discount-broker
ecclesiologist
educationalist
electrochemist
encyclopaedist
exchange-broker
fifth columnist
flamenco dancer
French polisher
general manager
handicraftsman
High Court Judge
horticulturist
house decorator
house furnisher
house physician
hydrotherapist
king's messenger
language master
leading counsel
leather-dresser
maître de ballet
manual labourer
market-gardener
marriage broker
medical officer
merchant-tailor
metallographer
money-scrivener
Mother Superior
music publisher
naval pensioner
painter-stainer

palaeobotanist
pavement artist
pharmacologist
plastic surgeon
pneumatologist
prima ballerina
property master
question master
reception clerk
representative
rheumatologist
schoolmistress
ship's carpenter
spectacle-maker
spectroscopist
sports mistress
station manager
store detective
superintendent
sword swallower
systems analyst
tallow chandler
timber merchant
tobacco planter
town councillor
traffic manager
troubleshooter
turf accountant
under-secretary
vice-chancellor
vivisectionist
water-colourist
weather prophet

15

agriculturalist
ambulance driver
ancillary worker
arboriculturist
assistant master
attorney general
Bow Street Runner
cabinet minister
casting director

charge d'affaires
Christy minstrel
cinematographer
commission agent
company director
crossing-sweeper
dancing mistress
diamond merchant
domestic servant
forwarding agent
funeral director
gentleman-farmer
geomorphologist
governor-general
graphic designer
hackney coachman
heart specialist
helminthologist
instrumentalist
insurance broker
jack-of-all-trades
musical director
numismatologist
ophthalmologist
palaeontologist
physiotherapist
platform-speaker
plenipotentiary
police constable
police inspector
portrait-painter
prestidigitator
professional man
programme seller
provision dealer
queen's messenger
railway engineer
recording artist
resurrectionist
school inspector
science mistress
scripture-reader
sleeping partner
song-and-dance man
speech therapist

stretcher-bearer supporting actor tight-rope walker
strolling player ticket collector vice-chamberlain

Trees and shrubs

2 & 3

ash
bay
ben
bo
box
elm
fig
fir
gum
koa
may
oak
yew

nipa
palm
pear
pine
plum
poon
rata
rose
shea
sloe
sorb
teak
toon
upas
whin

elder
erica
furze
genip
gorse
guava
hazel
henna
holly
iroko
Judas
karri
kauri
larch
lemon
lilac
maple
mango
myrrh
olive
osier
papaw
peach
pecan
pipal
plane
roble
rowan
salix
savin
sumac
thorn
withy
yucca
zamia

6

acacia
acajou
almond
antiar
azalea
bamboo
banian
banyan
baobab
bog oak
bonsai
cashew
cassia
cherry
cohune
conker
daphne
datura
deodar
derris
durian
fustic
gingko
ginkgo
gomuti
jarrah
jujube
kamala
laurel
linden
locust
longan
loquat
mallee
manuka

mimosa
myrtle
nutmeg
orache
orange
pawpaw
papaya
peepul
platan
poplar
privet
protea
quince
raffia
rattan
redbud
red fir
red gum
red oak
sallow
sapele
sapota
spirea
spruce
sumach
tupelo
walnut
wattle
willow

7

althaea
ambatch
arbutus
bebeeru
big tree

4

acer
aloe
anil
bael
bass
bush
coca
cola
date
dhak
dita
gean
holm
ilex
jute
kava
kola
lime
ling

5

abele
alder
apple
areca
aspen
babul
balsa
beech
birch
briar
brier
broom
cacao
caper
carob
cedar
chico
cubeb
ebony

blue gum
bramble
bullace
cajuput
cajeput
camelia
catalpa
champac
conifer
coquito
cork oak
cow tree
cypress
dogwood
durmast
fan palm
filbert
fuchsia
genipap
gum tree
heather
hemlock
hickory
holm oak
jasmine
juniper
madrona
oil palm
palmyra
red pine
redwood
robinia
rosebay
sequoia
sourgum
soursop
spiraea
syringa
talipot
tea tree
wax palm
wax tree
wych-elm

8

allspice
barberry
basswood
bayberry
beefwood
bergamot
box elder
buddleia
calabash
calamite
carnauba
chestnut
cinchona
coolabah
coolibah
cork tree
corkwood
date palm
dwarf box
euonymus
evonymus
gardenia
guaiacum
guaiocum
hardwood
hawthorn
holly oak
hornbeam
inkberry
ironwood
japonica
kingwood
laburnum
lavender
magnolia
mahogany
mangrove
manna ash
mesquite
mulberry
oleander
palm tree
pear tree

piassava
pinaster
plum tree
quandong
rain tree
rambutan
red cedar
rosemary
rosewood
sago palm
saltbush
shadbush
silky oak
sourwood
sugar gum
sweet bay
sweet gum
sweetsop
sycamore
tamarack
tamarind
tamarisk
viburnum
wisteria
witch-elm
woodbine

9

ailanthus
algorroba
auracaria
azedarach
balsawood
balsam fir
bearberry
blackjack
bog myrtle
buckthorn
butternut
carob tree
casuarina
China tree
chincapin
coco de mer

coral tree
crab apple
crowberry
deciduous
eaglewood
euphorbia
evergreen
firethorn
flame tree
forsythia
hydrangea
ivory palm
jacaranda
Judas tree
kalanchoe
kapok tree
launcewood
macadamia
mistletoe
paulownia
pitch pine
plane tree
poinciana
poison oak
poison ivy
quebracho
rose apple
royal palm
sagebrush
sapanwood
sapodilla
sassafras
satinwood
screw pine
sour gourd
stinkwood
stone pine
sugar bush
sugar pine
sweet gale
tallow wood
thorn tree
tree heath
tree tomato
tulip tree

tulipwood
wax myrtle
whitebeam
whitewood
wych hazel

10

almond tree
arbor vitae
bird cherry
blackthorn
bladdernut
bottle tree
brazilwood
breadfruit
bunya-bunya
butter tree
buttonwood
chinaberry
coffee tree
coniferous
coral tree
cotton bush
cottonwood
Douglas fir
dragon tree
durmast oak
eucalyptus
fiddlewood
frangipani
gopher-wood
gomuti palm
grease bush
greasewood
greenheart
Joshua tree
mangosteen
mock orange
pagoda tree
poinsettia
prickly ash
pyracantha
raffia palm
rose acacia

rubber tree
sappanwood
sessile oak
sorrel tree
sour cherry
sugar apple
sugar maple
weeping ash
white cedar
whitethorn
wild cherry
witch hazel
yellow-wood

11

Aaron's beard
black spruce
black walnut
bottlebrush
burning bush
cabbage palm
cabbage tree
camphor tree
chaulmoogra
coconut palm
copper beech
cotoneaster
crepe myrtle
crape myrtle
cryptomeria
cypress pine
dawn redwood
false acacia
feather palm
honey locust
honeysuckle
Japanese ivy
lacquer tree
laurustimus
mountain ash
native peach
Norway maple
purple heart
pussy willow

service tree
slippery elm
spindle tree
stephanotis
talipot palm
tulip poplar
varnish tree

12

balsam poplar
balsam spruce
blackcurrant
blackjack oak
cherry laurel
Christ's thorn
creosote bush
cucumber tree
custard apple
golden wattle
rhododendron
rose of Sharon
monkey puzzle
Norway spruce
philadelphus
sea buckthorn
snowball tree
snowdrop tree
Spanish cedar
St. John's bread
swamp cypress
tree of heaven
umbrella pine
umbrella tree
wellingtonia
white currant
yellow poplar

13

bougainvillea
butcher's-broom
cranberry bush
cranberry tree
hemlock spruce

horse chestnut
Japanese cedar
paper mulberry
poison hemlock
royal ponciana
spike lavender
sweet chestnut
wayfaring tree
weeping willow

14 +

African mahogany
bergamot orange

cedar of Lebanon
flamboyant tree
flame-of-the-forest
flowering currant
Japanese andromeda
Jerusalem cherry
Lombardy poplar
maidenhair tree
monkey bread tree
mountain laurel
red-osier dogwood
silk-cotton tree
strawberry tree
turpentine tree
virginia creeper

United Nations members

2 & 3

UK
USA

4

Chad
Cuba
Fiji
Iran
Iraq
Laos
Mali
Oman
Peru
Togo
USSR

5

Benin
Chile
China
Congo
Egypt

Gabon
Ghana
Haiti
India
Italy
Japan
Kenya
Libya
Malta
Nepal
Niger
Qatar
Samoa
Spain
Sudan
Syria
Zaïre

6

Angola
Belize
Bhutan
Brazil

Brunei
Canada
Cyprus
France
Gambia
Greece
Guinea
Guyana
Israel
Jordan
Kuwait
Latvia
Malawi
Mexico
Monaco
Norway
Panama
Poland
Russia
Rwanda
Sweden
Turkey
Uganda
Zambia

7

Albania
Algeria
Andorra
Armenia
Austria
Bahamas
Bahrain
Belarus
Belgium
Bolivia
Burundi
Comoros
Croatia
Denmark
Ecuador
Eritrea
Estonia
Finland
Georgia
Germany
Grenada
Hungary
Iceland

Ireland
Jamaica
Lebanon
Lesotho
Liberia
Moldova
Morocco
Myanmar
Namibia
Nigeria
Romania
St. Lucia
Senegal
Somalia
Tunisia
Ukraine
Uruguay
Vanuatu
Vietnam

8

Barbados
Botswana
Bulgaria
Cambodia

Cameroon
Colombia
Djibouti
Dominica
Ethiopia
Honduras
Malaysia
Maldives
Mongolia
Pakistan
Paraguay
Portugal
Slovakia
Slovenia
Sri Lanka
Suriname
Tanzania
Thailand
Zimbabwe

9

Argentina
Australia
Cape Verde
Costa Rica
Guatemala
Indonesia
Kampuchea
Korea, North
Lithuania
Mauritius
Nicaragua
San Marino
Singapore
Swaziland
Venezuela

10

Azerbaijan
Bangladesh
El Salvador
Kazakhstan
Korea, South
Kyrgyzstan
Luxembourg

Madagascar
Mauritania
Micronesia
Mozambique
New Zealand
Seychelles
Tajikistan
Uzbekistan
Yugoslavia

11

Afghanistan
Burkina Faso
Côte d'Ivoire
Netherlands
Philippines
Saudi Arabia
Sierra Leone
South Africa

12

Guinea-Bissau
Turkmenistan

13

Czech Republic
Liechtenstein
United Kingdom

14

Papua New Guinea
Solomon Islands

15 +

Antigua and Barbuda
Central African Republic
Dominion Republic
Equatorial Guinea
Marshall Islands
St. Kitts and Nevis
St. Vincent and the Grenadines
Sao Tomé and Principé
Trinidad and Tobago
United Arab Emirates
United States of America

Weapons and armour

2 & 3

ABM
axe
bow
dag
das
gat
gun
gyn
ram
Sam
TNT
V1
wad

4

ammo
arms
ball
barb
bill
bolo
bolt
bomb
bren
butt
cane
club
colt
cosh
dart
dirk
épée
fang
flak
foil
gaff
ICBM
jack

helm
kora
kris
mace
mail
mere
mine
nuke
piat
pike
Scud
shot
slug
Sten
tank
tock
tuck
whip
Z-gun

5

A-bomb
aegis
ancus
ankus
armet
armor
arrow
aswar
bacyn
baton
bidag
bilbo
birch
bolas
boson
brand
buffe
crest
CS gas

culet
estoc
flail
fusée
fusil
gipon
grape
gupti
H-bomb
hobit
imber
jupel
jupon
keris
khora
kilig
kilij
knife
knout
kukri
kylie
lames
lance
lasso
latch
lathi
luger
Maxim
noose
pilum
poker
pouch
prodd
razor
rifle
royal
sabre
salet
salvo
shaft
shell

skean
skene
sling
spear
stake
staff
stave
stick
sword
tachi
targe
tasse
tawse
visor
vizor
waddy

6

ack-ack
air gun
aletes
amukta
anlace
armlet
barkal
barong
barrel
basnet
baston
bhanju
bodkin
Bofors
bonnet
bracer
bridle
brugne
buffer
bullet
calote
camail

cannon
carcas
carrel
casque
cassis
celate
cheeks
crenel
crinet
cudgel
cuello
cuisse
dagger
daisho
dragon
dualin
dum-dum
dusack
exocet
feltre
glaive
gorget
gusset
hanger
heaume
helmet
homing
jezail
katana
kerrie
khanda
kikuki
kodogu
lancet
lariat
lassoo
lorica
mascle
massue
Mauser
mazule

mesail
morian
morion
mortar
musket
muzzle
napalm
pac one
pac two
parang
pellet
petard
pistol
pom-pom
pop gun
powder
primer
qillij
ramrod
rapier
rocket
salade
sallet
saturn
scythe
Sea Cat
semtex
shield
sickle
stylet
sumpit
swivel
tabard
talwar
target
tonite
tulwar
VGO gun
umbril
Webley
zipgun

7

ailetes
anelace
assagai
assegai
ataghan
awl-pike
bacinet
balasan
baldric
balista
barbute
bar-shot
basinet
baslard
bayonet
bazooka
belfrey
biliong
blow gun
bombard
bourdon
brasset
Bren gun
buckler
calibre
caliver
caltrap
carabin
carbine
carreau
chakram
chalcos
chauces
chopper
cordite
corslet
couteau
crupper
cuirass
cuisses
culeset
currier
curtana

curtein
cutlass
djerrid
dualine
dudgeon
dussack
elf-bolt
Encorder
espadon
fauchon
fendace
firearm
fire-pot
frontal
garotte
garrote
Gatling
gauchet
gouchet
gunlock
greaves
grenade
gunshot
halbert
halberd
hand gun
harpoon
hatchet
hauberk
hoguine
holster
javelin
kastane
kindjal
langrel
laniers
long bow
Long Tom
lyddite
machete
missile
Mons Meg
morglay
murrion
mursail

musquet
oil bomb
panache
panoply
patriot
placard
poitrel
Polaris
pole-axe
poniard
punt gun
quarrel
rabinet
roundel
scourge
Sea Dart
Sea Hawk
shashqa
shinken
shotgun
side-arm
sjambok
Skybolt
Sten gun
surcoat
teargas
torpedo
Trident
twibill
vamplet
ventail
visiere
Walther
warhead
wind-gun

8

allecret
amusette
Anschutz
armament
arbalest
arbalist
arbalete

arquebus
attaghan
atom bomb
axe-knife
balister
ballista
bardings
bascinet
baselard
basilard
basilisk
baudrick
birdbolt
blowpipe
bludgeon
brassard
brassart
brayette
broad-axe
Browning
buckshot
buff coat
burganet
burginot
burgonet
cabasset
calthrop
canister
carabine
cartouch
cascabel
case-shot
catapult
chacheka
chamfron
champons
chanfron
chausses
cladibas
claymore
cod piece
colleret
colletin
corselet
crinière

crossbow
culettes
culverin
damaskin
deringer
destrier
dynamite
eel-spear
elf-arrow
falchion
falconet
fauchard
field-gun
fireball
firelock
fireship
gadlings
garrotte
gauntlet
gavelock
gunflint
gunpaper
gunsight
gunstock
hackbutt
halecret
hail shot
half-pike
hand-pike
haquebut
hassegai
howitzer
jambeaux
jazerant
land mine
langrage
Lewisite
Lewis gun
magazine
mangonel
mantelet
Maxim gun
munition
oerlikon
ordnance

organ gun
paravane
paterero
pauldron
Pauly gun
pectoral
pederero
petronel
phosgene
pistolet
plastron
poignard
portfire
pyroxyle
querquer
radar gun
repeater
revolver
ricochet
ringmail
sabatons
scabbard
scimitar
scorpion
shamshir
shrapnel
siege-gun
solarets
solerets
spadroon
spontoon
springal
stiletto
stinkpot
stone axe
stonebow
sumpitan
The Baron
testière
tomahawk
Tommy gun
umbrière
vambrace
vamplate
volcanic

whin-yard
yataghan

9

ack-ack gun
aerial gun
angel-shot
arrowhead
artillery
automatic
aventaile
backpiece
badelaire
bainbergs
beinbergs
ballistic
bandeleer
bandolier
bannerole
bastinado
battleaxe
Big Bertha
Blue Water
boar-spear
Bofors gun
bomb-chest
bombshell
booby trap
boomerang
Brown Bess
cannonade
cartouche
cartridge
chain-mail
chain-shot
champfron
chassepot
chaussons
columbiad
defoliant
demi-lance
Derringer
detonator
doodle-bug

epaulette
espringal
face-guard
falcastra
fish-spear
flagellum
flamberge
flintlock
Francisca
garde-bras
gelignite
grapeshot
green fire
guncotton
gunpowder
habergeon
hand-staff
harquebus
hausse-col
headpiece
heelpiece
knobstick
Landridge
matchlock
mazzuelle
Mills bomb
minute man
munitions
musketoon
needle-gun
poison gas
pom-pom gun
pourpoint
quaker-gun
rerebrace
sabatynes
shillalah
slingshot
slung-shot
small-arms
small bore
spring-gun
starshell
stinkbomb
sword-cane

teeth arms
trebuchet
truncheon
turret gun
volley gun
ward staff
welsh-hook
wheel lock
xyloidine
zumbooruk

10

ammunition
arcubalist
artillator
aventaille
banded mail
banderolle
banderilla
barrel helm
battery gun
blind shell
Blue Streak
Bowie-knife
brandestoc
brichettes
brigandine
broad arrow
broadsword
burrel shot
cannonball
cannon shot
coat armour
coat of mail
colt python
cataphract
cross-arrow
demi-cannon
dive bomber
field-piece
fire-sticks
flanchards
flick knife
flying bomb

Gatling gun
grainstaff
harquebuse
hand cannon
hand mortar
iron bullet
iron cannon
knobkerrie
lambrequin
Lee-Enfield
letter bomb
limpet mine
machine gun
Minie rifle
mustard-gas
paixhan-gun
pea-shooter
powder horn
pyroxyline
rocket ball
Sidewinder
six-shooter
small sword
sticky bomb
sword stick
Winchester

11

anti-tank gun
basket sword
blunderbuss
bow and arrow
breastplate
breaststrap
brigandyron
brigantayle
chapel de fer
chlorine gas
contact-mine
Dahlgren gun
depth charge
elephant gun
espallières
grande-garde

gun carriage
gun howitzer
hand grenade
harping iron
hawk missile
Holstein gun
Jacob's staff
Kelver cable
khyber knife
Lochaber axe
misericorde
morning star
neutron bomb
nuclear bomb
plate armour
powder chest
safety-catch
scale-armour
Snider rifle
sporting gun
Steinbuchse
Thompson gun

12

Armstrong gun
battering ram
boarding pike
breech loader
bridle cutter
cartridge box
curved dagger
demi-culverin
fire carriage
flame-thrower
floating mine
fowling-piece
Hotchkiss gun
hydrogen bomb
Lancaster gun
magnetic mine
Mills grenade
mitrailleuse
muzzle-loader
poisoned dart

quarterstaff
revolving gun
rocket-mortar
sharp shooter
Stokes mortar
suicide plane
sword-bayonet
tracer bullet
trident spear
wheel-lock dag

13

aerial torpedo
arming doublet
ball-cartridge
brass knuckles
chiefton tank
Churchill tank
cruise missile
duelling sword
guided missile
high-explosive
holster pistol
Kentucky rifle
knuckleduster
leather cannon
mortar carbine
nuclear weapon
Orgelgesschutz
percussion cap
poisoned arrow
sharpened pole
sub-machine gun
submarine mine
throwing knife
two-edged sword

14

blank cartridge
Brunswick rifle
duelling pistol
incendiary bomb
miniature rifle

nitroglycerine
rocket launcher
sawn off shotgun
small-bore rifle
stone-head spear
two-handed sword

Perkins steam gun
Raytheon missile
swivel musketoon
wheellock pistol

16 +

anti-personnel mine
anti-satellite missile
automatic machine gun
ballistic missile
Der Grosse Pumbart Von Steyr
double-barrelled shotgun
double-edged knife
double-edged sabre
double-edged sword
heat-seeking missile
muzzle loading rifle
Nordenfeldt machine gun
Schofield Smith and Wesson
shoulder launcher
Springfield rifle
volitional repeater

15

anti-aircraft gun
anti tank grenade
bolt action rifle
bulletproof vest
holster revolver
imbricate armour
lachrymatory gas
Mannlicher rifle
matchlock musket
Maxim machine gun
missile launcher
Molotov cocktail
Partridge mortar
pepperbox pistol

Weather

3	4					
		eddy	lour	veer	cloud	gusty
		fair	melt	warm	draft	humid
col	bank	flaw	mild	west	drift	light
dew	bise	föhn	mist	wind	dusty	lower
dry	bora	fret	pelt		eager	misty
eye	bore	gale	puff	**5**	eagre	muggy
fog	calm	gust	puna		ether	north
hot	cold	haar	rain	balmy	Eurus	Notus
ice	cool	hail	rime	blast	flake	rains
icy	damp	haze	scud	blink	flood	rainy
low	dank	hazy	smog	blowy	foehn	sleet
sky	dark	heat	snap	brume	foggy	slush
sun	dewy	high	snow	buran	fresh	snowy
wet	dusk	hoar	spit	chill	front	sonde
	dull	iris	thaw	cirri	frost	south
	east	knot	vane	clear	gibli	spate

spout
stone
storm
sunny
virga
windy

6

arctic
aurora
Auster
boreal
breeze
bright
buster
chilly
cirrus
cloudy
colder
deluge
floods
flurry
fogbow
fogdog
freeze
frosty
ghibli
hyetal
icicle
isobar
isohel
kamsin
mizzle
mizzly
nimbus
samiel
seadog
sea fog
serein
shower
simoom
simoon
squall
starry

stormy
sultry
sunbow
sunset
torrid
trades
trough
vortex
warmer
welkin
winter
wintry
zephyr

7

backing
blowing
bluster
broiler
cat's paw
Celsius
chinook
climate
clouded
cumulus
cyclone
dewdrop
drizzle
draught
drought
dry-bulb
etesian
fog bank
freshen
hailing
isogram
isohyet
isoline
kamseen
khamsin
meltemi
mistral
monsoon
pampero

pelting
pouring
rainbow
raining
sea fret
set fair
sea haar
sea mist
showery
sirocco
sizzler
snowing
squally
stratus
summery
sunglow
sunless
sunrise
sunspot
tempest
thawing
thermal
thunder
tornado
twister
typhoon
veering
wintery

8

aerology
autumnal
black ice
blizzard
clear day
clear sky
cloudlet
cold snap
cold wave
cumulous
dead calm
dewpoint
doldrums
downpour

easterly
east wind
elements
fireball
flooding
fogbound
fog patch
forecast
freezing
freeze-up
head wind
heat wave
high wind
iceblink
icebound
isobaric
isopleth
isotherm
levanter
libeccio
light air
lowering
millibar
overcast
rainfall
raindrop
rainy day
scorcher
sea storm
snowfall
snowbank
spitting
sunburst
sunlight
thundery
thermals
tropical
twilight
variably
velocity
westerly
west wind
white out
wildfire
williwaw

wind cone
windless
wind rose
windsock

9

advection
afterglow
anemology
anthelion
atmometer
barometer
barograph
baroscope
cloudbank
cloudless
cloud rack
cold front
crosswind
drizzling
dry season
dust devil
dust storm
fresh gale
hailstone
hailstorm
hard frost
harmattan
heavy rain
hoarfrost
hurricane
hygristor
ice needle
isallobar
isotheral
Jack Frost
lapse rate
libecchio
lightning
mare's
  tail
meltwater
moonlight
north-east

northerly
north-west
north wind
nor'wester
occlusion
pea-souper
pyrometer
raincloud
rained off
rained out
rain guage
rainstorm
sand storm
scorching
snowblink
snowbound
snow drift
snow eater
snowflake
snowstorm
solar wind
south-east
south-west
starlight
storm belt
tidal wave
trade wind
updraught
unsettled
warm front
whirlwind
whole gale
wind-chill
wind force
wind gauge
wind scale
windstorm

10

aerography
anemograph
anemometer
anemometry
anemoscope

antitrades
atmosphere
black frost
Cape doctor
centigrade
changeable
clear night
cloudburst
cloudscape
convection
cumuliform
depression
Euroclydon
Fahrenheit
hot climate
hyetograph
hygrograph
hygrometer
hygroscope
ice station
isopiestic
land breeze
March winds
mare's tails
radiosonde
Scotch mist
storm cloud
strong gale
sweltering
thundering
tramontana
tramontane
turbulence
visibility
warm sector
water cycle
waterspout
weather eye
weatherman
weather map
wet chinook
wet weather
white frost
willy-willy

11

altocumulus
altostratus
anemography
anticyclone
atmospheric
cats and dogs
cold climate
cold weather
downdraught
dull weather
equinoctial
etesian wind
freezing fog
fresh breeze
foul weather
ground frost
hyetography
lowering sky
low pressure
mackerel sky
meteorology
mild weather
rain or shine
rainy season
stiff breeze
storm centre
storm signal
sunny spells
temperature
tempestuous
thermometer
thunderbolt
thunderclap
tourbillion
troposphere
warm weather
weathercock
weather vane
white squall

12

April showers
atmospherics

cirrocumulus
cirrostratus
cumulonimbus
easterly wind
freezing rain
gentle breeze
high pressure
Indian summer
lightning rod
meteorograph
moonlit night
nimbostratus
slight breeze
starlit night
storm brewing
storm warning
strong breeze
thundercloud
thunderstorm
tropical heat
tropical rain
weather glass
weather house
westerly wind
white rainbow
wind velocity
windy weather

13

autumn weather

ball lightning
Beaufort scale
cumulostratus
electric storm
frosty weather
galeforce wind
heat lightning
magnetic storm
north-east wind
northerly wind
north-west wind
occluded front
peal of thunder
precipitation
roll of thunder
south-east wind
southerly wind
south-west wind
stratocumulus
summer weather
thundershower
torrential rain
weather report
weather symbol
wintry showers
wintry weather

14

air temperature
aurora borealis

blustery shower
chain lightning
freshening wind
mackerel breeze
meteorological
moderate breeze
Northern Lights
sheet lightning
southern lights
sunny intervals
torrential rain
weather station

15 +

aurora australis
barometric pressure
Beaufort wind scale
bolt of lightning
centigrade scale
come rain or (come) shine
Fahrenheit scale
forked lightning
lightning conductor
mean temperature
microclimatology
prevailing winds
radiometeorograph
southerly buster
tropical climate
wind-chill factor

Wedding anniversaries

3

tin (10th)

4

gold (50th)
iron (4th)

lace (13th)
ruby (40th)
wood (5th)
wool (7th)

5

china

(20th)
coral (35th)
fruit (4th)
ivory (14th)
paper (2nd)
pearl (30th)
steel (11th)
sugar (6th)

6

bronze (8th)
copper (9th)
cotton (1st)
flower (4th)
silver (25th)

7

crystal (15th)
diamond (60th)
emerald (55th)
leather (3rd)

8

platinum (70th)
sapphire (45th)

15 +

silk and fine linen
(12th)

Wines

(including grape varieties and wine-producing regions)

3 & 4

asti
Aszu
brut
Bual
cru
Döle
fino
hock
port
sec
seco
sekt
vin
vino

5

aroma
Byrrh
Corvo
Crépy
cuvée
Fitou
Médoc
Mosel
Rioja
Rully
secco
Tavel
Tokay

6

Alsace
Bandol
Barolo
Barsac
Beaune
Ben Ean
Cahors
Cassis
Chénas
Chinon
Claret
Cornas
Corton
Dingac
Frangy
Graach
Graves
Málaga
Morgon
muscat
Quinta
Saumur
Volnay
Wehlen

7

acidity
Aligoté
auslese

Banyuls
Barbera
bouquet
Caldaro
Chablis
Chianti
Clairet
Cotnari
demi-sec
dry wine
Eiswein
Falerno
Fendant
Fleurie
Fronsac
Gaillac
Inferno
Lutomer
Madeira
Malmsey
Margaux
Marsala
Martini
Moselle
Musigny
Oloroso
Orvieto
Othello
Pomerol
Pommard
Pouilly
Recioto

red wine
Retsina
St. Amour
Sasselo
Schluck
Sercial
Vouvray

8

Bordeaux
Brouilly
Burgundy
Condrieu
Dubonnet
Echezaux
essencia
Frascati
Gigondas
Juliénas
Mercurey
Montagny
Montilla
muscadel
Muscadet
muscatel
Pauillac
Piesport
Pol Roger
Riesling
rosé wine
Sancerre

Santenay
Sauterne
spatlese
Sylvaner
tastevin
Valencay
Valgelia
Vaudesir
Verdelho
Vermouth
vin blanc
Vin Jaune
vin leger
vin rouge
Vin Santo

9

abboccato
Anjou wine
Ayler Kupp
Bardolino
Blanc Fumé
Bollinger
Bourgogne
Bourgueil
Champagne
Chialetto
Clairette
Corbières
Côte-Rôtie
Domestica

Est! Est! Est
Hermitage
Kreuznach
Lambrusco
Meursault
Minervois
Montlouis
pétillant
St. Emilion
St. Raphael
San Severo
Steinwein

10

Barbaresco
Bernkastel
Beaujolais
Bull's Blood
Chambertin
Chiroubles
Lakes Folly
Mâcon Lugny
Manzanilla
Mateus Rosé
Montrachet
Rhine wines
Rhone wines
Richebourg
Rivesaltes
Taittinger
Vinho Verde

11

Aloxe-Corton
Amontillado
Bocksbeutal
Bonnes Mares
Chianti Putto
Clos-de-Bèzes
Clos St. Denis
Commanderia
Egri Bikaner
Maurodaphne

Monbazillac
Moulin-à-Vent
Nierstiener
Pouillly-Fumé
Saint Julien
Vega Cecilia
Vin de Paille
Vin de Graves
vin mousseux
vintage wine

12

Asti Spumante
Blanc de Noirs
Château Canon
Château Gazin
Château Pavie
Côtes-du-Rhône
Frecciarossa
Hickinbotham
Petit Chablis
Pouilly-loche
Romanée-Conti
Saint-Emilion
Saint Estephe
Saint Raphael
still Moselle
Valpolicella
vin ordinaire
Virginia Dare
Vosne-Romanée

13

Beerenauslese
Blanc of Blancs
Château Ausone
Château Bélair
Château Chalon
Château Coutet
Château Dauzac
Château d'Yquem
Château Figeac
Château Kirwan

Château Lafite
Château Lagune
Château Langoa
Château Latour
Château Meyney
Château Nissac
Château Palmer
Château Pouget
Coteau Dulayon
Clos de Vougeot
Entre-deux-mers
Liebfraumilch
Moselblumchen
Muscato Mabile
Pouilly-Fuissé
Qualitatswein
Rhine Riesling
Scharzhofberg
sparkling wine
Touraine wines
Wild Irish Rose

14

Château Boscaut
Château Caillou
Château Climens
Château Giscour
Château Grillet
Château Guiraud
Château Lamothe
Château la Tâche
Château Margaux
Côtes-du-Ventoux
Gamay de la Loire
Gewürztraminer
Henkell Trocken
Lacrima Christi
Moet and Chandon
Quarts de Chaume
Rothbury Estate
Santa Maddelena

15

Château Belgrave
Château Rieussec
Clos de Jacobins
Côtes-de-Provence
Côtes-du-Vivarais
Crozes-Hermitage
Gruner Veltliner
haut poitou wines
Mersault Charmes
Morey-Saint-Denis
Passe-tout-Grains
Sacramental wine
Saumurchampigny

16

Chambolle Musigny
Château Batailley
Château Desmirail
Château Haut Brion
Château Lascombes
Cremant de Cramant
Gevrey-Chambertin
La Roche Aux Moines
Les Forts de la Tour
Monteé de Tonnerre
Muscato de Setubal
Pouilly Vinzelles
Savigny-les-Beaune
Schloss Schunburn
Zinfandel Essense

17

Charmes-Chambertin
Château Beausejour
Château Calon-Segur
Château Magdelaine
Corton-Charlemagne
Côtes-du-Roussillon
Nuits-Saint-Georges
Ockfener Bockstein
Wehlener Sunnenhuhr

18

Blanquette de Limoux
Château Cheval Blanc
Château Lafon-Rochet
Domaine de Chavalier
Muscat de Frontenac
Schloss-Rockelheim
Zeller Schart-Katze

19 +

Brunello de Montalcino
Chassagne-Montrachet
Château de Brane-Cantenac
Château Carbonnieux
Château Chasse-Spleen
Château la Fleur Petrus
Château la Gaffelière
Château Latour-Figeac
Château Mouton Rothschild
Sauvignon de Touraine
Vernaccia de Oristano
Trockenbeeren Auslese

Grape varieties

3 & 5	Syrah	Saumur	Catawba	8	Delaware
Flora		Shiraz	Chelois		Malvasia
Gamay	6		Cinsaul	Baco	Nebbiolo
KWV		7	Fendant	Noir	Rulander
Steen	Merlot		Furmint	Carignan	Sylvaner
	Muscat	Aligoté	Gutedel	Charbond	Viognier

9

Chasselas
Columbard
Clairette
Nederburg
Pinot Gris
Pinot Noir
Trebbiano
Ugni Blanc
Vernaccia
Zinfandel

10

Chardonnay
Fleur du Cap
San Giovesi

11 & 12

Chenin Blanc
Fulle Blanc

13

Cabernet Blanc
Cabernet Franc
Montepulciano
Müller-Thurgau

14 +

Gewürztraminer
Emerald Riesling
Thompson seedless

Wine-producing regions

3 & 4

Ahr
Alba
Aude
Dao
Jura
Nahe
Ohio
Saar

Apulia
Bandol
Cognac
Cyprus
Graves
Greece
Limoux
Marche
Oregon
Sicily
Umbria

Bordeaux
Burgundy
Bulgaria
Dalmatia
Gigondas
La Mancha
Lombardy
Mersault
Monterey
Piedmont
Provence
Slovenia

Côte de Nuit
Napa Valley
Rheinpfalz
Santa Clara
Valdepenas

11

Finger Lakes
Württemburg

12

Amador County
Barosa County
Hunter Valley
New York State
Yakima Valley

5

Anjou
Baden
Blaye
Bourg
Loire
Mâcon
Medoc
Mosel
Paarl

7

Almaden
Côte d'Or
Fronsac
Hérault
Penedès
Pomerol
Romania

9

Alto Adige
Alto Douro
Bourgueil
Champagne
Corbières
Hawkes Bay
Lake Garda
Languedoc
Mendocino

13 +

Alameda County
Castell di Jesi
Emilia Romagna
Entre-Deux-Mers
Pleasant Valley
Washington State

6

Alsace

8

Abbruzzi
Auckland
Bergerac
Blenheim

10

California

Index and cross-reference listing